Contents

South Sefton
6th Form College

information &
communication
technology

for edexcel applied A2 level single award

chris.guy_sean.o'byrne

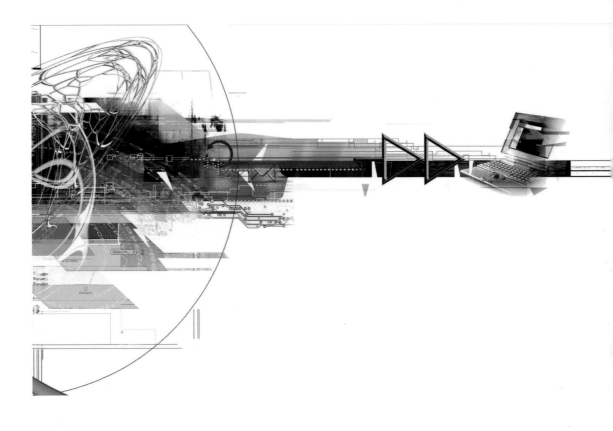

Hodder Murray

A MEMBER OF THE HODDER HEADLINE GROUP

The Publishers would like to thank the following for permission to reproduce copyright material:

Photo credits
p.86 © Royalty-Free/Corbis; p.93 Dominic Burke/Alamy; p.103 © Bettmann/Corbis; p.144 © Eriko Sugita/Reuters/Corbis; p.173 Steve Connolly; p.175 © Canon Europa N.V. and Canon Europe Ltd 2002–2005; p.185 *t* Panasonic Consumer Electronics UK, *b* Sony Europe.

Acknowledgements
All Microsoft screenshots © 2006 Microsoft Corporation; p. 74 and p.120 Gantt Project, Copyright © 1989, 1991 Free Software Foundation, Inc. 51 Franklin Street, Fifth Floor, Boston, MA 02110-1301, USA, http://ganttproject.sourceforge.net; p.77 Oyster Card © Transport for London; p.110 PRINCE © 1997 - 2005 all rights reserved - Key Skills ILX, Nantwich, Cheshire CW5 6GD, www.prince2.com; p.153 FINGABOX, www.redboxentertainment.com.

Every effort has been made to trace all copyright holders, but if any have been inadvertently overlooked the Publishers will be pleased to make the necessary arrangements at the first opportunity.

This high quality material is endorsed by Edexcel and has been through a rigorous quality assurance programme to ensure that it is a suitable companion to the specification for both learners and teachers. This does not mean that its contents will be used verbatim when setting examinations nor is it to be read as being the official specification – a copy of which is available at www.edexcel.org.uk

This material is solely a reference resource. It is not intended to be, nor should it be used as, a revision or study guide for any Edexcel Limited qualification or assessment.

If you are interested in revision or study guides please contact Edexcel Limited directly.

Although every effort has been made to ensure that website addresses are correct at time of going to press, Hodder Murray cannot be held responsible for the content of any website mentioned in this book. It is sometimes possible to find a relocated web page by typing in the address of the home page for a website in the URL window of your browser.

Hodder Headline's policy is to use papers that are natural, renewable and recyclable products and made from wood grown in sustainable forests. The logging and manufacturing processes are expected to conform to the environmental regulations of the country of origin.

Orders: please contact Bookpoint Ltd, 130 Milton Park, Abingdon, Oxon OX14 4SB. Telephone: (44) 01235 827720. Fax: (44) 01235 400454. Lines are open 9.00–5.00, Monday to Saturday, with a 24-hour message answering service. Visit our website at www.hoddereducation.co.uk

©Chris Guy, Sean O'Byrne 2006
First published in 2006 by
Hodder Murray, an imprint of Hodder Education,
a member of the Hodder Headline Group
338 Euston Road
London NW1 3BH

Impression number   5   4   3   2   1
Year   2010 2009 2008 2007 2006

Cover photo © Robert Harding Picture Library Ltd
Typeset in 11/14pt Clearface BT
Printed and bound in Italy

A catalogue record for this title is available from the British Library

ISBN-10: 0 340 92651 1
ISBN-13: 978 0 340 92651 2

Introduction

This book is intended to help you do everything necessary to achieve the highest possible grade in the Edexcel A2 Applied ICT Single Award qualification. To achieve accreditation, you need to complete the three compulsory AS units plus three A2 units.

You must take units 7 and 8 plus one chosen from units 10, 11 and 12. This book covers all five of these units so that it will be useful to all A2 students.

Unit 7

This unit builds on your experiences of using databases, which you will have covered in AS Unit 2. You will need to understand data modelling in the A2 unit and this is explained in this book. This part of the book demonstrates the development of a database so that the student can see the steps and the techniques needed in order to produce a database ready for assessment.

Unit 8

This is about project management. Students have to use project management software in order to plan the development of a software product. The software product can be the output from one of your optional units. The book demonstrates techniques using Microsoft Project and the CD contains another example of project management software that can be used to plan and control the activities that go into a project.

Unit 10

This unit is about multimedia. The CD contains software that might be helpful in editing the files used in a multimedia project. This part of the book follows through an example multimedia project in order to demonstrate the stages and techniques involved.

Unit 11

This unit is about producing a spreadsheet product. This part of the book describes the planning stages and execution of a spreadsheet project with examples of many of the techniques that might be useful in producing a spreadsheet for assessment.

Unit 12

This unit is about customising applications. Its main focus is on how to program in a spreadsheet and in a database management system using an event-driven programming language. Students who wish to take their IT studies further should take this option. This is because many IT students do not learn to program at all and having some experience in programming will place you ahead of the game in any IT employment or higher education situation. The book covers many examples of programming techniques and many of the examples are also included on the CD.

UNIT 7
Using database software

Database applications

Aims

■ To introduce Unit 7

■ To explore features of a database application

Introduction

Event.mdb This file is used through Unit 7.1 to allow you to explore some of the features of a relational database. It is likely that your own database will be simpler than this one.

In Unit 2 of the AS course, you looked at transactional websites and how databases played an important part in the back office processes of running an online shopping site. In this unit you will learn about the design and construction of databases. Later, you will be developing a database for an end user.

This unit is externally assessed, so you do not produce an eportfolio. The assessment will be in the form of an assignment set by the awarding body in which you will be required to design, implement and test a relational database. You will be given a functional specification and some data to start the database.

The assessment will take place (under controlled conditions) for 10 hours over 3 weeks. During the production of the database you will need to respond to feedback from others, but the solution must be your own work.

The pre-release files for the Unit 7 examination will be available 3 working weeks before the actual examination.

There are many uses for databases both large and small. A small company might keep employee details in a database. Your school or college will have a management system that contains lots of information about students. It needs to keep things such as:

▶ name and address
▶ contact numbers
▶ examination entries
▶ timetable details
▶ registration information
▶ notes about students.

Even in a large school, a database such as this is small when compared with systems such as those possessed by the Inland Revenue. Their system has many details about everyone who has a national insurance number.

The Driver and Vehicle Licensing Agency (DVLA) database contains details about every car and driver in the UK. It has millions of records. It is used to gather information about drivers such as:

▶ number of points on their licence
▶ medical details that affect driving

▶ vehicles they can drive
▶ licence expiry date
▶ photograph.

It holds the following details about cars:

▶ MOT date
▶ colour
▶ make
▶ model
▶ tax expiry date
▶ fuel used
▶ engine size.

These are only examples of details it holds, but you can appreciate just how big this database must be.

Coombes Wood Events is a company that organises training events in locations around the country. It employs a number of people who deliver the training. The database is used to hold all the information relating to the events.
    Some of the functions of the database are:

● Recording the location of events
● Recording the names of people attending events
● Recording the names of employees delivering events
● Invoicing those attending
● Working out the fees paid to employees.

The database structure

A very simple database called a flat file database is made up of one table. The table contains a number of records, each consisting of fields.

In the example in Figure 7.1, the table consists of 4 records, each with 3 fields holding data.

Relational databases consist of more than one table holding data with relationships defined between them. A relationship is a link or connection between tables allowing interaction between the tables. See also Unit 7.4. Relationships allow the database to be used in a more productive way and, if used correctly, this reduces the amount of duplicated data held.

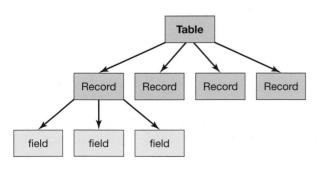

 Figure 7.1

> **CASE STUDY**
>
> Coombes Wood Events needs to hold details of which employee is organising each event. The employee details are held in one table and the details of events in another. By defining a relationship between the two tables, the employee details are linked to the event organised by that employee.
>
> If you examine Figure 7.2, you will notice that the events table simply has a field for the employee's ID number – it does not store employee details. This is linked to the EmployeeID field in the table of employees.

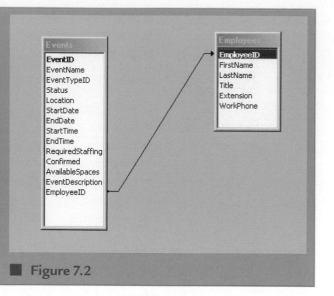

■ Figure 7.2

The structure of a database is important for users even if they cannot see it, because this determines how the database functions as a whole and how it turns the data it stores into information in the required format. When planning a database for a particular application/purpose, the overall structure is designed at a very early stage, taking into account the client's requirements.

It is unlikely that the person using a database will be an IT expert, so ease of use must be considered when designing the database system. In this unit, you are the IT expert designing the database and you must take account of user feedback. One of the most important aspects of this feedback will always be ease of use. If a database is easy to use then less training will be required and users can benefit from the system more quickly.

The user interface

The user interface is the point of interaction between the database system and the human user. It is of the greatest significance because it determines how easily the user can make the database do what is required.

The user interface is made up of the screen images and also devices such as the mouse, through which the user interacts with and controls the computer or, in this case, the database, which is stored on the computer system.

There are several kinds of user interface including:

▶ A command-driven interface, where you enter commands using a keyboard. In Figure 7.3, the command is dir/p, which displays a directory of files and subdirectories.

■ Figure 7.3

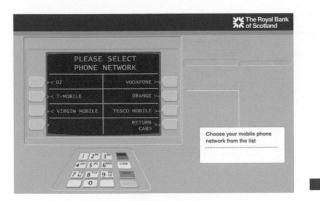

▶ A menu-driven interface, where you select commands from menus displayed on the screen. ATMs (cash machines) usually have this type of interface.

■ **Figure 7.4**

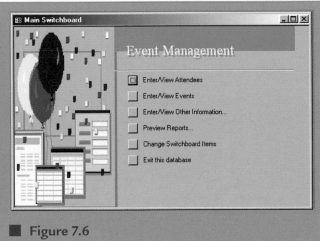

▶ A graphical user interface (GUI), where you interact with the computer using icons or menus.

■ **Figure 7.5**

CASE STUDY

Richard, the manager of Coombes Wood Events, asked for the database to be designed with a very simple user interface because he does not find using computers easy. The database was set up for him using a feature of Microsoft Access called Switchboards, which are very easy to use. The user is given a set of choices and simply clicks the button to select that choice.

■ **Figure 7.6**

Another part of the user interface is where the users enter the data into the system. Again, this needs to be presented in a format that the user finds easy.

In the Coombes Wood database, all the data entry screens are set up as forms, with very clear labels and text boxes to enter the data.

On the form, there are other features that make the database easy to use. For example, there are three buttons at the bottom left of the form. Once the details of an attendee have been entered, the next thing to do is register that person at an event. This is done by providing a button for this purpose, so the user does not have to go back to the main switchboard but can perform that operation straight from the current form. If the attendee has been on other courses, then these are shown on this form, again avoiding the need to go into other parts of the database or change screens.

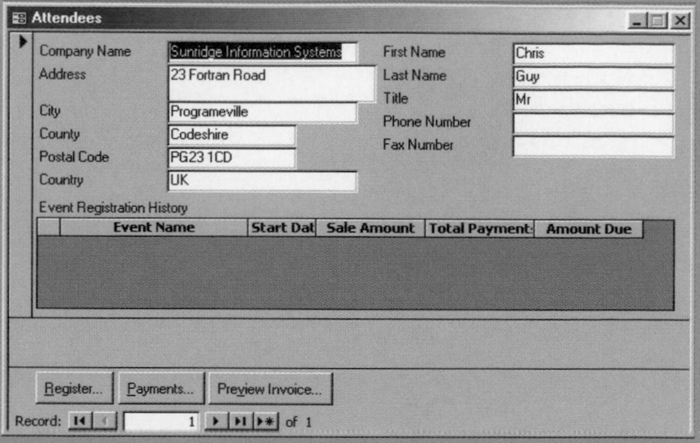

■ Figure 7.7

As you will have seen in this short introduction, there is a lot more to designing an effective user interface than just putting a few choices on a menu system. A good design looks at other features and tries to make the whole process of using the database as easy as possible.

Measures used to protect the quality of the data

> **VALIDATION** the process of checking data by the computer system as it is input to ensure that it conforms to predetermined rules. Validation can ensure that data is reasonable but it cannot ensure that it is correct.

A database is only as good as the data it contains. If there are errors in the data then the output cannot be relied on. It is impossible to remove all possibility of errors but a good database can help to significantly reduce both the number of errors and the impact of these errors on the information produced by the database system. Checks can be built in that perform VALIDATION of data as it is entered.

In the database for Coombes Wood Events, part of the company information is the current rate of sales tax (VAT). There is a validation check built in so that this cannot exceed 100%. If a value that is too high is entered then a message is produced.

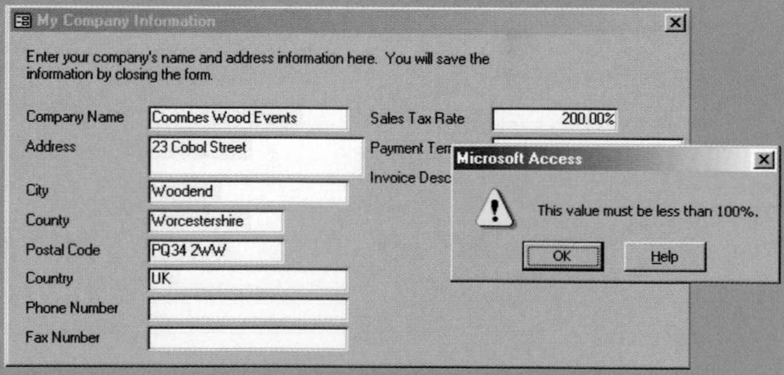

■ Figure 7.8

You will learn more about **validation** on **pp. 42–5**

Further information on **data formats** can be found on **pp. 35–9**

In your assessment task, you must make sure that you build validation checks into your final database, so that any data that is imported into your system is checked for suitability.

Data formats can also be used to ensure the quality of data. By setting the correct data format for a field, you can help to make sure that the data entered is of the correct type and format. For example you can make sure a user enters a date in the desired format, since there are lots of ways to enter this:

▶ 17/07/05
▶ 17/5/2005
▶ 17th June 2005
▶ 5/17/2005 (American).

By setting the exact format when setting up the database you can avoid problems later.

Types and forms of output

Good database design will consider the needs of the user when deciding the type and form of output from the database. Sometimes the output needs to be printed, on other occasions it is better on screen.

The exact form of output from a database should be discussed with the end user before the database is implemented. The user's needs must be taken into account – it is no good printing out huge lists of information only to find that it is of little use to the user.

CASE STUDY

The switchboard shown allows the reports to be previewed before printing.

Reports form the basis for printed output from this database. The ability to preview these reports means that they can be looked at on screen and then printed if needed. This feature was added at the request of Richard who wanted to cut down on wasted printing in the office.

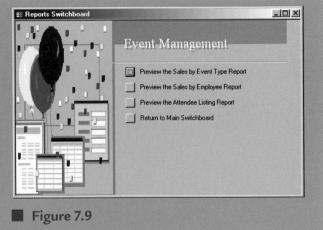

■ Figure 7.9

Methods used to extract information

The main ways of extracting information from databases in Microsoft Access are queries and reports. Queries are used to select subsets of information from tables; reports are used to present printed information in ways best suited to the user's needs.

In the example database, if someone needs to find all the events attended by a particular person, a query would be used to find all the entries in the table relating to that person.

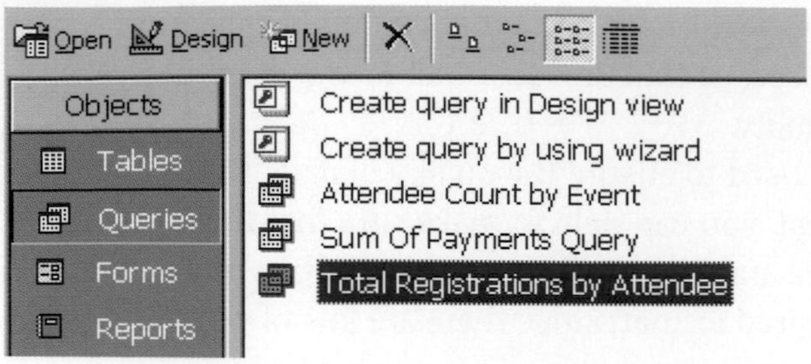

Figure 7.10 The names of the queries used in the database

When a police officer stops a car, he requests details from the control room. A query is used to search the police database for the ownership details of the car.

In the case study, some reports are based on the results of queries so that the information selected is displayed in a more user-friendly way. Some of the data entry forms, such as the one in Figure 7.7, combine the results of queries into the form to improve the way the form presents information. The part of the form displaying other events attended is based on a query in the database.

In the assessment, you will be required to extract information in a way that meets the requirements given to you and to present it in a format that is suitable for the purpose.

Functional specification

Aims

- ■ To examine how to produce a functional specification
- ■ To introduce a database that will be developed in following units

Introduction

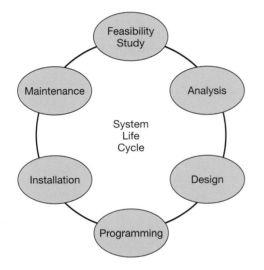

■ Figure 7.11

Databases like the one you have been looking at in Unit 7.1 can be very complex. Large commercial databases are even more complicated. This means that they must be designed very carefully from the start, since it could be expensive to fix them later if they do not perform as expected. A large business that depends on a complex system could lose millions of pounds if the system does not do its job properly. In extreme cases it might lead to the collapse of the business.

The process of building a database needs to be carried out using a systematic approach so that nothing is forgotten or left to chance.

As with any computer system it needs to go through the system life cycle.

CASE STUDY

The owner of a new DVD hire shop asked a friend to set up a database for his shop which is opening soon. He asked for a database to hold customer names and addresses and details of the DVDs in his shop. His friend set up a database to do this. His friend produced the database and an application to handle it. The day before the owner opened the store, he asked his friend for a demonstration.

His friend demonstrated how:

- Customer details could be entered.
- Lists of customers could be produced sorted in many different ways.
- DVD details could be entered.
- Lists of DVDs could be produced sorted in many different ways.

The shop owner was very impressed. 'How do I loan out a DVD to a customer?' he asked. 'Do what?' came the reply.

The database application did many things with the DVD and customer details, but the vital task of tracking DVD loans was not available. The opening of the store had to be delayed.

If only the two people in that short case study had heard of a functional specification, a lot of trouble could have been saved. They should have spent time together talking about the database and recorded in some way exactly what the database application needed to do when it was finished.

A functional specification is a formal way of identifying the requirements and recording in as much detail as possible exactly what is expected of the application.

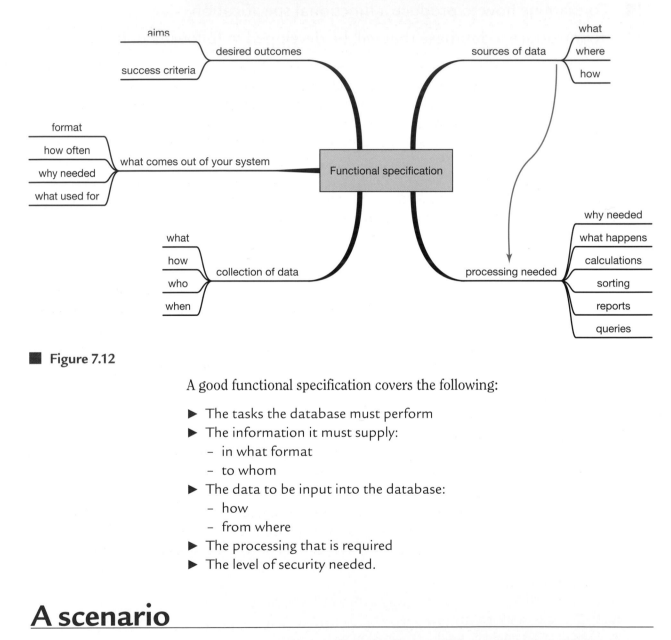

Figure 7.12

A good functional specification covers the following:

► The tasks the database must perform
► The information it must supply:
  – in what format
  – to whom
► The data to be input into the database:
  – how
  – from where
► The processing that is required
► The level of security needed.

A scenario

In the next few sections of this book, you will be working through the stages of the construction of a database. The database is to be set up for Karen who is the owner of DS driving school in the town of Butroc. Her business employs a number of instructors who each have their own car. At present, Karen works in the office, taking bookings for lessons. She takes these in several different ways. She records all the appointments in an appointments

Functional Specification. doc Use this file as you read this unit to help produce your final document.

book. Her instructors have to check each day and transfer their appointments to their own diaries. Mistakes are often made in copying the appointments. Missed appointments are the biggest source of complaints from customers.

Karen would like any new system to help avoid missed appointments and make it easier for drivers to be given their lists of appointments.

This is only a brief background to the situation. As you read through the following sections, more information will be provided. It is your job to complete the functional specification using the information provided.

The tasks the database must perform

The first stage of a functional specification is to arrive at a clear list of tasks that the database must perform before the client will accept it. The list of tasks can end up being quite long but the list should be as complete as possible.

You need to be prepared to spend some time producing this list – the clearer you are at this stage, the easier things will be later.

The views of the client are absolutely vital at this stage. There are a number of different ways that you can collect these. Sometimes, the person who is leading the project describes the tasks and this person may not be the end user of the database. You should try to find out the needs of the end user, so that the list of tasks represents these needs as well.

Interview

This is not the same as a job interview, but is simply an occasion when the analyst who is looking into the problem sits down with the client or the users of the system and asks some questions about the tasks they do now and how they see the database helping to carry out those tasks in the future. It is a good idea to make a list of questions you would like to ask, but you should be prepared to change your questions and to ask more if the need arises.

Notes from an interview with Karen
- Missed appointments are a problem.
- Must be able to give instructors a list of appointments.
- Some women clients only want female instructors.
- Some customers need automatic cars.
- Some customers like a particular make of car.
- It would be useful to know if a car's tax is running out.
- A learner only has two years before needing to retake the theory test.

Questionnaire or survey

This is a good way to collect information if you need the views of a lot of people. Also, questionnaires ask the same questions in the same way so that the answers are easier to process. Questionnaires need to be carefully constructed to collect correct and useful information.

The instructors and Karen's secretary were all given questionnaires about the present system. Here are some responses:

- Instructors do not like having to look in the appointments book each day.
- All of the instructors have copied appointments incorrectly into their diaries at some point.
- Karen's secretary once lost a page out of the appointments book.
- Lessons last one hour.
- The gap between lessons depends on the distance from one customer to the next.
- Instructors would like a list of their customers at intervals so they do not have to keep lots of copies of forms.

Observation

Simply watching the job being done and making some notes about the kind of tasks performed and what information is collected can produce a lot of useful information.

Notes from observations in the office
- A new customer came in to the office.
- Karen checked his (provisional) driving licence and noted the date of issue.
- Karen asked the customer to fill in a form to collect details of the name and address.
- She looked at the certificate from the theory test.
- She looked at the appointments book and booked a two-hour introductory lesson.
- She wrote the details down in the appointment book.
- She photocopied the details twice, once for the files and a copy to the instructor.

The information the database must supply, in what format and to whom

Remember how a lack of thought produced an inefficient database in the DVD library? With any luck, that is not going to happen to the database you are building for Karen and her employees. A database contains data held in such a way that it can be turned into information for different purposes. To turn data into information it needs to be given meaning. Data can be given meaning in different ways:

▶ context
▶ format
▶ labels.

How the output is produced and how it looks must be taken into consideration during the design of the database system and clearly defined in the functional specification. For example, it is possible to display a list of an instructor's appointments on a screen. This is very useful to Karen when booking an appointment, but the instructor who wants today's appointments might prefer it printed so that the information does not need to be copied, which was a problem with the old system.

> The instructors do not like having to copy out the diary every day. Your database could provide a list of lesson appointments at the start of each day to help them. It would also be useful to give them a weekly printout on a Monday, even though changes might happen on a daily basis. It would be useful to them to have this information.

The data to be input into the database, how and from where

Looking at the output required gives you a good idea of the data that is needed to generate that output. For example, you cannot expect the database application to print a list of customers whose theory test expires in the next month if the date they passed is not stored. In the notes from the interview, this is needed to warn customers if they are nearing that date since they will need to take the test again or pass a driving test before then.

The desired output needs to be studied carefully to make a list of the data items required to produce each of them. Some items of data will clearly be used in several outputs, but if you do not have the data in the system then you cannot use it. This seems obvious, but you need to be very careful to make sure that you include everything you will need at this stage.

In making up this list, you have to remember that this kind of data is covered by the Data Protection Act. This law states that you can only gather enough information to carry out your specified purpose and you should not keep any unnecessary data.

The data for your system also has to be collected before it can be input, so it is a good idea at this stage to examine who will collect the data and how they will do so. You should already have noted that a new customer is asked to fill in a form. This is one way of collecting data for your system.

The processing that is required

Turning data into information will not happen by itself. You will need to consider what processing is needed to produce that output. Some reports will need calculations to be performed, for example a customer's age can be calculated using their date of birth.

Karen would like the system to provide discounts for people who buy six lessons at a time. This requires two calculations to be performed, firstly to work out if the customer is buying more than six lessons and then to work out the discount.

To produce a list of female instructors, you will need to use some method of selecting only the records of the female instructors.

To give each instructor a list of appointments for a day, you need to select the instructor, the day, and sort the results into time order.

The level of security needed

DATA SUBJECT A person whose details are stored on a computer system and who can be identified from them.

DATA CONTROLLER A person or organisation that holds personal data on a computer system.

THE DATA PROTECTION COMMISSIONER An official appointed by the UK Government to oversee the operation of the Data Protection Act.

Security must be taken into account when dealing with personal information. The Data Protection Act states that data users must take care to prevent unauthorised access to the data.

Most databases can assign different levels of security to different users and sections of the database. For example, some fields might not be visible to some people, others might be set to be read-only. This means that they cannot be changed.

Karen does not want the instructors changing customers' names and addresses because she thinks this might lead to more mistakes being made. Some of them are very poor typists and spellers.

Users can have different levels of access so that menus, and other features are only available to people with the right level of access.

Database development

Aims

■ To examine some of the stages needed to design, develop and query a working database

Principles of database design

Analysing data

Once it has been decided what a database has to do, we then have to determine what data is needed in it and where that data will come from. The world is full of data and information. Some of it is relevant to your database and some is not. Much of the data that you will need to put into a database is messy and disorganised. You cannot proceed with creating a database until you have organised the data in a logical way.

One way to make a start is to note down all the data items that will be needed in the output. For example, in the driving school, we shall need at least the following:

■ **Figure 7.13**

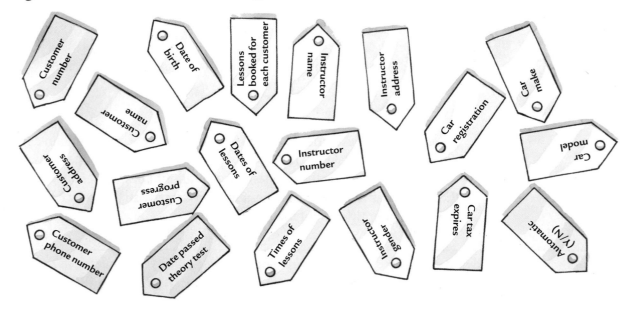

If we look through this data, we can see that some items belong together. For example, the customer number goes with the customer name, address and the phone number – all these have something to do with the customer. Similarly, there are lots of details that all have something to do with the instructor. Other items of information have something to do with the lessons being booked.

We can start to sort out this data if we try to attach each data item to something. This something is what is called an 'entity'. An entity is a real-world 'thing' about which we hold data. An entity might be a person, a car, a lesson, an invoice or a hotel booking. The point is that each data item belongs to an entity and only one entity. Each entity will normally be represented in a separate table.

A collection of data items about an entity becomes a table in a database.
Each data item is called an **attribute**. You may be more familiar with the term **field**, which applies to an attribute in a table.

An entity

Name ....

Address ....

Date of birth ....

NI number ....

Bank account number ....

It is not always easy to decide which entity 'owns' each data item. For example, if we have customers, instructors and lessons, which of these would own the total bill for 10 lessons? The answer is often that a new entity is required. A process called normalisation can be applied to decide exactly where each data item should belong.

Sorting out all this data is called data modelling. There are various techniques for doing this.

Further information about **normalisation** and **data modelling** can be found in Unit 7.4

Data models

Databases can be extremely complicated. They can very easily contain dozens if not hundreds of tables. This is before we even start to create the software that we need to handle the database. Organisations are so dependent upon their databases that it is vital to design them properly so that they can be handled efficiently without the risk of errors.

ACTIVITY

Another straightforward situation is a library borrowing system. A library system can, at the most basic level, work with just three tables – books, borrowers and loans. It isn't too difficult to decide what data goes into what table.

List the attributes needed in each of the three tables for a library borrowing system.

However, if the library system is to be really useful, it will probably take into account reservations, the ordering of new stock, the relative popularity of different books, topics or authors and many other things that go with running a library. What extra tables would be required to cope with all this?

It doesn't take long for a serious commercial database to generate complicated structures. This is why we need methodologies in order to tell us how to work out what to do. There are lots of different methodologies available for designing database systems.

The importance of modelling

It is sometimes tempting for students to produce databases from scratch without thinking too much about what goes into what table. Producing models might not seem to be the most interesting aspect of setting up a system. But, even with a small database, such as one you might make for an assignment, things can easily get out of hand. A lack of planning can seriously upset the later stages when a database is implemented. It can be very difficult and time consuming to put errors right later. You may have to create a whole new set of data.

Database creation software

Databases are extremely important to organisations and can be very complex. Because of this, it is not surprising that there are lots of examples of software designed to make their creation and manipulation easier. Many of these examples are aimed at professionals and cost enormous amounts of money. Fortunately, there are examples which cost much less and are perfectly good for:

▶ small scale databases
▶ businesses that do not have specialist development staff
▶ teaching purposes.

Most IT students throughout the world learn their database techniques with Microsoft Access. This is produced for PCs and is capable of being used for big projects as well as the smaller scale examples above.

   Microsoft Access is an example of a database management system (DBMS). It allows the creation and manipulation of relational databases. It fulfils the basic requirements of relational database management systems, for example there is separation of the data from applications. The applications are the modules, queries and macros created by the database developer.

 Figure 7.15

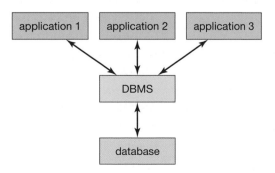

In a relational database, data is **independent** from the applications. The applications must work through the DBMS.

Figure 7.16

WIZARD   An interactive software tool that asks the user
questions and then creates something such as a table or
carries out an action such as installing software.

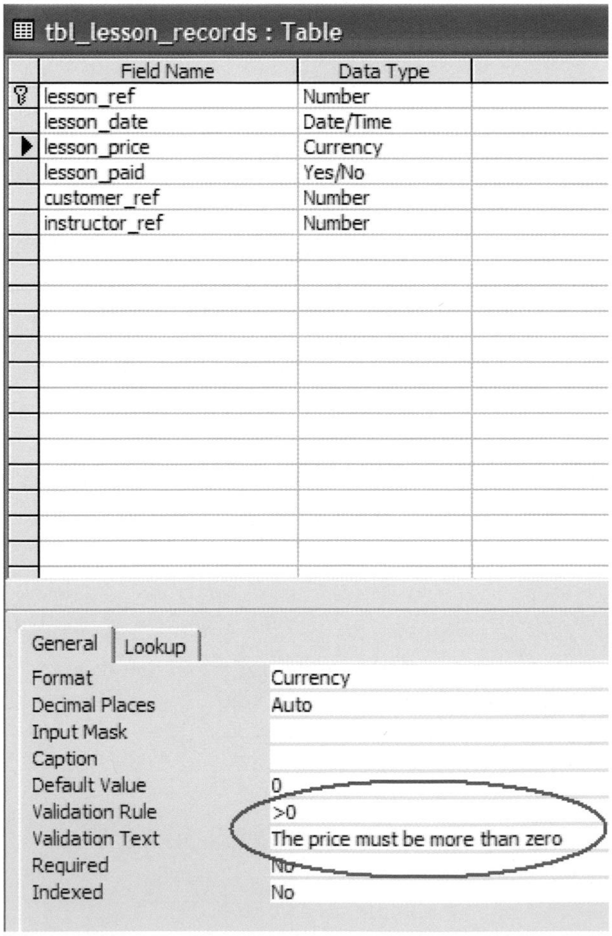

Figure 7.17

The requirement that applications must work via the DBMS means that the data is protected from being damaged by new applications. The DBMS can prevent accidental changes being made that would have an impact on other applications.

A DBMS such as Access provides a set of tools and building blocks for creating, updating and manipulating the database.

The main building blocks that a DBMS such as Access provides are visible as soon as the software is started up.

The main component parts that you will use in creating a fully functional database are:

▶ tables
▶ queries
▶ forms
▶ reports
▶ macros
▶ modules.

In many cases, Access provides WIZARDS to help you create a particular component very quickly.

Tables

Without tables, there will be no relational databases. These must be carefully designed so that they correspond to the entities that have been modelled.

Access has many useful tools to help create tables that work together. It also allows a lot of validation rules to be set up when the tables are created.

Data entry and validation

A database that contains inaccurate data can be worse than useless. A great deal of care must therefore be taken to make it as likely as possible that the data entered is accurate.

Various validation techniques can easily be built into a relational database created by DBMS systems such as Access.

Table design

We have seen that during table design, it is possible to set a wide variety of validation rules and create suitable user-friendly messages to go with them. These issues were examined in depth in Unit 2 of the AS level book.

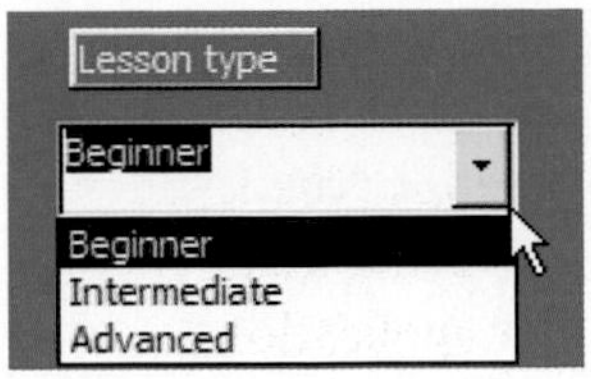

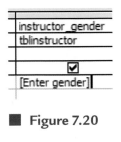

Figure 7.18

Selection from a list

Sometimes only certain data items are acceptable. One example may be that when selecting the type of lesson, only certain types are permitted. In this case, the data is selected from a list so that unacceptable data cannot be entered.

The contents of the drop-down list can be dynamic. In other words, they can change according to circumstances. For example, if a customer has already passed the basic driving test, only advanced lessons are then available.

Queries

These are mainly used in order to extract a subset of the data according to the requirements of the user. Queries can also be used to link tables together so that related data in different tables can be extracted and presented. Queries are normally attached to forms or reports so that the data selected is presented in the format required. Queries produce recordsets which can be generated when a selected group of data is required.

Queries can be created by using a tool called Query By Example (QBE), also known as the Query Design Screen. This is a grid where the tables needed are collected, the fields selected and the conditions entered so that when the query is run, the query extracts the data required.

Figure 7.19

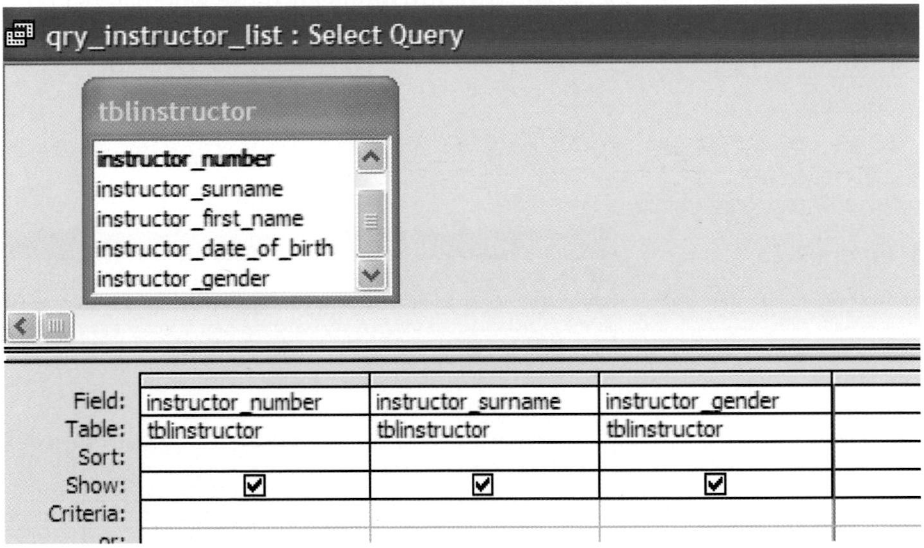

qry_instructor_list : Select Query

tblinstructor

instructor_number
instructor_surname
instructor_first_name
instructor_date_of_birth
instructor_gender

Field:	instructor_number	instructor_surname	instructor_gender	
Table:	tblinstructor	tblinstructor	tblinstructor	
Sort:				
Show:	☑	☑	☑	
Criteria:				
or:				

Queries, like all Access objects, can be varied in many ways to produce a wide range of useful results.

instructor_gender
tblinstructor

☑
[Enter gender]

Figure 7.20

Parameter queries

Sometimes you want to select a different group of data each time that you run a query. For example, you may want to show all the female driving instructors in the driving school. All you have to do is to put your instruction to the user in square brackets in the criteria box.

When the query is run, the prompt comes up for the user:

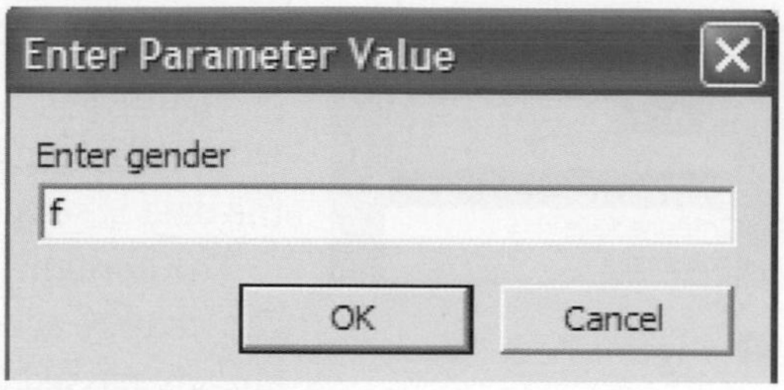

Enter Parameter Value

Enter gender

| f |

OK   Cancel

■ Figure 7.21

When the query is run, the required recordset is displayed.

■ Figure 7.22

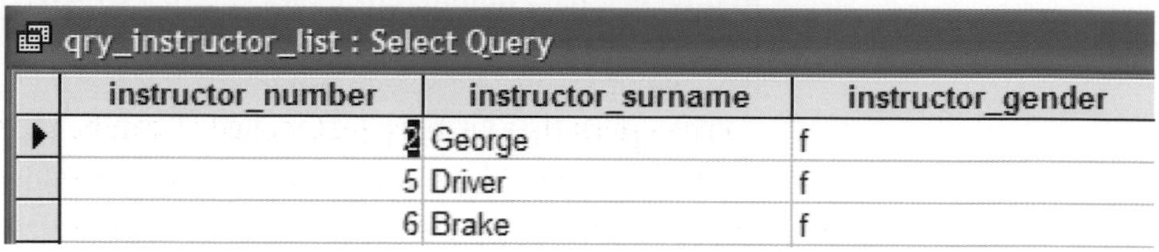

■ qry_instructor_list : Select Query

instructor_number	instructor_surname	instructor_gender
2	George	f
5	Driver	f
6	Brake	f

Queries can also be set up to perform calculations. Suppose you had details of all the lessons that had taken place in the driving school and you wanted to work out 10% discounts for those who had paid on time. You could set up a column in the query design grid that contains an expression such as:

```
lesson_price*.1
```

■ Figure 7.23

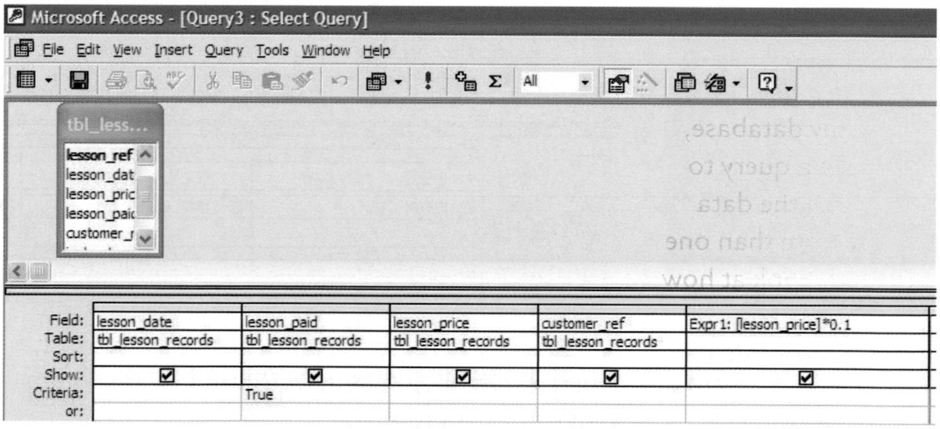

Microsoft Access - [Query3 : Select Query]

File   Edit   View   Insert   Query   Tools   Window   Help

tbl_less...

lesson_ref
lesson_dat
lesson_pric
lesson_paic
customer_r

Field:	lesson_date	lesson_paid	lesson_price	customer_ref	Expr1: [lesson_price]*0.1
Table:	tbl_lesson_records	tbl_lesson_records	tbl_lesson_records	tbl_lesson_records	
Sort:					
Show:	☑	☑	☑	☑	☑
Criteria:		True			
or:					

How did we select the records of lessons that were paid for?

This column in the query would show how much refund to give.

■ Figure 7.24

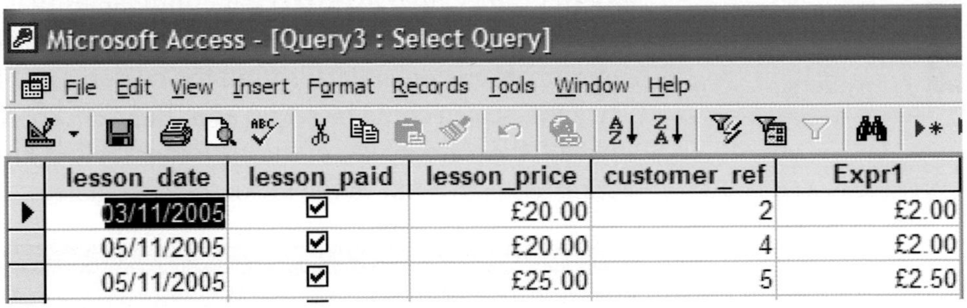

Microsoft Access - [Query3 : Select Query]

File   Edit   View   Insert   Format   Records   Tools   Window   Help

lesson_date	lesson_paid	lesson_price	customer_ref	Expr1
03/11/2005	☑	£20.00	2	£2.00
05/11/2005	☑	£20.00	4	£2.00
05/11/2005	☑	£25.00	5	£2.50

Lots of other calculations can be done in queries. The help pages that come with Access give many examples. Just click on Help and enter 'query calculations' into the search box.

The query that we have just looked at can be represented as a statement in Structured Query Language (SQL). This is particularly useful if we want to create a query during the running of a program. The code for this can be seen by selecting the View by SQL option from the menu. The table we are looking at has been named tbl_lesson_records.

```
SELECT tbl_lesson_records.lesson_date,
tbl_lesson_records.lesson_paid,
tbl_lesson_records.lesson_price,
tbl_lesson_records.customer_ref, [lesson_price]*0.1 AS Expr1
FROM tbl_lesson_records
WHERE (((tbl_lesson_records.lesson_paid)=True));
```

Multi-field searches

In the query design grid, there is a box where selection criteria can be applied. Filling in these makes sure that the recordset produced shows only the data that is wanted.

Range searches

The query design window is very versatile. It can be used to extract data that falls in a certain range. The word 'between' can be used almost as in ordinary language. To find all the customers with birthdates within a certain range, the query can be as in Figure 7.25.

ACTIVITY

In any database, make a query to search the data on more than one field. Look at how the SQL version deals with this.

■ Figure 7.25

Query1 : Select Query

tblcustomer

address2
postcode
telephone
level
date_of_birth

Field:	surname	forename	address1	date_of_birth
Table:	tblcustomer	tblcustomer	tblcustomer	tblcustomer
Sort:				
Show:	☑	☑	☑	☑
Criteria:				Between #01/01/1960# And #02/02/1978#
or:				

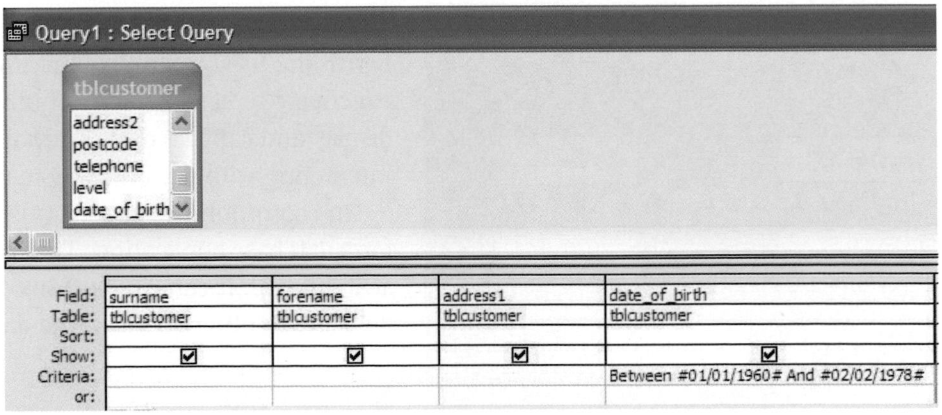

Using more than one table

Queries can be used to extract data from tables that contain related data. We can, for example, extract lesson details from the lesson records table and the appropriate customer details from the customer table all in the same query. The QBE screen could be set up as in Figure 7.26. Notice that the tables are linked – the primary key of the customer table is linked to the same field acting as FOREIGN KEY in the lesson records table.

ACTIVITY

Make a range query and look at the SQL code equivalent.

FOREIGN KEY A field used to link one table to another. It is not the primary key in the linked table.

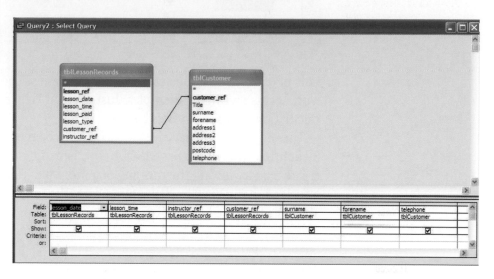

■ **Figure 7.26**

When this query is run, the details from both tables are displayed. You can base a report on such a query.

■ **Figure 7.27**

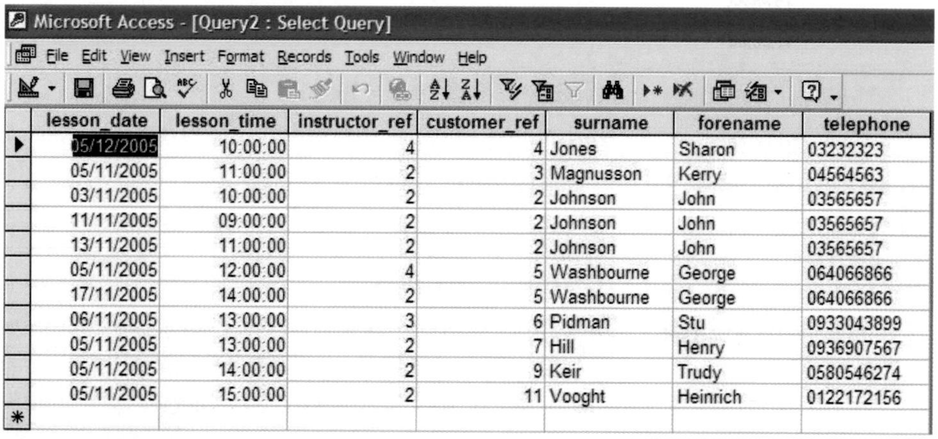

lesson_date	lesson_time	instructor_ref	customer_ref	surname	forename	telephone
05/12/2005	10:00:00	4	4	Jones	Sharon	03232323
05/11/2005	11:00:00	2	3	Magnusson	Kerry	04564563
03/11/2005	10:00:00	2	2	Johnson	John	03565657
11/11/2005	09:00:00	2	2	Johnson	John	03565657
13/11/2005	11:00:00	2	2	Johnson	John	03565657
05/11/2005	12:00:00	4	5	Washbourne	George	064066866
17/11/2005	14:00:00	2	5	Washbourne	George	064066866
06/11/2005	13:00:00	3	6	Pidman	Stu	0933043899
05/11/2005	13:00:00	2	7	Hill	Henry	0936907567
05/11/2005	14:00:00	2	9	Keir	Trudy	0580546274
05/11/2005	15:00:00	2	11	Vooght	Heinrich	0122172156

portfolio_tip

You should make sure that you use some multi-table queries in your database solution.

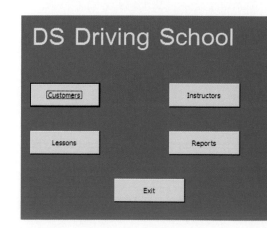

Forms

Forms are used to provide the user interface. They are effectively screens, which contain the controls needed to display and capture data. They also provide a means of interacting with the database in a user-friendly way.

One common use of a form is to provide a starting point for a database application. This is sometimes called a switchboard. It can use buttons or menu items in order to navigate to other forms in the database application.

■ **Figure 7.28**

Reports

These are the printed output from the database. They are usually based on queries but they also provide ways of grouping and sorting data as well as many formatting features. Reports can be customised to provide lists, invoices or any other document that contains data from the database.

portfolio_tip

Before you can complete a switchboard, make sure you plan what it should do and that all the reports and forms it uses have been built.

Customers

Ref	Surname	Forename	Address 1	Address 2	Pcode	Tel	Level	DOB
1	Gregory	Henry	17 High Road	Banbury	B56 6TG	05675665	B	21/11/1967
2	Johnson	John	5 The Ridge	Mapperley	NG67 7Y	03565657	I	07/03/1989
3	Magnusson	Kerry	7 Underhill Drive	Jamestown	JM8 7YY	04564563	I	08/04/1952

■ Figure 7.29

Lessons

	Time	Ref	Surname	Forename
December 18				
	09:00:00	2	Johnson	John
	10:00:00	2	Johnson	John
	10:00:00	4	Jones	Sharon
	11:00:00	2	Johnson	John
	11:00:00	3	Magnusson	Kerry
	12:00:00	5	Washbourne	George
	13:00:00	6	Pidman	Stu
	13:00:00	7	Hill	Henry
	14:00:00	5	Washbourne	George
	14:00:00	9	Keir	Trudy
	15:00:00	11	Vooght	Heinrich

■ Figure 7.30

Reports can group the output so that related information is presented together. For example a list of lessons could be produced for the management so that all lessons booked at the same time are shown together.

You should always make sure that the title of the report is meaningful. If you let the wizard make a report (often a good starting point), you will get a report heading and also column headings that are not meaningful to the reader. You should take the time to correct these to make them human-friendly.

Invoice **DS Driving School**

Dr

Washbourne

75 Caravan Road

Camberley

Surrey

17/11/2005

Lesson type

intermediate

Total cost

£25.00

■ Figure 7.31

Reports can be used for a great many purposes. It is easy to adjust a report and add extra details such as labels to make an invoice.

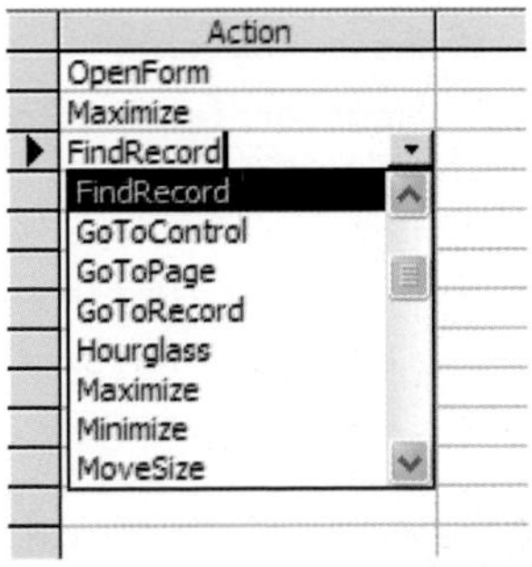
Action
OpenForm
Maximize
FindRecord
FindRecord
GoToControl
GoToPage
GoToRecord
Hourglass
Maximize
Minimize
MoveSize

■ Figure 7.32

Macros

The interface of the DBMS provides lots of menu-driven commands that allow the user to sort and display data as well as open tables and queries and create lists of various sorts. If a particular sequence of actions is often required, the actions can be stored in a macro which can then be replayed whenever required, without having to carry out the actions by using the menus.

Macros can be built up from a limited set of actions that can be selected from a drop-down list.

Macros can be attached to objects in the database and made to run when events occur such as clicking a command button or selecting an item from a menu.

Modules

If macros do not provide the degree of control required in processing data, it is possible to write programs to carry out any actions that might be necessary. In Access, a programming language called Visual Basic for Applications (VBA) is available.

■ Figure 7.33

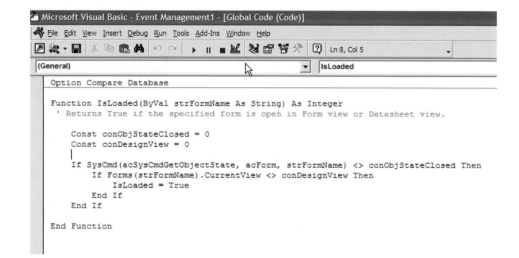

portfolio_tip

Although it is very instructive to look at the SQL, there is no expectation that any programmed solutions need to be included in this unit.

Some actions can be programmed by using another language called Structured Query Language (SQL). This is available in many database management systems. Access provides a version. It is particularly useful in creating RECORDSETS. SQL statements are an alternative way of setting up a query and are very valuable when creating queries within a VBA or other program.

Here is a short piece of VBA code that uses an SQL statement in order to create a recordset called rst_batch. The SQL statement is shown highlighted.

```
Public Function batch()
    'this function is called when all the flagged customers are to
    be matched

    Dim sql_batch As String
    Dim rst_batch As Recordset
    Set dbs = CurrentDb

    sql_batch = "SELECT basicdata.ID, basicdata.match_this_time FROM
    basicdata WHERE basicdata.match_this_time= " & True & ";"
```

```
Set rst_batch = dbs.OpenRecordset(sql_batch)

If rst_batch.RecordCount > 0 Then
With rst_batch
.MoveLast
.MoveFirst

Do While Not .EOF
key = rst_batch!ID
goget (key)
MsgBox ("Ready for next client?")
.Edit
rst_batch!match_this_time = False
.Update

.MoveNext
Loop
End With
Else: MsgBox ("Nothing to do")
End If ' end process if no data to be processed
End Function
```

RECORDSET A subset of a database. It has no physical reality, it is just a display of selected items that already exist in the tables.

At this stage, there is no need to become too concerned about all the detail in this piece of code, although it is really quite simple when you study it. You will look at VBA in more detail in Unit 12.

Menus

Many users prefer to work with drop-down menus because they are familiar with them from lots of other applications. Often it is a good idea to provide your users with the option of using a menu or a set of buttons.

Most database management systems such as Access allow the creation of customised menus. You can also easily produce them with object-based programming languages such as Visual Basic, Java or C#.

Figure 7.34 shows how a standard menu has had the daily operations of a driving school added to its menu bar.

■ Figure 7.34

When the daily operations option has been selected, by clicking on it or by pressing Alt-D (notice that the D has been underlined), it leads to a normal drop-down menu as in Figure 7.35.

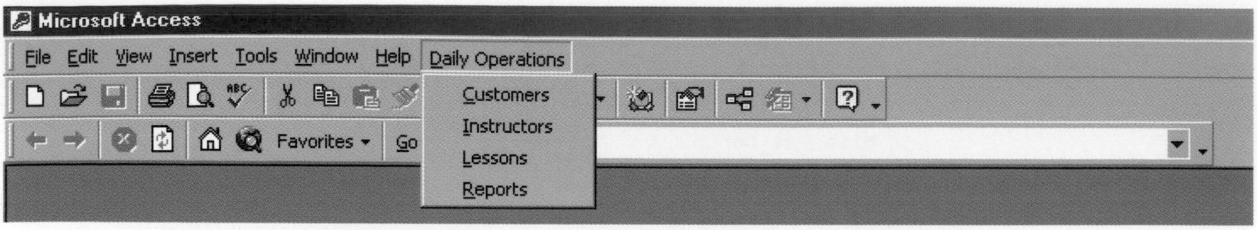

Microsoft Access

File Edit View Insert Tools Window Help Daily Operations

Customers
Instructors
Lessons
Reports

Favorites ▾   Go

Figure 7.35

Testing structures

Once you have designed the data structures that you need for a database, you should test them as far as possible so that errors do not occur later, when they will be more time consuming to fix.

Most 'testing' at this stage is really checking to make sure that:

▶ data is not repeated in tables except where required for links
▶ linked fields are the same data type
▶ each table has a primary key, chosen by the developer to avoid a default being created by the software
▶ text fields are no longer than necessary.

Proper testing will take place once you have created the planned database using the appropriate software. At that time, you can make sure that the required data will in fact be accepted, bad data is rejected and that the links are correct. This will be covered in more detail in Unit 7.5.

Data modelling

Aims

- To become familiar with the terms entities, attributes and relationships
- To use normalisation techniques in order to construct an efficient database model

What is a model?

DATA STRUCTURE
A methodical way of representing data so that it can be processed efficiently.

Usually in computing terms, a model is a representation of reality. Often it is a set of mathematical expressions or DATA STRUCTURES which attempt to mimic reality so that data processing can occur. We have seen that real-life information is messy, so we have to construct models in order to impose order on all this information. We have to turn information into data. When constructing databases, we model reality so that we can produce an efficient set of data that can be processed in the way we need.

Why structure?

When we are setting up a computer system to do a job such as organising the activities of a driving school, there are lots of items of information that we need to use. We listed these on page 15 in Unit 7.3. Some of this information is needed for one purpose only, such as when the tax on a car expires. We need to know this so that we renew it in time.

Other information has lots of uses. The customer name is needed to give to the instructor when booking a lesson. It is also needed when producing bills or when writing letters to the customer.

If all this information were just placed any old how in a filing cabinet, it would take ages to find what you needed.

ACTIVITY Have you ever been seriously inconvenienced because something you urgently needed wasn't in the right place or you didn't know where to look? List some examples and the consequences of losing vital articles of information.

If you couldn't find what you needed, you wouldn't know if the information was ever there in the first place or whether it had just got lost. This is why well-organised offices use filing cabinets and other methodical storage methods.

Making decisions about structure

It is not always obvious how you should organise things or information. Think about a collection of CDs or DVDs. Once you have several hundred of these, finding what you want to listen to or watch can be very time consuming. Many of us make systems to help us organise our possessions or our documents. Do you categorise your CDs by artist or genre? If you store them by artist, what do you do if you have a CD that has lots of different artists on it? Do you store important documents in different files according to whether they are to do with insurance, cars or official documents?

CASE STUDY

Greg is fed up with all his household documents being difficult to find. He spends a weekend sorting them out. He buys lots of new pocket files and a filing cabinet. He labels some of his files:

- mortgage
- house insurance
- car
- official documents
- receipts
- financial.

At first all goes well. It is obvious where to put the house insurance policy, the mortgage statements and the receipt for the new washing machine. The passport is no problem, neither are the children's birth certificates. What about the old bank statements? No problem, that's financial. The pet insurance documents? Change house insurance to just insurance and put them there? What about the guarantee for the microwave? It's a bit like a receipt so maybe it goes there. The electricity bills? They are official documents, aren't they? Or not?

Even with a system, things get complicated and you forget how you categorised things. Sometimes there just doesn't seem to be a system that works.

ACTIVITY

Come up with two or three different ways to categorise the goods in a supermarket.

When making a database, it is vital to get the categorisations right. If you make mistakes in the planning, it can take absolutely ages to sort out the problems. Big database projects get so complicated that they sometimes never work properly.

CASE STUDY

Use a search engine to look at the disastrous story of the planned NHS database.

Another system that had problems when launched was the online version of the 1901 census database. The problem here was one of underestimating the load put on the system. It failed within an hour of its launch and was down for repairs for almost eight months. Not only was extra hardware needed but a restructuring of the database to make searching more efficient.

It is really difficult to plan large database projects. This is why there are methodologies to help the designers get it right.

Relational databases

Most modern databases are built on the relational model. There are alternatives but relational databases combine a number of important benefits.

Relational databases are composed of many tables. The tables are linked together so that related data in different tables can be found. The idea is that as far as is possible, data is stored only once. This is so that no matter what activity is going on, the user knows that the data being looked at is the one and only copy of the up-to-date data.

Data redundancy

In the driving school scenario, each time a lesson is booked, the instructor gets a print out of the customer's name and address as well as the time of the lesson. This is so that the customer can be picked up from home if required. If the database stored the name and address every time that a lesson was booked, these details would be stored maybe 30 or 40 times. Apart from the wasted space, what if the customer moved address? Would it be necessary to go back through all the records and update the address every time? With a relational database, the address is held just once and only one adjustment need be made.

The unnecessary repetition of data in a database is called redundancy and every effort is made to avoid this.

Suppose a list of lessons is required which includes the names and addresses of the customers.

lesson_date	instructor_ref	customer_ref	surname	forename	address1	address2	postcode	telephone
03/11/2005	2	2	Johnson	John	5 The Ridge	Mapperley	NG67 7YH	03565657
05/11/2005	2	3	Magnusson	Kerry	7 Underhill Drive	Jamestown	JM8 7YY	04564563
05/11/2005	4	4	Jones	Sharon	5 High Street	Townsville	TV78 7YV	03232323
05/11/2005	4	5	Washbourne	George	75 Caravan Road	Camberley	GU2 6FR	064066866
06/11/2005	3	6	Pidman	Stu	8 Pelham Street	Colchester	CO8 7KL	0933043899
17/11/2005	2	5	Washbourne	George	75 Caravan Road	Camberley	GU2 6FR	064066866
05/11/2005	2	7	Hill	Henry	47 Pinewoods Avenue	Harborne	B77 8RE	0936907567
05/11/2005	2	9	Keir	Trudy	10 Brimstone Close	Bewdley	DY 79 8UB	0580546274
05/11/2005	2	11	Vooght	Heinrich	56 Dark Lane	Guildford	GU7 3SW	0122172156
11/11/2005	2	2	Johnson	John	5 The Ridge	Mapperley	NG67 7YH	03565657
13/11/2005	2	2	Johnson	John	5 The Ridge	Mapperley	NG67 7YH	03565657

■ **Figure 7.36**

If we stored all this data exactly as it appears in this list, we would be storing the name, address and telephone number for John Johnson three times as he has three lessons booked.

Data independence

Another great benefit of using a relational model for a database is that the data can sit there and be accessed in all sorts of ways. In the early days of computing, data was saved in different ways depending on the ideas of the programmer. If the program was updated, the data often had to be altered as well.

With data held in separate tables, it is a lot easier to make changes to the software that handles the database. It may not be necessary to change the structure of the tables or perhaps only in a small way.

Entities

An entity is something about which we store data. It normally has some sort of real-life identity but it doesn't have to. In the examples that you need to work with in this specification, there will not be any need to get into abstract ideas. The entities will usually be easy to understand.

An entity translates into a data table. In the DS Driving School example, some entities are physical objects and it is easy to visualise them:

► customers
► instructors
► cars.

Some entities are not physical such as:

► lessons
► car services.

We will see that often, as we develop ideas about what a database must be able to do, we find that more and more entities are needed. Most real-life databases have very many entities. Entities proliferate in order to keep data redundancy under control.

Attributes

These are the items of data that we store about each entity. They describe the entity. In the past, you have probably called them *fields* in a data table.

Attributes include such examples as surname, date and time.

Primary key

The primary key is the attribute which uniquely identifies an individual example of an entity. We usually choose reference numbers to make a primary key. So, in the case of the entity 'customer' in the driving school example, each individual customer is identified by a customer reference number. Sometimes a primary key is a compound key. This is when it is made up from two or more attributes. A hotel room booking can be uniquely identified by giving the room number and the date, so the two items together can uniquely identify a booking.

Relationships

Data in different tables – about different entities – is often related. For example, there is a relationship between a driving-school customer and a lesson. The lesson 'belongs' to a customer in a sense.

It makes no sense to keep all the details of a lesson together with all the details of a customer – as we have seen, this leads to storing a lot of information many times. So, we create a relationship that lets us look up the repeated data in the appropriate table. We do this in Access by making links.

In Figure 7.37, we can see that a relationship exists between the primary key customer_ref in the tblCustomer table and the same data in the

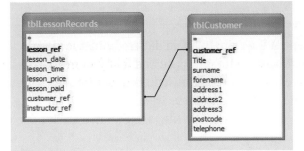

Figure 7.37

tblLessonRecords table. The attribute customer_ref in the tblLessonRecords table is called the foreign key. It is not unique as a foreign key, but customer_ref is unique for each record in the tblCustomer table where it is a primary key.

The use of attributes to form relationships is the only place where you will normally see duplicated data in a well-designed relational database.

Relationships come in three sorts: one-to-one, one-to-many and many-to-many.

Figure 7.38

One-to-one

If every occurrence of an entity is always matched by one occurrence of another entity, we have a one-to-one relationship. An example would be if we had an entity, customer, and another entity, telephone, and every customer had one and only one telephone number, not shared with anyone else. We can draw this as in Figure 7.38.

If we find that we have a one-to-one relationship, we may as well put the data all in the same table.

Figure 7.39

One-to-many

This is the usual type of relationship in a relational database. It means that every occurrence of an entity is matched by more than one occurrence of a related entity. An example from the driving school is customer and lesson because each customer has many lessons but each lesson only has one customer. We draw this as in Figure 7.39.

Figure 7.40

Many-to-many

When we are planning our database, we sometimes find that planned entities have a many-to-many relationship. This means that for every occurrence of one entity, there is more than one occurrence of a related entity. Also, the relationship is the same the other way round. If we had an entity, customer, and an entity, car, we would find that a customer might use more than one car and each car is used by more than one customer. We represent such a situation as in Figure 7.40.

Many-to-many situations are best avoided when constructing data tables. They make processing difficult, if not impossible. The way to fix many-to-many problems is to create a new table that acts as a link between the two entities. In this case, we would create an entity, and hence a table, such as **booking**. Each customer has many bookings, each car has many bookings, but each booking has only one car and only one customer.

Figure 7.41

Producing a set of workable one-to-many relationships is a vital stage in the construction of a relational database. There is a formal method for doing this called *normalisation*.

Normalisation

Normalising a database is essential if we are to avoid data redundancy. We do not want redundancy because it wastes storage space and leads to errors. The principles of normalisation were devised by Edgar Codd in 1970. These principles were a set of rules and if a database obeys them, it is said to be normalised. The idea is to simplify the content of the tables so that each table contains details about only one entity.

The process of normalisation takes place as a series of stages. As each stage is completed, the database is said to be in first, second or third normal form. You only have to work to this level, although further stages are possible.

We shall take a look at a brief example from the DS Driving School to illustrate the essential points about normalising a database.

Suppose we are constructing a simple database to store details of lessons as in Figure 7.42.

We would probably store additional details at least including the following:

► Customer number
► Customer forename
► Customer surname
► Customer address
► Customer phone number
► Date of lesson
► Time of lesson
► Instructor number
► Instructor name
► Instructor address
► Instructor gender.

Lesson summary

Instructor	Date	Time	Forename	Surname
Connolly				
	05/11/2005	10:00:00	Sharon	Jones
	05/11/2005	12:00:00	George	Washbourne
George				
	03/11/2005	10:00:00	John	Johnson
	05/11/2005	11:00:00	Kerry	Magnusson
	05/11/2005	13:00:00	Henry	Hill
	05/11/2005	14:00:00	Trudy	Keir
	05/11/2005	15:00:00	Heinrich	Vooght
	11/11/2005	09:00:00	John	Johnson
	13/11/2005	11:00:00	John	Johnson
	17/11/2005	14:00:00	George	Washbourne
Guy				
	06/11/2005	13:00:00	Stu	Pidman

■ **Figure 7.42**

If we were storing this in a simple table, we would set up a set of records where each record equals one lesson. Part of the table is shown in Figure 7.43.

instructor_surname	forename	surname	address1	telephone	customer_ref	instructor_ref	lesson_date	lesson_time
Connolly	George	Washbourne	75 Caravan Road	064066866	5	4	05/11/2005	12:00:00
Connolly	Sharon	Jones	5 High Street	03232323	4	4	05/11/2005	10:00:00
George	John	Johnson	5 The Ridge	03565657	2	2	13/11/2005	11:00:00
George	John	Johnson	5 The Ridge	03565657	2	2	11/11/2005	09:00:00
George	Heinrich	Vooght	56 Dark Lane	0122172156	11	2	05/11/2005	15:00:00
George	Trudy	Keir	10 Brimstone Close	0580546274	9	2	05/11/2005	14:00:00
George	Henry	Hill	47 Pinewoods Avenu	0936907567	7	2	05/11/2005	13:00:00
George	George	Washbourne	75 Caravan Road	064066866	5	2	17/11/2005	14:00:00
George	Kerry	Magnusson	7 Underhill Drive	04564563	3	2	05/11/2005	11:00:00
George	John	Johnson	5 The Ridge	03565657	2	2	03/11/2005	10:00:00
Guy	Stu	Pidman	8 Pelham Street	0933043899	6	3	06/11/2005	13:00:00

■ **Figure 7.43**

We can see that the instructors' names are repeated as are customer details. This leads to the redundancy problems we have already looked at. In this screen shot, we can see only the instructor's surname but, in reality, we would probably want to know more about each instructor such as the forename, address and gender. We will keep it as simple as we can at this stage.

USING DATABASE SOFTWARE

32

Stage 1 – Remove repeating attributes

We shall take out the instructor surname (and anything else to do with the instructor). We shall put this in a new table and call it **Instructor**. We can write it like this:

Instructor (<u>Instructor number</u>, Instructor surname, Instructor forename, Instructor gender)

We underline the instructor number because that will be our primary key.

We now have the rest of the data like this:

Customer (<u>Customer number</u>, Customer forename, Customer surname, Customer address, Customer phone number, Date of lesson, Time of lesson)

We have customers and their lessons stored under the primary key Customer number.

The tables are now in first normal form.

Stage 2 – Make all attributes functionally dependent upon the primary key

Basically, what we need to do is to make sure that in each table, all the attributes have a one-to-one relationship with the primary key. In the case of the Instructor table, this is correct. An instructor, identified by a number, has one surname, one forename and one gender.

There is a problem with the Customer table. A customer, identified by a number, has one forename, one surname, one address, one phone number and ... lots of lessons! What we need is another table. We shall call it **Lesson** and remove into it anything that is unique to a lesson.

So, we get:

Customer (<u>Customer number</u>, Customer forename, Customer surname, Customer address, Customer phone number)

and

Lesson (<u>Lesson number</u>, Lesson date, Lesson time)

We now have one-to-one relationships between all the attributes and their respective primary keys. They are in second normal form.

Stage 3 – Remove any attributes not dependent upon the primary key

What you need to remember here is that every attribute in a table must be dependent upon *the key, the whole key and nothing but the key*. Another way of looking at it is each attribute must contain information about the entity referred to in the primary key. When this is true, the database is said to be in third normal form.

In our DS Driving School example, we already have this situation so our database is already in third normal form.

To show how there can be a problem, in this table of information about cars, the company's country does not change with each different car – it gives us no separate information about a particular car – it tells us about the company not the car. To make this table into third normal form, we would need to create another table containing the company country and remove that field from this table. The company name could provide the basis for a link.

Company	Company country	Model	Colour	Registration number
Citroën	France	C4	Blue	VX56ABC
Ford	UK	Ka	Blue	VB52XYZ
Ford	UK	Focus	Red	BN53ZZZ

When you are designing data tables, it is important to break down the data into small units. Many inexperienced database designers set up fields such as 'Name' or 'Address'. This can make processing very difficult later. Suppose we need to send a mailing to everybody in a particular town. It is much easier to do this if the town is stored separately from the rest of the address. It is usual to split the name up into title, surname and forename – sometimes the initials too. Addresses are often split into at least three lines and another for postcode.

Creating a relational database structure

Entities, tables, attributes and fields

In Unit 7.4, we took a close look at how a database can be modelled using entities and attributes. The entities are the 'things' about which we store data. The attributes are the data items that we store about the entities.

When we actually create a database, we turn these ideas into reality. We make a separate table based on each of the entities and we make fields to represent the attributes. For example, we can create a table of cars, with fields such as make, model and colour.

Field types

To a computer, data is just data. It is all stored as bit patterns, 0s and 1s, otherwise known as binary digits. That is it – there is no meaning at all. We, as human users however, want different collections of data to represent totally different things. There is no problem to this, we can say that a particular group of bits represents a number, a letter, an instruction, a picture or a cabbage if we want. We make the rules.

In Figure 7.44, a part of a computer's memory is shown diagrammatically, to demonstrate that we can treat different parts of it differently.

program instructions	letters	whole numbers	fractional numbers

■ Figure 7.44

When we design a database, we set up our rules at the time of design. This way, when the data is processed, we get out of the system what we want. For example, if we want to add up some numbers, we have to establish that the data is in fact represented as number data and not as letters.

The decision we make about what a particular item of data, stored as binary digits, represents is called determining its data type.

There are hundreds of different possibilities for data types, but in any particular system, there are usually limits. Also, the names given to data types

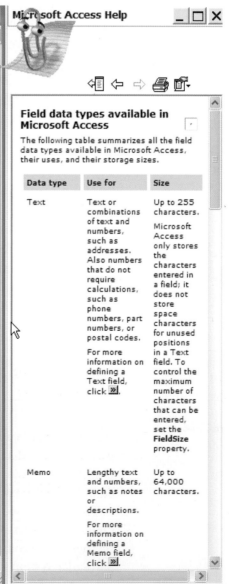

Figure 7.45

may vary a little according to the system being used. For example, in Access there is a data type called Text. In most programming languages, this would be called String. When we are talking about data types in a data table, we more commonly talk about 'field types'.

When a field is created in a data table you have to decide what field type it is to be. In Microsoft Access, there are several possibilities.

The main types shown in Figure 7.45 take care of most decision-making when setting up fields, but they can lead to further choices which may need to be carefully considered. Choosing the field type not only affects whether you get the right output, it also affects the amount of storage space taken up and the speed of processing.

We shall now look at some of the main data types available in database management systems. The examples are based on Microsoft Access.

Figure 7.46

instructor_first_name	Text
instructor_date_of_birth	Date/Time
instructor_gender	Text

General | Lookup
Field Size   1
Format
Input Mask

■ **Figure 7.47**

If at any time you need to know more about data types you can always look up plenty of useful facts in the help pages that come with the database application.

Text

This type is probably the most commonly used. It allows the storage of any character that can be typed. Letters, numbers and symbols can all go in as text. You can enter up to 255 characters in a text field. However, you do not always want to store that many. Relational database management systems store data in fixed-length fields. If you do not tell Access anything, it will reserve the maximum 255 characters for each and every item that you store in that field. If you store a name such as 'Fred', the four letters go in then the rest of the allocated space is wasted. It is better to limit the size of text fields to what you think will be the maximum you will need.

In the DS database, the instructor gender is stored as Text in one character, because we only need to store 'M' or 'F'. By coding this data, we also speed data entry and reduce the likelihood of making typing errors.

People often make mistakes in using text fields. If you need to sort numbers into order or perform calculations, then a text field won't work. You *can* store numerals in a text field but the computer does not treat them as proper numbers. It treats them as the characters 0–9 – just the visual representation of numbers.

ACTIVITY

Set up a table with just one field. Call the field anything you like but set it up as text data. Enter the numbers 1 to 30. Then sort them. See where 1, 2 and 3 are. Why is that?

Memo

If you need a long comment in a record, you can use a memo field. This allows the storage of up to 64 000 characters. A suitable example in the driving school scenario would be a field to hold notes about the progress of a customer.

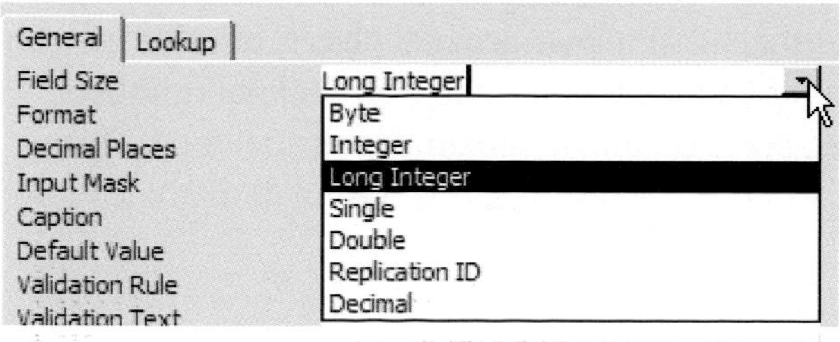

General | Lookup
Field Size   Long Integer
Format   Byte
Decimal Places Integer
Input Mask   Long Integer
Caption   Single
Default Value   Double
Validation Rule Replication ID
Validation Text Decimal

■ **Figure 7.48**

Number

If you need to do sorting or calculating, you need a number data type. But there are different number types all available under the heading 'Number'.

You can look up the details but some of the main facts are shown on the following page.

Number type	Meaning	Uses
Byte	Integer taking up 1 byte of storage.	Whole numbers up to 255. Use integers where you don't need decimal places as they take up less storage and process faster.
Integer	Integer taking up 2 bytes of storage.	Whole numbers up to 65 535.
Long Integer	Integer taking up 4 bytes of storage.	Whole numbers up to 4 294 967 295.
Single	Number with decimal point.	Use whenever you need fractional numbers. Single and double are the equivalent of floating point in some programming languages. In a floating point number, the number is stored in two parts, the mantissa or fractional part and the exponent (the power to which it is raised).
Double	Large number with decimal point.	For very big numbers where greater precision is required.
Autonumber	This is automatically assigned as a unique number. It takes 4 bytes.	Can be useful for a primary key.

Don't make the mistake of choosing a number field type if you have data with leading zeros or spaces or dashes in it. Telephone numbers have these, so must be stored as text.

Boolean

This is also known as Yes/No data. Useful for fields where only true or false data is needed, such as whether someone has paid a bill or not. Boolean data only takes up 1 bit of storage as it can be represented by 0 or 1.

Date and time

There are various ways that computer systems store dates. They can cause confusion, especially as Access has a special Date/Time data type that serves the purpose of storing dates and times.

Date/Time data takes up 8 bytes of storage. It is stored as a number. This makes it possible to perform calculations. For example, you can find out the date 20 days on from today by using the expression i. The function Now finds the date and time currently recorded on the computer's system clock.

You can choose how the date or time will look when displayed and what part of it you need to show by setting its format. You can also decide whether a time is to be shown in 12- or 24-hour format, with or without the seconds.

Currency

Many databases need to store data about sums of money. It is natural to choose one of the number formats that allows decimal places, but this is not a good idea. When calculations are done by a computer on decimal numbers, some values cannot be stored precisely and approximations are made. This can lead to errors which get worse if the results of one calculation are fed into another and so on.

General Date	19/06/1994 17:34:23
Long Date	19 June 1994
Medium Date	19-Jun-94
Short Date	19/06/1994
Long Time	17:34:23
Medium Time	05:34 PM
Short Time	17:34

Figure 7.49

Example

If £1.57 is divided by 3, the result will be 52.33333333 pence. Depending on the data type used to store this, the result might be stored in a rounded-down form, i.e. 52.33. If this result is now multiplied by a large number such as 200, the result will be 10 466 instead of the more accurate 10 466.66667. Further multiplications will increase the difference between the accurate figure and the approximate one.

The special currency format stores the two sides of the point as separate integers. This means that no approximations occur and the results will be exact.

The currency format also automatically displays whatever currency symbol, such as the pound (£) or dollar ($), is set up in the system configuration.

Other data types

Databases often need to store sounds and pictures. For example, a database of music CDs might contain a short extract from each one.

The DS Driving School database may need to store photos of the instructors. In this case, the data type OLE object is available. This can be linked to any suitable file such as a BMP picture.

■ Figure 7.50

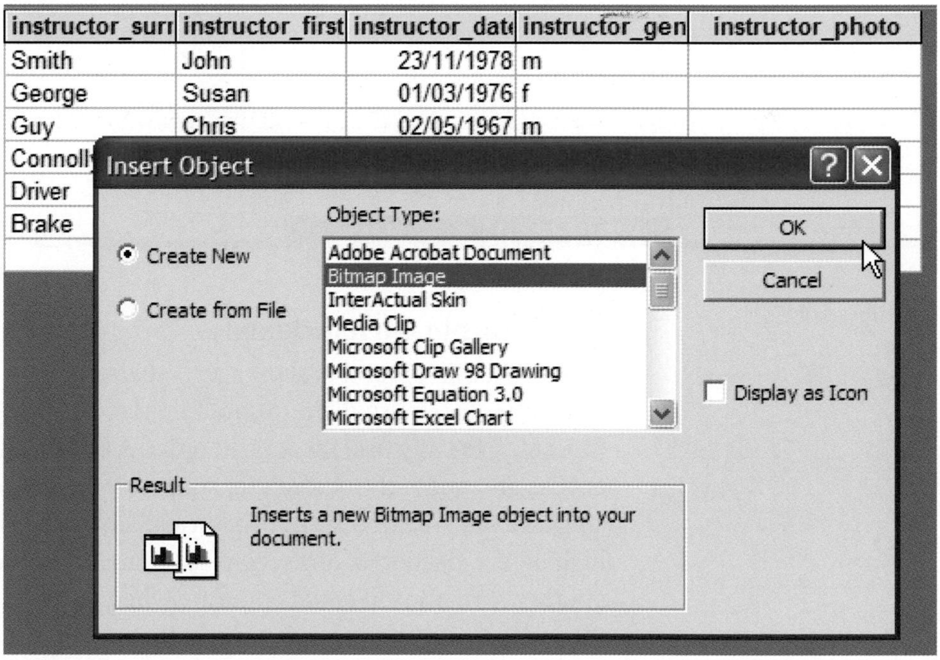

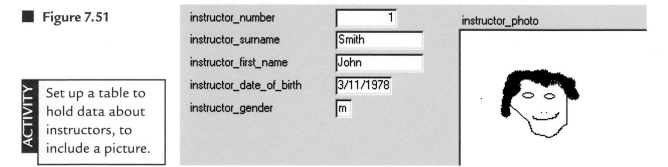

The images can then be displayed on forms or reports.

■ Figure 7.51

ACTIVITY

Set up a table to hold data about instructors, to include a picture.

Indexes

Many databases make use of indexes. They work just like the index in a book. When the database software is looking for a record, it first of all looks it up in the index. It then uses the index to go straight to the part of the data table where the record is stored. This way, it does not have to look through all the data that goes before the required record.

You can create an index on any field or on many fields. So, if you have a table with lots of records and you often need to search for someone's surname or a reference number, you can add an index to that field to help speed up the search.

Access lets you create indexes in table design view by simply selecting the field or fields you want for an index and then you choose Yes from the 'indexed' field in the design screen.

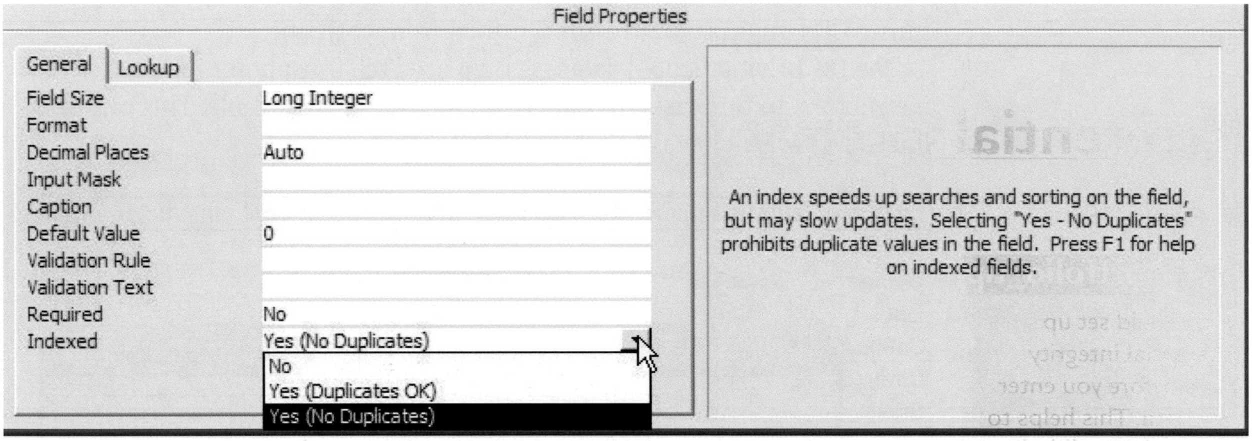

Field Properties

General	Lookup
Field Size	Long Integer
Format	
Decimal Places	Auto
Input Mask	
Caption	
Default Value	0
Validation Rule	
Validation Text	
Required	No
Indexed	Yes (No Duplicates)

No
Yes (Duplicates OK)
Yes (No Duplicates)

An index speeds up searches and sorting on the field, but may slow updates. Selecting "Yes - No Duplicates" prohibits duplicate values in the field. Press F1 for help on indexed fields.

■ Figure 7.52

The trouble with indexes

You might think that it is always a good idea to have indexes on lots of fields. After all, you can use them to speed up searches. But, nothing is for free! Indexes, to be any use, must be in order. A book index isn't much help if all the entries are randomly located! So, suppose you index a table on surname. The software will create a list of surnames in alphabetical order so it can quickly look up the location of any record searching by surname. Then you add another surname – it could come anywhere. The software then has to re-build the index to put the new surname in the proper place and that takes time.

So, indexes can be a good idea if the database doesn't change much. If it is updated a lot, it will spend most of its time re-building indexes and you will lose the advantages of quick searches.

Relationships

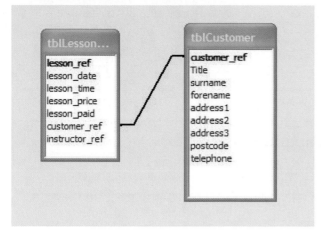

Figure 7.53

In Unit 7.4, we had a look at how tables are planned so that they work efficiently with minimal data redundancy. The idea is that if data is required from a different table, the database software can find it correctly.

So, if the name and address of a customer is required to be displayed alongside lesson details, all that we need to do is to make a link between the lesson table and the customer table.

We can do this permanently for the whole database by using the relationships facility.

We can also set them up to apply to a particular query. In either case, when they are in place, the software will always associate the right customer with the one referenced in the lesson table.

Referential integrity

portfolio_tip

You should set up referential integrity rules before you enter any data. This helps to ensure data validation.

Suppose we have a relationship between a lesson and a particular customer. Maybe customer number 2 has booked lots of lessons. What if we delete customer number 2 from the customer table? There will now be lots of lesson records that do not connect to any customer details. This can cause big problems in processing the data.

We get around this by enforcing *referential integrity*. If this is set, then it will be impossible to delete or change records in such a way that they no longer match linked records in other tables.

If you try to delete a record from the lesson table where there is a reference to lesson details in the lesson records table, referential integrity rules will not allow it.

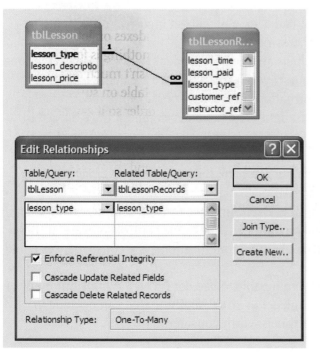

Figure 7.54

Figure 7.55

Validation techniques

Aims

- To understand the importance of validation
- To learn about some validation techniques

What is validation?

Validation is the process of checking that data input into a computer system is acceptable. It is carried out automatically by the software according to whatever rules have been set up by the software designer. Validation is carried out at the time of input.

Validation does not ensure that the data is accurate, only that it conforms to certain rules. So, if a validation check ensures that someone's surname must not contain numerals, it will reject the name B8nd. However, if the name is Bond and the operator types in Moneypenny by mistake, the check will not detect the error.

The importance of validation

You will probably have heard the expression 'GIGO' – Garbage In Garbage Out. This means that if you input bad data, you will get incorrect output, no matter how accurate the processing is.

Organisations and individuals are more dependent than ever on their stores of information. In the AS course, you learned that we are living in an information age, where information has become possibly the most valuable commodity for many organisations. The rapid development of IT has led to this situation.

An organisation can lose vast amounts of money or even go bankrupt if its information is not right. Imagine if a bank regularly made overpayments to creditors because of software errors.

Errors can be life threatening. Every time we fly on a commercial airliner, our lives are in the hands of autopilot and air traffic control software. If these systems have inaccurate data about aircraft locations, the consequences could be very grave.

Databases are particularly vulnerable to bad data. There is constant input of new data and this is always subject to error. Anything that can be done to minimise the risk of input errors is worth considering.

> **ACTIVITY**
> How could that error have been prevented?

Sometimes, bad data can be embarrassing. There was once a case where someone entered the word 'Deceased' in the record of a customer who had died. The trouble was, she entered it in the surname field. So, when a letter was next sent out to the customer, it started 'Dear Mr Deceased'. The man's widow was not pleased.

Validation techniques

When you create your database for assessment, it must include some validation techniques. In most cases, these can be set up at the time of table design. Some validation techniques are better applied on the forms used to collect data and transfer it to the underlying tables.

Presence check

Sometimes a field *has* to be filled in because if it is not, the record makes no sense at all or it cannot be used for its intended purpose. For example, if you make an airline booking online, you must supply your name, address and email address as well as flight and credit card details. If any of these are missing, the transaction cannot be made.

Access makes it easy to insist that a field is always filled in. All you have to do is to set the 'Required' property of the field to 'Yes' in the table design.

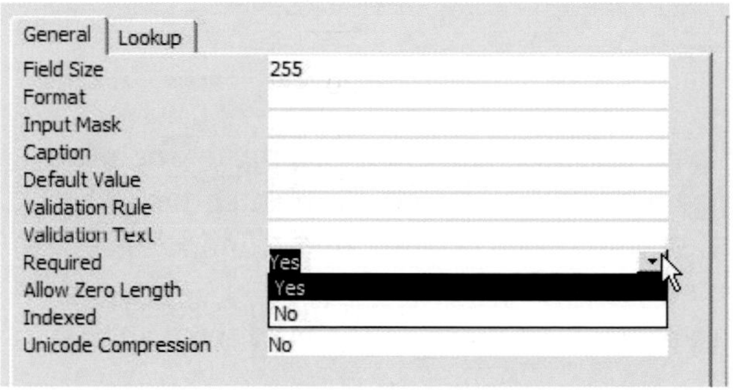

Figure 7.56

Range check

Some data items must fall within prescribed limits. One example could be where a very popular concert limits ticket sales to four per applicant. The booking system can be set up to make sure that all sales are no more than that number. In another example, the date of birth can be checked on job applicants so that nobody below 18 or older than, say, 65 can be entered into the applicant data file.

Where it is necessary to restrict data entry in this way, a **range check** is used. In this, the limits are set so that anything outside these limits is rejected.

The software will warn the user if the wrong data is put in and will not allow continuation to the next field.

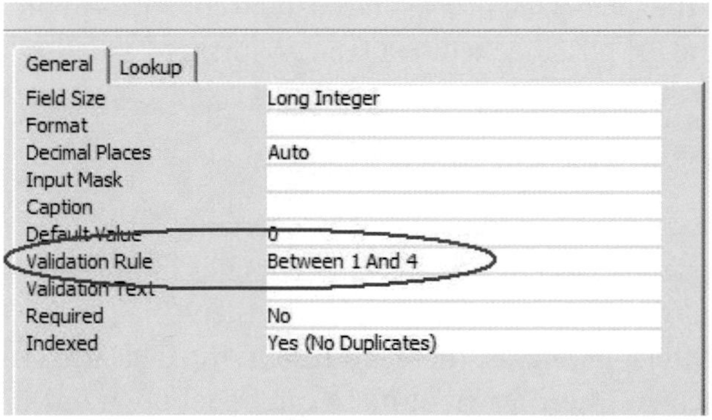

Figure 7.57

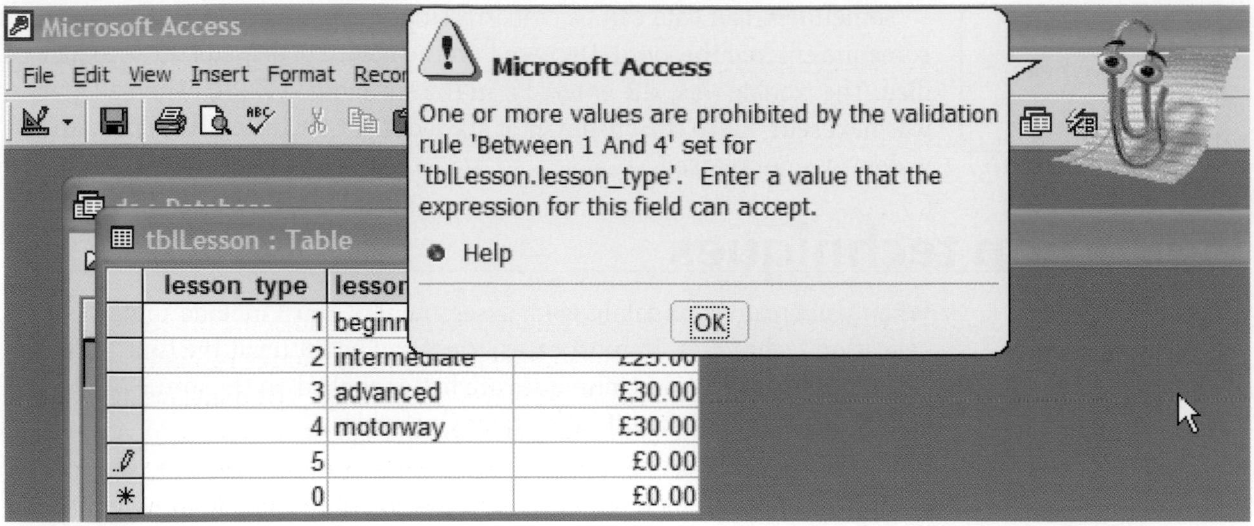

Figure 7.58

File lookup check

When you call your bank or insurance company, you will probably be asked your account number or policy number. The operator can enter this and immediately bring up the rest of your details. These can be confirmed as being accurate by asking you questions.

The software can be set to ask these questions and validate them against the stored details.

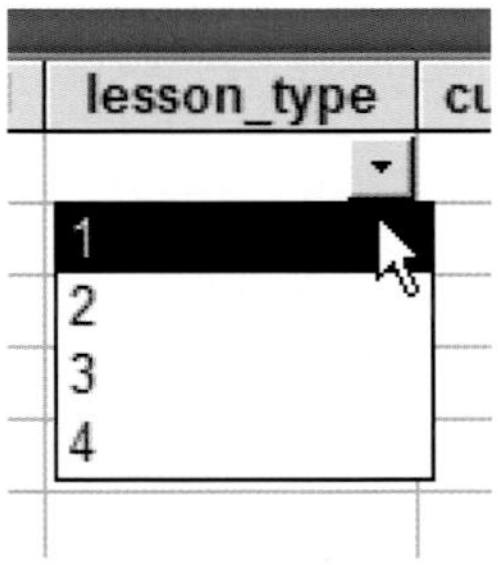

List check

In many cases, the data that is permitted to be entered is a limited choice. It makes sense to arrange that nothing else is permitted to be entered in that field. In the DS Driving School example, there are only four types of lesson. So, entering 5 is not permitted. The values can be looked up in another table and the link can be made in the table itself or a list box can be constructed on a form. Figure 7.59 shows the list box attached to a table. A further validation rule can be added to prevent the operator typing in an illegal value.

Figure 7.59

Figure 7.60

Think of some more real-life examples where format checks are useful.

Format (picture) check

Data often has to conform to a certain pattern. For example, recent UK car number plates have two letters, followed by two numbers then three more letters. In Access, there is a field in the table design screen where an input mask can be set up in order to force data to conform to a certain pattern. In Figure 7.60, it is set to LL (two letters), 00 (two numbers), then LLL. Any data entered that does not conform to the pattern is not accepted so some types of mistake can be avoided. This check, just as with all validation, does not ensure that the registration number is the right one, just that it is in the correct format.

Format checks are useful for postcodes and some telephone numbers too.

Length of data check

Databases nearly always have limits set on the size of data that can be entered into a given field. We have already seen in Unit 7.5 that it is a good idea to limit text fields in order to economise on storage space. In Access, setting a limit on the size of a text field automatically prevents the entry of data that is too long.

Other checks

There are many other ways in which data can be validated. Sometimes methods are invented specially for a particular situation. One commonly used method is called a check digit. To make a check digit, the digits making up a data item are processed in some way in order to generate an extra digit. They may be added together then divided by a prime number such as 11. This yields a remainder which is added on to the end of the data item. When the data item is input, the same process is gone through and if a mistake is made anywhere in the data item, the check digit will probably be wrong and an error message can be displayed.

Programmers can invent many other ways in order to make data entry as reliable as possible, but errors will always occur, particularly when data is being entered by humans. That is why wherever possible, it is better to use machines to read data.

The user interface

Aims

- To examine features of a user interface
- To implement some of those features in the case study database

Introduction

A well-designed and easy-to-use interface is essential if a system is going to be accepted easily by new users. Good design will help users not only to enter data easily but will also assist in keeping the data as accurate as possible. In the previous chapter, you looked at how validation techniques are used to reject data that does not fit certain rules. Here you will learn some additional ways to help keep data accurate.

You will also be shown ways to design and implement user-friendly interfaces.

Input Masks

Use the sample database called Masks.

ACTIVITY

Load the form Customers and type in some forenames.
Try using caps lock or the shift key when typing.

An input mask is used in text boxes and in fields in database tables to control the format of the data that is entered. Controlling the format also provides a degree of control over the values that can be entered.

A simple mask can be used to help in the entry of names on a form or table. By setting up a mask, you can force a capital letter for the first letter of the name and lowercase for the rest. The mask will also stop numbers being entered.

Whatever you do, the first letter is always upper case and the rest are lower case – you cannot enter numbers or any other characters. This happens automatically and makes the task of entering names much quicker. The user does not have to think about using the shift key and can just concentrate on spelling the names correctly.

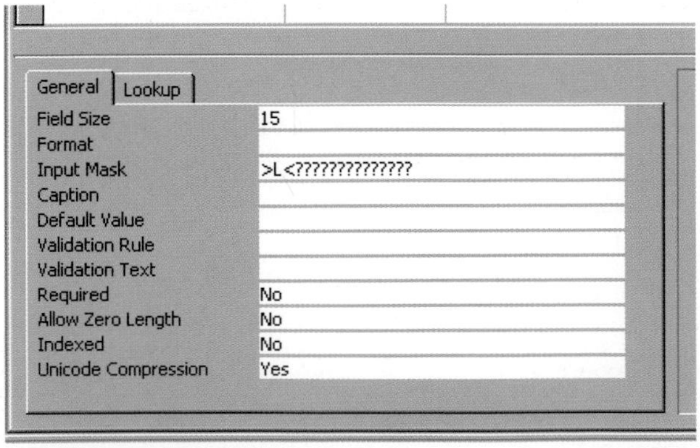

How is this achieved? Take a look at the properties of the forename field.

Next to Input Mask, you can see a strange looking pattern **>L<??????????????**. This pattern gives the database software some instructions about how to format this field:

> means change what follows to upper case.
L means a letter MUST be input.
< means change what follows to lower case.
? means only a letter can occupy this position but it can be left out.

General	Lookup
Field Size	15
Format	
Input Mask	>L<??????????????
Caption	
Default Value	
Validation Rule	
Validation Text	
Required	No
Allow Zero Length	No
Indexed	No
Unicode Compression	Yes

■ Figure 7.61

ACTIVITY

Use the table of mask characters below to see if you can produce a mask that would accept the surname O'Byrne.

There are 14 ?s because the maximum field size is 15 characters.

This mask works well for forenames but is no use for surnames. O'Byrne would be rejected because the apostrophe is not a letter.

The postcode field is another good example of how an input mask can be of use. Postcodes are a real pain to type as they have capital letters and numbers mixed together. This means you have to use the shift key quickly and accurately or you end up with something like:

► WR£$ %GH
► Wr34 5gh
► wr34 5Gh.

Using an input mask for a postcode field raises some problems – postcodes are not consistent, they can have a number of different patterns. The following are all examples of postcode patterns used in the UK:

► B2 5AF
► MP21 2PQ
► WC1A 4PW.

You must allow for all possible data patterns in your input mask, otherwise the user will be prevented from entering correct data.

ACTIVITY

Use the Masks database and try to enter the following as postcodes:

● WR£$ %GH
● Wr34 5gh
● wr34 5Gh
● B2 5AF
● MP21 2PQ
● WC1A 4PW

See how easy it is!

Open the table in design mode and study the mask for the postcode. Can you work it out?

The code for an input mask controls what the user can type into the field and how much they can type. The basic codes in Access are:

Character	Description
0	Digit (0 to 9; entry required; plus [+] and minus [–] signs not allowed).
9	Digit or space (entry not required; plus and minus signs not allowed).
#	Digit or space (entry not required; spaces are displayed as blanks while in Edit mode, but blanks are removed when data is saved; plus and minus signs allowed).
L	Letter (A to Z; entry required).
?	Letter (A to Z; entry optional).
A	Letter or digit (entry required).
a	Letter or digit (entry optional).
&	Any character or a space (entry required).
C	Any character or a space (entry optional).

Character	Description
. , : ; - /	Decimal placeholder and thousand, date, and time separators (the actual character used depends on the settings in the Regional Settings Properties dialogue box in Windows Control Panel).
<	Causes all characters to be converted to lower case.
>	Causes all characters to be converted to upper case.
!	Causes the input mask to display from right to left, rather than from left to right. Characters typed into the mask always fill it from left to right. You can include the exclamation point anywhere in the input mask.
\	Causes the character that follows to be displayed as the literal character (for example, \A is displayed as A).

To create an input mask on a form is simple if you have already created one for the table on which it is based. Any forms you create will copy the input mask onto the form. So it is a good idea to plan for input masks before you start.

If you need to change or add an input mask once a form is created:

1 Open the form in design view.
2 Right click the field in and choose Properties.
3 Select the Data tab and go to Input Mask.
4 Enter the Input Mask code.

Drop-down lists

Drop-down lists provide a user with a fixed set of options from which to choose data items for a field. They are used where the choice of data to be entered is limited to a list of predetermined items.

1 Open the Masks database on the CD.
2 Open the customer table and place the cursor into the field for payment method.
3 Enter a couple of records using the drop-down list.

You had three choices, Cash, Cheque, or Card. These are the only ways a customer can pay for goods, so the choice is limited to these.

This list was set up in the field design as in Figure 7.62.

To use this method:

1 Select the field you want to use with a list.
2 Click the Lookup tab.
3 Next to Row Source Type, choose Value List.
4 Next to Row Source, type in the choices separated by semi-colons.

This method is good for a list that will never change throughout the life of the database. If the list needs to be edited by the user then this method is not suitable – you cannot expect the user to edit field properties.

It is possible to use another table to provide the items for the list. This way, any changes in the lookup table will then also be made in the drop-down list.

General	Lookup	
Display Control	List Box	
Row Source Type	Value List	
Row Source	Cash;Cheque;Card	
Bound Column	1	
Column Count	1	
Column Heads	No	
Column Widths		

■ Figure 7.62

ACTIVITY

1. Load the Masks database and open the Customer form. Notice the drop-down box containing the names of items. There are four items in the list.
2. Open the Items form and add a new item of your choice. Close the form.
3. Return to the Customer form and the drop-down box should now include your extra item.

Notice how this time the Row Source Type is set to Table/Query and the Row source is set to the table used to produce the list.

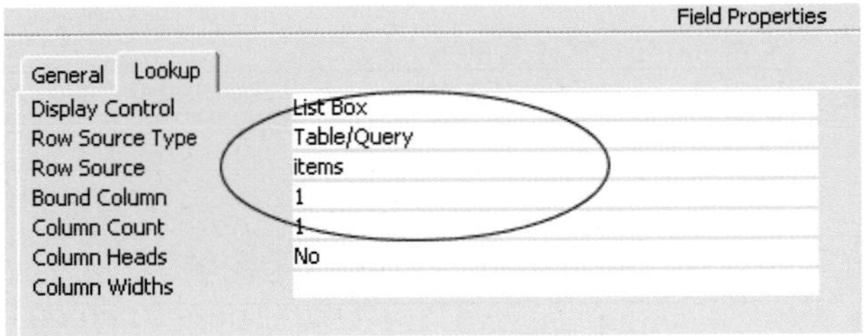

Field Properties
General
Lookup
Display Control
List Box
Row Source Type
Table/Query
Row Source
items
Bound Column
1
Column Count
1
Column Heads
No
Column Widths

Figure 7.63

Option buttons

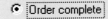

Order complete
Order complete

Figure 7.64

ACTIVITY

Load the Masks database and the Customer form. The field indicating that the order is complete uses an option button. Try it out.

Option buttons can be used on forms in Access to provide a quick way of making a choice. The field needs to be a Yes/No field since the button provides for only two states. Either the button is selected or it is empty.

In Figure 7.64, the order is either complete or it is not complete. The user simply clicks the button to complete the field. In the table, this is recorded as true or false.

Option buttons are useful because they are simple to use and the user has only to click the button to make a selection. This helps reduce mistakes when data is input.

Command buttons

Command buttons can be placed on forms to provide access to a range of events. It is possible to run macros or event procedures written in program code.

Buttons make complex processes available to people because they are programmed for them. You, as the system author, will be able to use wizards or to record macros and then assign them to buttons; the user simply clicks the button.

Buttons are a standard interface item. Most people are familiar with them and should be able to use them without training. Buttons should be given a caption that makes it obvious what action will be performed.

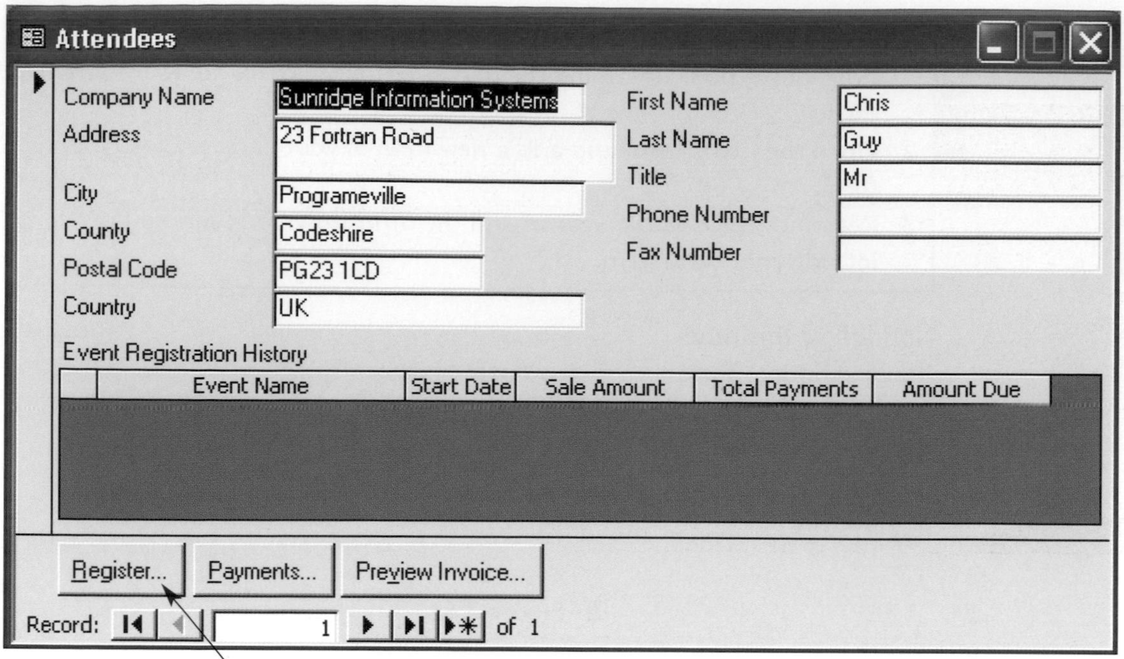

```
Attendees

Company Name    Sunridge Information Systems    First Name    Chris
Address         23 Fortran Road                 Last Name     Guy
                                                Title         Mr
City            Programeville                   Phone Number
County          Codeshire                       Fax Number
Postal Code     PG23 1CD
Country         UK

Event Registration History

         Event Name        Start Date   Sale Amount   Total Payments   Amount Due



Register...   Payments...   Preview Invoice...

Record:  |◄  ◄            1   ►  ►|  ►*   of 1
```

```vba
Private Sub Register_Click()
On Error GoTo Err_Register_Click
  If IsNull(Me![AttendeeID]) Then
    MsgBox "Enter attendee information before registering for an event."
  Else
    DoCmd.DoMenuItem acFormBar, acRecordsMenu, acSaveRecord, , acMenuVer70
    DoCmd.OpenForm "Registration"
  End If

Exit_Register_Click:
  Exit Sub

Err_Register_Click:
  MsgBox Err.Description
  Resume Exit_Register_Click
End Sub
```

■ **Figure 7.65**

The button called 'Register' on the form in Figure 7.65 runs the code shown under the image. The code might look complicated, but it is really quite simple:

1 It checks that an AttendeeID has been entered. If there is no AttendeeID then an error message appears.
2 It saves the information.
3 It opens the registration form.

All this can be done manually by going back to the switchboard but the button makes the whole task easier for the user.

Switchboard

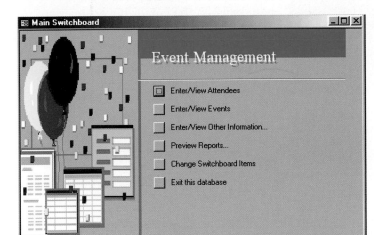

A switchboard is a feature often used in Microsoft Access database applications. It is a simple graphical interface that presents the user with a series of options. Clicking the button selects the option.

■ **Figure 7.66**

ACTIVITY

1 Open the event management database on the CD.
2 Look at the options on the switchboard.
3 Try the different options to see what they do.

When you tried the options out, you will have seen that each item on the switchboard can do one of several operations, for example:

▶ Load another switchboard.
▶ Run a report.
▶ Load a form.

The events database loads up and minimises the normal Access windows. The user can work without using the Access windows that you are familiar with. It is possible to turn off all other functions and menus, so that the user ONLY has the switchboard and nothing else. Doing this allows the designer to control who does what, by setting up different switchboards for different people. This can improve the security of the system by restricting the options available to different users.

Instructions

It is a fact that many people do not read instruction books! Most people prefer to try out the system and find their way through it. Some might say that this helps the learning process.

It is possible to build systems so that they are self-documenting. Forms can be self-explanatory by good design. By using labels on forms or names on buttons that are meaningful it is possible to indicate what they do.

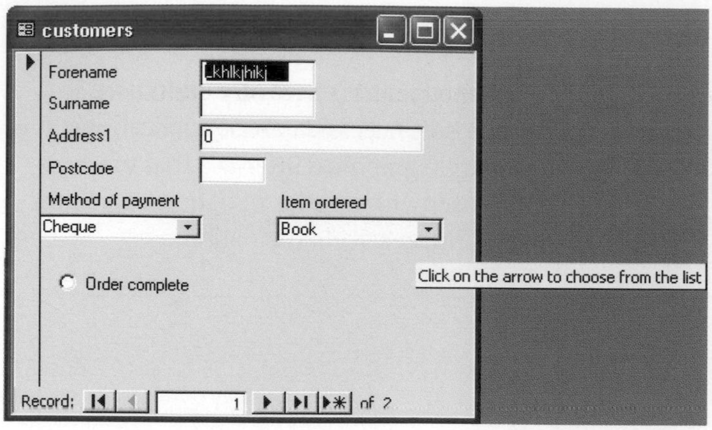

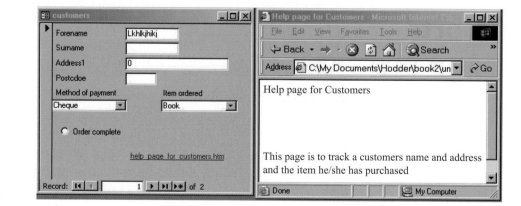

In Access, it is possible to build in further help in the form of tips which will pop up when the cursor hovers over an object.

In the Masks database, hovering over the Item ordered field produces a message that explains what to do.

■ Figure 7.67

Help screens

Another way to provide help is to use buttons to bring up custom help pages with details of how to best use the form that is currently on the screen. The method for doing this varies from package to package.

Basically, a button will activate a text box which will appear on screen. In some cases, it is possible to use hypertext links to web-style pages giving help. This method will give the users a more flexible approach to information.

Figure 7.68 shows an example of a help screen using hyperlinks on the form.

■ Figure 7.68

Error messages

Very often, if you let the system provide error messages, the messages are not helpful. The software works out that something is wrong, but cannot always be precise. This sometimes result in a catch-all type of error message such as the one in Figure 7.69.

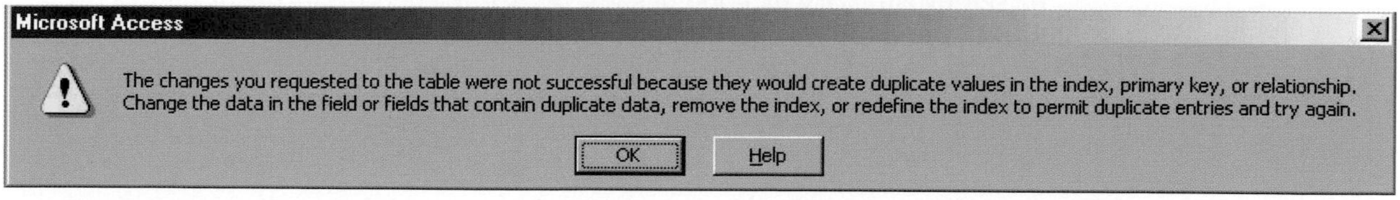

Microsoft Access

⚠ The changes you requested to the table were not successful because they would create duplicate values in the index, primary key, or relationship. Change the data in the field or fields that contain duplicate data, remove the index, or redefine the index to permit duplicate entries and try again.

OK   Help

■ Figure 7.69

This message was produced because the primary key field was left blank in a table, but it also mentions duplicates and relationships. So, unless the user understands the software and can work out what is happening, it is not very useful.

Wherever possible it is better to trap errors on forms and produce your own error message.

Figure 7.70

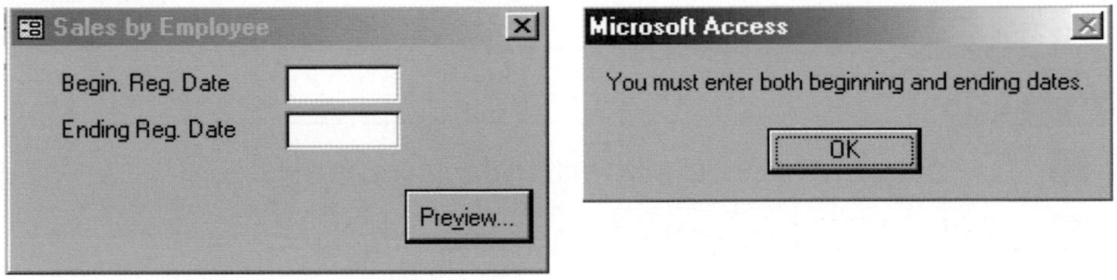

Clicking the preview button on the form in Figure 7.70 produces the message box shown, with a very clear message for the user. This was set up in the event procedure for the button.

When building your database you will need to try to minimise the possibility of invalid data being input by using validation checks in the fields on your forms.

Further information on **validation checks** can be found on pp. 42–5

You can make it easier for information to be selected from your database and displayed by creating menus. You can also use them to control how much or how little users are allowed to see and do with your data.

Reports

Your output should be in the form of meaningful information, using titles, columns, lines and other layout features that improve readability. You will incorporate calculations such as totals and running sums into reports when necessary.

Testing

Aims

■ To emphasise the importance of testing

■ To look at strategies for testing

Introduction

portfolio_tip

Testing is often the poorest section of work done for assessment by students. Plan your testing carefully and follow a plan to ensure that your database is thoroughly tested.

Testing is one of the most important stages in the development of a database. All databases should be tested before the user puts the final product to full use. Testing needs to be carefully planned so as to cover all possible outcomes.

The first tests are often called alpha testing. This is done in-house by the programmers or sometimes there are staff who are employed just to carry out testing.

Next comes the beta testing which is done by selected users, who report back any comments to the developers.

A good test strategy should cover functionality of the database and also the error handling facilities.

The solution meets all the requirements of the functional specification

ACTIVITY

Devise a questionnaire for the users of the DS Driving School database to collect their opinions of the solution.

At the start of the development process, a functional specification was drawn up. This needs to be looked at again during the testing process, to ensure that all the aims and objectives have been met. You should try to involve the user in part of the testing, to ask the question, 'Does the database application do what you expected?' It is often difficult to test the database under real conditions but every effort should be made to place the system under realistic load conditions.

The final product should be reviewed carefully alongside the original specification. Feedback from the user might mean changing a few things at this stage, but it is better to make changes before the database goes live. Consider which aims have been met and the extent to which they have been met. Are there any aims that have not or could not be met?

All menus work properly

Testing the menu system can be very repetitive but each option needs to be tested. Can the user navigate the structure efficiently or are there dead links? Every menu should have a way to reach the one above it, if there is one, and the main menu.

During the design of the database, a map of the menu structure should have been drawn up. This should be used to check the route through all the menus to make sure nothing has been missed out.

Validation checks prevent unacceptable data from being entered

General	Lookup	
Format		Currency
Decimal Places		Auto
Input Mask		
Caption		
Default Value		
Validation Rule		>0
Validation Text		The price must be more than zero
Required		No
Indexed		No

■ **Figure 7.71**

In Unit 7.6, you looked at the process of validation and the types of checks that can be built in through the use of the field validation property.

In the DS database on the CD, the price of a lesson has a validation rule to ensure that the price of a lesson is greater than zero. When testing the database, this rule needs to be checked to see if it is working. To do this, attempts should be made to enter values that will be rejected and values that will be accepted. For example:

▶ 0 (zero) should be rejected
▶ –2 should be rejected
▶ 1 should be accepted.

---

portfolio_tip

Simple mistakes are often the hardest to find, so look for them and test everything carefully.

Make a list of all fields which have validation rules and then you can use the list to make sure that all rules are tested.

ACTIVITY

Load the DS database and try the above values in the price of a lesson field.
Take some screen shots of your results.

Again planning is vital. All validation rules should be tested. It is easy to make a mistake and have a field that is not able to accept good data due to a simple mistake, such as using the wrong symbol, for example >16 instead of <16. Such mistakes are easy to make but can be hard to correct once the database is handed over to the user.

The database can cope with normal, extreme and abnormal data

The testing needs to cover all possible data that could be entered into the database. The driving school could have a field that holds the marks a person achieved in the theory test. The test is always out of 35 marks. The field would be set up to validate the number entered. The validation rule would be set up to hold marks from 0 to 35 inclusive (although those who scored 0 should not be driving!).

► **Normal data** such as 23 or 15, will be accepted and should not produce an error message. Numbers at the limits should also be checked: 0 and 35 are examples of normal data at the limits as defined by the rules.

► **Extreme data** falls outside the normal limits. –50, 45, and 96 are examples that could be used here. Data that is just outside the boundaries should also be entered: –1 and 36 are the numbers to use in this case. Although it seems unlikely that anyone would deliberately enter –1, it is easy to touch a key in error.

► **Abnormal data** is the type of data that is not expected. For example, a user might enter **thirty** as a mark or, more likely, hit the space bar in the middle of a number such as 25.

Only by testing with three types of data can you be confident that your database will stand up to a user when the database is in place. Here is an example of a test plan for this field:

Reason for test	Data type	Data entered
Not an integer	Abnormal	thirty
Out of range	Extreme	–30
Out of range	Extreme	50
Good data	Normal	32
Boundary	Normal	35
Boundary	Normal	0
Boundary	Extreme	–1
Boundary	Extreme	36

You will notice that the table includes *incorrect* data as well as good data. You must test with this type of data to prove that it is rejected by your system.

Output from the database is complete, accurate and in the required format

Once the database has been tested with a variety of data types and is accepting the data correctly, the output needs to be tested. To do this a quantity of good data needs to be entered into the system so that the output is realistic and represents the type and quantity of data the user expects.

All of the various outputs provided need to be tested so planning is vital. Look back at the functional specification and the list of outputs. Some will be printed and some will be on screen. The output should be checked against the data to ensure that it is accurate. For example, if a list of female driving instructors is printed, does it:

► show only female instructors
► show all the female instructors
► contain all the information required?

If any of the outputs reveal errors, then the source of the error must be found, the problem corrected and then the test repeated to ensure it is correct.

It is a good idea at this stage to involve the user in commenting on the output, by asking, 'Is the format as expected?'

Other people can use it without help

The best way to see how easy a system is to use is to test it out on others. Someone who has not seen that database system before should try it out to see how easy it is to use. Feedback on ease of use can then be looked at to review the database. It is often the case that someone else will see issues that you as the designer did not see because you are so familiar with the whole product. It is a bit like spotting your own spelling mistakes.

For the assessment, you are required to involve others in the testing and evaluation process and to use that feedback to modify your database.

In the end of unit task, you will have to import CSV files into tables that you have constructed. When you have set up the structure, you will need to test it prior to importing the data to make sure that it will reject invalid data. That way you will be sure the imported data has been correctly imported.

ICT skills

Aims

■ To revisit the skills covered in the unit

■ To give examples of how to carry out the tasks listed

Play the 'how to' video called Name.

In this unit, you have developed a number of skills in planning and developing databases. The assessment that you will undertake involves developing a database to a specification given to you by the awarding body. You will also need to import a set of data into the system you have set up and then test the database. You must also obtain and act on feedback given to you by others.

On the CD with this chapter is a series of video clips, which will talk you through the process.

Construct tables to represent entities

In Unit 7.5 you looked at how entities are represented by tables in a database. In Microsoft Access there are three ways to set up a table:

▶ Design view
▶ Using a wizard
▶ Entering data.

Design view

The most effective way to control the structure of a table is to use the design view. In this way you can enter all the necessary information in exactly the way you have planned. Each attribute in the table can be given the properties you intend.

Play the 'how to' video called Design.

■ Figure 7.72

Using a wizard

The wizard holds many possible types of attributes for a table. It is a way of helping users to set up tables quickly. It is good to use if you are not sure how to set all the properties yourself. However it does not give you full control over the format of the fields.

■ Figure 7.73

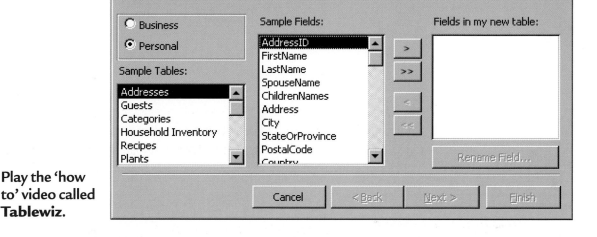

 Play the 'how to' video called **Tablewiz.**

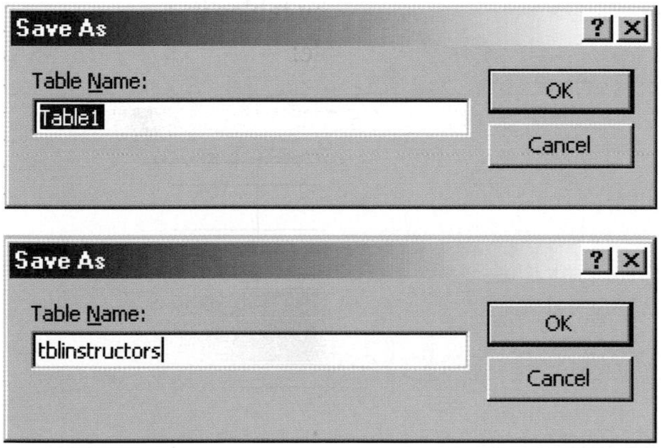

■ Figure 7.74

Entering data

It is possible simply to enter the data into a table and let Access decide how to format the data for you. This method is not recommended, because you do not have much control over the structure of the table.

Whichever method you have chosen, when the attributes are entered, you will be asked to save the table and at this point, Access will suggest a name such as **Table1**. You should not accept this *default* name but always give the table a name that is meaningful. Normally, you will choose a name that starts with the letters **tbl** so that it is easy to understand what the object is later on.

Define the fields in each table to represent attributes

In your design, you should have a number of attributes for each table. The attributes will become the fields you are going to use.

The best way to enter the fields into your table is to use the design view (see Figure 7.72).

Play the 'how to' video called Fields.

Start the design view and enter the name of each field into the design of the table. When the design for the table is complete, exit the design view and save the table.

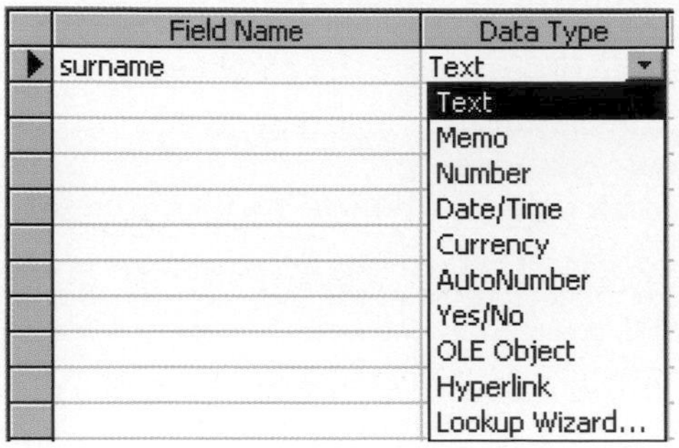

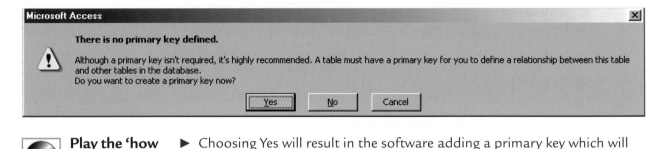

■ Figure 7.75

 Play the 'how to' video called Fieldtype.

Define appropriate data types and formats

When you are using the design view to set up a table you choose the data type and format of each field. You looked at field types on pages 35–9.

Once the name of the field has been entered, choose its data type from the pull-down menu next to it.

Define primary keys

If a table needs a primary key you should select this before you quit the design view. If you do not, then Access will try to choose one for you. It is better to set up your own primary key rather than let the software do it for you.

■ Figure 7.76

Microsoft Access ✕

⚠ **There is no primary key defined.**

Although a primary key isn't required, it's highly recommended. A table must have a primary key for you to define a relationship between this table and other tables in the database.
Do you want to create a primary key now?

[Yes] [No] [Cancel]

 Play the 'how to' video called Primary.

▶ Choosing Yes will result in the software adding a primary key which will almost certainly be unsuitable.
▶ Choosing No will leave the table without one.
▶ Choosing Cancel will go back and let you select one.

Create relationships between tables

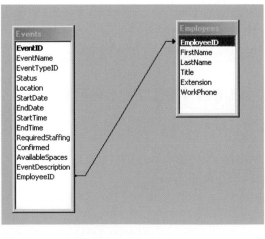

On pages 30–1 you looked at relationships.

To add a relationship, drag a field name from one table to the field you want to relate it to in the other.

■ Figure 7.77

 Play the 'how to' video called Relationships.

Define searches and sorts (single and multiple fields and tables)

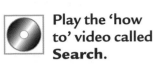

Play the 'how to' video called Search.

On pages 20–3, you looked at setting up queries in Access. When you set up a query, it is a way of searching the database so that it matches the data that you enter as an example in the design grid. You can also specify how you want the information to be sorted.

This query from the DS database searches for an instructor of a particular gender. The user is prompted to enter the gender.

■ Figure 7.78

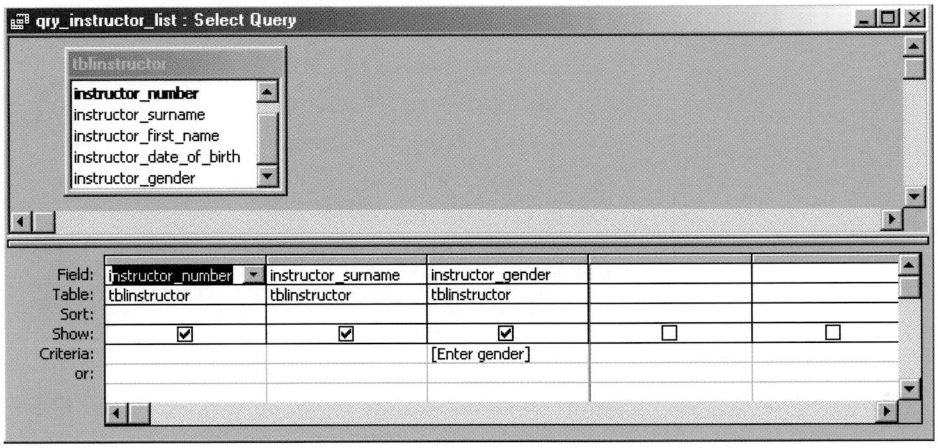

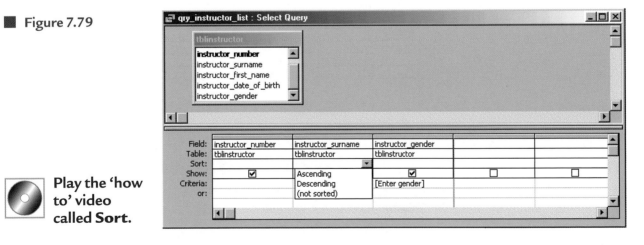

To sort the list produced by the instructor surname field, choose how you wish to sort the list using the sort facility.

■ Figure 7.79

Play the 'how to' video called Sort.

Use relational logic in searches

Often you need to make searches that combine different conditions. For example, you may need to make a list of all the lessons that have been paid for that also cost less than £25. This combines two conditions, lesson_paid=True AND lesson_price<25.

In the query design grid, this looks like this:

■ **Figure 7.80**

Field:	lesson_date	lesson_time	lesson_price	lesson_paid
Table:	tblLessonRecords	tblLessonRecords	tblLessonRecords	tblLessonRecords
Sort:				
Show:	☑	☑	☑	☑
Criteria:			<25	True
or:				

Although the query design grid does not make this clear, the two conditions are both required and they are linked by an AND relational operator. This is clear if you look at the same query in SQL view.

```
SELECT [tblLessonRecords].[lesson_date],
[tblLessonRecords].[lesson_time],
[tblLessonRecords].[lesson_price],
[tblLessonRecords].[lesson_paid]
FROM tblLessonRecords
WHERE ((([tblLessonRecords].[lesson_price])<25) And
(([tblLessonRecords].[lesson_paid])=True));
```

There are other relational operators that you can use such as OR and NOT. OR allows a search where either of two (or more) criteria are matched. NOT looks for cases where a criterion is not matched. It is often easiest to set up these conditions in SQL view.

You can make the change to OR very easily in the SQL view or you can enter the OR condition in the OR cell in the design grid.

■ **Figure 7.81**

Field:	lesson_date ▾	lesson_time	lesson_price	lesson_paid
Table:	tblLessonRecords	tblLessonRecords	tblLessonRecords	tblLessonRecords
Sort:				
Show:	☑	☑	☑	☑
Criteria:			<25	
or:				True

Import data from and export data to other databases and applications

In the assessment you will need to import data into your tables. The best way to achieve this is to set up the tables using the design specification and then to import the data into each table as necessary.

To import data into a table use the **Get External Data** option.

■ Figure 7.82

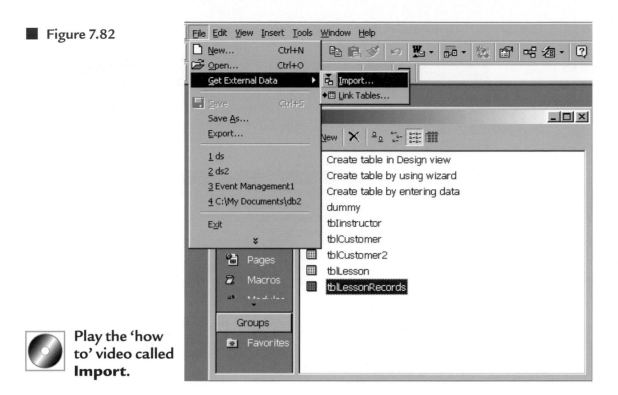

Play the 'how to' video called **Import**.

Figure 7.82 shows importing data into the Lesson records table.

Use macros to automate common tasks

Common tasks such as printing a report or sorting a table can be written into macros to make things quicker for the user. Macros can perform many tasks and are easy to set up.

■ Figure 7.83

■ Figure 7.84

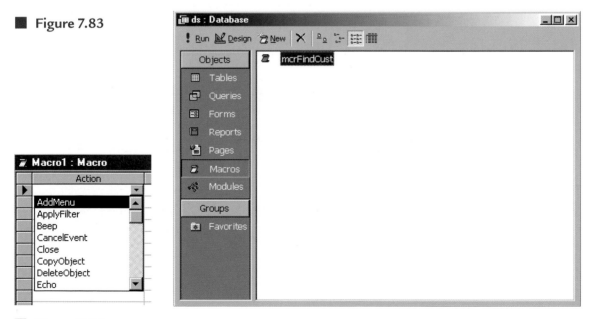

First select the macro object button.

Then select the type of operation to perform.

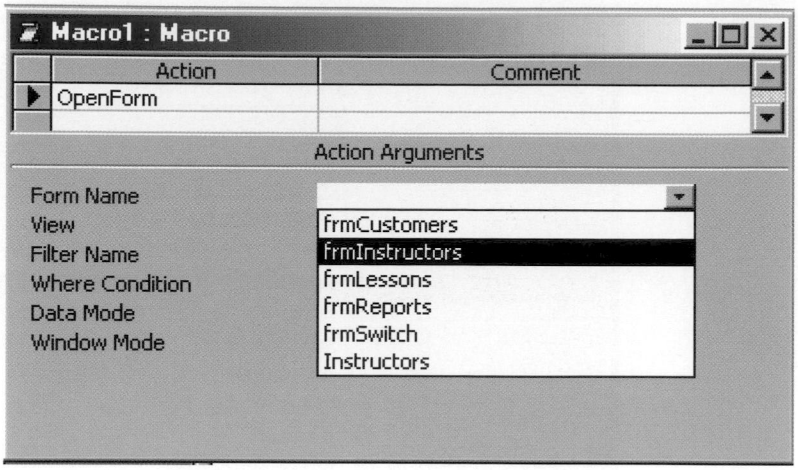

Play the 'how to' video called Macro.

Figure 7.85 shows that the macro will open the form frmInstructors.

Use wizards effectively

Wizards can save you a lot of time by setting up forms, reports and other objects for you very quickly. The **Forms** wizard is particularly useful in setting up forms from tables or queries quickly and easily. Sometimes wizards can be less useful, particularly if you want to customise your layout.

Often, the easiest thing to do is to use a wizard to create a layout and then edit the layout afterwards in design mode to produce the effect you need.

■ Figure 7.86

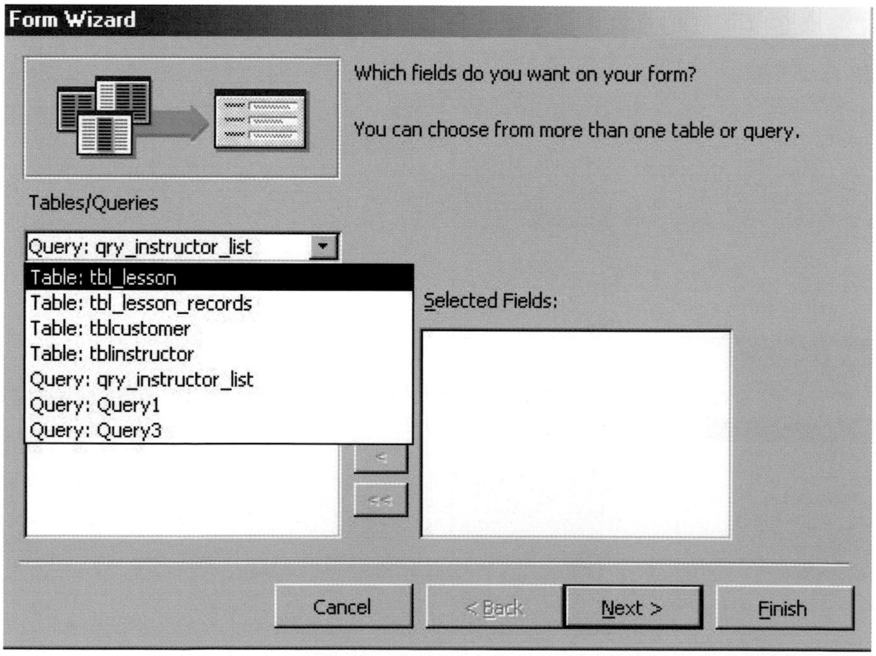

First you choose the table or query on which the form is based.

Play the 'how to' video called Wizard.

Then choose the fields to include. In this case, surname and forename have been selected.

Forms and reports

While working through the earlier chapters in this unit, you will have seen many examples of how to create forms for various purposes to deal with the control of a database and also for the entry of data into the database. Forms make up the user interface for the whole database system.

Reports are used wherever printed output is required. Both forms and reports can be set up from scratch or they can be based on tables or queries. We have seen how wizards can be extremely useful in setting them up quickly so that you only have to make slight adjustments later.

The specification lists a number of skills involving forms and reports that you should have picked up while working through this unit. These are listed here with a few comments that should be borne in mind whenever you are working on them.

Data-entry forms

Forms can enable the entry of data into single and multiple tables

If two or more tables are related, you can make a single form to accept data for each table. This is probably not going to be useful very often, especially if you have a one-to-many relationship. Alternatively, you can base a form on a query, where the query is based on more than one table. That can be very useful where you want to update the data in related tables.

Forms should have appropriate field lengths

If you use the form wizard to make a form, the amount of space allocated to each field may not be appropriate. You should go into design view and adjust this according to the needs of the data table.

Forms should provide clear labelling of fields

If you set up a form with a wizard, each field will 'inherit' the field name and apply it as a label. So you might get a form that has customer_number as a label. You should go through such automated labels and replace them with user-friendly labels such as Customer Number.

Forms should provide instruction fields where necessary

If it is not obvious what is supposed to be entered into a field, then extra instructions should be placed on the form as a label.

Forms should include validation checks on field entries as appropriate

In earlier chapters, you have seen several examples of how to apply a wide range of validation checks on forms. You should use these as much as possible in order to make sure that the data entered is as reliable as possible.

Forms should enable the selection and entry of data from built-in lists where appropriate

Adding combo boxes and list boxes is further help in the construction of forms that are as well-protected as possible against the entry of bad data. There have been several examples of these in earlier chapters.

Forms may include calculated fields

Often, you want a form to display a calculated result. You may input a price of an item and how many have been ordered. On forms, it is easy to add extra fields where the data source is calculated from other fields by using an expression.

The discounted price shown in Figure 7.88 was produced by entering an expression into the field as shown in Figure 7.89.

Lesson calculator

Lesson type   1
Lesson description   beginner
Lesson price   £20.00
Discounted price: £15.00

■ Figure 7.88

Discounted price: =[lesson_price]*0.75

■ Figure 7.89

Forms can make use of automated number fields (counter fields)

If you set up a data table that contained an autonumber field, this can be shown on a form to give the user feedback on the current position in the table. An autonumber field cannot be edited.

Text Box: lesson_date

| Format | Data | Event | Other | All |

Format . . . . General Date
Decimal Places . . . . General Date   19/0
Visible . . . . Long Date   19 J
Display When . . . . Medium Date   19-J
Scroll Bars . . . . Short Date   19/0
Can Grow . . . . Long Time   17:3
Can Shrink . . . . Medium Time   05:3
Left . . . . Short Time   17:3
Top . . . .
Width 1.455cm
Height 0.45cm
Back Style . . . . Normal
Back Color . . . . -2147483643

■ Figure 7.90

Forms can use date and time fields

You should make sure that at some stage, you set up fields based on dates and times. You can alter the format displayed on the form so that the user is in no doubt how the data is to be entered.

If the user enters a date in one format such as 12/12/05, the form can be set to convert it automatically to another format such as 12 December 2005.

Reports should have suitable headers and footers

It is always useful to add information to a report in order to make its purpose clear. So adding headers and footers can ensure that each page has a reference point to remind the reader what it is about.

If you use the report wizard, it will add headers and footers for you but you can always alter them in design view if you so wish.

The footer in Figure 7.91 shows how the page number and the total number of pages can be automatically generated.

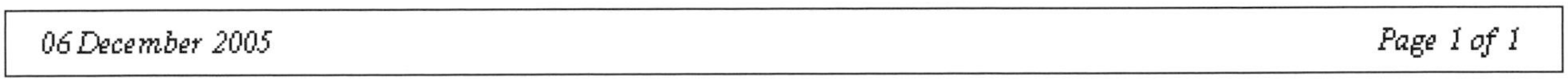

06 December 2005	Page 1 of 1

■ **Figure 7.91**

This was produced by the following expressions:

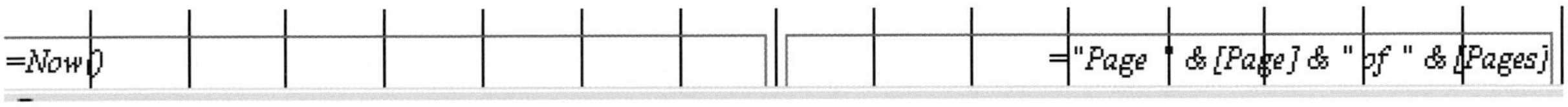

=Now() ="Page " & [Page] & " of " & [Pages]

■ **Figure 7.92**

Reports should have an appropriate format and layout

Again, the wizard will give you plenty of help in making a report look good. Sometimes, you need something completely different. For example, Access is good at making invoices or school reports. You can add logos and any design that you want so that the printout is exactly as you want it. The wizard defaults are helpful and save a lot of work but don't always stick rigidly to them.

Reports should often have sorted data grouping

You can arrange the output on a report to be grouped at various levels. So, you can have all the customers of one driving instructor grouped in alphabetical order under his name and the instructors themselves arranged in alphabetical order. All things are possible!

Reports can include calculations and total fields

By using expressions, it is possible to produce calculations at report print time. The process is just the same as for making calculated fields on forms. Remember that calculations on reports are not stored unless you write program code to do it.

Reports can include specified queries

Don't forget that a report can be based on a table or a query. In fact, many of the most useful reports are based on tables linked by a query that also extracts just a subset of the data.

UNIT 8
Managing ICT projects

Examples of projects

Aims

- To introduce Unit 8
- To examine some examples of projects

Introduction

This is a compulsory unit for the A2 award. It is assessed by means of an eportfolio.

During the AS course you completed two projects, an ebook about life in the information age and an eportfolio about databases. With these, you had to plan and implement your work over a period of time. You should have developed some experience of planning and developing projects for yourself during this time. This unit looks at some formal project management tools and some of the systems that can be used to manage a large project.

During this unit, you undertake a user-focused project for your final assessment. You will need to work with others during the project development to gain experience of managing a group of people.

You must use project management software for this unit. There are many alternatives available for this; Microsoft Project is one example and its use is illustrated in Unit 8.7.

On the CD with this book is a piece of software that you can use for project planning. It is called GanttProject and it is open source software. It will carry out all the planning functions you require.

The CD contains GanttProject in a folder ready to install.

Assessment evidence

Your portfolio will be assessed for five pieces of evidence. Further details of the contents of your eportfolio are given later in the unit and as tips throughout the unit.

Evidence 'a'

This covers the research and project proposals for a new software product. You will need to draw up a proposal and present it to the management group. (This is one time you need other people involved.) Following the presentation, you need to draw up a project definition that defines the scope of the project. You will agree this after the presentation. You must involve other people to act as stakeholders: senior manager, reviewer and customer. If you can work with 'real' stakeholders, it would be better but if not you will need to have someone acting the part. Your teacher could act as the senior manager, a fellow student as a reviewer and someone else as the customer or user.

Evidence 'b'

You need to produce a detailed project plan and use this to monitor the progress of the project and communicate this to the others during the project development.

Evidence 'c'

You need to keep detailed records showing how you managed the project, including how you organised meetings to report project progress. You will need to hold meetings of your project board and keep minutes of the meetings.

Evidence 'd'

This is the production of a software product according to the project plan and the delivery of it according to the time scale set. The software should meet the objectives agreed at the start of the project.

Evidence 'e'

For this, you carry out an end-of-project review with the management team. This needs to be a critical review using feedback from the end-of-project review meeting. You will need to arrange a meeting of your project board to finally sign off your project.

Project requirements

To fulfil the requirements of this unit there must be a real product being produced by you. It is a good idea therefore to combine this unit with the optional unit that you choose:

▶ Unit 10 Using multimedia software
▶ Unit 11 Using spreadsheet software
▶ Unit 12 Customising applications

You will then have a real project to complete and produce evidence for two units at the same time. You will need to remember this in your planning of a time scale.

A project is not a never-ending process. It needs to take place over a set period of time, with review points and milestones set along the way. Any project will involve people in a variety of ways and roles.

The awarding body requires you to carry out a project that will need at least 10 weeks and, whilst the software is not the main focus, it needs to be substantial enough to present a challenging project.

> **portfolio_tip**
>
> The work in your eportfolio is **not** a team effort, the work **must** be your own, but you need the experience of working with others to demonstrate communication skills.

CASE STUDY

Sunridge Information Systems recently replaced their head office network. This was a major project for them and involved changing their entire network over to new machines.

Initial idea to change

The idea to change came from a need to update the current system. There were several issues that led to the initial idea:

The servers were becoming short of storage space.

The system was slow because some of the machines were quite old.

Staff often complained of the time taken to carry out tasks. They often compared the computers with their home computers, which were much quicker.

Proposal

The IT director and systems manager met with the managing director and the finance director and it was agreed that research would take place so that a proposal could be put to the main board of directors at the next meeting in one month's time.

The finance director looked at how the deal could be financed, and the IT director contacted several companies to obtain provisional quotes for a system. At the meeting it was agreed that the project would go ahead. The ideal time for such a radical replacement of the system was identified as the summer months when many staff take annual leave. This gave a time scale of nine months to complete the project.

Planning

The IT director now produced a detailed list of requirements for the new system. This included three new file servers, 250 new computer systems and a new suite of software.

Three quotes from different companies were compared. Then, changes to the infrastructure were required so quotes for cabling were required as well as the new computers. The quotes varied widely, but cheapest is not always the best. So the IT director produced a document comparing the quotes and recommending which company to choose. This was presented to the board of directors at a special meeting. They then gave the go-ahead for the orders to be placed.

The order for the goods needed to be placed three months before the installation date to allow for the building of the systems and delivery to take place.

At the same time, the installation dates were agreed with the suppliers' engineers who were going to install the system. The installation would take around five days and included the transfer of data from the old servers to the new ones and the setting up of user IDs on the new system.

Included in the cost of the new system was six days of training for the network manager, split into three days of pre-delivery training then, one month after delivery and commissioning, there would be another three days of training. This had to be put into the plan for the project.

Installation and commissioning

Some of the setting up could be done with the old system still running but the last two days of the commissioning required the entire system to be down. This needed separate planning so that the staff could continue to work during the shutdown. Key staff that needed to have a computer system were loaned laptops and printers for the two days. Important files were copied onto these the day before the system closed down.

During the shutdown the old and new machines were swapped out and the data transferred from the old system to the new one. The process was much slower than expected, and extra technical staff were needed to unpack and set up the new workstations. The IT director had to some extent underestimated the size of the task. Fortunately a budget had been set aside for contingencies such as this. In any planning it is a good idea to allow some extra resources in case the unexpected happens.

Project review

At the end of the project, a review took place. This found that the new system was set up as planned and within the budget set. Performance of the system was as expected and the project had met all its objectives. It was noted that the commissioning and deployment of the workstations took longer than expected and it was agreed that if such a major change were to happen again, which in the world of IT is very likely, then more time would need to be allowed for the changeover or more staff employed on a temporary basis to assist with the setting up of new machines.

Large IT projects

The Oyster card system

One example of a large IT project is the Transport for London Oyster Card system. Transport for London and London Underground wanted to create a smart card ticketing system to make travel in London faster, and more convenient for people who regularly use buses and the Underground.

Using the cards means that tickets are not needed on buses and movement through ticket gates at Underground stations is faster. A smartcard called Oyster is at the centre of the system. The card can be read automatically by readers on every bus and at all Underground stations. The card only needs to be touched on a reader to be seen by the system.

Some of the objectives were:

▶ fewer queues
▶ more reliable equipment
▶ less frustration
▶ less violent crime
▶ fewer heavy loads of cash to collect from buses and stations
▶ faster processing of passengers
▶ reduced fraud – as tickets cannot be copied easily.

Seven different companies bid for the contract, worth about £1 billion. The contract was not just to set up the project but to run it for ten years as well. It is the largest such project in the world at present.

The Oyster card can be 'charged' with money at many different retail outlets and stations. Each time it is used, the appropriate fare is deducted from it.

The system was set up and is now running successfully. The project directors are now looking to extend the system so that cards can also be used in cashless transactions to buy items such as newspapers at the outlets where the cards are topped up.

For more information on how Oyster works, follow the link:

http://www.tfl.gov.uk/oystercard

The 1901 census online

The National Records Office undertook another large project. The project was to make the results of the 1901 census available online so that people could research their ancestors from home rather than having to travel to London or regional offices. The project started in 1998.

The idea was to make 175 million records available across the Internet. Initial searches would be free then charges would be made to access the detailed information.

The first major task was to scan and digitise millions of documents from the original census. Some of the work was contracted to the prison service, which used prisoners to scan and load data onto the system. The rate at which this was carried out led to some concerns that the project would not be ready to go live on 1 January 2002. A further £2.9 million was made available to employ another firm to finish the task.

A progress review in 2001 decided the project was back on schedule to launch in 2002. The system went live at midnight on 1 January 2002. Within hours, the servers crashed and the system was taken offline. Several attempts were made to go live again but it was almost 11 months before the system was fully operational. The volume of hits experienced by the site had been vastly underestimated. The system was designed for 1 million users with a peak of 1.2 million per 24 hours. But, by midday on 2 January 2002, 1.2 million users **per hour** were trying to access the site. The system had to be shut down and did not fully reopen until 21 November 2002 although it was partly available at regional offices during this time.

Despite the earlier failure, the system is now up and running and is said to be successful.

For a review of the system produced by the National Audit Office follow the link:

http://www.nao.org.uk/publications/nao_reports/02-03/02031259.pdf

The characteristics projects have in common

Time scale

All projects must have a fixed time scale.

- ▶ Sunridge had 9 months to introduce the new system.
- ▶ Oyster cards were introduced in 2 years but the project runs for 17 years.
- ▶ The census system had 3 years to digitise the data and go live.

Resource management

All of the projects involved the management of resources.

- ▶ Sunridge had to manage the purchase of the new computers, the installation and the replacement of the old computers.
- ▶ Oyster had to fit terminals in thousands of buses and underground stations, make millions of cards available and set up a system to manage this.
- ▶ The census project had to set up a website and necessary communications to hold and service the database. They also had to manage the digitisation of millions of records.

Budget restrictions

- ▶ Sunridge set aside £350 000 for the project. It cost £330 000 in the end because the IT manager negotiated good discounts with the equipment suppliers.
- ▶ The Oyster card project was financed by the company who won the contract to set it up. The total cost is estimated at £1 billion.
- ▶ The census database budget needed to increase as the project developed because the initial setting up cost more than the estimated cost. More money was needed after the launch to set up more equipment to meet demand.

Project team

A project team was appointed in each case to oversee the project. The size of the team was different in each case.

- ► Sunridge had a team of three people in the company to introduce the new system.
- ► Oyster card needed thousands of people to install the equipment and write the software to run the system. There are still thousands of people working for the project now because it is an ongoing system.
- ► The census database used subcontractors, including the prison service, to implement the system. They needed to change parts of the team as the project moved forward.

Good communications

- ► The Sunridge team being very small, were in daily contact. Communications with the suppliers was made at regular intervals to ensure the suppliers were aware of deadlines.
- ► The management team for the Oyster project held regular review meetings to monitor progress and set targets for the contractors to meet.
- ► The census database team monitored the project at intervals and made changes as needed. For example they found the prison service was not meeting targets so they employed another firm to digitise the data.

External agencies

All of the projects involved external agencies.

- ► Sunridge needed computer suppliers, the cabling company, and installation engineers as well as temporary staff from an agency at the last minute.
- ► The Oyster project involved a wide range of equipment suppliers and installers and employed a team of programmers to write the software for the system.
- ► The census database used the prison service to digitise the data. They then employed another company. They also needed system suppliers and installation engineers for the web-based system.

Critical success factors

Good communication is essential to good project management. Reviews need to be held regularly and action taken to correct things that are not going to plan. The census team realised that the prison service was too slow to digitise the data so changed the supplier. Trust in outside agents to deliver on time is crucial to success. The IT director of Sunridge did not accept the cheapest quotes but looked deeper into issues such as ongoing support.

Planning is important for any project; the time spent planning is never wasted. Small projects like Sunridge might need weeks of planning. Larger ones such as Oyster need years of planning and testing before the system is ready.

Training staff to use and cope with the new system is vital. The best system in the world will fail if the staff and users are unable to cope when it goes live.

Working to time is vital to the success of any project. Some projects fall behind time from the start because of a lack of appreciation of how long it takes to carry out certain tasks. Some tasks are more critical to the success of a project than others. A method known as critical path analysis is often used in the planning of a project. This looks at the tasks that need to be performed and identifies the ones critical to making progress. Some tasks can be completed at any time, others cannot start until preceding tasks are completed. A critical task is one that will hold up the entire project if it is not completed on time.

For example, in the Sunridge case, it took three months for the delivery of the equipment. Obviously the installation cannot take place if the equipment is not delivered. So ordering the equipment three months in advance is a critical task. Other tasks such as training can take place while waiting for the equipment.

Reasons why some projects fail

The failure of a new system will cause havoc regardless of the scale of the project. The failure may be total, partial or temporary. The failure of the census system was corrected over time, but could have been avoided.

There are a number of factors that contribute towards the failure of a project:

▶ insufficient resources
▶ a lack of human intervention
▶ incomplete specifications
▶ ambiguous specifications
▶ poor budgeting
▶ poor monitoring
▶ inadequate predictions of usage.

Poor planning might result in a failure. All the resources could be available but the project management was not clear and responsibility was not allocated effectively.

The initial analysis might not take account of factors that might affect the project. The census project did not expect the amount of interest it created. The press launch was scaled down to reduce interest, but the interest was there and the publicity surrounding the system failure generated more interest resulting in an unmanageable situation.

The public expectations of computer technology is high. Often people expect more of computers than they are capable of delivering. Many projects fail to take account of this. The system works as expected by the developers, but is a failure in the eyes of the public.

In a Government project, a very positive picture of a system may be portrayed on the Government agency's website, but reality tells a different story.

Some projects fail because they are let down by others. A supplier could go into liquidation at a vital point in the project or supplies might not arrive on time. The project team has very little control over such events, but contingency plans might help to reduce the impact, as can the careful choosing of outside suppliers you involve in a project. Cheapest is not always best.

Stakeholders

Aims

- To introduce the people involved and who are affected by projects
- To examine the roles and responsibilities of stakeholders

Introduction

Even small projects can involve a number of people or organisations. These are called stakeholders. They all have some interest in the project or are affected by it in some way.

Senior management

The senior management team of a large company is made up of a number of people, each with their own specialist jobs within the company. Some examples are:

- Business manager
- Finance manager
- IT manager
- Service manager

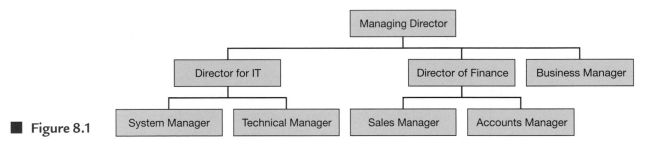

■ Figure 8.1

Each of these will have their own perspective on the project and might be looking for outcomes that affect them in some particular way.

They will have a major input into the initial stages of a project. They will need to set clear planning, budgetary, and overall goals for the project. With the exception of the IT manager they may not fully understand the nature of an IT-related project and will need to take advice about this.

The senior managers must take an active role in the project from the outset. Their role is to control and lead the business and they are ultimately accountable for the success or failure of the project.

They need to have a detailed knowledge of their business. They should have the expertise and experience in the areas for which they are responsible. They also need the ability to influence the direction of a project.

Customer or client

portfolio_tip

Your software project needs a real client. You will need evidence of how you consulted with them to identify their needs.

portfolio_tip

Be realistic in what you can produce for your client. Do not aim for a system that requires skills and techniques you do not have or are not able to acquire in the time allowed for the project.

The customer or client is the person or company that the final product is being produced for. From the start, their ideas and perspectives are of the utmost importance. It must be clear from the start exactly what they want.

The needs of the customer must be clearly identified at the start of the project. The customer needs clear and impartial advice. Often customers have a good idea of what they want, but do not have a clear idea of what is possible within the constraints of the system. Today people expect a lot from IT systems because the power of IT is growing fast.

The customer must therefore be involved in the project from the outset and will need to be kept informed of the progress of the project. Their views will be needed at various points in the project development as well as at the end point review.

What the customer received: What the customer wanted:

■ Figure 8.2

User

A software project can have a wide variety of users depending on the nature of the product. In the case of a small project, the client and the user might be the same individual. However in the case of a large company the client is the company and the users would be members of staff in that company. In the case of a public system such as an online train ticket booking system the user could be anyone. The user is often the person most affected by the end product so they need to have an input at some stage in the project.

portfolio_tip

You will need evidence that you have consulted your user at various stages in the development of your project. You must also show that you have responded to user feedback.

Training needs must be identified and users then trained in the system's use, although clearly in the case of the online system mentioned before this is not possible. The user can still be provided with online help. A telephone support service can be called in the case of difficulty.

The project specification should include user needs and must be accurate and clear. During the development of the project, user opinions should be sought and, if necessary, follow-up action should be taken.

Any impact as a result of the new software must be evaluated from the user's point of view. In a big company, this could involve negotiations with trade unions about working practices.

Project manager

portfolio_tip

For assessment purposes, you will be playing the part of the project managers. You will be assessed on how well you planned, monitored and reviewed the project. You will need to collect evidence such as reports and presentations that you have produced. This should include minutes of meetings which you take when the project board meets.

The project manager is in charge of the project with the overall responsibility to deliver the final product on time and within budget. Much of the role involves the co-ordination of the project team and being a link between the team and the client. The manager needs to have the authority to make decisions about the project on a day-to-day basis.

Good communication skills combined with technical know-how are essential skills needed by project managers. They need enough technical knowledge to be able to understand the technical issues and to communicate with the technical members of the team. They need to create and monitor effective communications with other roles involved in the project.

At the end of the project, an end-of-project evaluation will be completed by the manager to assess how well the project was managed and if any follow-up actions are needed.

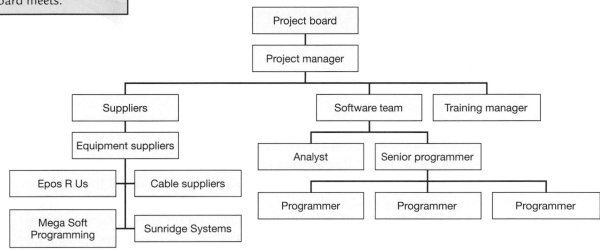

■ **Figure 8.3**

Team members

The project team is a group of individuals with the necessary skills to implement the project, under the direction of the project manager. The size of the team will vary with the size of the project. In your project, you will carry out most of the roles yourself.

A typical team for an IT project might include:

▶ **Systems analysts** who will work out how to use computers to carry out the desired tasks. Their work starts by talking to the client about what they need their IT system to do.

Once they have a clear picture, they design a system that can do the task well. The task is then broken down into small steps. They provide a design for the system so that the programmers can produce the software to make it work.

- ▶ **A senior programmer** who will lead the team of programmers. With a large project, they will use their experience of programming to allocate modules to different programmers. They will also provide advice and motivation to keep the project on time. They will liaise with the project manager to review progress.
- ▶ **Programmers** who will write the code and test the modules they have been allocated.
- ▶ **Installation engineers** who will deal with the technical side of setting up and commissioning the new equipment.

Peer reviewer

The idea behind peer review is that an individual often does not see the mistakes or flaws in his own work. This is because he has planned the project in a way that seems logical to him. Opportunities for improvement can often best be seen by someone else with expertise or experience in the field. Showing planning to others means that weaknesses that might go unnoticed are identified. Then, with advice and encouragement, he can be corrected before the project gets too far under way.

Supplier

If new equipment is needed, the supplier should ensure delivery of the goods on time. Part of the planning process is to liaise with suppliers and obtain quotes for supplies and services needed for the project. At the same time, the project manager needs to get a firm agreement on the delivery times.

Suppliers should also be able to advise on suitable products, although a project manager needs to be aware that the sales department of any supplier is interested in generating sales revenue. The supplier must also take an ongoing interest in the project because future business may depend on a successful outcome.

Project proposal

Aims

- To analyse the components of a project
- To persuade others that a project should be pursued

We have seen in Unit 8.1 how often IT and other projects – particularly in the public sector – fail. The reasons for failure are often to do with unrealistic expectations of a system or misunderstanding the requirements of the client.

What is always essential is to have a clear and realistic proposal that sets targets. These have to be specific, realistic, measurable, attainable and have a time scale.

The right people

There is a serious IT skills shortage in the UK. There are just not enough people who have the latest IT skills to take advantage of what IT has to offer businesses and society in general. In even more short supply are the people who can understand an IT project *and* communicate the essence of it to non-specialists.

In business situations, if someone has a good idea, then the management of the company will need to be persuaded that it is worth pursuing. IT systems can be horrifically expensive and if they are not efficient and effective, the company could incur big losses.

In the public sector, the situation is often reversed. Here, money is often no object. A flagship new system that will look good on a minister's CV can easily consume vast amounts of money, but will never face the ultimate test of market forces. This is one reason why many public sector IT projects fail.

What the project is about

Any new unit must start from a clear understanding of what it is all about. This seems obvious, but it is often overlooked. Fuzzy thinking at the start of a project can easily lead to unclear objectives and wasted effort.

In this chapter, we shall look at how to make sure that the requirements of a new project are kept as clear as possible. This way, everyone concerned, from the finance director to the programmer, is absolutely clear about what needs to be done and when.

Livewires is a company that supplies and installs computer network cabling. We met them in the AS book, when they were investigating new ways of producing quotes for customers. At the last meeting of the Board of Directors, the finance director reported that the dividend they paid to shareholders was rather low and that they might become more profitable if they diversified. He pointed out that there was a huge public interest in home networking and good money might be made if they tapped into this market as well as maintaining their traditional role as a supplier to businesses. To do this, they have opened a warehouse which sells networking equipment to the general public.

Livewires has an IT director. This is a good idea because it means that IT-related decisions can be discussed with a knowledgeable person at board level. Some companies put IT matters in the charge of the finance director who is briefed by an IT manager.

The IT director undertakes to investigate what is necessary in order to roll out an IT system that will allow the new business to function effectively with the existing activities.

Getting approval

In the case study, the finance director has asked the IT director to investigate the feasibility of a new IT system. Both directors now need to persuade the rest of the board that this expansion is a good idea. It may be that the rest of the board is sceptical about moving outside its traditional territory.

A meeting with the board will be required at some stage, in order to put forward the proposals. The two directors who are promoting this expansion need to be able to persuade their colleagues that the changes will benefit the business. The rest of the board won't care about the technology used as long as it brings cost benefits. So, work needs to be done to summarise these benefits and convince them that the changes are feasible.

The persuasion can be done by:

▶ producing reports
▶ talking to the others
▶ producing and running a presentation.

A presentation can be a good starting point because it encourages thinking in bullet points. A further advantage is that presentation software such as Microsoft PowerPoint has a number of pre-existing templates. These can be invaluable in reminding you what you should think of covering.

There are plenty of templates to choose from.

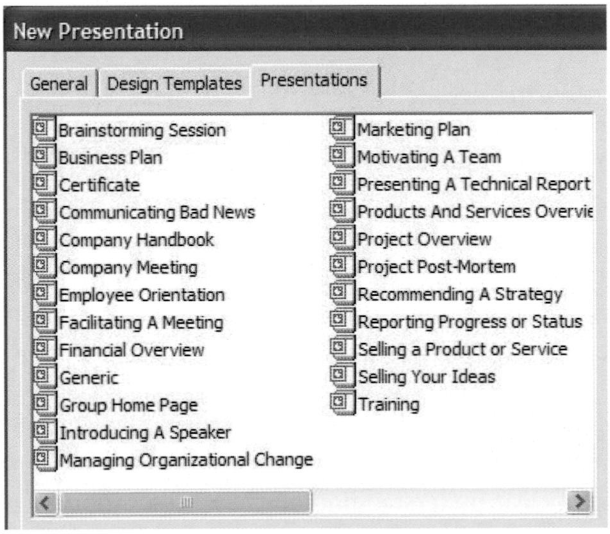

■ **Figure 8.4**

They can remind you of some important headings.

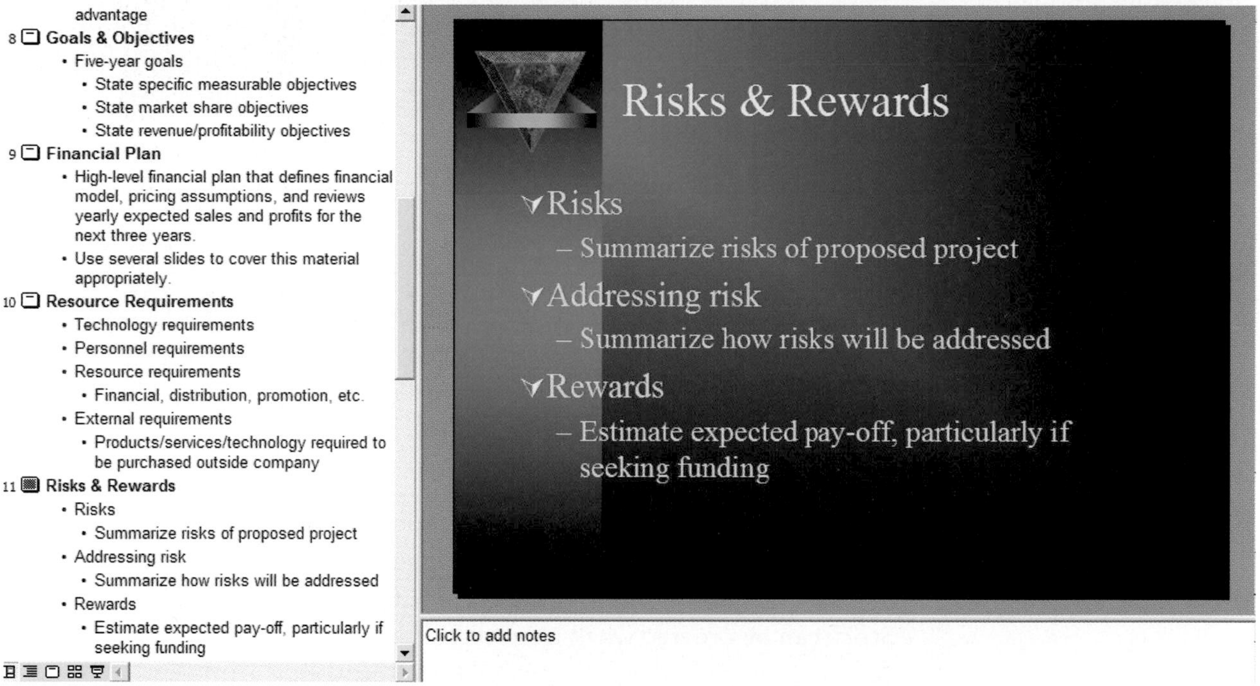

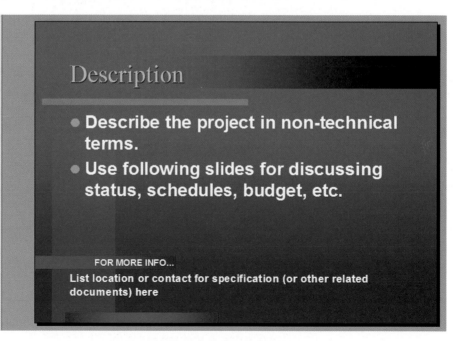

advantage
8 Goals & Objectives
• Five-year goals
• State specific measurable objectives
• State market share objectives
• State revenue/profitability objectives
9 Financial Plan
• High-level financial plan that defines financial model, pricing assumptions, and reviews yearly expected sales and profits for the next three years.
• Use several slides to cover this material appropriately.
10 Resource Requirements
• Technology requirements
• Personnel requirements
• Resource requirements
• Financial, distribution, promotion, etc.
• External requirements
• Products/services/technology required to be purchased outside company
11 Risks & Rewards
• Risks
• Summarize risks of proposed project
• Addressing risk
• Summarize how risks will be addressed
• Rewards
• Estimate expected pay-off, particularly if seeking funding
Risks & Rewards
Risks
– Summarize risks of proposed project
Addressing risk
– Summarize how risks will be addressed
Rewards
– Estimate expected pay-off, particularly if seeking funding
Click to add notes

■ **Figure 8.5**

They remind you how you should try to put your points across.

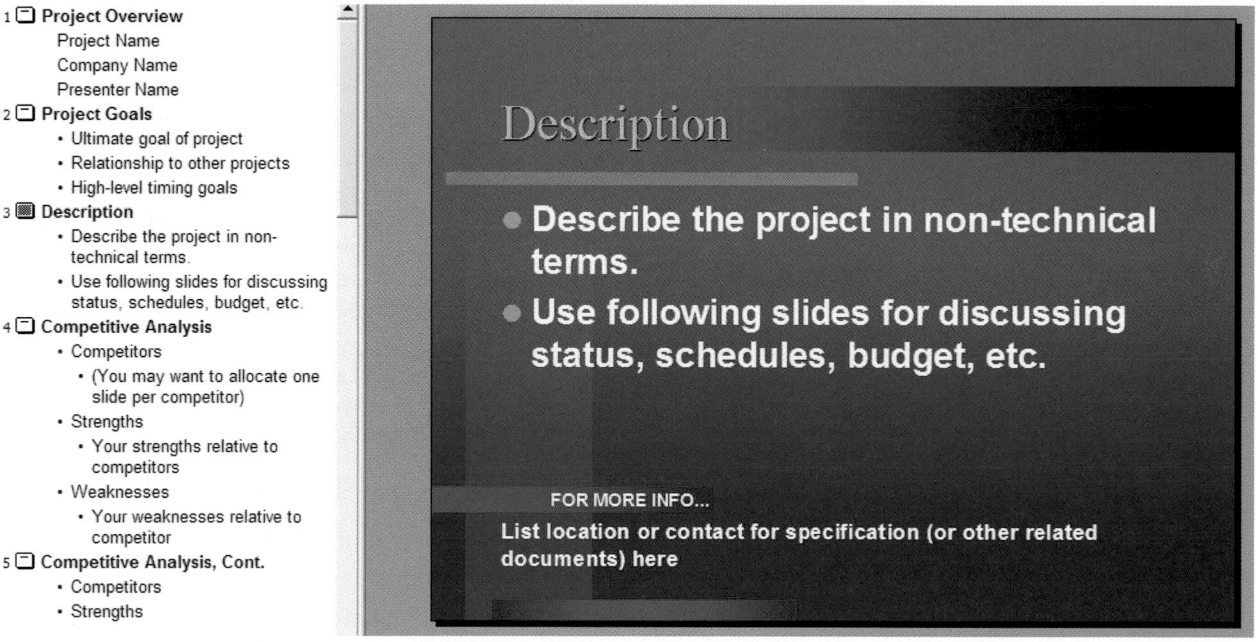

1 Project Overview
Project Name
Company Name
Presenter Name
2 Project Goals
• Ultimate goal of project
• Relationship to other projects
• High-level timing goals
3 Description
• Describe the project in non-technical terms.
• Use following slides for discussing status, schedules, budget, etc.
4 Competitive Analysis
• Competitors
• (You may want to allocate one slide per competitor)
• Strengths
• Your strengths relative to competitors
• Weaknesses
• Your weaknesses relative to competitor
5 Competitive Analysis, Cont.
• Competitors
• Strengths
Description
• Describe the project in non-technical terms.
• Use following slides for discussing status, schedules, budget, etc.
FOR MORE INFO...
List location or contact for specification (or other related documents) here

■ **Figure 8.6**

Remember, you may find good ideas in more than one category of template. In this case, we can use:

- Business Plan
- Project Overview
- Selling Your Ideas.

ACTIVITY

Produce a presentation for the board of directors summarising the needs of this project.

You should not just rely on presentations. Once you have marshalled your facts and opinions about the project, you can lay them out on paper to send to the other directors so that they can start thinking about them. You can also start to get your points across in more subtle ways. Conversations at lunch, in the corridor or over drinks can help to set the scene in a more relaxed way than in formal meetings.

What the project will deliver

The IT director must start out by deciding exactly what the new IT system is for. Vague ideas such as 'to increase efficiency' or 'to integrate the business' are no use. Specific requirements are essential although, in the early stages, the fine detail does not need to be examined.

The company is now trading in two distinct areas of business:

▶ **The original networking business** will continue to provide a service to businesses. It deals with fairly large contracts, which typically take several days or even weeks to fulfil. It takes time to wire up a large building. Stock can be ordered when a contract is agreed. Payment is made by the customer on delivery of the invoice when the work is complete.

▶ **The new retail business** is directed at individual consumers. The transactions will be smaller and unpredictable. Livewires needs to have sufficient stock at all times so that casual customers can get what they want on the spot, otherwise they will go elsewhere. An efficient stock-control system is needed to ensure this without tying up too much money in slow moving stock. Livewires did not have this problem before.

Dealing with casual customers also requires a Point of Sale (POS) system. Customers will expect to be able to pay by credit or debit card when they make their purchases. Again, this is new to Livewires. POS systems already exist for thousands of other retail businesses so it should be possible to buy in a ready-made system.

What benefits the project will bring and the potential risks

The new business brings some risks. It has a lot of potential but it is a totally different market sector to the old Livewires enterprise. The whole history of Livewires has been directed towards other businesses. It is now moving into retail sales to the general public.

A new IT system will potentially bring business information to the board of directors as well as supporting the day-to-day activities of the new combined company.

A new IT system should be able to:

▶ maximise the profitability of the new retail arm by allowing 'just in time' purchasing of stock

▶ provide communication between the retail outlets and the older part of the company

- provide a basis for later expansion into online marketing (a web-based ordering system)
- give the management team a much better overview of the finances of the combined company
- provide a stock control system
- print invoices
- record payments
- produce orders for new stock.

There are some business risks in the proposed new part of the business. What we are concerned with here are the risks involved in commissioning a new IT system.

Some of the more significant risks are that the new system:

- may not be able to integrate with the old system
- may not perform adequately and bring the projected business benefits
- may not be ready in time for the launch of the new combined enterprise
- may contain bugs that will cause problems for the new organisation.

Impact on personnel and practices

New staff will be hired in order to run the retail side of the business. They will need training in whatever new IT systems are produced. Existing staff will need to be aware of the extra dimensions to the system. The IT support staff in particular will need to become familiar with the new system so that they can help users and maintain the new system.

Often, output from a system needs to be 'tweaked' in order to satisfy managers. This means that spreadsheets or database queries are often set up to take output from an IT system in order to produce a particular report or presentation. The IT staff will need to be aware of exactly what output is going to be produced by the new IT system and in what file formats it can be delivered.

Projects can have unintended results too. A new system such as the London Oyster card can affect the way people do their jobs and this might lead to industrial unrest.

The functional requirements

It makes no sense to buy a new IT system unless it is clear what it has to do. Without this clarity of purpose, money will probably be wasted in buying functionality that is not required.

A retail business has completely different requirements to those of a business-to-business operation. It will firstly need a system to handle retail sales. There is no need for Livewires' own IT people to produce this. Such systems are already in use with many other similar businesses so they can be bought from various suppliers who have already developed them. All that will be necessary will be to:

- contact some suitable suppliers
- get quotes from them
- negotiate with them about the costs involved in customising their systems, installation and training.

EPOS

Most retail IT systems now involve Electronic Point of Sale (EPOS). These are the systems that allow the scanning of goods at a checkout, the production of an itemised receipt and the ability to take card payments. Everyone expects retailers to have this capability because they often do not carry enough cash with them to make large purchases.

■ Figure 8.7

ACTIVITY

Use a search engine to find three different suppliers of EPOS systems. Make a list of facilities that they provide and if possible try to determine their costs. In most cases, this may be difficult because costs are often negotiated with the client on the basis of their own special requirements.

Stock control

Any business that keeps stocks of materials or goods for sale needs to be completely aware of what is in stock and how much there is. If a business overstocks, it is tying up capital that could be earning interest. If it understocks, there is a risk that goods will not be available when the customers want them. If this happens, the customers will probably go elsewhere. A good computer-based stock-control system makes it easier to tread the fine line between over- and under-stocking.

A good EPOS system will automatically adjust stock levels when purchases are made. Some will carry out automatic re-ordering.

ACTIVITY

Carry out a quick online survey of companies that provide out-of-the-box stock-control systems. Do any of them integrate with EPOS systems?

ACTIVITY

Make a database structure that could support a stock-control system. What tables would be needed and what fields in these tables? Draw a diagram to show how the tables would be linked.

Hardware

The retail part of the business will need to purchase a wide range of hardware devices in order to operate the EPOS system and other new functions. They will need card readers at the checkouts as well as a server to handle all the transactions. The retail store will need to be wired up to allow the devices to be connected. As Livewires is already in this business, it will be able to organise this activity itself. This will need to be booked in as a job with the cabling section so that engineers will be available.

> **ACTIVITY**
>
> Make a list of hardware devices and other resources that will be needed in a retail store to allow EPOS and stock-control activities to be carried out.

Users of the results of the project

Retail staff

The staff in the retail store will need to operate the EPOS equipment. Some will need to operate the computers that update the stock figures and the retail prices. Initially, there will be one new appointment for someone to look after the networking involved, but it is expected that this will not require a lot of maintenance.

Warehouse staff

Any stock-control system requires human input from time to time. If the stock levels are automatically adjusted when deliveries and sales take place, then a stock check will sometimes be necessary to make sure that the reality reflects the calculations. It may be that damage or theft has resulted in the real figures being wrong. Warehouse staff will need to be able to change the figures to reflect reality.

> Who needs to have access to the warehouse data files? Should there be different levels of access for different staff? If so, why?

All the warehouse staff will have to learn how to use hand-held barcode readers which they will use to read product details from the shelves and record current stock levels.

How long the project will take

All projects need to have a time scale. Without this, there is always the possibility that they will over-run and that they will no longer fulfil their purpose. The IT director will eventually make a decision about who is going to implement the systems that they need. Once that decision has been taken, negotiations will take place about the time frame.

Livewires may insist upon penalties if the project is not completed in time. The time agreed with the suppliers must be realistic – some things are just not possible. However, if the IT system is not ready for when the store opens, then sales will be lost and the reputation of the company will be seriously affected.

The supplier of the systems may not be entirely able to dictate events. There may be a lead time for supplies to be obtained. Possibly the customisation of the software will need the attention of a specialist programming company that has no spare time at the moment.

ACTIVITY

Make a list of all the factors that could delay the implementation of an IT project such as Livewires' EPOS and stock-control system. Can you think of any contingency planning that could help to reduce the impact of late delivery?

When the project must be finished

The Board of Directors would like the systems to be ready and in place in two months. This is to coincide with the opening of the new retail store. The various managers all need to be informed of the time scale so that all the aspects of opening the store are dealt with fast enough to meet the proposed opening date. As well as installing the IT systems, the overall project will have to include:

ACTIVITY

What other activities will need to be coordinated in the commissioning of the new store?

- building work
- fitting out the store
- recruiting staff
- training staff

- decorating
- stocking the store
- advertising

Resources that are needed

The suppliers of the software system will be closely involved in advising Livewires about what resources need to be in place before the EPOS and stock-control systems can go live. Some of these resources have been mentioned already, but they will include:

- EPOS terminals
- cabling and ducting
- wiring cabinets
- network hardware
- servers
- electrical outlets
- connectivity to the rest of the company.

ACTIVITY

The network part of the EPOS system will require:

- hubs
- switches
- patch panels
- patch leads
- a router
- fly leads
- UTP cable
- UTP outlets.

Find out what each of these items is for and draw up a table of explanations.

In any modern network, there will be at least one server but usually there are many more than this. Servers are often specialised so that there may be a file and print server for day-to-day activities, an email server to deal with communications and a web server, if the company's website is internally hosted.

Outsourcing

Many operations these days are OUTSOURCED. This means that whereas in the past a company might have done certain jobs itself, it has become more cost-effective to pay specialist companies to do the work instead. This can lead to economies of scale and a reduction in the number of specialist staff employed.

CASE STUDY

British Airways, along with many other airlines, has outsourced its in-flight catering to an outside company. This freed it up to concentrate its efforts on the business of providing and selling flights. The company that took on the catering was able to provide meals at a lower cost because it could produce thousands of them for other customers as well.

The problem was that when the workers at the catering company had a grievance, they were able to cause immense damage by going on strike. This had nothing to do with British Airways, who lost a great deal of business because of it. If British Airways had kept the catering in-house, it would have had more control over its industrial relations.

Outsourcing is not all good news. It can mean a loss of control.

A company will normally be engaged in order to oversee the installation of a new system. This company will probably sub-contract many of the jobs to others. In this case, the cabling will be done by Livewires itself because that is their business. They will have to work closely with the supplier's project manager in order to provide everything that is needed.

The software suppliers will have their own suppliers with whom they have to coordinate and do business. They will buy the computers from outside suppliers because this is normally cheaper than making their own.

Much of the EPOS equipment will come from specialist suppliers. It will be necessary to make sure that they can deliver what is needed and on time.

The new system needs to link into the existing IT systems that Livewires already has in place. The easiest way to make this happen is over the Internet. For this, a reliable ISP has to be found. Someone will have to make sure that the ISP is capable of delivering the sort of service that is required.

A physical connection is needed to connect to the ISP. It may be that a separate telecommunications company has to be engaged to deal with this.

All these organisations and people need to be able to work together. Later, in Unit 8.7, you will see how software can be used in order to coordinate all these activities.

Ways of tackling the project

Livewires had a number of different options when it came to planning the EPOS and stock-control systems. There is seldom one absolutely right option. There are always judgements to be made and trade-offs of benefits versus disadvantages.

ACTIVITY

There is so much choice in everything these days! If you go to a supermarket to buy washing powder, you will probably be faced with 20 different brands, four or five sizes and a decision whether to buy biological or non-biological. Maybe you don't care, but at some stage you reach out and grab a packet. How do you decide? How do the manufacturers try to influence you?

Suppose you want to buy a printer. You need it to print high quality images from your new 6-million-pixel camera. You also want to print ordinary documents. Do you need a card reader as well? Do you need a DVD burner? Do you care about the print speed? Find out how many makes of printer there are that could do the job. How would you finally decide which one to buy?

Bespoke system

Livewires could commission a software company to create a system specially for them. It could get involved in discussions and many meetings in order to make sure that everything was exactly right for them. There are some advantages of this but there are more disadvantages:

▶ The software would take longer to produce.
▶ It would probably contain bugs that would need to be ironed out over time.
▶ It may not be compatible with other people's systems and this might make communication with others difficult.
▶ They would be locked in to one supplier for maintenance.

Off-the-shelf EPOS

There are so many companies that already have EPOS and stock-control systems that it seems silly to 'reinvent the wheel'. An existing system will be tried and tested and the maintenance would probably be cheaper because the supplier already has experience in the field. Best of all, the system is available right away.

The disadvantage might be that it would not be exactly right for Livewires but, these days, it should not be too difficult to get a system that can quickly be customised.

Methods of setting up the WAN

If Livewires wanted to include communication between its existing business and the new retail arm, a WAN would be useful. A WAN allows geographically distant sites to communicate as if there were no distance issues at all.

There are various choices here, of course. A dedicated link could be commissioned such that Livewires had exclusive access to a connection between its premises. This would be expensive – possibly extremely so.

A Virtual Private Network (VPN) might be the best option. This way, the Internet is used to provide connectivity, but a server – located anywhere – is used to provide the functionality and data access that Livewires requires. Login IDs and passwords can be used to maintain privacy.

ACTIVITY

Produce a document for the board of directors with your recommendations of how to tackle this project.

Definition of scope

Aims

■ To define what is included in a project

■ To establish a clear understanding of what the project must achieve

Someone has had a good idea or a problem needs to be solved. An IT solution has been suggested. The management has been persuaded that the IT solution is a good idea and has given approval for the spending of funds to finance the project. The project is ready to go. The people who came up with the ideas have already outlined the reasons for the project but now come the details.

For most organisations, new IT projects involve considerable costs and considerable risks. This is more acute than with many other types of project.

The reason for undertaking the project

A project starts and finishes with the client. This must never be forgotten by anybody involved in seeing the project through to completion. If the project does not satisfy the client, he will not want to pay and he will certainly not want to do any repeat business.

This must be uppermost in everybody's mind throughout the life of a project. It is very easy for those who work on small parts of a project to forget what it is for. For example, the programmers of a new system may get closely involved in some programming problem that lets them show off some new ideas or try out experiments that they have long been thinking about. Although these ideas may well benefit the efficiency of the product, they may have nothing to do with what the client wants.

In the Livewires scenario outlined in the last chapter, the purpose of the IT project was twofold:

▶ to provide an EPOS system for a new store
▶ to provide stock control.

But, there are other aspects that need to be tied down once the project is given approval. Is the EPOS system going to be linked to the stock-control system? Is the whole system going to have some form of integration with existing systems at Livewires?

If the answer to these questions is yes, then extra work will have to be done and the project will take longer. There will, crucially, be more to test as well as to put together. The project manager needs to be clear about all this so that the client (Livewires) is not disappointed.

The expected benefits to the organisation

ACTIVITY

Why might a customer choose to visit a store with EPOS rather than one without?

ACTIVITY

Produce a presentation for the directors of Livewires outlining the potential benefits of the new system.

This has already been argued at the project proposal stage. There are many reasons to install an EPOS system such as:

- customer convenience
- store reputation
- stock-control linkage
- itemised receipts
- accounting.

The stock control system will allow a greater degree of 'just in time' ordering which will improve the company's cash flow. It also allows greater precision in making sure that items are always in stock.

Finally, if the system is integrated into the existing IT systems that Livewires has, there will be better business information available to help the directors to make strategic decisions.

The objectives of the project

ACTIVITY

Make a list of other specific components – hardware, software and activities that will be needed for the proposed system at Livewires.

These have been hinted at throughout the planning stages. They need to be spelt out so that nobody involved forgets what they are aiming at.

Greater detail can be added here so that the project can be divided into separate jobs and the jobs assigned to different people. Some of the key objectives are:

- Point of Sale hardware to be available at ten checkouts in the new store
- software to support Point of Sale transactions
- networking to support the POS systems
- interfaces to allow the transactions and product updates
- software to allow cashless transactions
- connectivity to allow cashless transactions (they need to be connected to their bank and to credit agencies)
- provision of stock control software.

Key success criteria

The main criteria for success might seem pretty obvious – Livewires wants a system that provides:

- EPOS
- stock control
- reporting.

It is not enough to simply paint the broad picture. Some very specific points should be drawn up so that each member of the project team will know when the particular job is finished. There will be lots of these, even in a fairly straightforward project such as the Livewires example. The success criteria for a big project can be much more difficult to arrive at.

The London congestion charge is at first sight a fairly simple idea – even though it involves some rather clever IT. It was introduced with the stated aim of reducing traffic congestion in Central London – although there were unstated social aims behind this.

Every vehicle entering the congestion charge zone is photographed many times. Its number plate is decoded by special software and stored on a database. At the end of each day, the stored number plate details are matched against the details of those who have paid the charge. If there is a match, the relevant number plate records are deleted. Exempt vehicles such as buses are deleted. Otherwise, the registered keeper of the vehicle is sent a penalty notice and has to pay a fine.

What are the success criteria for an IT project like this? The obvious ones are from the point of view of the developers and are to do with whether it works as planned.

■ Figure 8.8

- Does the system catch all or most of the cars that enter the zone?
- Do the right or the wrong people get penalty notices?
- How many errors are discovered in sending out the notices?
- Can it handle the volume of data encountered?

The Mayor of London might have a different point of view. His success criteria might be:

- Does the congestion charge reduce traffic volumes?
- Is the system generating enough revenue to pay for itself and for other projects?
- Are more people using buses?
- Is the air quality measurably better?

One trouble here is that the first two criteria are contradictory. If fewer people drive into the congestion zone, the system will make less money.

Other people have yet other views. Businesses will want to be assured that the system will not harm their trade.

So, success criteria are often not what they seem and side effects are normal. Still, once a project has been given the go-ahead, they are needed in order to keep track of progress.

In the case of Livewires, the success criteria can initially include things such as:

▶ Do all cash terminals connect to the server?
▶ Is it always possible to contact the bank system for credit and debit cards?
▶ Does the reported stock level match the real stock level to within 10%?

Make a list of other success criteria you think are important to Livewires.

The constraints

It would be wonderful if a project could be endlessly expanded to provide more and more useful services. Livewires would no doubt like to have an online arm to its operations so that its retail sales could reach an even wider public. Some accounting functions could be integrated.

IT students will know about this sort of problem. Often when they are planning a practical project, they attempt to do too much and end up with an unfinished project. No project can do everything. There are always constraints on what is possible.

The two major constraints are going to be money and time.

There is always an upper limit on what can be spent on a project. If it goes over budget, the client will probably refuse to pay.

Time is important because most systems will lose their whole point if they are not ready on time. Livewires' EPOS system must be ready for the store's opening. There will probably be no backup manual solution for processing sales and anyway it would be very embarrassing if their first day were a flop.

There are plenty of other constraints too:

▶ Is there suitable hardware available?
▶ Is the system compatible with other linked systems?
▶ Is the system capable of dealing with the expected volume of data?
▶ Are there programmers available who can actually do the work?
▶ Are there likely to be any redundancies that might cause trouble with employees or unions?
▶ Could there be knock-on effects on the working practices of others in the company or outside it?
▶ Are the staff capable of being trained?

CASE STUDY

The Wembley Stadium project
The idea of building a showcase stadium for the nation has been hit by delay after delay. The initial budget was used up a long time ago. At the time of writing this book the project is a long way off target in terms of time and money.

ACTIVITY

Think of other constraints that could be added to the list.

Areas of risk

Suppose a builder started out on a project to build a new estate of houses. He buys the land – possibly at an enormous price – and then has to prepare the land, demolish any old buildings that are already there, design the new houses, obtain planning permission, order the materials, plan the stages of building, hire the workers, arrange for services to be laid on, ensure that he has proper title to the land, follow building regulations and countless other details.

After all that, he has to advertise and sell the houses to make a profit! This is all quite straightforward compared with an IT project! The reason is that although the builder has a lot to do, it has all been done before. There are plenty of people 'out there' who can do the various jobs. Also, at the end, he has houses to sell. Everybody knows what houses are and what to expect from them. They may differ in many ways and some may be of better quality than others but houses are buildings in which people live. They contain rooms and most houses have similar rooms for similar functions. A purchaser of a house knows what to expect.

Not so with an IT product! A typical IT product has never been made before. It may have some family resemblance with other IT products and as time goes on, there is more to compare it with, but each new IT product is unique. That is the whole point. If it were not unique, then the purchasers would buy something else.

Everyone knows what to expect from a house or a car or a washing machine. Software and even new hardware presents a whole new realm of possibilities. So it can be difficult to define in advance exactly what one hopes to get. Also, software is complex. A car may have between two and four thousand components. A moderately sized IT system will have hundreds of thousands if not millions of lines of program code.

Most projects have faults in them that escape the attention of the testers. We have come to expect faults which gradually get fixed over time. We would never accept faulty goods in other aspects of life.

Setting out expectations is therefore difficult and presents more of a moving target than most other projects that we undertake. Still, we have to try so that everybody who is involved in a project is as well informed as possible and knows what to do and when.

Many possible pitfalls have already been covered in the project proposals. The main risks to the Livewires project are:

▶ The project might not be delivered on time.
▶ The project might be over budget.
▶ The system might crash under load.
▶ The system might have faults that produce wrong stock figures.
▶ The system might be sabotaged by dishonest employees.

> **ACTIVITY** What measures can the project manager take to minimise some of these risks? You may want to discuss these with other students and come up with a plan.

The project roadmap

This is a rough estimate of what will be delivered – for example, when resource requirements such as people, materials, equipment and time might be needed.

The project manager will have to make a plan so that everything is in the right place at the right time. This can be done using various methods and diagrams are particularly helpful in keeping an eye on progress and communicating this to associates and clients.

It is crucial to be aware of the order in which tasks must be performed. It is no use if the EPOS software is written but there is no network cabling ready so that it can be installed. The networking can be done at the same time as the programming. This is because different people are involved. However, the same programmers will be working on the two parts of the software so these tasks must follow each other.

The easiest way to organise a project is to use special project management software such as Microsoft Project. This allows tasks to be inserted and resources allocated as well as automatically adjusting links so that if one task overruns and another task needs to follow, the consequences can always be made clear.

One view of part of the Livewires planning looks like a network diagram as in Figure 8.9.

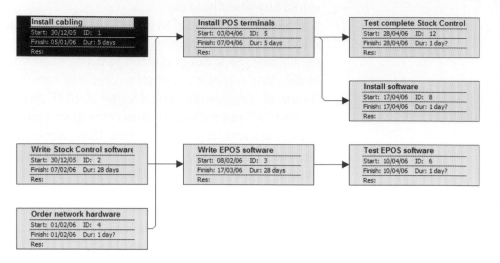

Project management software allows the incorporation of the resources required into the plan. People are regarded as a resource and it is desirable to make sure that they are not double booked and that they have time to carry out their tasks.

Other resources such as equipment can also be factored into the plan and the software can show if there are any clashes in requirements that would prevent the plan from moving forwards.

The project's stakeholders

Lots of people are involved in any medium to large-scale project. They all have a point of view and they all have something to lose if things do not go according to plan.

The stakeholders in the Livewires project include various people employed by Livewires itself. The IT director has put his job on the line over this project and will be in trouble if it fails.

The project manager has his reputation to consider. If the project does not get delivered on time, he will lose future opportunities.

The users of the system need to have the right tools to do their jobs – if the results are unsatisfactory, their working lives may suffer.

The software company needs to be fully informed of the points of view of the other stakeholders so that it can produce what is needed to the satisfaction of all other parties.

> **ACTIVITY**
>
> For the London congestion charge system, make a list of all the stakeholders who had a point of view regarding the success of the project.

Interim review points

It is dangerous to wait until the end of a project before reviewing. To be sure that everything is on track, there need to be points where current progress is assessed. Without this, there is a danger that when the final delivery time comes, everything is not ready.

ACTIVITY

Suggest points where the Livewires project should be reviewed and who should be involved.

When students are producing IT projects, a wise teacher sets intermediate deadlines so that there is not a sudden crisis right at the end when it becomes clear that everything is way behind schedule.

The road map mentioned in Figure 8.9 shows some of the tasks involved in the Livewires project. It would be sensible to review progress with quick briefing sessions from time to time. These should not be too often otherwise they would interfere with the actual accomplishment of the tasks. Also, it is wise not to distract too many of the participants in a project.

The project deliverables

A project may have many objectives but some of them might follow on from the actual delivery of a system. In the Livewires example, the system is finished when:

- ▶ it is installed
- ▶ it is tested
- ▶ the data is input
- ▶ the staff are trained.

The suppliers have now done their bit. They have supplied what is 'deliverable'. It is now up to the retail store to make use of the system to achieve the company's longer term objectives.

The quality criteria for the deliverables

The deliverable aspects of a system must be defined from a quality point of view from the outset. That way, there is a basis for accepting the system – or not. If there is a dispute between the client and the supplier, this can only make sense if there is an established level of quality that was agreed at the outset.

It could be that a certain number of transactions can take place using the EPOS system at the same time. The production of errors might be a factor in the quality criteria. It would be reasonable to expect the calculations of stock levels and of customers' bills to be 100% accurate.

ACTIVITY

Make a list of other quality criteria that the EPOS system must meet.

Usability could be a factor. A typical checkout operator should be able to be trained in a reasonable time to use the system with few mistakes being made. The interface must be intuitive and friendly enough for this to happen.

Speed of response is an issue. It is not much use if every time an item is scanned, the checkout operator has to wait a minute for the item's identity to be looked up on the server.

The target completion date

We have seen that in most business cases, this is absolutely crucial. It is common for IT projects to overrun because they are often more complex than they seem. But, as more and more reliance is placed on IT systems, completion dates need to be adhered to more carefully than ever.

Project organisation

Aims

■ To look at ways in which project team members can communicate successfully

The bigger a project becomes, the more difficult it is to coordinate. The more people there are involved, the harder it is for them to communicate. If they do not communicate, then the project may well develop in different directions and the end product may not be what was required or it might even fail completely.

It is the responsibility of the project manager to make sure that the team is coordinated, but this is made easier if the members of the team have some ground rules to follow so that they all understand each other.

These rules can include the format of reports. They may be set out as a questionnaire so that everything is covered. The rules will also cover when reports have to be made. This way the whole team will always be up to date with events. In addition, there will be rules that cover a range of activities and these will be examined in this chapter.

Storing documents relating to a project

Students of IT will already be well versed in following sensible rules for the storing of documents. In the AS part of this course, documents will have been collected, organised and stored for the ebook part of the work.

Even in the information age, there is no getting away from paper documents. Although more and more records are being stored electronically, some documents are still needed. They are needed for use away from a computer and also for legal purposes.

ACTIVITY

Think of reasons why paper documents are still necessary for legal contracts. Can you think of how eventually even this situation may be transferred to electronic format?

The trouble with paper documents is that they can only be in one place at one time. If a team is working on a project, they will all need to have access to some of the documents. For example, progress reports from one group, such as the programmers, will be of interest to the other groups, such as the testers and installers as well as the project manager and the client.

One way to make sure that all team members have access to the latest documents is by making photocopies of reports and circulating them to those who need to know. This is still a very widespread means of communicating with a team and it works well. You can read them anywhere and you have a permanent copy.

ACTIVITY

Make a list of a few duplicated documents that have been circulated to you or your teachers over the last few weeks. What were they about and can you think of a better way of communicating the facts?

There are always disadvantages to using paper communication like this. It is so easy to lose the paper. If you get lots of memos and reports, it is very tempting not to read them, to file them 'somewhere' until they are out of date and then throw them away. Your teachers will probably be familiar with this as they get bombarded with all sorts of memos and instructions from heads, principals, local authorities and the education department.

Paper also takes up a lot of space. It is difficult to find documents you want – especially if there are lots of them. Storing data electronically is so much easier but you cannot get away from documents. You need to have a good system for categorising documents, filing them away and also for getting rid of ones you don't need any more.

You can learn from a PC operating system. You set up folders to hold documents for different categories of information. A project manager could have a hierarchical system something like this:

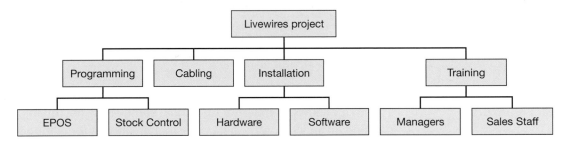

■ Figure 8.10

This is exactly how the relevant information could be organised on a PC hard disk but in this case, you would use boxes, folders and files.

Unfortunately, it is harder work re-categorising paper files – you cannot drag and drop when you change your mind!

A well-run IT project will not circulate unnecessary paper memos as they make a lot of work.

Nowadays, it is usually preferable to communicate within a project by email. That way backups can be made, material can be categorised and re-categorised and searches can be made. Crucially, it is much easier to delete redundant information.

Some software can be set up automatically to sort documents relating to a project. Microsoft Binder is an example of this.

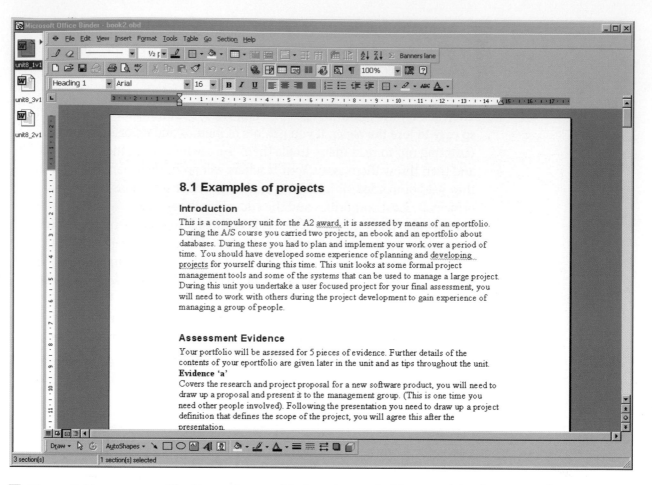

Figure 8.11

The image shows a binder set up to hold some of the documents for this book. Clicking on an icon on the left opens that document for editing in the normal way. Options are included to do things such as adding a common footer to all documents, or numbering pages sequentially starting at the first document.

Protecting information from accidental damage

portfolio_tip

Remember you need to show you have used standard ways of working. Making a backup is a standard way of working. It is a good idea to have at least two backup copies.

This is easier if the information is stored electronically. Any information you have in a paper system is vulnerable. You might throw away an important document or lose the lot in a fire or burglary. A careless member of staff might shred the wrong documents. With computer documents, you can and should make backups, then not only is it so much easier to keep track of what is going on, but you also do not lose important data.

Computer stores of data can be protected in other ways too. Important files can be made read-only or hidden to make them safe from accidental deletion. Different people can be given different access rights so that there are fewer opportunities for carelessness.

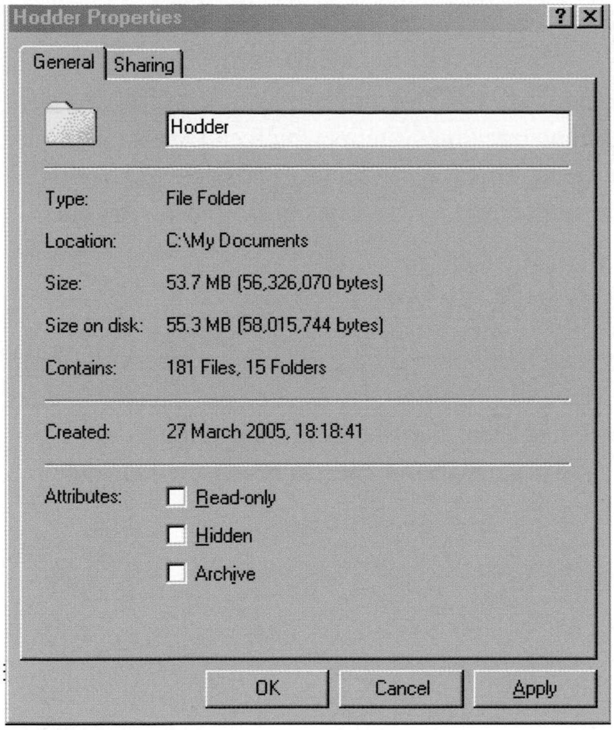

Figure 8.12a

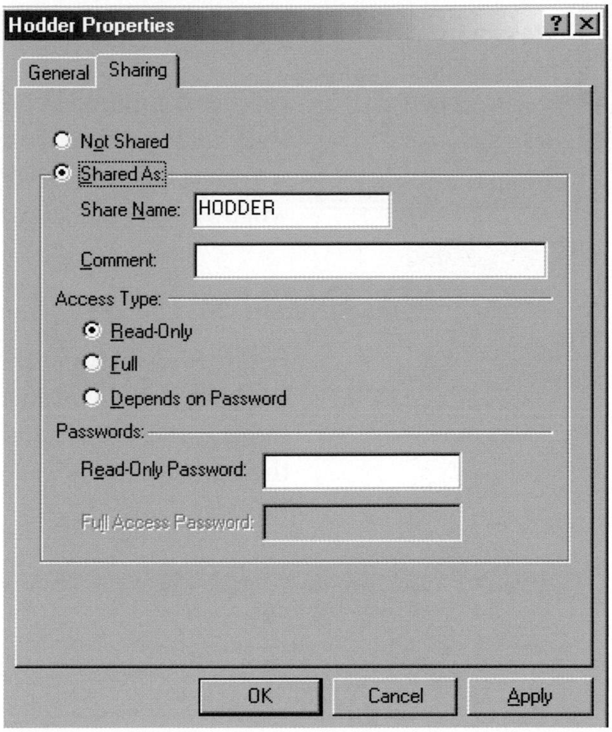

Figure 8.12b

Make a list of ways in which a paper-based filing system can be protected against accidental damage.

The figures above show how folders and files can be protected. Figure 8.12a shows the basic settings for hidden and read-only; Figure 8.12b shows how a folder can be shared and different levels of access given to others.

Communicating with stakeholders

Apart from the participants in a project, it is also necessary to give feedback to those who will use the system. The client will be reassured if he gets regular news of how the project is progressing. Those who will have to organise the implementation of the system will also be better able to plan their activities if they know about delays. Again, it is easiest to do this via electronic methods.

Mailing lists can easily be set up with any email software. With them, it is possible to have different groups that can overlap if necessary and send them reports at regular intervals with no great effort and with no danger of forgetting anyone. As with paper documents, these should be well targeted and only sent when needed, as regular boring bulk emails get deleted without being read!

One of the authors used to receive an IT trade magazine sent every week and always skimmed through it to see if there were any interesting articles – sometimes there were. It changed to electronic distribution by email and it is so much easier just to delete it – one less job to do!

ACTIVITY

Make a list of some of the stakeholders in the Livewires project.

Do you get regular newsletters in your emails? Do you read them?

If paper communication methods are used to communicate with the stakeholders, there are document-tracking systems which can keep a record of what has happened to documents. This way, it is always possible to check whether each person who should receive a report has in fact been sent one.

Using software to organise a meeting

Figure 8.13 shows how Microsoft Outlook can help organise a meeting. Chris is trying to invite Sean and Steve to a meeting. He can see his availability next to his name. If Sean and Steve had their diaries online then Chris would see their availability as well. In large organisations, meetings are often arranged this way.

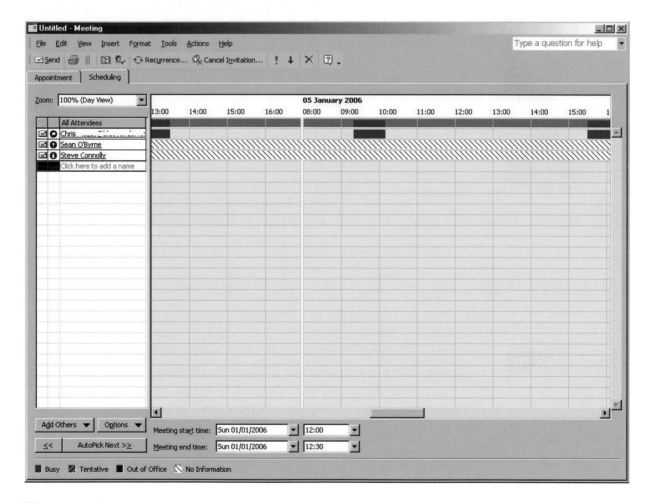

Figure 8.13

Reporting on progress

Few projects run completely according to plan. There are often unexpected delays or sometimes things get done faster than expected.

The building of the Empire State Building in New York City was started in 1930. It was scheduled to be built in 18 months at a cost of $43 million. In fact, it was built in under 15 months and at a cost of $24.7 million.

Not many projects these days can compete with that for efficiency.

■ **Figure 8.14** Health and Safety at Work 1930

The people involved in each part of a project need to communicate with the project manager at regular intervals so that the overall progress of the project can be made as effective as possible.

For a small project, this might simply mean the project manager making a phone call or sending an email every week. In bigger projects, it will be formalised so that section leaders have to send in reports every so often in order to communicate progress. Meetings will also need to take place at intervals throughout the project. These meetings should be minuted and actions to be taken clearly recorded.

In the Livewires scenario, it is probably sufficient to hold informal communications. It is worth remembering that, although communicating progress is essential, time spent communicating progress is time not spent on the project itself. These things have to be carefully balanced.

portfolio_tip

You will need to show how well you communicated the progress of your project to others involved.

Holding reviews

If a project is a big one or if there have been many unexpected problems, it is sometimes helpful to review what has happened in the light of the original plans. Maybe the dates set for completion were overambitious. Maybe the programmers have hit upon a problem that is taking a long time to sort out.

A complete re-think can sometimes help to get everyone together and look at the whole project. They may be able to help each other to come up with solutions or maybe the parameters need to be changed.

Phases of a project

Aims

■ To look at ways of breaking a project down into manageable stages

Introduction

Any complex task is easier to handle if it is broken down into smaller stages. There are many reasons for this.

▶ Different tasks can be assigned to different people and teams. This makes the best use of their expertise and also allows tasks to proceed at the same time.
▶ Problems can be isolated more easily and sorted out.
▶ Project managers can more easily plan the timing of the project by looking at the timing of the component parts.

> If you have produced IT projects before, you will already be familiar with some of the main stages of project planning.

Planning takes time. It can also be a bit frustrating when you are keen to get on with the job. When you are setting up a small project, it can be very tempting to skip the planning. This is a bad idea because, even in a small project, you can waste a lot of time if you start work on something in the wrong way or the parts of the project do not work together. With large projects involving many people, planning is absolutely vital.

You can devise your own methods for planning a project and in some ways you will always have to do this. After all, each project is different and the people involved will be different too. You may have to take capabilities and personalities into account.

But projects have been with us as long as humans have worked together. Even IT projects have been around quite a long time now. Because of this, people have discovered that there are certain ways of organising projects that work. Project management has become a discipline that can be learned.

There are many standard project management methods. They have been devised to work in different situations. In some cases, they have been devised to work with particular types of software, such as the building of an Oracle database application.

Some methods have been created by government and public bodies. One commonly used methodology in the UK is called Structured Systems Analysis and Design Methodology (SSADM). Whatever method is used, sticking to it can help a great deal. If all the members of a team are following, say, SSADM, they will all follow stages and produce documents in a standard way. This helps them to communicate and saves time that might otherwise be lost in misunderstandings.

All project-planning methods divide the project into stages. These stages have undergone convergent evolution so that similar stages can be recognised in most methodologies. We shall now look at what goes on in some of these stages. These stages are taken from a typical software development methodology. In any organisation, there will probably be rules and processes that are unique to them.

portfolio_tip

You should be ready to break your own project into parts along the lines of those covered in this unit.

Analysis

Strategic study

We have already seen that new projects can develop from a perceived need or maybe a good idea. Most often they will arise from the business needs of an organisation. From time to time businesses will undertake a strategic study where they look at where they are going. In this, they may make big decisions and plans for the future. In Livewires' case, they decided to expand into retail sales. In Sunridge Systems, they decided that they needed to upgrade their IT equipment. A strategic study can lead to another stage called a business study where the business activities are examined to see how they fit together into the company's strategies.

The result of these studies will be a general definition of a system. No details are needed yet, just an overview of what the system is supposed to achieve. In the Livewires scenario, this would be the decision that EPOS and stock-control systems are needed, with some rough ideas about how these would help the business to operate more effectively.

Once the project has been decided upon, it is usual for it to be defined in these general terms in a document. There are common methodologies in use that define what documents are needed. One methodology is called Projects In a Controlled Environment (PRINCE). In PRINCE terminology, this document is called a Project Initiation Document (PID).

PRINCE (now PRINCE2) is widely used in UK government projects. These web links show what is required in a PID.

portfolio_tip

Make a PID for your own project.

http://www.prince2.com/p2structure.html
http://www.ogc.gov.uk/sdtoolkit/reference/documentation/p05_pid.html

An example template of what a PID looks like can be seen on the next link:

http://www.ogc.gov.uk/prince2/downloads/prince%20templates/
projectinitiationdocument.rtf

Investigation and feasibility study

Once a project has been commissioned, there will need to be an investigation. This is to find out more about exactly what problems need to be solved, whether a solution is possible and whether a solution is affordable.

Potential users may be consulted and the tasks that need to be covered are looked at in greater depth. The outcome of the investigation is a feasibility

ACTIVITY

In your own project, draw up a list of possible problems that might be avoided with some careful planning.

study. This document will examine the costs and benefits of the proposed system and in particular look at any risks that there might be in following up the project. Likely risks would be expenditure, time delays, problems with training staff, compatibility with old systems and many more potential issues.

In real-life projects, sometimes the feasibility study may recommend not to proceed with a project.

Requirements analysis

The next stage of analysis will be a set of documents that describe what the system is supposed to do from a business point of view. In the Livewires example, these will include material such as:

Figure 8.15

Livewires Co. Ltd.
EPOS System Requirements

1. To commission a new EPOS system to allow the efficient functioning of at least ten checkouts in the new retail store.
2. The system should be capable of handling 5000 stock items.
3. The system should be able to process customer purchases by scanning bar codes.
4. The scanning rate should be fast enough to allow up to ten items to be scanned per minute.
5. There should be separate access to the system to allow staff to alter stock items and their prices.
6. The system should print out an itemised bill for each customer.
7. The system should link with the stock-control system.

portfolio_tip

You will need to produce a detailed specification for your system. When writing the specification, remember that you measure the success of the project by looking back at this document. So make sure it is realistic for you to achieve.

The next step is to set out how the system is to achieve what is expected of it. We need to look at the functions it is to perform in more detail and the data that underlies the system. We shall need to start looking at data structures and where the data will come from.

This document must serve two purposes – to provide instructions for the IT specialists who are going to develop the system and also to show to business managers so that they understand that they are going to get what their business requirements demand. It is not easy to write in such a style as to serve both these purposes.

Decisions can also be taken at this stage about the sort of equipment that will be needed and, crucially, the computer platform that will be chosen. Maybe it will be a Windows PC system or possibly a Unix set-up will be more robust.

Initial design

The system now needs to be designed. This can also be split into many stages. We are now concerned with exactly how the new system will be constructed.

One easy way to look at the design stage is to first of all appreciate that the designs will probably be passed onto other people who will actually construct the system. This means that an adequate design must be in detail and must be written by someone who understands the development environment.

Another way to look at the design process is to think of designing an Access database. Access is very helpful here because it has separate features to help you design and make:

- tables
- forms
- reports
- queries
- macros
- modules

You can also learn from Access by looking at the design screens that it provides. The level of detail that is shown is going to be a minimum for passing on instructions.

An example of the detail can be seen in Figure 8.16. This shows just some of the detail required, such as position of controls on a form, the names of data fields and the properties of these objects.

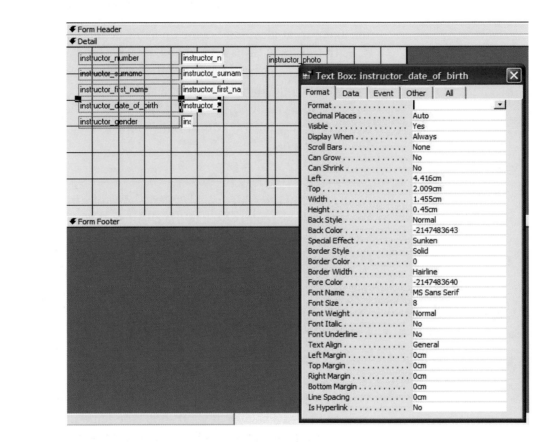

■ Figure 8.16

Each of these will need to be designed. If you are producing a different project such as a website, you need to look in a similar way at the component parts. They will include such things as:

- HTML pages
- JavaScript or other scripting modules
- Images
- Flash movies
- Applets
- Sound files
- PDF files.

Unit 7.3 contains much detail on database design principles.

ACTIVITY

Produce a design for your system, set up as a series of mini-specs.

Again, each of these needs to be designed.

No matter what you are producing, it is likely that you can split it into the interface, the processing and the data. At the end of the design process, you will have what is called a mini-specification. This is an exact specification of a part of the system that can be passed to a programmer (or developer using tools such as Access).

Unit 7.3 contains much detail on database design principles.

Development

Prototyping

Prototyping is an extremely useful tool in the initial stages of a project. It is the production of non-working demonstrations of what the system might look like. It simulates the intended system and is a very clear way of showing the client what ideas have come up in a way that is easily understandable.

With modern GUI-based systems, it is easy and quick to make some realistic mock-ups before going to the trouble of producing the processing that will underlie the interfaces and reports.

Prototypes can be adjusted in the presence of the client or the user so that the analyst can go away with specifications that are more in tune with what the client wants.

Iterative development

At all stages of the system analysis and hopefully in the design stages too, there should be reports back to the client so that any deviations from what is required are spotted early. Also, improvements can be made on the basis of the way in which the project is developing.

The design gets passed to the programmers for coding. Sometimes, coding will not be required and the developers might use Access or other application generators to produce the product. Either way, they will need clear design plans so that they produce exactly what is required.

Testing

Testing is crucial to the success of every project. Projects done by students are very often tested badly if at all. It should be remembered that the purpose of testing is to reveal errors. A good testing process will seriously attempt to 'break' the system. This is why most software developers employ separate testers – the programmers who wrote the program often don't want to see their lovely code fail and may not test it rigorously enough!

As we have seen, projects are produced in modules. This makes it a lot easier to test them. Each module can be tested as it is produced. If the modules are small enough, there is not too much to test at each stage.

Testing will be carried out according to a set plan. The tests will be numbered and the documentation of the test will include:

▶ the test number
▶ the test case (what the test is trying to show)
▶ features to be tested
▶ features excluded from test

- ▶ pass/fail criteria
- ▶ the test data (what data will be fed in to the test)
- ▶ the test procedure (how the test is carried out)
- ▶ the test log (a detailed report on what happened).

Companies differ in what they require in a proper test document.

Formative testing

Testing done during development is sometimes called ALPHA TESTING and is used to feed back to the developers how their work is progressing. The test results will be used as a basis for removing bugs and improving the performance of the system. This testing could be referred to as 'formative' because it takes place during the 'formation' or construction of the system and not at the end when it is put together.

ALPHA TESTING Testing carried out during the development process by the development company or its agents.

Summative testing

At the end of the development of all the modules, they will be brought together to test that they work together. This is sometimes called integration testing. Modules that worked well in isolation may not perform as expected when linked to the rest of the system. Because of this, tests are carried out incrementally as the modules are joined together. Often there are problems in the passing of data between modules and these need to be ironed out as early as possible.

Although not a term in general use in system design circles, the term summative testing could be applied to tests which are carried out at the end of the development process.

It is important that the client is happy with the outcome of the testing so some of it will be done by the client under realistic conditions. If a version of the software is released before full testing has taken place so that a typical client can try it out, this is called beta testing. Sometimes customers are given special benefits in order to carry out beta testing.

Acceptance testing is another type of summative testing where the customer goes through some agreed checks to verify that the product fulfils the requirements agreed at the outset. This is often written into the contract so that when acceptance testing has been successfully carried out, this can be a trigger for payment.

Documentation

Any project generates vast amounts of documentation. We have seen that there is lots produced during the analysis and design stages as well as in the testing. This documentation is internal to the development company and is useful for the later tracking down of errors or as evidence that due process was carried out if there is any dispute with the client.

As well as this, there will be documentation supplied to the client. This is intended to help the client and all the users to make the best use of the system when it is installed.

In the past, all documentation was produced as a series of big manuals that were heavy to move about and traditionally difficult to read. Nowadays, much of the documentation for software is electronic.

Documentation can be supplied on a CD. This is helpful because it takes up little space and can easily be updated. Also, it can be written using hypertext so that the user can click on links to follow up any topic of interest. Some documentation is now web-based. This has the advantages of CD-based materials but it can be updated even more readily and can also collect data about the user, such as how often it is consulted and what problems are being looked up most.

We are also used to embedded documentation. Most PC software these days comes with built-in documentation that is accessible by pressing F1 or selecting Help from the menu. This is also written using hypertext and can be context sensitive too. This means that if we are working on a particular feature and request help, the system knows what we are looking for.

Despite all the virtues of electronic help systems, paper-based documentation remains essential as a complete reference for anyone who is installing or using a system. As such it is expected that it will contain at least some of the following sections:

ACTIVITY
Look at the context-sensitive help available to you in any piece of software. Rate it for ease of use.

- ▶ version information
- ▶ system requirements
- ▶ installation procedures
- ▶ troubleshooting procedures
- ▶ frequently asked questions
- ▶ tutorials with example data
- ▶ step by step instructions
- ▶ meanings of error messages
- ▶ ways to contact the development company.

Hand-over to customer

The completed system will need to be installed on the customer's premises. For a small system, this might simply mean handing the customer a CD with an installation wizard on it.

For bigger projects, there will have been a carefully coordinated plan of getting the premises ready, installing power and cabling, acquiring the furniture, the hardware, setting up and testing the hardware, installing and testing the software, entering or migrating the data and many other stages as well. The project manager will have made sure that all this took place at the right time. We have seen that the customer will have had involvement in the hand-over because some acceptance testing will probably be contractual.

It will probably be the case that there will be extra payments made to provide ongoing support so the signing off of the project may not be the end of the contact between the customer and the developer.

The customer might also decide to run the new system alongside the old one if there was an old one. This doubles the work but ensures that any teething problems won't affect the company activities. This is called parallel running.

Sometimes a pilot run is tried. This is where one part of the system is tried out before bringing in the whole package. In the Livewires case, there is no changeover process like this because it is a new system for a new business function – it has to work from day 1.

Project planning

Aims

■ To produce a project plan with suitable software

Introduction

Managing a project can be a highly complex task. As with most tasks, there are computer solutions to help. It is possible to plan a project using simple and familiar software tools such as a spreadsheet.

The tasks involved in a project can be listed and the dates of the project can be set out as headings. Then, it is a simple matter to shade in cells to illustrate when the tasks should be carried out. You can use different colours to indicate different people or teams.

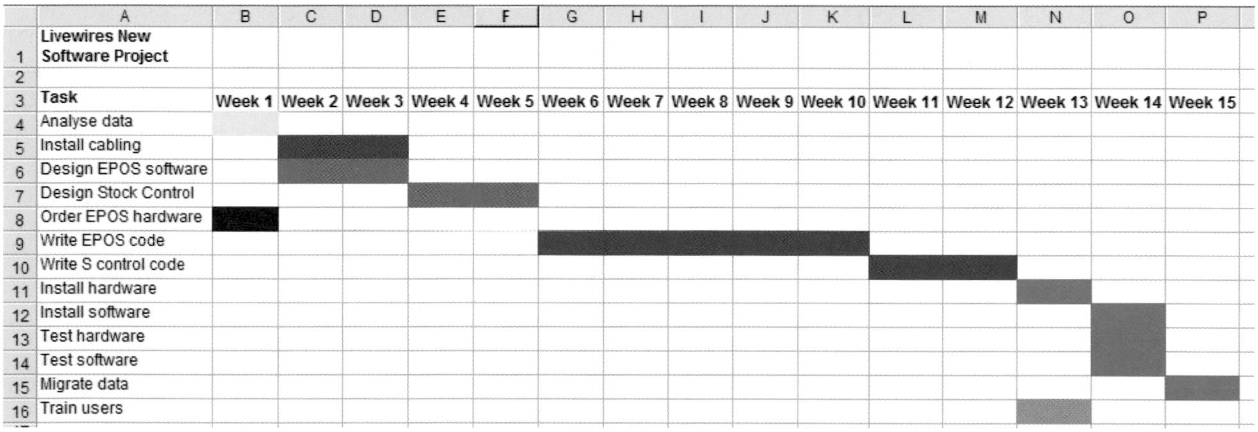

	A	B	C	D	E	F	G	H	I	J	K	L	M	N	O	P
1	Livewires New Software Project															
2																
3	Task	Week 1	Week 2	Week 3	Week 4	Week 5	Week 6	Week 7	Week 8	Week 9	Week 10	Week 11	Week 12	Week 13	Week 14	Week 15
4	Analyse data															
5	Install cabling															
6	Design EPOS software															
7	Design Stock Control															
8	Order EPOS hardware															
9	Write EPOS code															
10	Write S control code															
11	Install hardware															
12	Install software															
13	Test hardware															
14	Test software															
15	Migrate data															
16	Train users															

■ **Figure 8.17**

What we have here is a project planning diagram called a Gantt chart. These are much used in project planning in order to give a quick visual impression of the stages of a project.

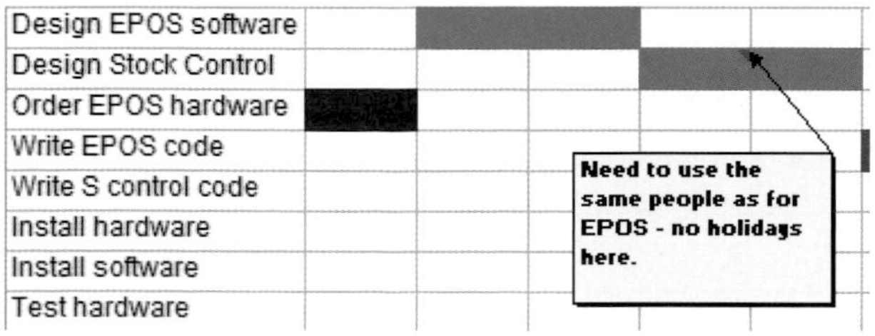

Design EPOS software			
Design Stock Control			
Order EPOS hardware			
Write EPOS code			
Write S control code			
Install hardware			
Install software			
Test hardware			

Need to use the same people as for EPOS - no holidays here.

■ **Figure 8.18**

As the stages of the project are passed, it is an easy matter to update the spreadsheet by changing the colours or by adding data such as a 1 to a cell when the task is complete. It is also easy to add notes to cells to record any special events or problems.

Although a spreadsheet can achieve quite a lot, it is not really designed for the task of project management. Its main advantage is that everyone has this software and most people can use it.

Another approach is to use a drawing package such as Microsoft Visio. This is an excellent piece of software that lets you make all sorts of diagrams and charts. Many of the illustrations in this book were made using it. It has the capability of producing Gantt charts – but it doesn't end there. You can organise a project while drawing your diagram and do things such as link activities and make changes to dates and the diagram will update itself automatically.

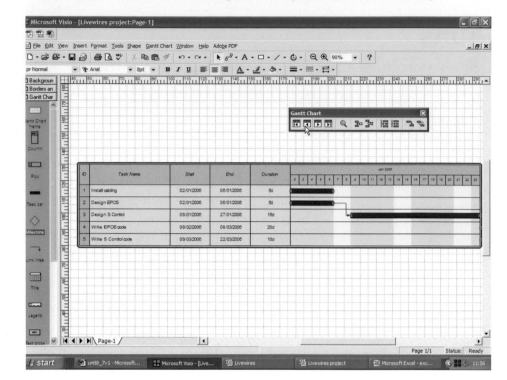

portfolio_tip

You must use proper project management software in the preparation of your own project plans.

There are many other capabilities in Microsoft Visio, but it is still basically a charting tool and there are alternatives.

Microsoft Project is a typical example of software that is designed from the start to organise projects. It can do all that Visio can and more besides. The rest of this chapter will look at how to organise a project using Microsoft Project.

The phases of the project

When you start project management software such as Microsoft Project, you are presented with a grid, rather like a spreadsheet. In fact, if you already have some work saved in a spreadsheet, you can copy and paste it or import it into Project.

The grid has spaces where you can enter the tasks that need to be performed. They all default to 1 day. The Gantt chart shows all tasks as starting on the same day at this stage.

	❶	Task Name	Duration	26 Dec '05	02 Jan '06	09 Jan '06
				M T W T F S S	M T W T F S S	M T W T F S S
1		Analyse data	1 day?		▓	
2		Install cabling	1 day?		▓	
3		Design EPOS software	1 day?		▓	
4		Design Stock control	1 day?		▓	
5		Order EPOS hardware	1 day?		▓	
6		Write EPOS code	1 day?		▓	
7		Write S control code	1 day?		▓	
8		Install hardware	1 day?		▓	
9		Install software	1 day?		▓	
10		Test hardware	1 day?		▓	
11		Test software	1 day?		▓	
12		Migrate data	1 day?		▓	
13		Train users	1 day?		▓	

At first, you enter how long each one will take. Later on, the software will help you to generate dates when these activities will take place.

When you add the timings of each task, the Gantt chart updates itself.

You can quickly enter values such as '1 week' by typing '1w'. The software adjusts it. You can also fill down as with a spreadsheet.

	❶	Task Name	Duration	26 Dec '05	02 Jan '06	09 Jan '06	16 Jan '06	23
				S M T W T F S	S M T W T F S	S M T W T F S	S M T W T F S	S M
1		Analyse data	1 wk		▓▓▓			
2		Install cabling	2 wks		▓▓▓▓▓▓			
3		Design EPOS software	2 wks		▓▓▓▓▓▓			
4		Design Stock control	2 wks		▓▓▓▓▓▓			
5		Order EPOS hardware	1 wk		▓▓▓			
6		Write EPOS code	5 wks		▓▓▓▓▓▓▓▓▓▓▓▓▓▓▓			
7		Write S control code	2 wks		▓▓▓▓▓▓			
8		Install hardware	1 wk		▓▓▓			
9		Install software	1 wk		▓▓▓			
10		Test hardware	1 wk		▓▓▓			
11		Test software	1 wk		▓▓▓			
12		Migrate data	1 wk		▓▓▓			
13		Train users	1 wk		▓▓▓			

The activities to be carried out in each phase

Once you have the main tasks set out on the grid, you can subdivide each major stage into sub-tasks. For example, the stage where the cabling is being installed might be divided up into drilling holes in wall for the cables, laying the cable runs and finally connecting up the connector boxes. You can make as many sub-tasks as are useful in managing the project. Each sub-task can be assigned its own time factor. To make a sub-task, all you have to do is to move to the task name cell below the task to be split and select Insert New Task. Clicking the Indent button relegates the task to the status of a sub-task.

The sub-tasks show up on the Gantt chart, indented under the main task.

■ Figure 8.23

⊟ Install cabling	3 days	Mon 02/01/06
Drill holes	1 day	Mon 02/01/06
Lay cable	3 days	Mon 02/01/06
Connect boxes	2 days	Mon 02/01/06

This now shows the sub-tasks as occurring at the same time. This may not be possible if the same people are used to complete all these tasks. We shall see later how to make sure that these tasks are made consecutive and not parallel.

Start date and end date of each activity

Using Microsoft Project, it is easy to enter the desired start and end dates for each task.

■ Figure 8.24

⊟ Install cabling	3 days	Mon 02/01/06	Wed 04/01/06
Drill holes	1 day	Mon 02/01/06	Mon 02/01/06
Lay cable	3 days	Mon 02/01/06	Wed 04/01/06
Connect boxes	2 days	Mon 02/01/06	Tue 03/01/06

Sometimes it is better not to insist on this and to let the software decide for you. That way, the important links can be established first and then the dates are calculated using those constraints.

Dependencies

In any project, there are plenty of constraints that dictate when things can happen. For example, the software cannot be written until it is designed. The data cannot be entered until the hardware and software have been installed. The cabling cannot be laid until the holes are drilled in the walls.

You can link tasks very easily with Microsoft Project. All you have to do is to highlight the related tasks and click on the Link Tasks button. That adjusts the Gantt chart to show the tasks as being consecutive and also alters the start and end dates.

■ Figure 8.25

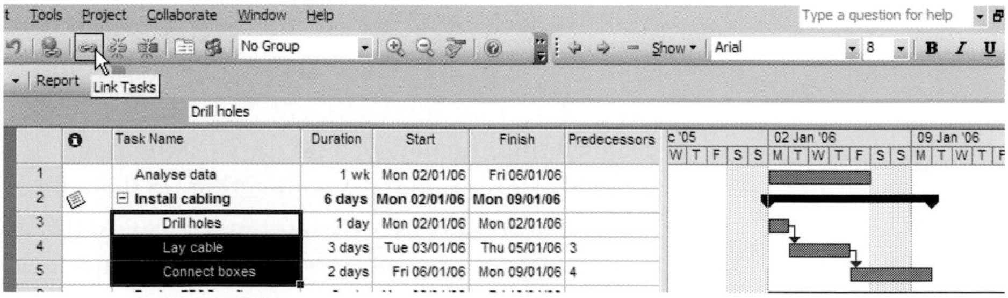

Notice that the column headed 'Predecessors' now indicates that Task 4 must be preceded by Task 3 and Task 5 by Task 4. This is one of the many benefits of using specialised software – all the relevant information is changed whenever you update the plan. You may notice also that Task 5 has been scheduled to take place in part over a weekend. You can arrange for this not to be possible if the people assigned to that task do not work weekends.

Resources required for each activity

The resources for each activity are usually going to be the people involved. You can add them at any stage by clicking on the 'Assign resources' button. Figure 8.26 shows how the engineers have been added to the resources required for installing the cabling.

■ Figure 8.26

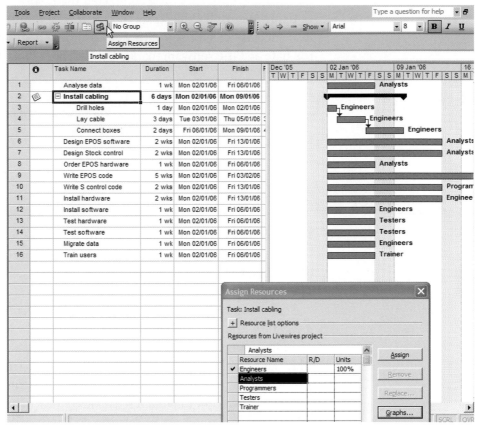

When the tasks have all been examined, the Gantt chart starts to show the project in all its complexity.

■ Figure 8.27

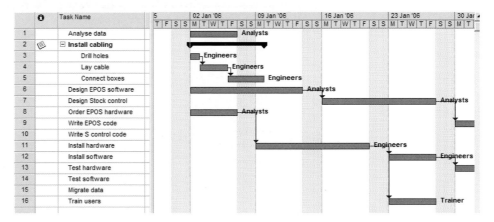

Dates of key milestones

Sometimes you need to keep an eye on events that are outside your control or there may be particular points in a project where something totally new happens. These events are called milestones. It may be that the programmers are from another company and may be delayed and you cannot begin installations until they have completed their work.

Using Microsoft Project, you can enter these milestones by adding a new task such as 'Receive software' and assigning it a duration of 0 days. You enter the date and the software marks it on the chart with a diamond symbol.

■ **Figure 8.28**

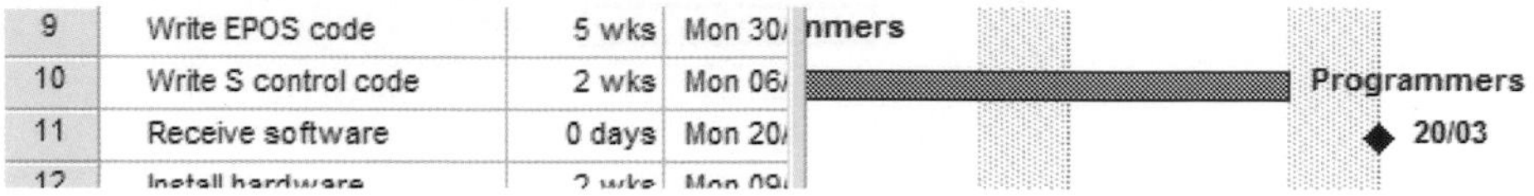

9	Write EPOS code	5 wks	Mon 30/	nmers
10	Write S control code	2 wks	Mon 06/	Programmers
11	Receive software	0 days	Mon 20/	◆ 20/03
12	Install hardware	2 wks	Mon 09/	

Potential risks

The main risks to a project are that the resources will not be available when they are needed. In particular, if the people you are relying upon to do a task do not complete it on time, then everything else will be thrown out of gear. The project could fail because of this.

The project management software cannot prevent circumstances like this but it can help to show you how things are going and whether you have built in enough contingency plans. The resource allocations can include spare people who can be drafted in if someone is not available. This is a budgetary decision that will incur greater costs, but the success of the project might be worth it.

We have seen how important it is to keep track of how the project is progressing. The software can help you do this by adding information to the tasks.

■ **Figure 8.29**

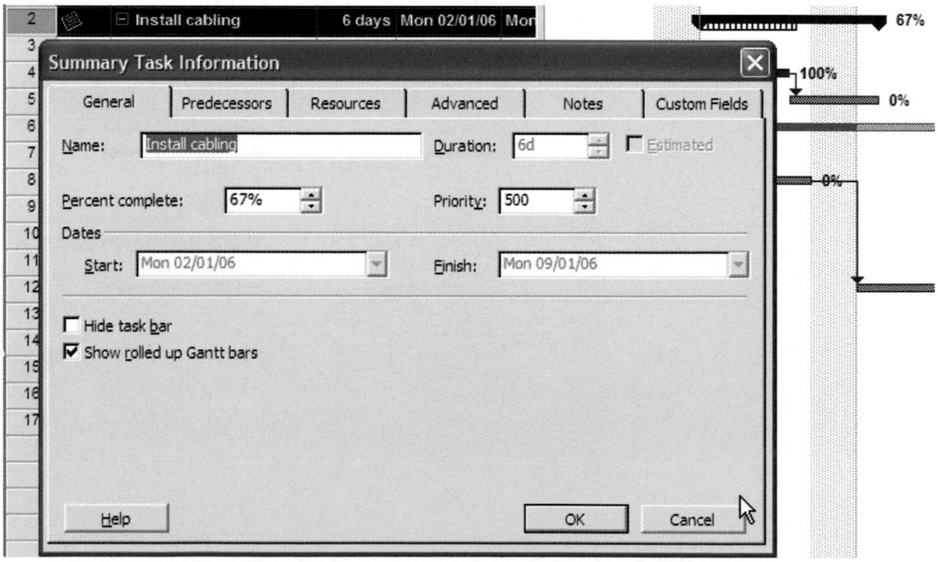

The Gantt chart has a view where you can see how things are going. When a task is complete, a tick is placed in the information box.

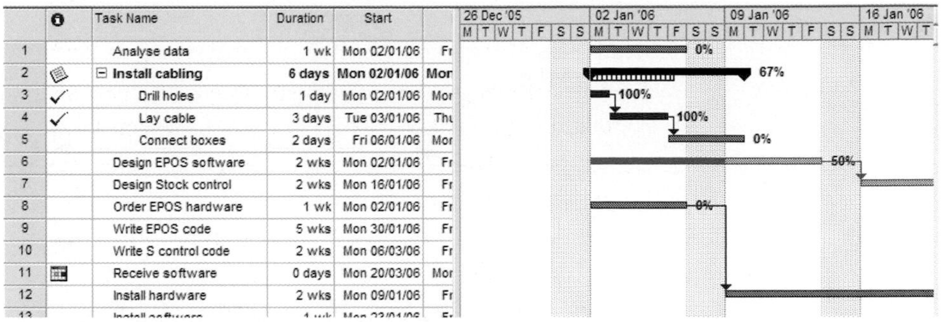

■ **Figure 8.30**

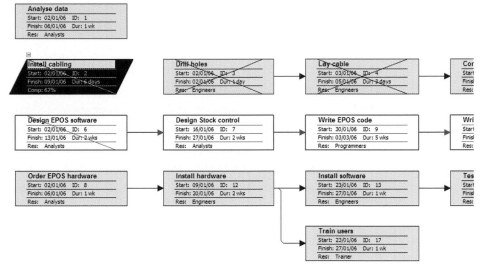

A network diagram is another view that you can produce to give a good overview of how things are progressing.

■ **Figure 8.31**

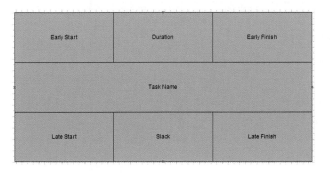

PERT chart

Throughout this chapter, much use has been made of Gantt charts in order to track the duration and progress of a project.

There are other ways in which you can plan projects. One technique is called PERT analysis. This means a Program, Evaluation, and Review Technique to estimate a task's duration. You can enter the best and worst cases into the software and it will calculate results accordingly.

You can set up diagrams with standard symbols to record tasks on this basis.

A fully developed PERT chart will show paths through a project with tasks identified and alternative paths shown. It is similar to the network view shown in Figure 8.31. PERT charts are good for showing the possible routes through a project whereas a Gantt chart is good at showing the timeline.

Early Start	Duration	Early Finish
	Task Name	
Late Start	Slack	Late Finish

■ **Figure 8.32**

 http://whatis.techtarget.com/definition/0,,sid9_gci331391,00.html

Project planning

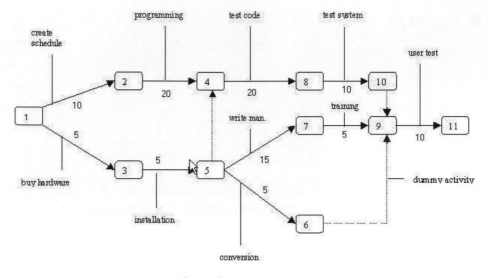

Project management techniques

The structured techniques and software tools shown in this chapter can be a great help in planning and managing a project. The downside is that they presuppose that people are happy with being organised to such a close degree. In reality, when a resource (person) is supposed to become available, it may be that he or she is busy with something else or doesn't want to do the work just now. It is never this easy to manage human beings and a wise project manager does not place too much reliance upon closely managed systems.

Project execution

Aims

- To look at the practicalities of carrying out the project
- To consider ways of measuring the progress of the project

Introduction

So far, this unit has been mostly concerned with planning stages and how to plan for a project. Time spent in planning is never wasted although sometimes the planning seems to take longer than the project. You have now reached the stage where all the planning is in place and you are about to carry out your project.

For this unit you are assessed on the planning and the way you carry out the project and the end review rather than the project itself, but you still need a project as suggested in Unit 8.1. It is best to use one of the optional modules that follow as the basis for this project.

The assessment for this section is in assessment criterion **c**.

Following the plan

ACTIVITY

Produce a presentation for your project board showing progress so far with your project.

At this stage, you will have a plan that you have produced and you will have obtained approval for the plan to go ahead. You can now start to build your software system using the plan that you have spent so much time devising. It is a good idea to keep a diary of what you have done as well as marking things off on the plan. That way you can go back and review your progress.

While you are going along, you need to keep track of the milestones you have reached and keep the other stakeholders informed as to your progress.

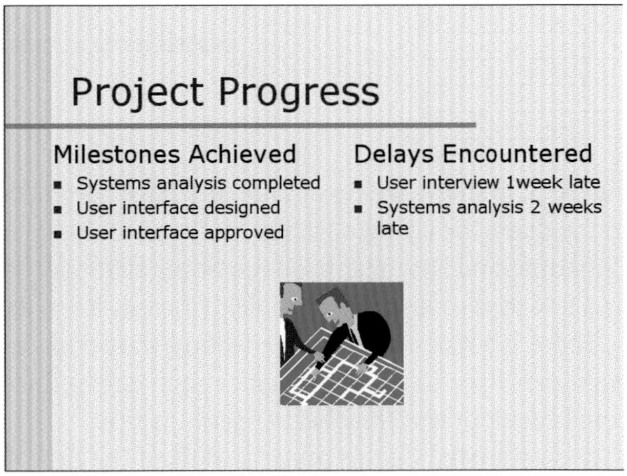

Project Progress

Milestones Achieved
- Systems analysis completed
- User interface designed
- User interface approved

Delays Encountered
- User interview 1week late
- Systems analysis 2 weeks late

■ Figure 8.34

Milestones

Most project planning methods involve the setting of milestones. These can be used as a method of measuring success and the progress of a project.

When you establish milestones, they need to be set over a measurable period of time. Milestones for your project might include completing an interview with a user or client or completing the design for your user interface.

When setting a milestone you should identify specific criteria that are easy to measure so you can be sure you have reached that point in the project. The example above of completing an interview is a clear milestone. When the interview is complete you know that you have reached the milestone.

An objective such as 'The user interface is easy to use' could not be used as a milestone since it is not an event or a point in time.

Binary milestones are the best to use. A task is then either **Done** or **Not Done**.

Problems

Even the best-planned projects run into problems. It could be that a task takes much longer than expected, or you might be hit by unexpected technical problems. What would happen if the system at your school or college were not available for several days due to technical faults? Would you be able to make up the time? Are there are other systems you could be using at home? If so, do you have the necessary files available or are they all on the system that is down? If you are following standard ways of working, then you will have a copy!

What if you become ill? No one can predict they are going to be ill (unless they know that their team will make the final of the World Cup!) Your planning must include some contingency time to allow for the unexpected.

■ Figure 8.35

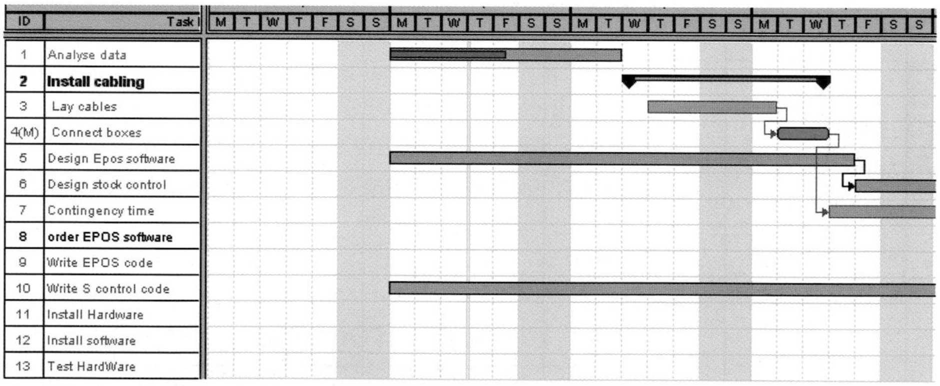

Figure 8.35 shows 4 days of time that have been allowed by the Livewires team. In the diary, the laying of cables and connecting takes place soon after the Christmas and New Year holidays. Some staff may have extended their holidays by a few days so it seems sensible to include a few days extra if needed.

There is a risk of snowfalls affecting transport at this time of year and the engineers have to travel a distance each day to the site. Poor road conditions could result in less time being spent on site.

It is estimated that as much as 80% of the time spent on a project is spent on unplanned work. The industry average for code production is 8–20 lines of correct code per day!

Changes to the specification are likely to occur as you go along. The user might want more features or new software on the network might force a change. Typically 25% change to the specification is to be expected.

Finally if you finish a stage before a deadline, don't tell anyone! It gives you more time for the next stage.

Recently, the new information system for the Scottish Police ran into problems.

The project is currently seven times over budget and three years late.

The system was to be a new central record of all criminal convictions and was ordered back in 1999. The plan was to go live in March 2004.

Investigations revealed the following problems:

- Poor understanding of system functions
- Specifications changed too often
- Over-optimistic setting of targets.

Other typical problems and precautions include:

▶ **Project lacks focus:** To avoid this make sure your initial aims and ideas are well thought out and listed clearly. Specify your aims in terms of practical outcomes that can be measured.
▶ **Product does not work:** The testing phase should be thorough. If you build your product in a modular way, make sure each module works before you start the next. Seek advice early on if you are having problems producing your product. Do you need to improve your own skills?
▶ **Product does not meet user needs:** Be clear from the start exactly what the user needs are. Consult the user during development and prototyping. Obtain clear feedback from the user, in writing if possible.

Effect of delays

Once the schedule starts slipping it's hard to get it back on time. Often things tend to get worse instead of better. This may be because the project was too ambitious or you simply underestimated the time needed for a task that occurred early on in the process. One thing is sure, a delay in one part of the plan will have a knock-on effect. In a large project, it is sometimes possible to bring in extra staff or even change the service provider. Alternatively, sometimes a decision is made to compromise on quality. A late running project might undergo less testing than was originally planned.

You cannot possibly come up with a checklist of all the risks your project might face. Assessing delays is a real activity; filling in a checklist and forgetting them will not make them go away.

In the previous example, Livewires built in extra time for installing cables in case of transport problems. In your case, you need to look at your own commitments in the planning process. Some examples might include:

▶ Work for other subjects – check deadlines against each other
▶ Do you know of any events such as a concert or play that might take you out of lessons for rehearsals?
▶ What is your own attendance record like?

As soon as you are aware of a delay in a project, you need to look at the impact of this on the rest of the project. A day or two here and there may not seem like much, but they all add up as the project goes along. Eventually you might end up weeks behind.

You should look at the reasons for the delay – is it that you simply did not work hard enough, or was the delay outside of your control? Is it likely to happen again? If this is the case, you need to take action to minimise the effect next time. If the system at college or school failed, make sure you are able to work on another system next time. If it is your own time management then look at how you are spending your time. Can you use it more effectively?

When you reach the end of each stage of your project, hold a review. What risks did you identify at the start? Keep a diary of what you did successfully to deal with each problem. Keep notes on what worked and what did not.

Hindsight is great, so use the benefit of it to decide what you would do next time.

The project software is a great tool to help if the project does go off track. You will be able to model different scenarios for bringing the project back on track by editing the dates of certain activities. You can also look to see if some tasks can run concurrently (at the same time) so as to reduce the overall timescale.

Deliverables

Aims

- To examine some ideas of the type of product you could deliver
- To look at the components of the system you are expected to deliver

In this unit, you need to produce and deliver a software project in a planned way. This involves producing a number of items known as *deliverables*. You have been advised to combine this unit with one of the others so this chapter will consider not only what the deliverables are but will contain examples of how this might be achieved in the other three units of the single award. If you are doing the double award then you will have a wider choice of units to use.

Software products

The main focus of the planning unit is obviously the planning itself. However you still need to deliver a software product. For the product to be 'delivered' means:

- ▶ it works
- ▶ it is suited to the user's needs
- ▶ the user has accepted the product.

CASE STUDY

In the Livewires project, the following could be examples of deliverables:

- A stock-control system that tracks stock levels
- A network of EPOS terminals in the retail outlet
- A working EPOS system.

portfolio_tip

Make sure you have a real end user for your software, and that you produce something that fulfils those needs. This is important if you are to achieve the higher mark bands.

Unit 10: Using multimedia software

The focus is using multimedia software to create a product. The product could be:

- ▶ a revision package
- ▶ a distance learning package
- ▶ an ebook for a child
- ▶ a computer game
- ▶ an interactive quiz.

To be successful, you should have created a product that is stand-alone and uses multimedia to enhance the product.

Unit 11: Using spreadsheet software

This unit requires you to produce a spreadsheet. It needs to be one that is complex enough to show that you can manage many sophisticated features of a spreadsheet. The final product will be a self-contained spreadsheet package. The package could:

► Analyse the changes in climate over a certain period of time.
► Help a small business to model the effects of changing energy suppliers.
► Be a theatre-booking system with a diagrammatic layout of the seats and automatic takings calculator.
► Analyse meals in a restaurant for the costs of the ingredients or their nutrient content.
► Model the effects of changing the number of checkouts in operation in a supermarket and the possible impact on profits.
► Model the likely effect on growth rates of different feeding regimes with farm animals.
► Compare the likely costs of a month's travel in London by paying for tickets directly, buying daily travel cards or using an Oyster card in its various forms.

You should make sure that whatever scenario you choose for your spreadsheet project, it contains a variety of advanced techniques and not just be a simple cost calculator.

Unit 12: Customising applications

This unit needs some programming skills. The product could use a spreadsheet or a database, but it will need customising using code. The final product will be a working solution enhanced by the use of code. The package could be:

---

portfolio_tip

If you are using work for other units as your project, remember that each unit needs to have its own eportfolio.

► a stock control system
► an employee payroll system
► a database for a garage to track servicing
► a spreadsheet that links with a database
► a spreadsheet to quote for re-roofing a house.

Documentation

An important aspect of any product is the documentation that goes with it. You will need to produce this documentation for different purposes as part of your deliverables. This chapter gives some ideas. Further detail is provided in the units themselves and you should look at those details as well so that the assessment evidence for the other unit matches that unit's mark bands.

User documentation

This will be aimed at the people who will use the system on a day-to-day basis. It must include instructions on how to use your product effectively under normal conditions. Sometimes simple things go wrong and error messages will appear. You should show the user how to deal with messages and give some idea of what might have caused them.

Unit 10

A simple set-up guide should be produced. Most of the package should be self-documented with online help. The guide you produce should enable someone to setup and run the package easily.

Unit 11

How to use the spreadsheet, what to expect from it and what is its main purpose. All need to be included together with examples of common errors.

Unit 12

How to load and use the package, including any menus, and data entry forms. Screen shots with examples will help here. Again examples of common errors and what to do about them should be included.

Installation documents

Before any of your projects can be used, they will need some kind of installation process, although it might only be how to copy the files needed onto another computer. Screen shots are a good way to illustrate this.

Some of the other units might need specific documents.

Unit 10

Work for this unit might need extensions such as the installation of Flash or video players. You should include this information in the documents.

Unit 11

Does the spreadsheet need macros to be turned on? If so, explain how to do this. Are any of the cells hidden or protected? You need to include this information if needed.

Unit 12

Does the spreadsheet or database need to be set up for first use? Does the software have any special requirement because of the programming that is integrated into it?

Technical documentation

Technical documents are aimed at experts who might have to improve or maintain your system in the future. Technical documents should always be enough to enable another expert to recreate your system from your paperwork.

Unit 10

For this unit, only technical specifications are needed for the machine that is able to run your product.

Unit 11

The technical documents should include formulae used, details of any macros and enough information to set up your spreadsheet or workbook from the start.

Unit 12

Here you will need to include the code for your customisation, with annotation and details of variables used so that another programmer can understand the code.

User training

In most projects, user training is a vital part of the end product, as important as the system itself. After all what is the point of having a fantastic system in your company if no one can use it? You will need to plan for user training in your project, and although you do not have to deliver formal user training as part of the work for the optional units, you should ensure that the user documents contain the training needs of people who will be using your system.

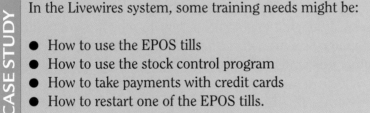

In the Livewires system, some training needs might be:

- How to use the EPOS tills
- How to use the stock control program
- How to take payments with credit cards
- How to restart one of the EPOS tills.

Training topics

You will need to decide on the topics that need to be covered during the training. This will depend to a large extent on the experience of the user. You will need to ascertain this during the initial stages of the project. You will need a clear picture of the client's present work force and their capabilities.

Does your system require any special topics covering things that might not be familiar? For example if you were training the staff of Livewires, you would need to know how to process a credit card under normal circumstances and how this relates to your system.

Training team

How large will your team need to be and what skills will they need? Do some of the team have special skills that are needed for some of the training?

Group that needs training

Different groups of people will need different types of training; the network manager clearly will need a different level of training from the shop floor staff at Livewires. How will you address the different needs of various groups?

Dates of training

You need to consider when it would be best to train the users in the Livewires scenario. The system manager will need training ahead of the installation so that it is supported as soon as it goes live. Some of the other staff may receive on-the-job training as the system is put into use.

Training medium

What training medium is best suited to the task – how will the training be delivered? The systems manager will need experience of managing a system. Are you going to do this on a simulation or on the live system? Clearly the manager will need some written material to refer to later – there will be a lot to remember and system management can be a complex business.

Budget

Is there a budget for training? You will need to tailor the training to fit the budget.

Training materials

Training materials will be needed. This could include such things as manuals, handouts and presentations. You will probably need training exercises to enable staff to practise the operations they will be performing.

Software

Will the training need any extra or adapted software? For example, if you are training staff in credit card transactions you might need to have some software that will simulate transactions.

Training feedback questionnaires

At the end of any training there is always a feedback form of some kind. You will need to think about the questions to ask and how this information can be used to help you plan future events.

Reviews

Aims

- To examine the use of reviews in project management
- To look at how reviews can be used to benefit the project

Reviews are a significant part of project development. Different types of review take place at different stages in the life of a project. This unit examines the type of review you will need to take part in and how to manage the different reviews.

Independent review

An independent review is performed by someone not connected with the project. The idea is to have someone from outside to look at the early stages of the planning and bring a different perspective to the project. For example, how often have you failed to notice a spelling mistake in your work? Usually people see what they think is there and can often miss the most obvious mistakes. In project planning people can easily lose sight of reality. It is easy to become overenthusiastic and promise too much. It is easy to become sidetracked by something you think is a very good idea but when looked at analytically it is often a lot of work for something that is cosmetic. It is easy to become overconfident and believe you can solve every problem. Misunderstanding user needs is also a danger in the early stages.

An outsider will have no previous involvement in the project and will look at it in a different way. They can check that the objectives are clear and understood by everyone and that progress reports match actual progress.

They should also check the assumptions that people are making and check these against the written documents.

An independent review can improve the chance of success and make sure that the outcomes are clear and unambiguous. It should also check to see if major risks and issues are identified early and so can be managed.

A good independent reviewer will be objective and constructive in the feedback that is given and not try to blame individuals for what they have not done.

Another advantage of this type of review is that very little of your time is required to carry out the review.

The reviewer will feed back to the project manager and to the senior management team running the project.

Livewires commissioned a review by a consultant from Sunridge Information Systems. An expert in EPOS and stock control systems looked at their plans. The expert suggested they that reconsider the number of EPOS tills they had planned for. In his experience a store of the size they proposed needed more tills. Another suggestion was to position the tills in different locations.

portfolio_tip

You must have evidence of feedback from others and be able to show how you responded to that feedback as part of your portfolio.

The person you need to carry out this type of review is someone with similar or better skills than yourself. They will certainly need to know about project planning and how to develop a software project similar to your own.

You should not be afraid of asking someone to help you in this respect and to make full use of their knowledge and expertise.

Your teacher or lecturer might give you feedback in this way, or you might use a fellow student.

Management review

From time to time, formal management reviews of your project should take place. These are part of the lifecycle of a project. The dates for these are usually agreed at the start of the project and in your case may be deadlines set by your tutor. These should be listed in your project plan and appear in the project definition.

Remember that management has the power to order work on a project to cease or change direction at any time.

If you are about to undergo a management review, you should prepare a Status Report ahead of the report date. It should include:

On the CD you will find a template for a project review.

- ▶ Tasks completed last week
- ▶ The status of the project as a whole
  - – Percentage of the project that is complete
- ▶ Tasks planned for next week
- ▶ A review of the schedule so far
  - – Milestones met
  - – Milestones not met
  - – Reasons why they were not met
- ▶ Review of the budget (not in your project)
- ▶ Issues that have been noted
  - – Description
  - – Action taken
  - – Additional action required
- ▶ Changes that have been made to initial brief
  - – Description
  - – Reason
- ▶ Date of completion expected

Preparing for a meeting

You will need to prepare for and present information at a formal management review. First you need to be clear about the meeting and its purpose. You will need to prepare information for the meeting so make sure that you know:

► the date
► the start time
► the end time
► the place.

Use the template to prepare your statement to the meeting, and make sure that you have enough copies for everyone at the meeting. You should find out:

► participants' names
► topics to be covered.

You might need to prepare an agenda for the meeting or you might have one sent to you if the management are running the meeting. Make sure that you can cover all that you need to go through in the time allocated and that you have identified any action items yourself. For any action item you should identify:

► the person responsible
► the deadline.

Following the meeting, minutes should be written up and posted by the date set at the meeting.

portfolio_tip

Make sure that you keep a record of the meetings you have held. These will be needed as evidence in your portfolio.

Close down and end-of-project review

Aims

- To learn how to set up and run an end-of-project review
- To examine the documentation produced for an end of project review
- To look at ways to gather information about your own performance and identify further development needs

portfolio_tip

You must include feedback from the user in your final evaluation. You must also include a review of your own personal skill development.

This unit looks at how to set up and run an end-of-project review. This is the final stage in the project documentation. The project is now complete and the final review will consider any lessons learned for future projects and evaluate the success or otherwise of the current project. The project manager will normally make a presentation to the project board outlining the outcome of the project. The review will include the evaluation from the user's point of view.

Completion

By this stage your project should be complete. If it is not, it is sometimes because of poor planning or because the project was too ambitious.

The plan should have specified dates for formal close down. In your case, this will coincide with the deadline for submitting your work to the awarding body.

The end-of-project review is sometimes called a project audit. The documentation produced here should contain summary information about the final project linked to the original project definition. It should show the date the project closed, who handed the system over to the client, and who from the client company accepted the final software product.

The review of the project schedule should show which milestones were met and which were not met. Reasons should be given why milestones were not met.

Documentation

For the final project review you will need to produce a document which evaluates the success or otherwise of the project. This document will form part of your eportfolio. It should include a summary of the main aims of the project and a review of the progress made. The document should start by outlining the original definition of scope. Each of the key success criteria should be addressed stating the degree to which each of them has been achieved.

For your eportfolio, your evaluation should be a critical one using feedback from the end user. You should confirm the success of the project by referring to each of the objectives specified in the initial documentation. You should also write about the effectiveness of the project, any lessons you have learned, and you should justify any changes you made to the original specification.

Review meeting

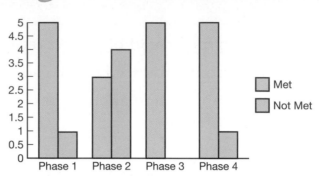

■ **Figure 8.36**

At the end of the project the project board would normally hold a final meeting to give all those involved the opportunity to air their views about the strengths and weaknesses of the project and to formulate a list of lessons learnt. The project definition should be referred to so that you judge the final outcome of the project.

Figure 8.36 illustrates the number of milestones met and not met during the phases of a project. Phase 2 clearly did not go well. The reasons would have been discussed at the project board meeting at the end of that phase. It would be appropriate at this stage to indicate any lessons learnt from that phase.

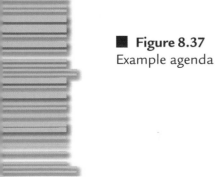

Livewires EPOS end of project review

Date 23/6/2005
Location Board Room head office

1. Apologies
2. Minutes of last meeting
3. Matters arising
4. Summary of information gathered
5. Results of surveys
6. Discussion of things performed well
7. Discussion of problem areas
8. Recommendations for future projects
9. Identification of solution opportunities
10. Review of risk management
11. AOB

■ **Figure 8.37**
Example agenda

ACTIVITY

Produce an agenda for the final meeting of the project board for your project.

Livewires is a forward looking company. Figure 8.37 shows that item 9 is called 'Identification of solution opportunities'. This is a polite way of saying how can things can be done better next time and who needs to improve their performance.

Before the installation the IT manager did not fully appreciate the complexity of software installation. He did not allow enough time for that phase. The result was that the installation ran four days behind schedule and other staff ended up working overtime to make up for the lost time so that the store could open on time.

The board identified an opportunity for the IT manager to receive some training in systems software installation, so that in future he would be better equipped to estimate the time scales involved.

The IT manager felt valued as an employee and welcomed the opportunity to develop his skills.

At Flaoly Supplies a major project ran behind schedule and many problems were encountered because the installation of the computer network was done to a poor standard. The IT manager worked very hard to correct the error and eventually rescued the system. However, at the board meeting he was blamed for the problems and made to feel as if he had totally let the company down. He therefore left the company at the earliest opportunity. The company found him very hard to replace and struggled for a long time.

portfolio_tip

You will need to set up the end-of-project review and encourage people to express their opinions of the outcomes of the project. You will need to take notes of the meeting and produce a summary of the main points. This will be needed in your eportfolio.

The review should show the degree of stakeholder satisfaction, which should be linked to the project definition. Any lessons learned during the project should be listed and explained.

SKOB Software services

Contact information.

Name

Phone

E-mail

Please rate the Software on each of the following:

	Excellent	Very Good	Fair	Poor	No preference
Value for money	○	○	○	○	○
Ease of use	○	○	○	○	○
Reliability	○	○	○	○	○
Quality	○	○	○	○	○
After-sale support	○	○	○	○	○

Figure 8.38 Part of an online customer survey form

portfolio_tip

In your evaluation, you must include an assessment of your own personal progress. You could include any new skills you have gained or how you have improved any of your existing skills. You should also comment on your performance as a project manager and identify any ways in which you could improve your performance next time. You also need to include the effectiveness of the project management methods you used.

You should use the meeting to gather information about your own performance and identify your further development needs. You should also comment on how you have learned to improve communication and identify ways that you might improve the deliverable products.

What could have been done better? If you did the same thing again how could you make it better?

- What were your expectations?
- How would you evaluate your performance?
- Have you improved your skills?
- What are your strengths?
- Were any risks not identified?
- What was the impact of these risks?

Figure 8.39 Suggested check list for the final review

Items	Response
Has the final review been conducted according to the agenda?	
Has the project board agreed that all possible objectives have been met?	
Have you made notes of the meeting?	
Have ideas for improvement been recorded?	
Have lessons learned been recorded?	
Have any changes from the original brief been noted by the project team?	
Has a report been written summarising the final project review meeting?	
Has the report been distributed to the board for review?	
Has feedback been provided and appropriate changes made?	
Have the results been recorded in your eportfolio?	

portfolio_tip

You should also check the assessment criteria in the specification to make sure you have provided all the necessary evidence in your work.

ICT skills

Aims

- To look at the skills needed to create a Gantt chart
- To consider how to share information with others electronically

The main focus of this unit has been the management of a software development project. Depending on the focus of the project, you will have acquired a number of new skills in the development of software. This unit looks at some of the IT skills needed to manage a project effectively.

 In a folder is a program called GanttProject for you to install.

One of the main pieces of software you will need is project planning software. Provided on the CD is a piece of software for project planning called GanttProject. This will enable you to plan the projects and produce evidence for your portfolio of the project's planning and progress. You can also use Microsoft Project which is a well-known project planning tool.

Set up and maintain a project plan

To set up a project in GanttProject, first load the program and select File → New Project.

This will load up the create project wizard.

On the first page, add details of the project so that when it is loaded you know what it is about and who is responsible for it. Click Next.

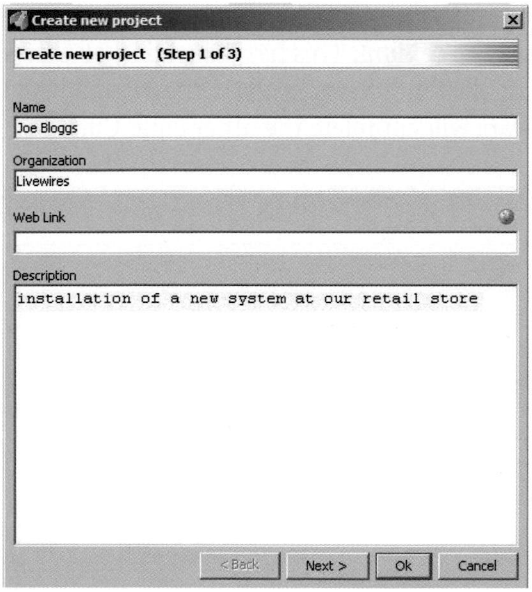

Figure 8.40

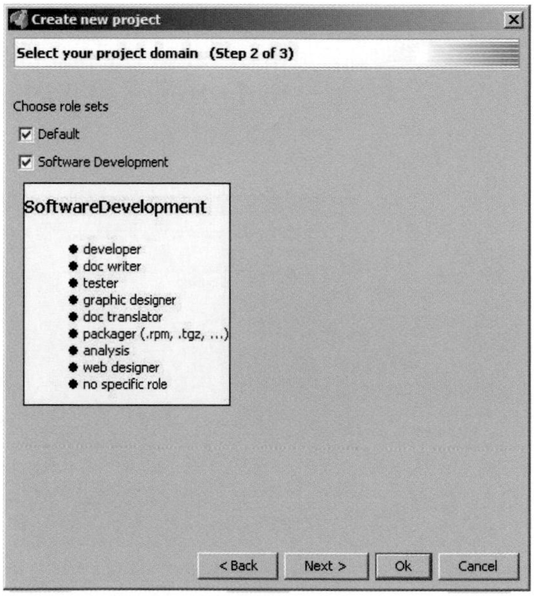

Figure 8.41

Click to indicate that you are doing a software project. This loads a set of predefined roles for you if you need to allocate them. Click Next.

This last setup page lets you add bank holidays to the plan. If you do, then the software does not count them as work days. You can decide if weekends are work days or not. If you tick them then they will not be used as working days. This means that if a task needs 10 days, it will go over two full weeks. Click OK to set up the project.

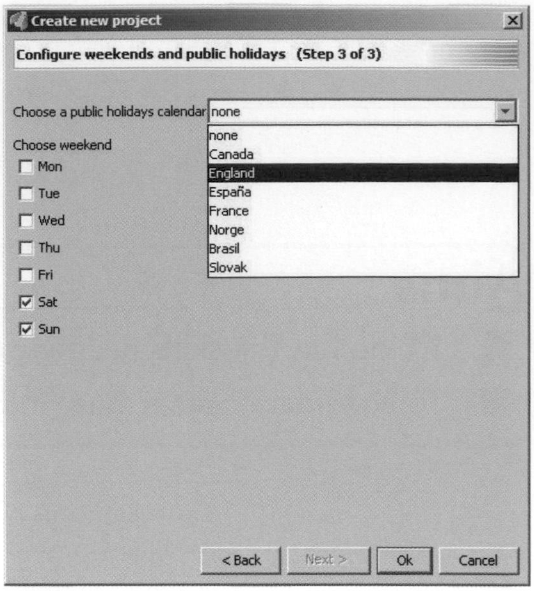

■ **Figure 8.42**

Add a first task

To add a new task, click the new task button on the task bar. A task of 1 day's duration will now appear. You need to edit the task, so click on the edit task button.

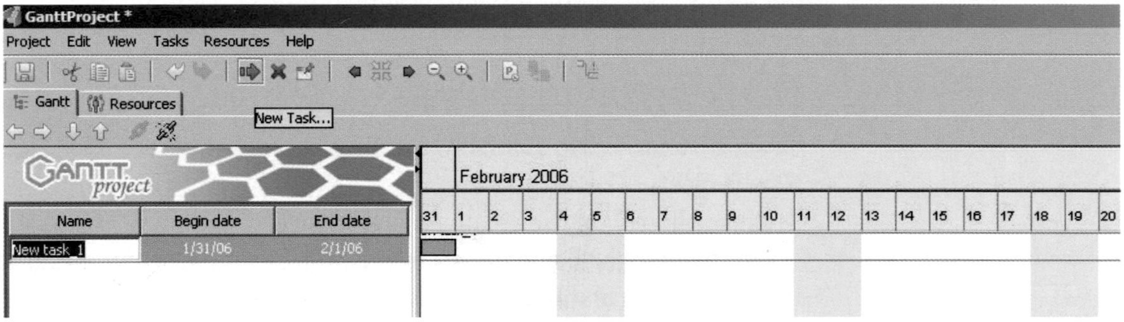

■ **Figure 8.43**

In this case, the first task is to install the cabling. This has a duration of 4 days so the Name and Duration boxes are filled in. Alternatively, you can set a begin and end date – either way the software will complete the other data. Click OK.

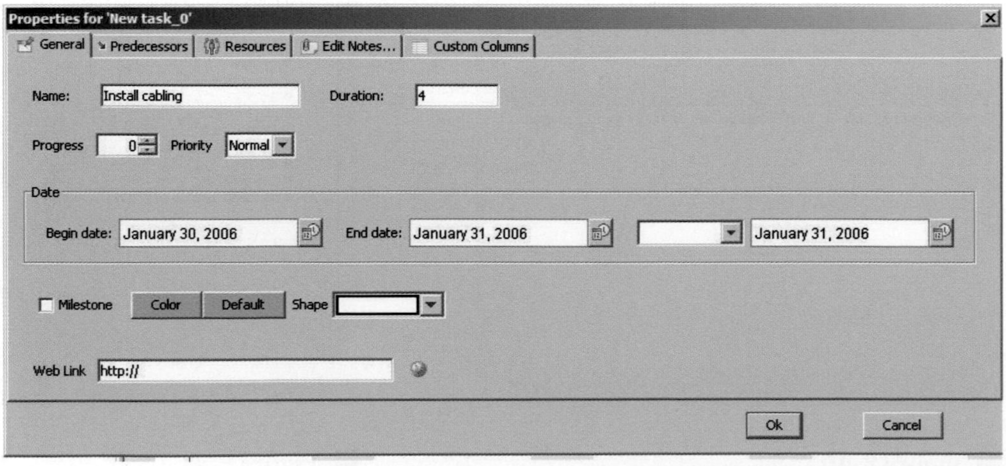

■ **Figure 8.44**

The first task has been added to the chart. Notice that the begin and end dates are in American format – month/day/year. The red line indicates today's date. This will be useful later on when you are looking at your progress.

■ **Figure 8.45**

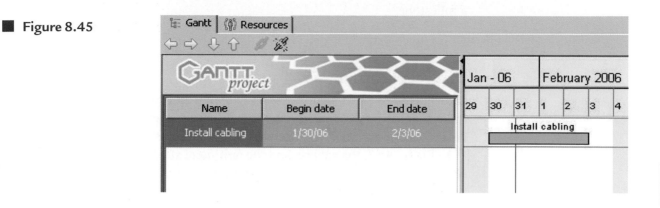

To add more tasks, repeat the process of adding new tasks.

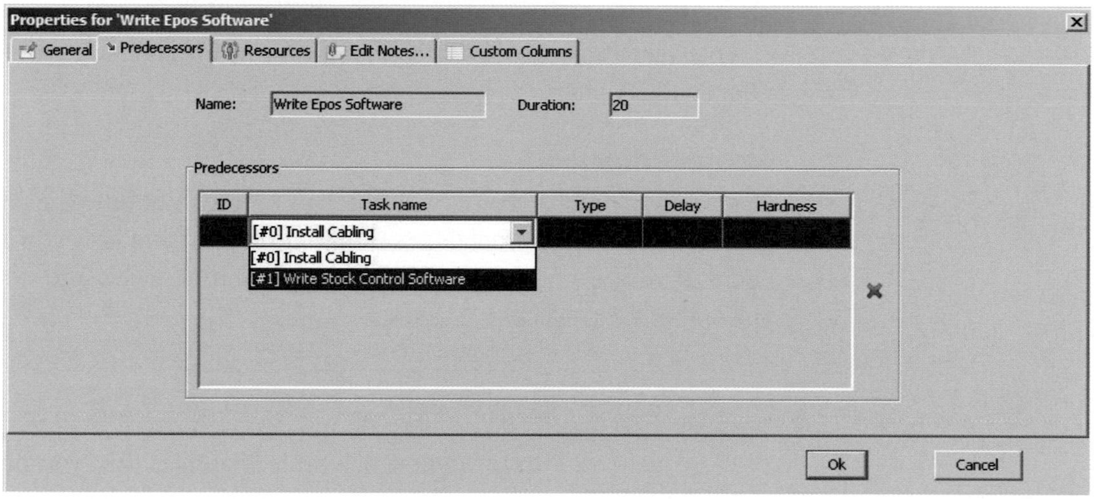

■ **Figure 8.46**

Add dependencies

Some tasks depend on other tasks being done first. The Write Epos Software task cannot take place until the Stock Control Software has been written. To add this fact to the plan, edit the Write Epos Software task and click on the Predecessors Tab. The drop-down menu is used to choose the preceding task.

■ **Figure 8.47**

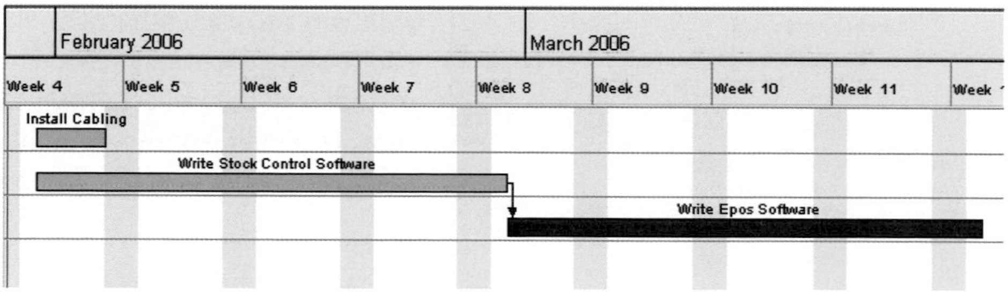

This shows up on the chart with a line linking the two, and the tasks are placed in sequence on the chart.

Add a milestone

Milestones can be set by placing a tick in the Milestone box when you edit the properties for a task. This changes the chart to show that a particular point is a milestone.

Other tools

Critical path analysis

Critical Path Analysis identifies tasks which must be completed on time in order that the project finishes on time. It helps to identify other tasks that can be delayed for a while if you need to catch up on missed tasks.

In Figure 8.47, the cabling and the writing of stock control software can run at the same time, but the Epos software cannot be written until the stock control software is ready.

PERT analysis

Program Evaluation and Review Technique (PERT) is a way of producing an alternative view of time estimates made for each project task.

The GanttProject software can produce one for you. Using the view menu, choose PERT chart.

Project diaries

Keeping a diary of a project will help you to track not only the progress of the project but also any problems you have dealt with and how you coped with them. It will be a useful tool when it comes to the review and evaluation at the end of the project.

Create and manage a shared work area

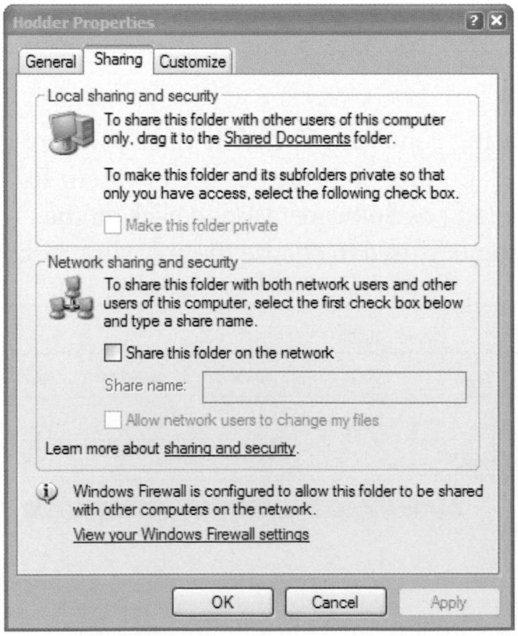

■ Figure 8.48

In the course of a project such as this, you need to be able to communicate with as many of the project team as possible. There are many ways that this can happen:

► email
► meetings
► website
► shared area on a network.

All of these are useful ways of keeping the team in touch with you and each other. The shared area method allows you to store documents in such a way that each of the members of the project group can access them at any time. Depending on how you have set the permissions for the area, members of the group will be able to:

► read the files
► read and change the files
► read, change and create new files.

If you are using a network at school or college, you may not have the access rights to set up such an area. You may need to ask the network manager to do this for you. However here is a quick guide to how it is done on a small network.

In the example, the Hodder folder is going to be shared:

1 Right click on the folder. Choose Sharing.
2 Put a tick next to Share this folder on the network.
3 If you want the group to change the files, add a tick next to Allow network users to change my files.
4 Give the Share a name so that the others can see it.

Present information to stakeholders

Formal reports

When writing a formal report, such as one to the project board, you should think very carefully about how you are communicating the information. In the case of your project, you need to focus on the stage you are at and progress made on the development of the software.

Your reports should be brief and to the point, but at the same time cover all the required information.

You should:

▶ use paragraphs
▶ keep paragraphs short
▶ present evidence of progress
▶ use images from the planning software.

■ **Figure 8.49** An example of how a project report contents page might look

Report to Project Board

Introduction:

I. Project outline
  A. User details
    1. User Profile
    2. User experience
  B. Purpose of Software
    1. Outline of Purpose
    2. User requirements

II. Project Specification
  A. Desired outcomes
    1. Output format
    2. User interface

Report templates are available in most word-processing packages, for example Microsoft Word.

Presentations

You should produce a presentation to help inform the project board of the progress so far. The idea of a presentation is to highlight the main points of your project development, and communicate these to others in an effective way. Your presentations should communicate effectively and convey information to the required audience.

An effective presentation will not have large amounts of text to read. It will highlight the main points using headings and bullet points. You are running a business meeting and you should concentrate on communicating the information in the most efficient way.

When you have completed your presentation, you should check it to ensure that it covers all the points you need it to cover for that meeting. It is a good idea to check the following:

► spelling
► size of text
► amount of information on each page
► that it covers the required information
► that each slide is clearly laid out.

portfolio_tip

Keep copies of any presentations as evidence for your portfolio.

UNIT 10
Using multimedia software

Multimedia applications

Aims

- To explore a range of ways in which multimedia is used
- To evaluate the effectiveness of a multimedia product

Introduction

This is an optional unit which is user focused. It is intended for students who would like to develop higher level skills in multimedia design and production. In Unit 1 you put together an ebook that used multimedia techniques. In this unit, you will develop your skills further and use new tools and techniques. You will be assessed on your ability to design, produce and evaluate a multimedia product. You can use this unit as a focus for Unit 8 – Managing ICT projects.

The power of computers has increased very rapidly in recent years. These advances have changed many aspects of our lives as you will recall from your work in Unit 1 – The information age.

Rapid developments in digital video and photography have made it easier to capture, edit and combine different types of digital images with sound and text to produce a multimedia end product. Multimedia is now used widely in business, education, industry and for entertainment.

Assessment evidence

portfolio_tip

Make sure that your criteria are SMART: specific, measurable, attainable realistic and time-constrained.

portfolio_tip

Make sure that you involve others in evaluating your prototype product and that you use their comments in improving the product.

For this unit you will design, produce, test and evaluate a multimedia product to meet a set of functional requirements that you will need to agree with an end user. Your work will be assessed on the following evidence:

a A functional specification that describes the context, purpose and audience for your product. You will need to describe in detail the product and set out clear measurable success criteria.

b A design for the product that meets the functional requirements and makes good use of multimedia design. It needs to include different multimedia components, some ready-made and some you made yourself. You will also need evidence of prototype solutions, which have been evaluated and improved on.

c A runtime version of a fully working multimedia product with instructions for users.

d Evidence of testing the project both formative and summative.

e An evaluation that measures the success of the product and your own performance.

To use and develop multimedia effectively, you need a computer that has:

- ▶ a CD drive for reading and, possibly making CD-ROMs
- ▶ a sound card so that sounds can be heard
- ▶ a processor chip powerful enough to keep up with video
- ▶ a colour monitor.

The basic specification is quite low and these days you will find it difficult to purchase a machine that does not have the necessary features.

Uses of multimedia

Multimedia products are designed to communicate information to an audience. They can be very engaging – dynamic, visual displays which will hold attention far better than just text. Multimedia can also benefit people who have difficulty accessing written words.

This unit focuses on the use of multimedia in a variety of fields and looks at the impact of its use as well as its advantages and disadvantages.

A multimedia application is one that uses:

- ▶ combinations of colours
- ▶ images
- ▶ sound
- ▶ text
- ▶ video.

Strictly speaking, TV is multimedia because it uses moving images and sound although most people would not think of TV as being multimedia because it does not involve using a computer to view it. A multimedia product can be something that the audience just watches or it can be made interactive so that the user becomes more involved in the way the product functions.

Education and training

Education is one of the biggest markets for multimedia products. The range of products available for schools is growing on a daily basis. There are materials available for every subject on the curriculum. Recent UK government policy has been to make money available for schools to buy such products.

A good education product will be fun to use so that the student will want to use it and at the same time it will cover the desired range of subject material. There are many products available and with Internet access it is possible to use multimedia via a web connection. There is a vast wealth of educational material available freely on the Internet. A good example is:

 http://www.schoolscience.co.uk/content/4/biology/abpi/heart/heart4.html

This page has lots of interactive elements on it. There is a movie, Flash animations which run when clicked and an interactive question section which prompts you if you give a wrong answer. This site contains many other pages which illustrate the use of multimedia.

It is not just schools and colleges that use multimedia as an educational tool. It is also used for training in business and in industry.

CASE STUDY

Reuters is a worldwide news and media agency. The company developed a multimedia package to train its staff in something called Transaction Products. It combines computer-based simulations with practical exercises. The package has been used to train staff all over the world.

CASE STUDY

The Heath and Safety Executive is a UK government body that monitors and promotes health and safety at work. It has developed a number of multimedia packages to promote its aims. One example is a package to improve knowledge of the Driving at Work Regulations amongst professional drivers. Many drivers found the traditional approach, which consisted of training lectures, boring and did not give them experience of applying the rules to real situations.

The package that was put together used a number of video simulations. The driver chooses a scenario, follows a video, then completes an exercise based on the video. They then complete a quiz on the scenario which is followed up by a debriefing video.

When questioned by a survey, driver comments included:

● Less boring than reading the books
● Better than just listening to a lecture
● The videos provide a better explanation than just words and pictures
● The situations are not real so mistakes can be corrected without danger.

■ **Figure 10.1**

Entertainment

The world of entertainment is a vast industry with many different aspects. The use of multimedia is widespread in the industry. A visit to the cinema is a multimedia experience – it combines rich sound and moving images.

Another area of entertainment is multimedia games. They have been around for many years and each week they seem to become more powerful and more sophisticated. The latest range includes very powerful hand-held devices capable of running video, animations and sound. As with all games, the user interacts with the system to produce changes in the game motion or action.

Mobile phones are the latest way to experience multimedia. Video phones allow video to be recorded, played back and sent to other phones. Phone companies offer packages that include online games and even live TV.

Interactive multimedia provides many opportunities for the use of multimedia in many ways and situations.

Marketing and advertising

The marketing and advertising industry makes use of multimedia in many ways, not just for selling and advertising items, such as on TV, but to market and advertise company services. The power of persuasive presentations is greater than printed literature because it makes audiences react by involving them more. Research has shown, and any teacher will tell you, that by combining sight and sound, retention of information is doubled. If you remember more then you will be likely to be persuaded to look further into the product or services.

Many websites use multimedia marketing and advertising. Company websites often contain presentations, images and sound. However this area is not just limited to the web, companies also distribute material on CD or DVD designed to be used either with a computer or a TV set. These can take the form of rolling displays at exhibitions or public areas such as shops. How many times have you stood by the till with one of those annoying product demonstrations featuring a spanner that fits everything or a set of boxes that keeps food in the fridge?

Holiday companies now offer interactive brochures that combine video tours with photographs of the destination.

Teleconferencing

This is a specialised form of multimedia allowing communication between two or more remote locations in both sound and vision. Teleconferencing can be carried out over an Internet connection or more likely using a dedicated telephone line such as ISDN.

Advantages:

▶ You do not have to be in the same location
▶ Travel is avoided
▶ A speaker can address many people.

Disadvantages:

▶ It is not the same as having the person in the room
▶ Immediacy is lost

- ► Cost of setting up
- ► Cost of telephone call
- ► Time differences can cause problems.

Publishing

Many magazines and books (like this one) now come with CDs containing multimedia products. Some books are available online or in CD format, providing a wider range of material and experiences for the reader. A printed book cannot contain any of the engaging forms of information that are available in multimedia. Some companies specialise in publishing multimedia on CD-ROM.

Most newspapers and news agencies now have online versions that can be searched for past news stories and contain links to similar stories. They often contain links to video accounts and slide shows of the news stories.

http://www.bbc.co.uk
http://www.cnn.com

Several well known encyclopaedias are available in printed form and multimedia. The multimedia versions include videos, sounds and images as well as search facilities.

Interactive television

The introduction of cable and satellite digital TV in the UK brought with it interactive TV (iTV).

Interactive TV is any television with a 'return path'. Information flows in two directions not only from broadcaster to viewer, but also back from viewer to broadcaster.

Interactive television allows lots of possibilities:

- ► TV-commerce: You will be able to buy goods without leaving the set.
- ► You can pause live TV.
- ► Films are available on demand.
- ► It is possible to choose different camera angles, for example during a Grand Prix.
- ► Viewers can vote on live shows.

There are many more possibilities and, as the market develops, more will become available. However all this comes at a cost. Viewers of satellite TV need to connect their boxes to the telephone line, so every time you interact you make a phone call even though you may not be aware of it.

CASE STUDY

QVC is a shopping channel on digital TV. It has been using TV-commerce since October 2001. Its interactive application provides a convenient way for viewers to purchase products. By pressing the interactive button they are able to use their account to buy a product featured on air. The average time required to complete a purchase is less than a minute. The application also has reduced costs because QVC interactive orders do not require call centre agents to be used – the customer is connected directly to the computer system. QVC now sells more goods via interactive TV than via the web.

Product demonstration

Multimedia product demonstrations are more than pictures of a product. They can take the form of a detailed look at a product and its features. An interactive multimedia product demonstration allows the user to look at the product in their own time in an individual way. Different consumers will be interested in different aspects of the product. A 3D presentation allows the customer to see and learn more about your product in detail. Customers can get a real-time experience and relate themselves to the product, producing a better rate of sales than still images.

Some products such as computer peripherals often have animations on CD in the form of a demonstration of how to connect and set up the peripheral. Tutorials are commonplace and demonstrate to the user how to use the peripheral effectively.

The CD with this book contains some product demonstrations in the form of How to... videos.

When looking at examples of multimedia you should evaluate the multimedia features used. How effective are they in putting across the message intended. Are they appropriate in quality and do they add to the overall effect? How effective is the design of the product? Is it attractive? Does it make you want to carry on or is it complex and off-putting?

Functional specification

Aims

- To examine the importance of the functional specification
- To examine the specification details required for a multimedia product

Introduction

portfolio_tip

To gain high marks in this section, make sure that your specification fully describes the product and covers its purpose, the context, and the intended audience. You must include specific and measurable success criteria.

Any software creation project must have a reference point. The functional specification is vital in describing the final aims of the project in terms of what the final product will do.

The specification should start with a description of the user's requirements and the purpose of the product. You will need to write down a set of success criteria in a clear and unambiguous way so that you have a clear picture of the direction you need to go right from the start. The clearer you are at this stage the more chance there is that you produce a product that meets the requirements. The functional specification explains to others, as well as yourself, what should be achieved. The document is not static however, and it is possible that you might want to update it when you have shown your prototype to the user.

The functional specification provides evidence for assessment criterion **a**.

As you work through the chapters of this unit, you will follow an example of project building a multimedia product. The CD contains some software and images for this purpose.

The purpose of the product

portfolio_tip

Your product needs to be challenging enough to encourage you to develop new skills beyond those you used in Unit 1.

portfolio_tip

Your product must be interactive and consist of a substantial integrated multimedia package. A series of unrelated tasks is not appropriate and will not fulfil the awarding body criteria.

In Unit 10.1, you learned about the many uses for multimedia products. You will need to be clear from the outset what is the intended purpose of your product. This needs to be agreed with the user before you go any further.

If, for example, the purpose is teaching a young child simple arithmetic, you will approach the design in a totally different way than for a product that explains astrophysics to a first year university student.

The following might be suitable products for you:

- ▶ A revision guide for a subject or topic.
- ▶ An interactive information point.
- ▶ A guide to your own town or a place that interests you.
- ▶ An adventure game.
- ▶ An interactive guide to a particular hobby or interest.
- ▶ An interactive story with different pathways and endings.

Sunridge Travel is an expanding holiday company. It is about to launch a new weekend away break to London. The director thinks it would be a good idea to have an interactive brochure produced. That will give prospective customers a guide to what they might see in a day's sightseeing around London.

The purpose of the guide is:

- To provide a photographic tour
- To persuade people to book the tour
- To act as a guide to some of the sights
- To provide information about the tour company.

The information the product must supply

portfolio_tip

When you plan this project, allow time to gather together your resources. However it is easy to become carried away in collecting pictures and sounds so make sure you do not spend too long on this. If you do then you may find the rest of your work is rushed.

One of the primary tasks of a multimedia product is to supply information in a variety of forms. You need to be clear from the outset exactly what information your product will supply. This varies according to who is using the multimedia product and you need to make sure that the information is suitable for your audience. You may need to spend some time collecting suitable information and researching for your project.

To produce a good multimedia product, you will need to collect a wide variety of images, sounds, drawings and video clips. You will need to use special software to edit the video clips and sounds to make them suitable for your product. It is a good idea to discuss with your user the exact requirements for the information to be provided. Once you have collected a range of suitable information and multimedia components you should ask the user to look at some samples to check that you are working on the right lines.

The London information package needs to contain the following information:

- Photographs of major tourist attractions
- Some video clips to illustrate aspects of London's attractions
- A map showing the locations of some of the attractions
- A slide show of images of London
- An itinerary for a typical tour
- A detailed review of one major attraction.

How the information must be presented

One of the advantages of multimedia is that the information can be presented in a wide variety of formats. This can help make information accessible to a wider audience. You need to specify exactly how the various bits of information will be presented. It is easy to say there will be a slide show, but how long will the slide show last, how many slides will be in it, how big will the slides be when they are displayed?

If you are displaying text, are there any requirements as to how the information must be presented? For example, the company might have a particular colour scheme associated with its products which you will need to reflect in your design.

The intended audience will also influence the way in which you present information. A young child will require the use of bright colours and short sentences. An adult will be able to cope with longer sentences and words, therefore more information can be presented in one go.

These may seem like minor details, but the more time you take to plan at this stage, the easier it will be later on.

CASE STUDY

The London package requires a slide show lasting between two and a half and three minutes and should show a photograph for a minimum of ten seconds. The show should run automatically and each photograph should be shown full screen. The photograph should be in colour. There should be background music and each slide should have a title so that the users know what they are looking at.

How the product will be used

Multimedia products can be used in a variety of ways. Some require the use of a computer while some need to be used away from a computer, perhaps on a DVD player connected to a television. The product you are going to produce needs to be interactive. It also needs to be viewed on a PC.

You will need to consider how the product will be used so that in the design stage you can ensure that it is fit for purpose. During development you will need to keep in mind how the product is going to be used. You may need to review your product once you have produced a prototype.

For example, the CD guide will need to be used in a variety of different computer systems by users with a varying range of computer skills.

This means that you will need to ensure that the final product is easy to set up and does not require any special software to run. It will need to run on any make of computer and be independent of the operating system used.

Specific aims might include:

► Runs on any computer.
► Has a 'home screen' from which the users can choose parts of the tour.
► Each part of the tour should return back to the 'home screen' automatically.

portfolio_tip

Include in your portfolio a detailed description of how the product you are producing will be used. Describe the scenario as well as the product itself. You should also describe the typical user.

How to judge the effectiveness of the product

When your project is complete, you will need to review the product to judge how well it performs the tasks you intended it to do. A good well-written specification will have a list of performance criteria that are expressed in such a way as to make the evaluation easier to carry out.

You must take account of others in your review, so in your specification you need to include details of how this will be done. A simple survey form for a test user to complete is a good way to do this. Users can complete the form as they look at the product.

Some things might not be easy for you to measure. For example, the tour company in the case study would consider the product effective only if it generated business. You might want to measure effectiveness by looking at how well it conforms to the specification.

Questions you could ask yourself:

► Did it hold the users' attention?
► Have the users retained any of the information?
► Does it perform as expected in a variety of situations?

Product design

Aims

■ To give an overview of the elements of design
■ To consider the importance of good design

Introduction

Once you have a clear specification for your product, you will begin to design your solution. During the design stage, there are many things that need to be taken into consideration. To produce a good multimedia product requires a lot of care at this stage. Good design leads to good products that fit the specification and work as they should.

You may find there are many ways of reaching the desired specification. You will need to try out some ideas and review them with your users before finally deciding the way in which you are going to finish your product. At this stage you should simply concentrate on what you would like the final product to look like. As you become more experienced in using the software you will be able to produce more detailed designs.

Your design contributes to assessment criterion **b** in the specification.

To achieve high marks, your design needs to be comprehensive and must satisfy all the functional requirements. You must show a full awareness in the design section of both the audience for your product and its purpose. You must make effective use of the different types of multimedia components, ready-made or original, and you must combine them to convey information effectively.

You should also produce some prototyping with evaluative comments at each stage. You must make full use of feedback from others.

Some of the headings in this unit are covered in more detail later on.

Structure and navigation

portfolio_tip

Try to produce a prototype of your user interface. Have someone look at it and make suggestions for its improvement.

Many developers create the structure of a product using their own ideas of how it should be organised. When you are planning the structure of the information, it is essential to stay focused on the needs of your audience and how they will be looking at the information. Try to group the different types of information in such a way that your audience might be able to understand it. Once you have grouped your content into distinct subjects, you will need to name these content areas. When deciding on labels for navigation items, think about the user. Keep them simple and as short as possible. Try not to be too clever or you might confuse. Your aim is to display information to the audience as efficiently as possible.

One way to improve your design is to make a site map or overall plan of your product. This will show how the interface will be structured, as well as how you will arrange the content in it.

Graphical design

Good graphical design is essential if your product is to look good and be user-friendly. Graphic design involves the effective use of colour and layout to create an overall effect. One consideration that needs to be kept in mind during graphical design is the method of navigation. It is likely that your navigation will use a menu of some kind. Perhaps a good plan is to use a window down the left of the page whilst displaying the information in a frame to the right.

■ Figure 10.2

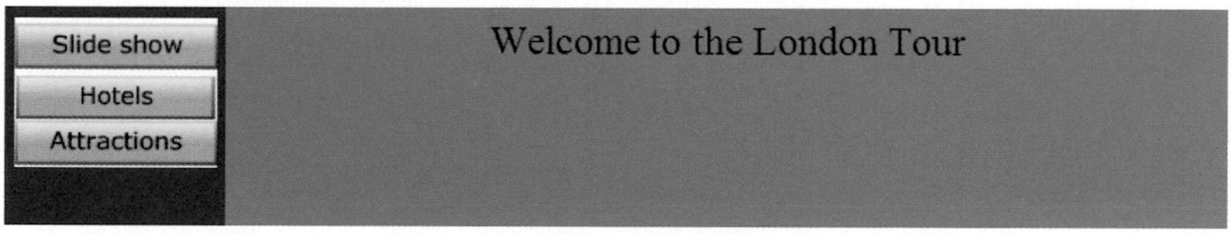

| Slide show |
| Hotels |
| Attractions |

Welcome to the London Tour

Navigation does not have to be achieved using complex structures. Simple graphics can often be used to create buttons which are a very effective means of navigation.

Careful choice of fonts, colours and backgrounds will make a simple yet attractive user interface.

Colours should be chosen carefully to provide a consistent look to the package. Good graphical design is based on the use of a limited range of complementary colours. Using too many colours produces a confusing and sometime off-putting interface. The colour scheme should enhance your product and its content, and not distract the users. Colour can be used to give users clues about navigation. Grouping of content, importance and relationships can be effective using colours.

Interactivity and user interface

To use your product to the greatest extent, the user must be able to interact with it in some way. The way in which your user interacts will depend upon many factors such as:

► The type of multimedia product.
► The computer platform on which it is to be run.
► The hardware available.
► The location in which the equipment will be used e.g. a railway station.
► The intended user.

The specification requires you to create a multimedia product that enables the user to interact with it. Your product is going to be used on a computer. Therefore you will need to design your interface to be used in that way. You can assume that the main way your user will interact with your product is with a mouse and a keyboard. The amount of interactivity will depend on the nature of the product. A learning package will need more interactivity than an information package, for example.

Good interfaces will help the user to decide what to do next. This idea of indirectly pointing users in useful directions is a part of all well-designed multimedia interfaces. Users should be able to see what is available to them on every screen.

The London tour package has a slide show. This can be constructed so that the user can interact with it. For example, buttons can be provided so that the slide show can be:

- played
- paused
- rewound
- fast forwarded.

■ **Figure 10.3**

Figure 10.3 is the prototype for a slide show viewer. You have been asked to evaluate the slide show interface from a user's point of view.

Make a list of some of the ways you might improve the slide show interface.

Use of multimedia components

CASE STUDY

The London package uses images and sound as part of the slide show. Video clips could be used to show some of the tourist attractions in action, for example a video clip of the London Eye.

Still images, video clips, sound and animations are all types of multimedia component. An effective multimedia product will use these components in a way that makes the final product attractive and effective.

You will need to incorporate all of these components into your final product so that you can demonstrate your skills in this area. Using the components effectively means they are used in a way that is appropriate to the product you are creating. Do not use them simply because you have to. During your design, try to think about how you can use the components in your product.

ACTIVITY

Make a list of some animations that might be included on the London tour CD.

Each component needs to be integrated into your product so that the user does not have to be concerned about the software that needs to be used. You will learn in the next few chapters how to do this. Your final product must be self-contained so you will need to make sure that the components are in a format that enables them to be copied easily, as well as making sure they fit within the limits given in the specification.

Layout and presentation

The layout and presentation of the final product will determine its success or failure. A product that is well laid out and easy to access will achieve its aims. A product that is poorly laid out will fail in its purpose.

How a page is laid out will determine whether a user understands your message or not. A good layout gives the entire product coherence. Users should immediately be able to find the information they need. A sloppy layout is a distraction, hiding your information and even confusing the users to a point where they will give up.

It is often tricky to make things line up on a page. Many packages have guides to help you to organise the layout. By displaying a grid on the screen, you can lay the objects out more accurately as well as making them line up properly.

Figure 10.4

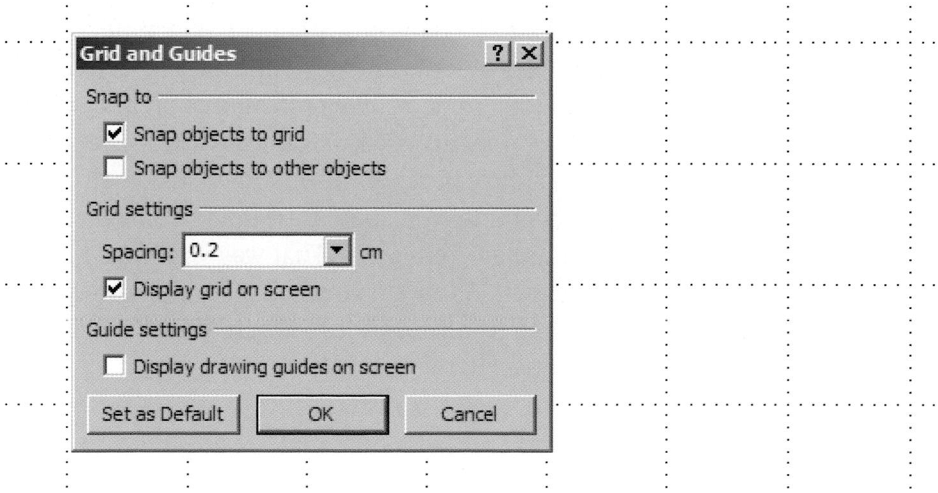

Figure 10.4 shows the guide set-up dialogue for a PowerPoint presentation. You can see that turning on the option to display the grid on screen has produced a grid of dots on the page. These dots will not show up on your presentation.

Using the grid helps to organise the space on a slide consistently. Using it throughout your development process will help you to place objects in an orderly and consistent way. A layout will look more professional if you use a grid to keep everything in line.

Using a grid is easy – just put the text frames and images inside the grid boxes. Then move the objects so that they touch the top or bottom of a grid box. The 'snap to grid' feature will help here. It means that you do not need to be too accurate. If you move close to the grid line and release the mouse button, the object will snap into place against the grid line.

Another aspect of good presentation is to use plenty of empty space around objects. This is known as white space. It makes the information more readable and is more pleasing to the eye. Do not put too much on a page.

Prototyping is useful in helping to produce a good layout. You will need to experiment with the tools available to you so that you are aware of the features that you can use. It is a good idea to try several initial layouts and then evaluate each one before deciding on the best approach. Remember that the layout should help the user get the most out of your product. Presentation also needs to be considered. The product must look good and not be full of spelling and other errors.

ACTIVITY

Look at some websites such as

http://www.bbc.co.uk.

Make a list of the features used to make the layout of the page effective.

Consistency

portfolio_tip

In your design, refer to the font type, size, colours, background, and layout that you will use for your entire product.

Consistency is the key to a good layout. You should make sure that your graphic layout is the same throughout. Try to give each page a similar look, using the same or similar backgrounds throughout your product. Often people like to show off with lots of different colours and background effects, using lots of fonts and word art in multi-coloured headings.

Take a look at a some professional products. You will rarely find features such as word art used. To produce a consistent design, choose a plain font and a simple background and then stick with it. If you need to draw attention to something, you should use bold or a larger size in the same font rather than use different fonts. That way your final result will look and feel consistent. Although you can use some variety, aim for consistency. The user learns to read your pages – where the title will be, what a colour means – and they understand your intentions faster.

Testing

It may seem odd to be talking about testing before you have even designed your package but it is a good idea to think about how you will be able to test the final product. If you determine how you will test the final product, then the design will benefit from it.

You can also test some of your work as you go along. This will help to make things easier at the end. Keep a record of what you test in this way and if things go wrong, use this as evidence that you have improved the product by fixing the problem.

It will not matter how good your end result looks or what your images are like. Even the latest HiFi surround sound will not make up for a product that simply does not work and keeps crashing all the time.

Prototyping

Prototyping is a way of combining design and testing into a developmental process that will result in a better end product. It will also help you to discover what is possible with the software you are using.

Prototyping is the building of a model of a system. In terms of a multimedia product, prototypes are used to help the designer to set up a product that is intuitive and easy for end users to manipulate.

Advantages of prototyping:

- It reduces development time.
- It involves the end user.
- You receive early user feedback.
- It improves user satisfaction.
- Potential training issues can be identified.

Disadvantages of prototyping:

- Sometimes it reduces the amount of analysis.
- Users might expect the finished system to have the same performance.
- It can leave unfinished systems due to too much time being spent on the prototype.
- Users, having seen the prototype, might expect the system finished sooner.

Refine your initial design and try out alternatives

Initial ideas can quickly be turned into a prototype that is functional even though it is not complete. For example, if you are not sure how a particular feature works, you can try it out and see if it seems effective or not.

For example the buttons in Figure 10.2 could be linked to blank dummy pages. The interface can then be tested to see how well the buttons perform and how easy it is to make the frames link together.

You could set up different versions of the page and then see which colour scheme or style is best. You might decide that the buttons do not look quite right and a different shape will look better or that the colour scheme is wrong.

portfolio_tip

Keep a record of all the testing that you do. If something does not work, then keep the evidence of how you made it work. This will show the development of your final solution.

portfolio_tip

If you are following this unit alongside Unit 8 – Managing ICT projects, then you should have evidence that a prototype has been shown to the project group and also have evidence of their feedback.

portfolio_tip

Keep a record of any prototyping you do and any refinements made as a result. You should also have some feedback from others on your prototype.

Test that the product is functional and works as expected

To test if your final product functions in the way you expect, you could build a prototype consisting of linked frames and pages but without the full content. It is sometimes a good idea to see if the structure is right before you go to a lot of trouble adding colour, precisely positioned images and text.

You can create the structure from almost blank pages and when you choose a structure that is acceptable, you can edit the pages in detail, adding the carefully chosen content and images knowing that the structure is in place and tested.

Check for ease of use

A prototype is a good way to evaluate how easy the site is to use. If the structure is set up, you can quickly arrange for a few people to try the navigation routes and the links to see how easy it is to move around the site. If they get lost in the pages and find the product difficult to use, you can correct it and resolve the issues before you do too much work on the pages.

Test for robustness

One of the most important things you need to do during testing is to try and make your product fail. You should set out to cause problems. That is the only way you can be sure that the final product is solid enough to survive in the hands of a user.

Building a prototype allows you to rectify any major problems before too much work is done. It also enables you to test out the possibilities of the software you are using to produce the product. You can find out how well it is able to produce a system that is truly independent of the system you are using.

Test users' response to the product

A good way to test the response of a system is to give the system to a variety of users with different levels of experience. However, it is too late to do this level of testing with the final system. That is why software is often released in what is known as beta versions. These are, in effect, a final version of the prototype. They are released to a range of users who undertake to try them out and report any problems. The more widely the product is tested at this stage the better the final product should be when released.

Structure and navigation

Aims

■ To examine different ways of navigating a system

Introduction

To enable the user to access all parts of your product, you need to plan carefully how the pages can be navigated. A navigation map can be used to help plan the structure of the entire product; it should show all of the pages and the connections from one page to other pages.

You should be able to see clearly how your material is to be connected. That way you will be able to establish links between them in a planned way. The navigation map is different to the storyboard you met in Unit 7, in that it does not provide as much detail about the contents of the individual pages.

You also need to plan how the files will be organised on the disk you supply. If you are working to standard methods all your files will have meaningful names and be set in folders that make it easy to see where everything is stored.

In effect, you have two sets of maps. A logical map which shows how the pages are connected and a physical map which shows how the files are organised on the disk.

Hierarchical

This structure is very much like a tree. You move from top to bottom, by moving down one branch at a time. As you go down, more branches are available. This method of navigation allows you to group things together. The topmost page is a menu, which leads the user to sub menus.

Figure 10.5 shows such a structure.

■ **Figure 10.5**

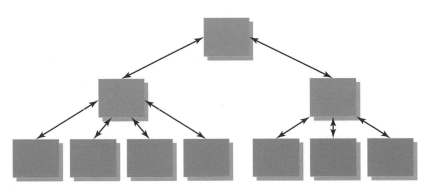

The information could also be represented in text form. For example, part of the London CD may have the following structure.

1. Main menu
  1.1. Places to visit
     1.1.1. London Eye
     1.1.2. House of Commons
     1.1.3. St James Park
     1.1.4. British Museum
  1.2. Shows
     1.2.1. The Lion King
     1.2.2. Les Misérables
     1.2.3. Fame

Linear

In a linear system the user has less choice of movement. Navigation is sequential, moving from one page to the next. This is useful for a simple system where the user needs to experience the pages in the order the designer wishes. Sometimes this is an appropriate method of linking pages. There is less flexibility for the user but more control of their experience.

■ Figure 10.6

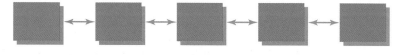

In Figure 10.6, the user can move in two directions, forwards and backwards.

It is possible to combine the two methods in different sections of the product. For example, on the London CD, the user might go the start page for a walking tour and be able to take a virtual walk by looking at images of the sights in the same sequence as they would come across them as they walked along (see Figure 10.7).

■ Figure 10.7

Graphical design

Aims

- To consider the importance of good graphic design
- To look at examples of graphic design

In this unit, you will learn about some of the features of good graphic design. Good design will make your end product much more user friendly. Good design is not difficult; it requires the application of some simple techniques and a careful approach to layout.

User interface

The user interface is the point of contact between your user and the system you have produced. It is often referred to as the human–computer interface (or HCI). Its design is the most important aspect of the multimedia system you are creating. During its design you must keep in mind who the user of your system is likely to be and their probable level of computer skills.

For example, a product aimed at five-year-old children will need images to click on, such as a picture of a printer, rather than words.

Some ideas for good design:

- ▶ Do not have too much on any one screen.
- ▶ Arrange images symmetrically.
- ▶ In something like a slide show, make all the images the same size.
- ▶ Group similar activities together.

The Gestalt principle

The Gestalt principle is that people use a top-down approach to organising data. This principle should influence how you organise graphical information on the screen. The Gestalt principle identifies the criteria that people use to group items together when displayed. Correct grouping makes it easier for a user to locate an item. For example, all the buttons to do with navigating the menus, such as back, forward, and main menu, should be grouped together. This allows the user to learn the interface more quickly. There are several ways that items can be grouped to make access easier. Colour, drawing frames and highlighting can frequently be used to assist in this.

■ Figure 10.8

Figure 10.8 shows a poorly designed user interface for the London CD. Some of the problems are:

▶ Items are not balanced on the page.
▶ Menu is cluttered.
▶ Buttons are confusing in layout.

ACTIVITY

Write a critical evaluation of the page saying what you think is wrong with it and then make a sketch showing how you would lay out the page. Give reasons for your choice of final layout.

Effective use of colour

Choosing the correct colour scheme can make a big difference to the quality of a multimedia product. If you have watched TV programmes about selling and improving a house, you may have noticed that they often recommend that you choose neutral colours for decoration.

People's attention is drawn to bright, basic colours, but after a short time the eye becomes tired. If you want to get attention very quickly, then use bright colours. However if you are trying to present specific information that needs to be well understood or the page needs to be read carefully, bright colours will not help.

Eye fatigue is more likely to occur at the yellow and red end of the spectrum, and will spoil concentration as well as reduce the time that someone will spend using your product.

Only use bright colours for important information that must stand out. Use the saturated colours where you want people to look first. Colour can be used to help when density of text is a problem. If there is a lot of text on a page it can be broken up and clarified by the use of colour to pick out the most important parts.

One last tip is that you should start by designing in black and white. If the pages are not effective in black and white then colour will not help – change the way it is laid out first.

Contrast

Contrast is the amount of difference between the lightest and darkest areas of an image.

High contrast makes text easy to read, that is why black on white is used for word processing. Too little contrast makes text difficult to see.

The effect of contrast on text is easy to see in Figure 10.9.

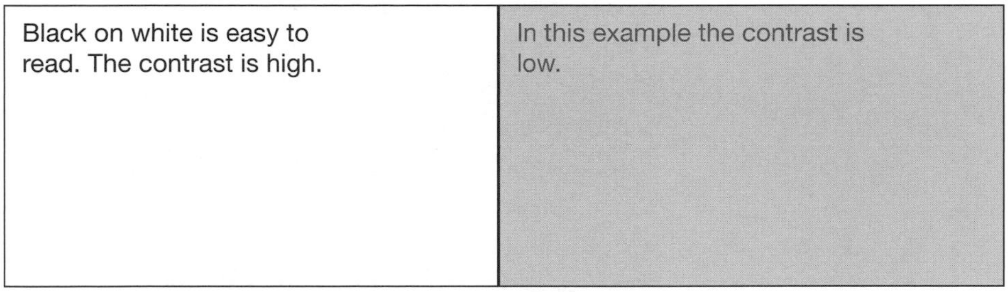

■ **Figure 10.9**

Black on white is easy to read. The contrast is high.	In this example the contrast is low.

When using photographs, the contrast will affect how clear the image is. Sometimes a dark image can be improved by changing the contrast. You will see how to do this later, in Unit 10.7. Figure 10.10 shows the effect of changing the contrast of an image.

■ **Figure 10.10**

 These images are available on the CD in a folder called contrast images.

Notice how the images can be changed by adjusting the contrast. In the image above the London Eye is almost invisible but the trees are lighter and show more detail.

Pattern

Patterns can be used to good effect to make things stand out, however be careful with text positioned over patterned backgrounds. The patterns will hide some of the text as it passes over areas with low contrast. Figure 10.11

■ **Figure 10.11**

shows how a pattern can make a page totally impossible to read. So use patterns carefully.

Patterns can be used in the actual text to create artistic effects for things like opening screens, but be careful as it is easy to over do this type of thing.

Background and borders

Borders can be used to make things stand out or to separate groups of items. A user can easily be guided to look at a particular part of the page by using borders. Sometimes borders can be used to make frames around things when you need a visual effect. One example is to put a border that looks like a picture frame around a photograph.

A background is the colour or pattern that is behind the elements on a page. Text and images appear to be on top of the background, the colour of which should be carefully chosen to complement the elements on the page. A good background will make the elements on the page stand out clearly and not interfere with the clarity. If you are using bright text on a dark background, then use a bold, non-serif font.

Images and patterns are often used as a 'watermark' background. This usually makes reading more difficult and sometimes almost impossible.

Web-safe colours

Browser-safe colours, or the palette as it is sometimes called, is the range of colours built into the major web browsers such as Mosaic, Netscape, and Internet Explorer. There are slight differences between the versions for Macs and PCs. The palette only contains 216 colours rather than the full 256 that are available because 40 colours vary between Macs and PCs. So for true cross-platform use you are left with just 216 colours.

The origin of such a limited colour scheme lies with the early computer displays that could use only 256 colours. Most systems today use far better video cards capable of millions of colours. You really only need to use the limited range of colours if your user has an older machine.

The impact of layout on the overall effect

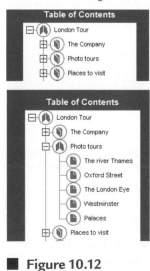

Figure 10.12

The layout of a page will affect the ability of the user to access information on it. This is a critical factor in the design. Layout factors include:

▶ the number of links
▶ alignment
▶ grouping
▶ density of text and images.

Too many links will confuse the users. It is better to use more pages that are linked or a menu that expands and collapses as needed to reduce the number of visible options at any one time.

Figure 10.12 shows a menu structure that can be expanded as the user accesses items. The user is not confronted by too many options but has the flexibility to expand the menu if needed.

Composition

White space is the blank areas between objects on the screen. Even if your background is green it is still called white space! White space should be used consistently throughout the product. Too much white space will make a page seem empty and unimportant, perhaps suggesting that content is lacking. Too little white space however and the page will seem like a jumbled mess.

Shape

The screen is pretty much a fixed shape – there is no getting away from the fact that you have to make your product fit the rectangular screen.

However, you can use shapes for items such as buttons and icons to group them together or make them stand out.

Balance

Think about a seesaw. When two children are of equal weight, they balance each other. Also two small children on one side can be balanced by a large child on the other side.

Balancing the appearance of a screen works in the same way, not just in relation to the size of objects but also the visual appearance of lightness or darkness.

The images on the pages of this book are set out to create a balanced appearance on each page.

Formal balance

Formal balance is symmetrical: items on the left side of the screen are the same shape, size and colour as the items on the right side of the screen. Formal balance is much easier to design. Many large buildings use this form of balance, with a line of symmetry down the centre of the building.

Informal balance

This is usually asymmetrical, where a number of smaller items on one side of the screen are balanced by a single large item on the other side. A darker image needs to be balanced by several lighter items.

Creating a good looking asymmetric screen is more difficult. It depends a lot on personal taste and skill. It is not just about size but colour, distance and position.

How fonts can enhance or detract from readability

Most computers have a very wide range of fonts and styles available to use. Some are very fancy; some are very plain. If you look at a few professional websites you will notice that they use simple fonts most of the time.

Styles

Style can refer to the use of bold, italic and underline when using text. There is a range of preset styles available to use for items such as headings.

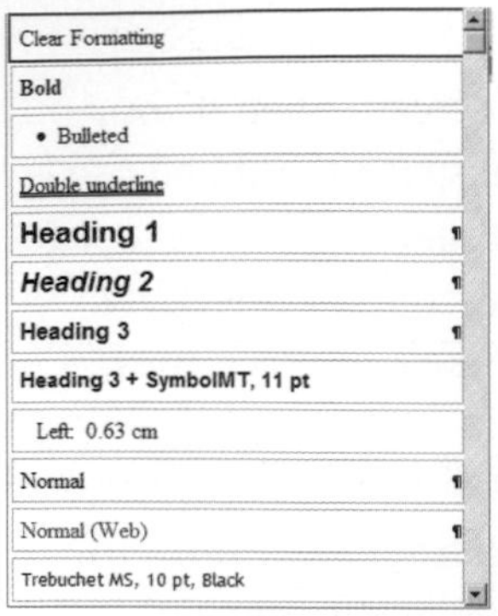

Figure 10.13

The image shows a drop-down menu from Microsoft Word which gives access to a range of styles including headings of various sizes.

It is often better to use a change in style rather than changing the font to make something stand out.

Typefaces

There are many thousands of fonts or typefaces available as downloads from the web. It is very tempting to use lots of different fonts, and to make thinks look very fancy by using decorative fonts. Often fancy fonts can make the information difficult to read.

For example:

This is written in a nice looking fancy font that looks like I have handwritten this line.

Fonts like this have their uses but only in a limited range of applications, for example if you want to make it look like someone has signed a document. But a whole page of this font would make the reader give up very quickly.

Professional products normally use plain simple fonts that are easy to read. It is accepted that variable-width fonts are easier to read than fixed-width fonts.

A serif font is normally easier to read than a sans-serif font, because the individual characters differ more from each other.

Text in UPPERCASE LETTERS or CAPITALS is difficult to read in complete sentences. It should be used for no more than about 10 characters at a time, to pick something out.

Emphasis

There are several ways you can emphasise something so that someone's attention is drawn in a particular direction. You can use:

- ► **bold**
- ► underscore
- ► CAPITALS
- ► *italics*
- ► colour
- ► highlighting
- ► negatives

Consideration of presentation method

Your brief is to produce a multimedia product that will be viewed on a computer. The user must be able to navigate around easily.

The size of PC screens may vary from one user to the next. However all screens with the same resolution will display the same image, the only difference will be the size of the image. The specification for your product is that it should display correctly on a monitor set to 1024 × 768 pixels. You should work on your design based on that resolution.

As mentioned before the design needs to be suitable for your intended audience. Your specification should state the target audience. Different audiences will have different requirements.

Consistency

If you look at the website of a large organisation, you notice the same colour scheme is used throughout the site and the font use is consistent from one page to next.

To improve your product, choose during the design stage a limited font range and a colour scheme. Stick to it as you develop the product.

It might help to produce some prototypes using different colour schemes to show to users. Seek their opinions on the overall effect and then decide on the final scheme.

Consistency can mean other things too, e.g. layout of page, where the menu is, navigation links.

The importance of a corporate image

Often a corporate font family is used with corporate colours throughout the product. Most large companies have a corporate colour scheme. A company is often recognised by its corporate image and you will need to find out if your user has a corporate scheme. If the company has a logo then it is likely that this will appear on all the pages somewhere so plan for this in your design. This adds a constraint on the developer, who needs to allow for it on every page.

Interactivity design

Aims

- To examine ways of making a product interactive
- To learn how to create and add interactive items

Introduction

The files for this unit are in a folder called Demo Pages.

There are many ways to make a product interactive. This chapter looks at a range of methods to allow your user to interact with the product.

You are working towards making a product that is able to run using standard browser software. The product will therefore need to behave like a website, so this unit is going to look at using a web authoring package to build the interface to the package.

There are sample pages on the CD to illustrate the use of the features in this unit. The pages have been constructed using Dreamweaver, but most other packages function in a similar way.

Buttons

Buttons provide a very natural and intuitive interface. Even very young children will know that buttons are there to be pressed. Buttons come in a very wide range of designs and can be grouped together or arranged in a pattern to give an indication of their function.

■ Figure 10.14

Software such as Dreamweaver provides an extensive range of button designs. Figure 10.14 shows some examples of buttons that can be made from available designs. Some have captions on them to describe their function, such as the 'About us' button. Others need no caption, such as the '+' button. When loaded in the browser, these buttons animate and make a clicking sound when pressed.

ACTIVITY

Load the file **button demo** from the CD.

Move the mouse over the buttons to see the animation effect. Try clicking the buttons and notice the effect.

You will need to choose a button style that will be suited to the users of your package. Also remember to be consistent, do not mix too many different button styles.

■ **Figure 10.15**

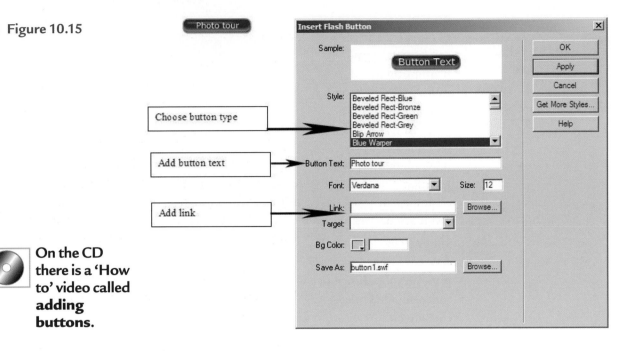

On the CD there is a 'How to' video called **adding buttons**.

Image maps and hot spots

Hot spots are areas, defined in a graphic or picture, that contain a hyperlink. It is possible to set the whole picture as the link or a part of it, depending on the effect you want to create. Hot spots do not show up in browsers. Users can only see a hot spot is present when the mouse pointer changes appearance as it is moved over the graphic.

■ **Figure 10.16**

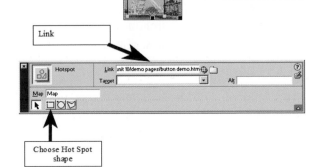

On the CD is a 'How to' video showing the hot spot being added.

Figure 10.16 shows a hot spot being added to an image. In this case, only part of the image is the hot spot.

ACTIVITY

The CD contains a file called Hot Spot Demo. Load the file and move the cursor around.

You will see the pointer change as it hits the hot spot.

Try clicking on the hot spot.

On the CD is a file called map demo.

ACTIVITY

Load the file and, using Figure 10.17 as a guide, try out the image map.

A graphic with hot spots is called an image map. They are a good way to present a user with lots of choices. The user might need some prompting to investigate the map by moving the mouse pointer over it since it will not always be obvious that there are hot spots.

Figure 10.17 shows a photograph with hot spots defined. The hot spots are linked to other photographs showing more detailed images of the wheel.

You will notice that the image map alone does not give any clues to the user. This could be used as a design feature to encourage someone to explore the page.

■ Figure 10.17

Text links

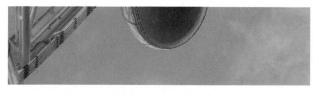

Back to image map

■ Figure 10.18

Text links are simply pieces of text – a sentence or a word – that form a hyperlink to another part of the product. Most people are familiar with this kind of link, however try to use a word or sentence that describes what the link does.

Rollovers

A rollover image is made up of two images. The top image is displayed when the page loads but, as the mouse is moved over the image, it changes to show the other image. A rollover can be used quite effectively to draw the user's attention to something.

■ **Figure 10.19** The two images for the rollover

Before starting to make a rollover you need to have two images that will form the layers of the image.

Select Insert → Interactive Images → Rollover Image, then identify the top and bottom images. You can also make the image a link if you wish by entering a link to follow.

The Rollover file on the CD shows a rollover button made from the two photographs in Figure 10.19.

There is a 'How to' video on the CD showing this process.

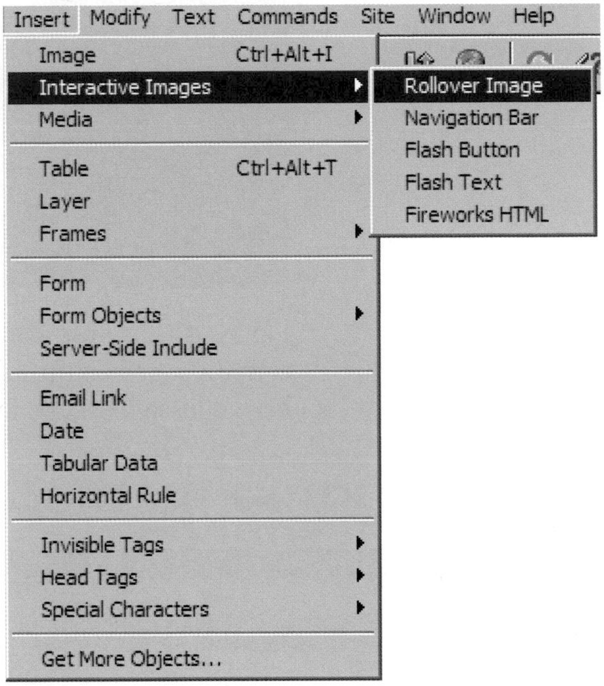

■ Figure 10.21

■ **Figure 10.20**

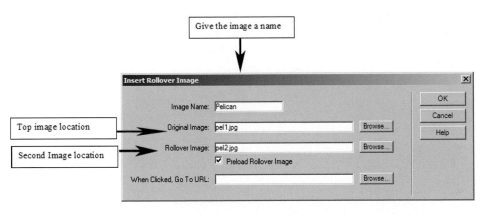

Give the image a name

Top image location

Second Image location

Insert Rollover Image

Image Name: Pelican
Original Image: pel1.jpg Browse...
Rollover Image: pel2.jpg Browse...
☑ Preload Rollover Image
When Clicked, Go To URL: Browse...

OK
Cancel
Help

Menus

A menu is a list of choices presented to the user. Most people are familiar with the idea of a menu. If you have a complex product then it is best to use a series of menus to avoid confusion.

While it is common to use drop-down menus in many packages such as word processors, in a multimedia product such as the London CD, menus can be made up of buttons on a page or in a frame at the side of the window. Menus can also be found along the top or bottom of pages.

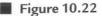

Figure 10.22 shows a prototype of the London tour start-up page. The menu is in the frame on the left and is presented using text links. The colours have been chosen to match the company's coach livery.

User response methods

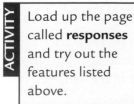

■ Figure 10.23

ACTIVITY

Load up the page called **responses** and try out the features listed above.

Users can respond to the system in a number of ways depending on how much information you need. There are several standard components with which many people are familiar.

Text boxes

These allow the user to type in text from the keyboard – the user is free to type in anything. They can be limited to one line or the box can be larger and scroll to take more than one line of text.

List boxes

These present the user with a list of choices to choose from. They are useful when you want to limit the range of responses.

Radio buttons

Radio buttons can be chosen by clicking on them. When you click on a radio button, the button becomes shaded to show it has been selected. Radio buttons collect a Boolean value: they are either selected or not. Only one radio button can be selected out of each group.

Check boxes

Check boxes are similar to radio buttons in that they are either selected or not selected. However you can select more than one check box in a group.

Image capture and manipulation

Aims

- To examine ways of capturing still images
- To learn techniques for manipulating images

 On the CD is a package called GIMP. Instructions for installation are in a text file called Gimp Install in the Gimp folder.

This unit looks at a variety of techniques and ideas for capturing and manipulating still images. These images might be photographs or drawings. There are many packages available for this. The one used to illustrate this unit is called GIMP. It is on the CD for your use.

Capturing ready-made images

■ Figure 10.24

TWAIN Technology Without An Industry Name is a standard for communications between imaging devices and computer software.

Ready-made images could be in a variety of formats including:

- ▶ paper
- ▶ photographic slides
- ▶ photographic negatives.

The most common way to capture images of these types is to use a scanner. A flat bed scanner, such as the one in Figure 10.24, is quick and easy to use. The image to be scanned is placed on a glass plate and the top of the scanner is closed to keep the document still and flat. If you are scanning something thick, such as a book, most scanners allow the top to be removed.

To capture the image you might use dedicated software that came with the scanner or you might scan directly into the software you are using. Most up-to-date software will accept images from TWAIN devices, such as scanners or digital cameras. GIMP is able to receive images in this way.

Scan a paper image

From the GIMP file menu choose Acquire and then TWAIN.

This will load up the scanner software and allow the image to be scanned directly into the GIMP image software for you to manipulate. When scanning an image, a number of settings can be used to control how the image is scanned.

Cropping

If you only need part of an image, it is pointless scanning the whole page. It results in a file size much bigger than you need and you will still need to crop the image later.

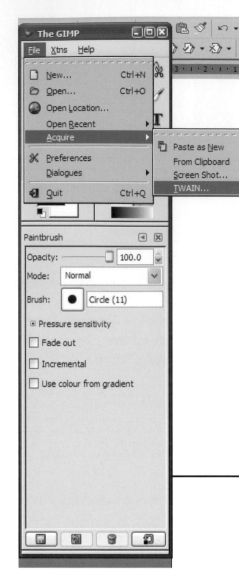

■ Figure 10.26

In the old photograph in Figure 10.26, only the head and shoulders of the boy in the centre is required, so a frame is drawn around the area to be scanned.

■ Figure 10.25

Image resolution

Image resolution is normally given in dots per inch (dpi). The more dots per inch that are scanned, the more detailed the final image will be or the more you can enlarge the image before it loses detail. However the greater the resolution, the bigger the file size will be. The cropped image above would use 12.8 Mb if scanned at the scanner's full resolution of 1200 dpi, but only uses 75 Kb if scanned at 75 dpi.

If you are scanning an image to be viewed on the computer screen, then you should scan at a low resolution, since the image on screen is only around 75 dpi. This will keep the file size of your product to a minimum and help the processes that use it to run more quickly.

Output size

When setting the resolution, you need to consider the size of the final image you require. If you need to enlarge the scanned image, then you must scan at a high resolution; for example an image scanned at 150 dpi becomes 75 dpi when doubled in size.

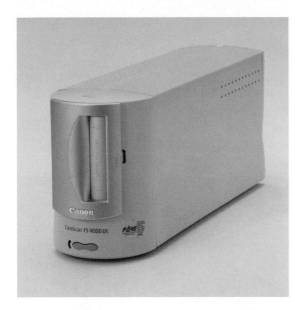

Figure 10.27

Scan other images

Other images such as negatives and slides require a special type of film scanner. This needs to be able to scan at very high resolutions, since the image from a negative is very small and it needs to be made much bigger to be of use. The film scanner in Figure 10.27 can scan at 11 000 dpi whereas most flat bed scanners are limited to around 1200 dpi.

Capture from digital sources

Images that are already in digital format are easy to capture. Such images might include those that follow.

Video still

Many video playback programs will allow you to capture a still image at any point. The resultant image is often referred to as a 'video grab'. This image is often not of a very high quality. Video images are often of a low resolution because of the need to store many images per second to record live movement.

Pictures on CD

Image libraries are often supplied on CD. Capturing such an image can be as simple as copying the image to your hard drive, or you might want to load it into your graphics package and make changes such as cropping the image first.

Pictures on a website

Pictures on a website can normally be captured by right clicking the image and choosing Save Picture As. However, you need to be careful that the image you are capturing is the genuine image and not simply a thumbnail image of much smaller size.

Screen shots

Many of the illustrations in this book are captured from the screen. The best way to do this is to use imaging software. GIMP can capture screen images in two ways:

▶ **Whole screen** This captures the whole of the screen with everything on it. This is good for evidence in eportfolios!
▶ **Window** This captures the selected window. This is good for capturing part of the screen only.

Once you have captured the screen image you can then crop it to display only the part you need.

> Remember that when you use a ready-made image of any kind, you must respect the rights of the copyright holder. You should acknowledge your sources of images and, if necessary, obtain permission for them to be used.

Back to image map

Figure 10.28

Creating original images

Use a digital camera

Many different types and makes of digital camera are now available – the chances are you will have one in your phone. They are now fast replacing traditional cameras; one high street retailer is now no longer selling film-based cameras.

■ **Figure 10.29**

Digital cameras come in many shapes and sizes. The image quality will vary according to the quality of the camera and its resolution. The resolution of cameras is measured in megapixels. Basically the higher the number of megapixels, the better the resolution of the camera and the bigger you can make the images. Once again, you should note that your product is going to be on screen so the resolution need not be particularly high.

Once you have captured your image, you will need to download your image to the computer. This can happen in many ways. Most cameras will simply connect to the USB port and can be treated as an extra disk drive. Images are simply copied to your hard drive. Some have removable cards that can be placed in a card reader on the computer and copied.

> **ACTIVITY**
>
> On the CD are two images in a folder called **resolution**. They were both taken on the same day and location, with two different cameras.
> Load up the two images and compare them for quality.
> Which is the better quality?

Use graphics software

If you need a drawing or diagram, you might need to use some form of graphics software to create your own image.

GIMP has many tools to enable you to produce high quality drawings. The tools include:

► brushes
► fixed shapes
► text
► fill
► crop.

Load up the GIMP software. Move the mouse pointer over the various tools to see what they are called.

The best way to learn to use a piece of software like GIMP is to experiment with the different options to see what can be achieved.

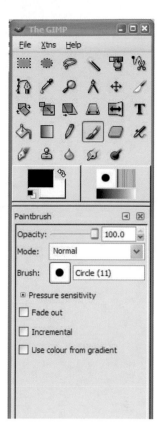

■ **Figure 10.30**

Manipulating images

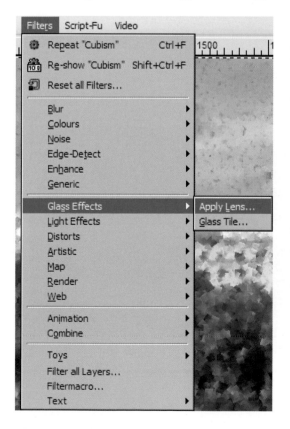

■ Figure 10.31

Filters

A filter is a tool that modifies an image in a certain predetermined way. There are many filters available. Think of them as special effect generators.

Some examples are:

► Blur
► Glass effects
► Artistic
► Map
► Render.

GIMP has many filters built in and many more can be downloaded!

On the following page are some examples of filters in use.

Figure 10.32
Original image

Figure 10.33 Using
a lens effect

Figure 10.34 Using a cubist filter

These images are on the CD in a folder called Filters.

ACTIVITY

Using a graphics package, load up the original image on the CD and experiment with different filters.

There are also specialised filters that can help to enhance images.

In Figure 10.35, the first image is from a series of 50 images captured over a period of 2 minutes with a webcam and a basic telescope. It is of low resolution and the detail is not clear.

The second image is the result of applying filters and stacking the images in layers in

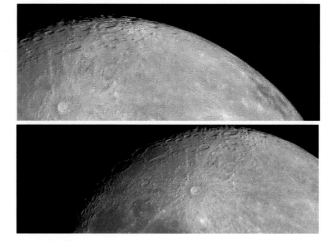

Figure 10.35

GIMP. The final image is a composite made from all 50 images. Notice how the detail is brought out in this way.

Resize

Resizing an image is when you make it bigger or smaller. In applications such as Word, you will be familiar with using the handles at the corners and on the sides of images to resize them. Image processing software provides different ways to resize an image by providing information about the new size of the image. The software will scale the image to preserve the quality. This is a

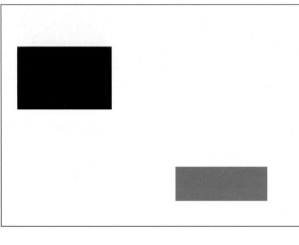

■ **Figure 10.36**

much better way of resizing images because it alters not only the size of the image on paper but also the storage size of the image.

Crop

Cropping an image is when you select only part of an image by cutting out the parts that you don't want. On page 174, you were shown how to crop an image in the scanner. Cropping an image in a package such as GIMP removes the unwanted portion of the image and reduces the file size. Cropping can be done in a variety of ways.

▶ **Freehand selection** You draw an area to crop using a freehand tool and crop the image to the shape.

▶ **Rectangle** You draw a rectangle to crop to.

▶ **Auto crop** The program crops to the edges of a defined image.

▶ **Zealous crop** The image is cropped to the defined edges, but the program removes any blank areas in the centre as well.

Here are some examples of cropping images.

■ **Figure 10.37** Original image

■ **Figure 10.38** Auto crop

■ **Figure 10.39** Zealous crop

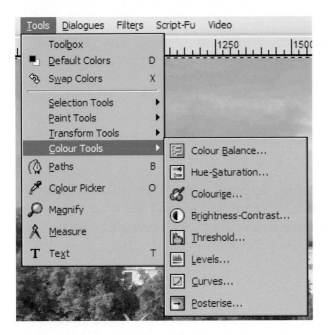

Figure 10.40

Colour

There are many tools available to help manipulate the colour of an image.

The menu in Figure 10.40 shows the main colour controls in GIMP.

Colour balance can be used to correct the colour of an image. If you have ever taken a photograph indoors without a flash, it most probably looks like Figure 10.41.

Figure 10.41

The image has a yellow orange colour cast caused by the lights in the room. The human eye corrects for this so you do not notice it, but the camera does.

It can be corrected by changing the balance of the colours in the image. When corrected, the image looks like this. In this case, the camera looks silver again.

Figure 10.42

> **ACTIVITY**
>
> The best way to investigate these effects is to load up one of the images on the CD and experiment with the various tools.

Characteristics and uses of bitmap and vector graphics

Graphic images on a computer can usually be divided into two types:

▶ bitmap graphics
▶ vector graphics.

Scanned images and images taken with a digital camera are normally bitmap files. Drawings constructed with packages such as CorelDRAW are saved as vector graphics.

Bitmap images are a collection of dots or pixels that form an image. Each pixel has its own colour. Images in bitmap form are usually saved in one of the following file formats:

► BMP
► EPS
► GIF
► JPEG
► TIFF.

Vector graphics are images that are described using mathematical definitions rather than a collection of pixels. They are usually small files because they only contain the formulae to recreate the image. Vector drawings can be resized without loss of quality. They are ideal for company logos, maps and objects that need to be resized.

Image resolution

Image resolution has been discussed in various places in this unit already. Here is an example of how image resolution affects quality.

The image on the right in Figure 10.43 is enlarged from an image taken with a camera using 5 megapixels. The one on the left is from a 1 megapixel camera enlarged to the same image size. Notice the difference in detail.

■ **Figure 10.43**

Bitmap images, such as photographs, need large amounts of storage space if they are stored in the format in which they were originally captured.

Compression is used to make the images take less storage space and make them easier to transport. There are two major types of compression: lossy and non-lossy.

Lossy compression

Image-processing software will remove information that is not visible or is too much for the human eye. Lossy compression can give a very high degree of compression, often 5–30 times. However the original information is lost from the image.

JPEG is a form of lossy compression used by most cameras.

Non-lossy compression

Non-lossy compression retains all the original information in the image. As a result, the compression ratio is much lower. With rates averaging 20–30%, formats that support non-lossy compression are GIF and BMP.

Video

Aims

- To look at methods of capturing video clips
- To learn how to edit video clips
- To examine ways of saving video clips

Introduction

Video recording has been around for many years but it has become far more accessible and cheaper to use in recent years. Many camera phones will now produce reasonable quality video for use on small screens.

In this unit, you need to capture and edit videos that you have made yourself and make use of them in your final product.

For assessment purposes, you must be able to capture (record) video yourself as well as make use of some ready-made video clips. You will need access to a video camera of some kind and a means of editing the clips once you have captured them.

If you are using Windows XP with Service Pack 2, then there is a video editing package already provided called Movie Maker. This chapter will illustrate the editing process using that package.

If you use ready-made video clips, you will need to check the copyright and acknowledge your sources as part of your standard ways of working.

Capturing ready-made video clips

Ready-made video clips can be found on many websites. There are also some available on the CD accompanying this book which you can use. The best way to capture a video clip is to download or copy it to your hard drive and this way you can access it at a faster speed for editing.

To download a clip from a website the best way is to right click the link and choose Save Target As from the menu.

Figure 10.44 shows a video being selected for download. Under the video title is some information about the clip. The numbers 320x240 refer to the dimensions of the video in pixels. This one will be quite small when played on screen. The next number is the length of time it takes to play

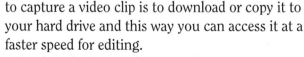

London.mpg

320x240 - 2:16 - 27.8MB

Open Link
Open Link in New Window
Save Target As...
Print Target

Show Picture
Save Picture As...
E-mail Picture...

■ **Figure 10.44**

the video – 2 minutes and 16 seconds. The third number is the size – 27.8 Mb is quite a large file to download; even with broadband it would take several minutes to download.

Recording original video clips

There are many types of camera available for recording your own video clips. Most digital cameras are able to record short video clips, although some of the cheaper models cannot capture the sound as well. Digital cameras are really designed for capturing still images so the clips they capture tend to be low in resolution to keep the storage requirements to a minimum. The videos tend therefore to be short and of low quality.

Digital video cameras range in price and quality from a few hundred pounds to many thousands for a professional camera. The advantage of a video camera is that it is designed for the job and the video will be of high quality, often with stereo sound. Depending on the type of camera used you will have to download or import the video from the camera to the computer. Movie Maker is able to capture video from cameras which are normally connected via a Firewire interface.

The camera shown at the bottom in Figure 10.45 records directly to a DVD. This allows the recorded video to be placed in the computer's disk drive and transferred quickly to the computer.

Hints for good recording:

■ **Figure 10.45**

▶ Always make sure the camera is steady. If possible, put it on a tripod to make it completely stable.
▶ When recording, never shoot a clip for less than 10 seconds. Anything shorter and the viewer cannot take in the subject material.
▶ Light levels make a big difference – try to shoot when there is good light.
▶ Most cameras have a zoom lens. Try not to zoom in and out with the camera recording. It is best used to frame the shot and then record.
▶ When moving the camera across a scene do it very slowly, to give the viewer time to take in what is displayed.

Editing video clips

On the CD is a movie called London tour. Clips called Bridge1 and River1 are in a folder called Video.

Editing video clips can be great fun. Editing can be used to remove the sections of the clip you do not need and to build several clips into a longer video. Movie Maker will allow you to add titles, sounds and music and then produce a video using them all.

This section will lead you through the process of producing a short video. All the clips and images you need are on the CD. A final example of a movie made with them is also on the CD.

ACTIVITY

Play the final video from the CD.
Follow through the directions in this section to have a go yourself.

Stage 1: Loading the files

The first stage is to set up a project and import the files you need. You are going to import the files River1 and Bridge1 together with an image.

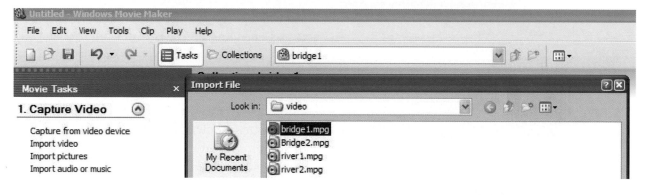

■ Figure 10.46

Choose Import video to load the videos from the CD. Do this for both videos, then choose Import pictures and add the picture Image 075(0).jpg.

■ Figure 10.47

When you have finished, the screen should look like Figure 10.47 with the three objects on the screen ready to be used.

ACTIVITY

Load the images as shown ready for use.

Stage 2: The storyboard

The storyboard is the area at the bottom of the screen where you can assemble the clips and images in the order that you intend to use them. You simply drag them into the frames on the storyboard.

■ **Figure 10.48**

The picture of the Westminster Clock Tower is first, followed by the bridge clip and then the river clip.

Stage 3: The timeline

This shows the length of time each event lasts and enables you to adjust the length of the clips by trimming the beginnings and endings if needed. It shows the music and sound tracks for the final video.

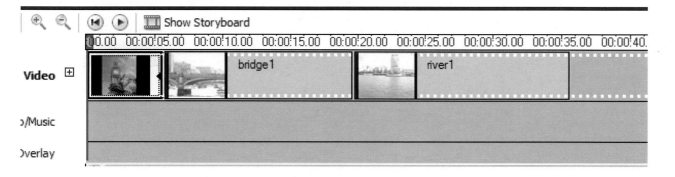

■ **Figure 10.49**

To adjust a clip, click on the beginning or the ending of the clip and drag the cursor to the new point on the time scale.

Stage 4: Adding the titles

From the side menu choose Add Title. The first title on the blue background is made by clicking on Add title before the movie. Once added, the length can be adjusted using the timeline.

Stage 5: Changing the sound

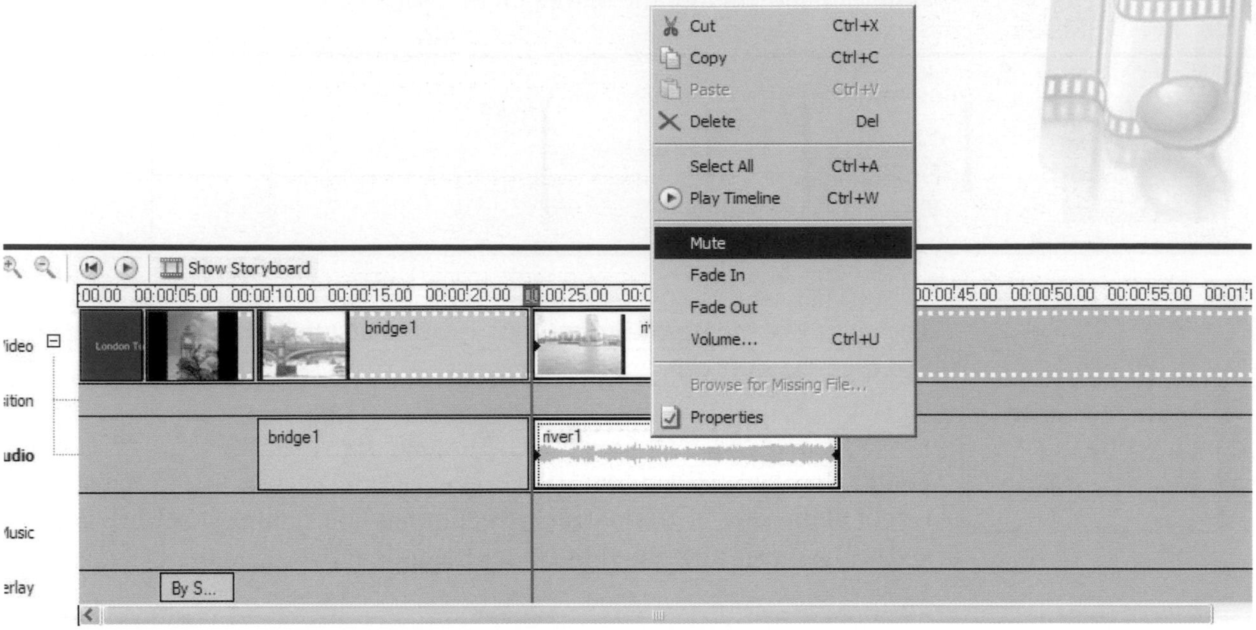

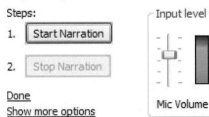

Figure 10.50

ACTIVITY

Mute the sound on each clip.

The original sound on the videos is just background noise so we are going to mute the sound for each clip. Select the clip and then right click. Choose Mute from the menu.

Stage 6: Recording the narration

Narrate Timeline

Drag the playback indicator on the timeline to an empty point on the Audio/Music track, click Start Narration, and begin your narration.

Steps:

1. Start Narration

2. Stop Narration

Done

Show more options

Input level

Mic Volume

Learn more about narrating the timeline

Figure 10.51

Start the narration by placing the timeline cursor at the start of the Bridge1 video then click on Record. Watch the timeline move as you record your narration. If you get it wrong do not panic; press stop, do not save it, then start again. When you have finished the narration, play the video back to hear what it sounds like.

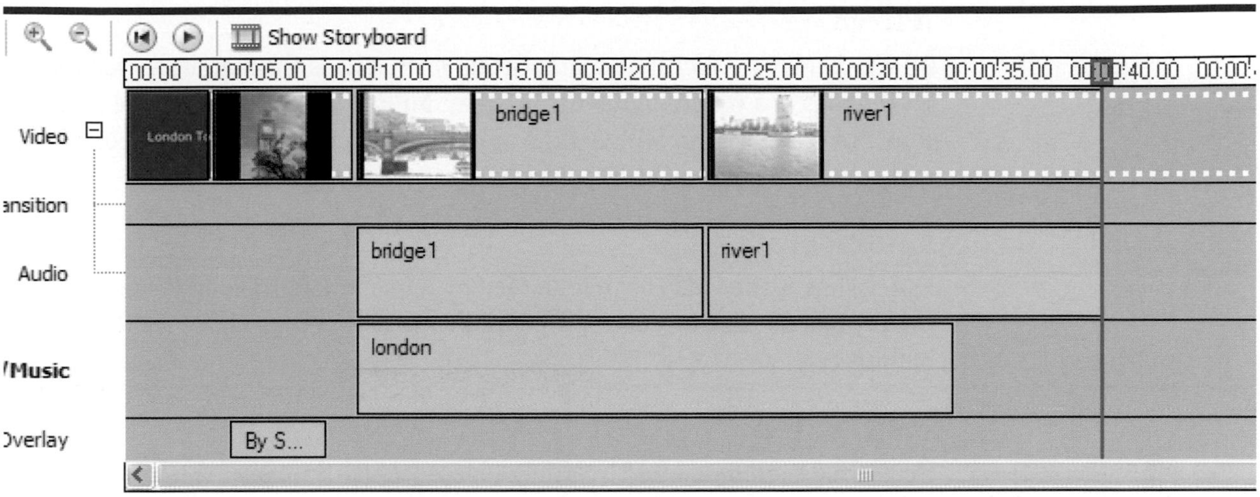

[Timeline interface]

Show Storyboard

| 00.00 | 00:00:05.00 | 00:00:10.00 | 00:00:15.00 | 00:00:20.00 | 00:00:25.00 | 00:00:30.00 | 00:00:35.00 | 00:00:40.00 | 00:00: |

Video — London T... / bridge1 / river1

ansition

Audio — bridge1 / river1

'Music — london

Overlay — By S...

■ **Figure 10.52** The final timeline showing the completed movie

Stage 7: Recording the movie

In the Finish Movie section of the menu there are several choices. You are going to save your video to 'My Computer'. Select the option to give your movie a name and then wait while the movie is recorded as a file. Depending on the power of your computer and the length of the video, this can take some time.

 Each of the above activities is demonstrated on a 'How to' video on the CD.
   If you are not sure what to do, watch the 'How to' video. They were all made using Movie Maker.

Using appropriate file formats

There are several video formats which all have their own particular uses. In the end, you need to choose the one which gives you the best quality within the storage capacity available to you.

AVI

There are numerous AVI file formats. They all make use of CODECs (COmpressor/DECompressors) to make the file size smaller. They compress the video by reducing the frame size from 720×480 pixels to 240×160 pixels. They also reduce the number of frames per second and change the colour, contrast and intensity.

File sizes are reduced, but so is the quality. Sometimes a video cannot be viewed because the user does not have the same CODEC as was used to encode the file.

MPEG-1

MPEG-1 (Moving Picture Experts Group format 1) is an industry standard. It has a frame size of 352×240 pixels. At this size it uses about 10 megabytes for each minute of video, so a typical CD can hold about 1 hour of video.

MPEG-2

MPEG-2 (Moving Picture Experts Group format 2) is the standard used for DVD and is of a much higher quality than MPEG-1. The file sizes are three to four times larger than MPEG-1, i.e. 40 megabytes per minute of video. A DVD can contain 2 hours of MPEG-2 video.

QuickTime

QuickTime is the video format devised by Apple. It is flexible in terms of quality and file sizes. A player for QuickTime videos is available for the PC platform.

Real video

Real video is intended for streaming videos in real-time over the Internet. The viewer will download the first section of the video and begin to watch whilst the remainder is downloading in the background. Real video can give high quality at large window sizes with relatively small file sizes. File size varies according to the quality and size chosen at the time the file is created.

Windows Media Format (WMF)

WMF is a Windows format for streaming videos. It gives high quality audio and video. The file size can be varied according to the size and quality of the video.

Sound

Aims

- To learn how to record live sound
- To learn how to edit and manipulate sound

Introduction

Sound recording has been around for many years more than video. Sound can be recorded in a variety of ways. In this unit, we are looking at recording directly to the computer.

In this unit, you need to use sound clips that you have captured and edited yourself and make use of them in your final product.

 On the CD is a piece of software called Audacity for sound editing.

For assessment purposes, you must be able to capture (record) sound yourself as well as make use of some ready-made sound clips. To help you with this, there is a piece of software called Audacity on the CD which will allow you to record and edit sounds in many interesting ways. You will need the software and a microphone to complete this section.

If you use ready-made sound clips, you will need to check the copyright and acknowledge your sources as part of your standard ways of working.

Recording live sound

This section will demonstrate how to record sound using Audacity and a microphone.

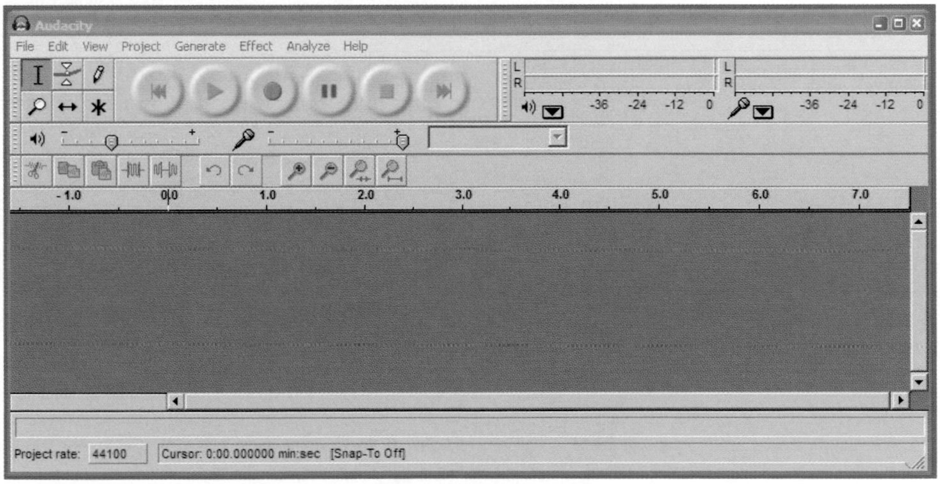

Figure 10.53

Figure 10.53 shows the empty window for Audacity. There are buttons at the top for the basic play and record functions. To record a sound with the microphone, press the record button. Do not worry if you make a mistake – you can delete or edit the sound later. Each time you press record, a new channel is opened and the recording starts on that channel.

Once you have recorded the sound, press play to listen to the sound.

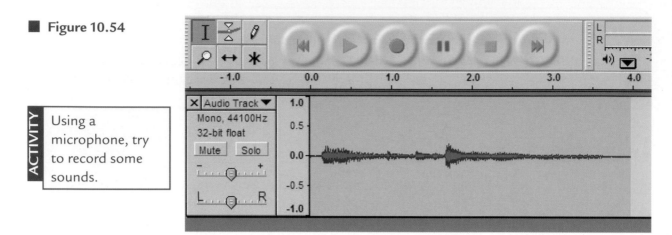

Using a microphone, try to record some sounds.

Figure 10.54 shows the wave pattern of a recorded sound. In this case, it is a piano playing.

Importing pre-recorded sound

There is a selection of sounds recorded using a microphone on the CD in a folder called Sound. In this section you will import the sounds ready for editing in the next section.

■ Figure 10.55

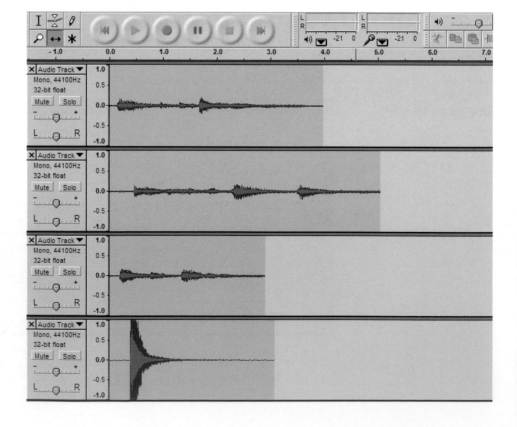

Open Audacity and from the project menu choose Import Audio. Navigate to the CD folder and import the file Piano1.wav from the disk. The screen should look like Figure 10.54.

Repeat this until you have loaded the following sounds:

▶ Piano2.wav
▶ Piano3.wav
▶ Cymbals.wav.

Your final screen should look like Figure 10.55.

Now try the play button. All four tracks will play together and it should sound terrible! This is because all the tracks are playing simultaneously and they need to be organised by editing.

Cutting and editing

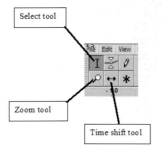

■ **Figure 10.56**

In order to make the sounds you have imported into a better-sounding piece of music you need to use editing techniques to build up a final piece which you will then save to disk.

To do this, you are going to use the tools at the top left of the screen.

The tools you will use are the select tool and the time shift tool. You might also need the zoom tool to help place the sounds more accurately.

Choose the select tool. Then drag the sound wave on the second sound track to the right to line up with end of the first sound. This will provide a rough alignment of the tracks – you will adjust it later.

■ **Figure 10.57**

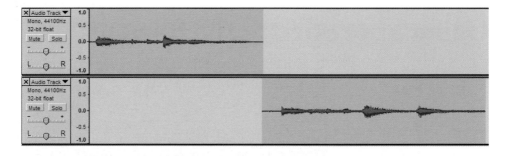

Now repeat this with the other sounds until the screen looks like Figure 10.58.

■ **Figure 10.58**

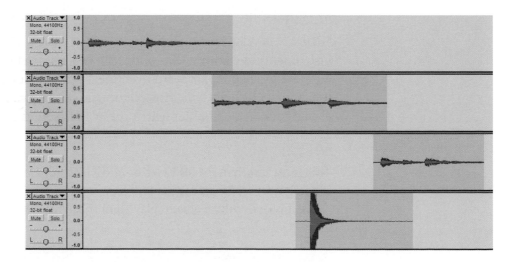

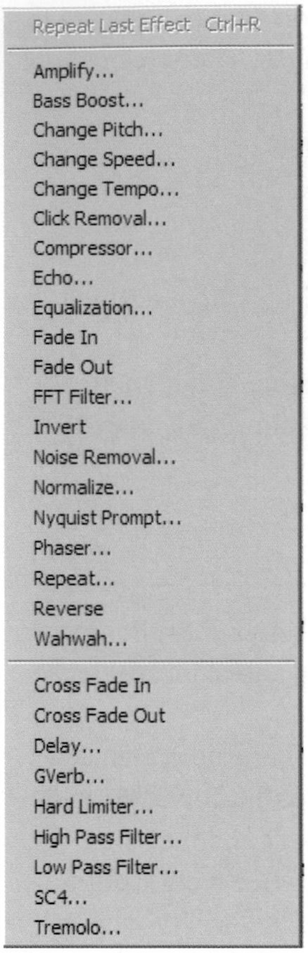
Repeat Last Effect Ctrl+R
Amplify...
Bass Boost...
Change Pitch...
Change Speed...
Change Tempo...
Click Removal...
Compressor...
Echo...
Equalization...
Fade In
Fade Out
FFT Filter...
Invert
Noise Removal...
Normalize...
Nyquist Prompt...
Phaser...
Repeat...
Reverse
Wahwah...
Cross Fade In
Cross Fade Out
Delay...
GVerb...
Hard Limiter...
High Pass Filter...
Low Pass Filter...
SC4...
Tremolo...

■ **Figure 10.59**

Now try playing the sound. You might need to move the tracks about a bit to make the final product sound OK. You can listen to the finished product by playing the file Music james1.wav on the CD.

Once a sound has been recorded digitally, it can be manipulated using the computer to make changes to the sound. The menu in Figure 10.59 shows some of the things that can be done with the sounds.

The best way to find out what these effects can do is to try them out for yourself. Highlight, with the Select tool, all or part of a track and try making some changes. For example, load up cymbals1 and reverse the sound track.

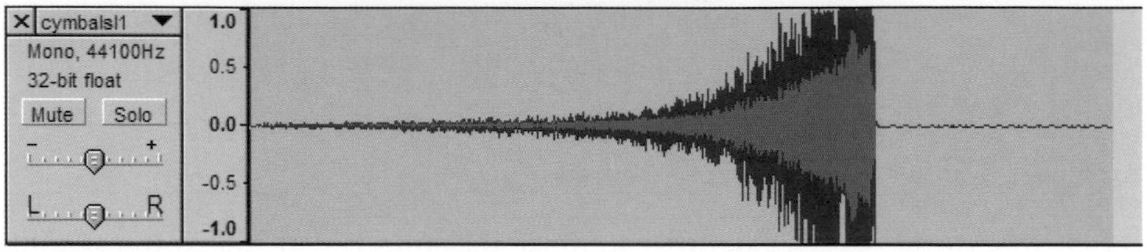
cymbals1
Mono, 44100Hz
32-bit float
Mute
Solo
L
R
1.0
0.5
0.0
-0.5
-1.0

■ **Figure 10.60**

Try playing it back and listen to the new effect created.

All of the activities described in this unit are available as 'How to' videos on the CD.

Using appropriate file formats

As with video, sound files can be stored in a variety of formats – some are compressed and some are not.

WAV

Files ending in .wav are stored in an uncompressed format. This was originated by Microsoft. It can store sound with varying sample levels. The files can be quite large.

MIDI

MIDI was developed as an industry standard protocol that allows electronic instruments to communicate with each other and with computers. A MIDI interface will allow a keyboard to connect to a computer or another keyboard. It is not strictly a file type. However music can be saved in MIDI format and played back on a computer with a compatible sound card.

MP3

This is an acronym for MPEG-1 or MPEG-2 audio layer 3. MP3 is the file extension for a compressed sound file.

Most people will be able to play all of these file types on their computers.

Using compression and codecs

Audio compression is used for a number of reasons including:

- reducing file size so that more audio files will fit on a particular medium
- reducing file size so that files will download from the web faster
- reducing data rate so that files will stream over the Internet.

Compressed audio files vary in size and quality depending on five settings:

- sample rate
- bit depth
- number of channels – stereo, mono, surround sound or multi-channel
- choice of audio compression codec
- audio compression codec settings.

Animation

Aims

- To learn about the different types of animation that are possible
- To produce an animated GIF from images

Have you ever drawn pictures in the corners of a book? Making the pictures slightly differently from one page to the next creates the effect of a moving image when flipping through them with your thumb. An animation is produced from a series of still frames that are put together in a sequence to give the effect of movement. There are many software packages available that will help in producing animations.

Stop frame animation

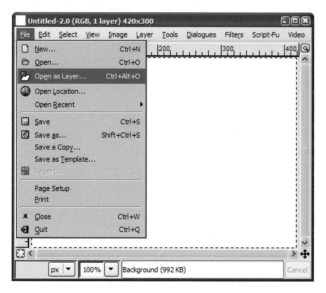

■ Figure 10.61

 On the CD is a folder called animation2.

Sometimes called 'stop motion' animation, this is the kind of animation used in the Wallace and Gromit films. In these animations, the models are moved in small incremental changes. A camera takes one frame at a time. The animator adjusts the figure, then the camera takes another. Industry standard animations use 25 frames per second (fps), making movement appear 'natural'. One minute of animation needs about 1500 stills. That's why it takes years to produce a film like Wallace and Gromit.

Load the web page called **animation**. The animation was created from the 57 still images of the London Eye in the folder called frames. The only difference between this and real stop frame is that the wheel moved itself! The animation was created by loading each image as a new layer into GIMP and then saving it as a GIF file. GIMP recognises the layers and creates the animated GIF for you using a wizard.

ACTIVITY

Using GIMP and files on the CD try to create your own animation.

Tweened animation

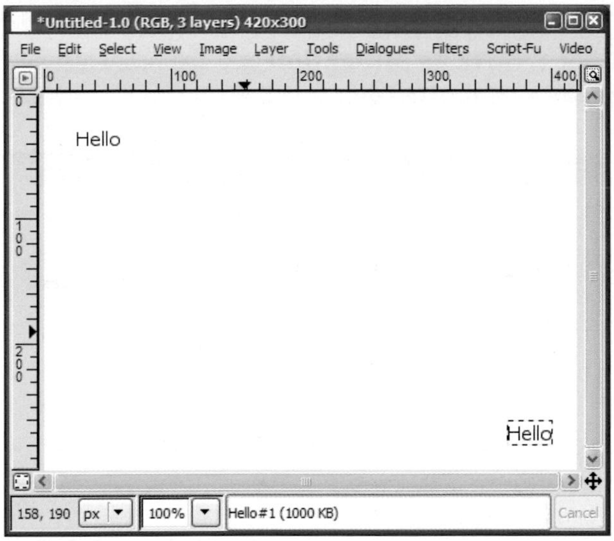

Figure 10.62

Figure 10.63

This is a made-up word to describe a technique of creating animation using a computer and software to fill in frames.

An animation is created by taking two different frames (called keyframes). These are positioned on the screen in the start and finish positions and the software automatically creates additional frames between them. When the frames are played back you have an animation.

To do this using GIMP:

1 On the first layer, place the word 'hello'.
2 Create another layer with the word 'hello' on it but at the opposite corner. You now have something like Figure 10.62.
3 On the video menu, choose the move path option and define the movement path as shown in Figure 10.63.

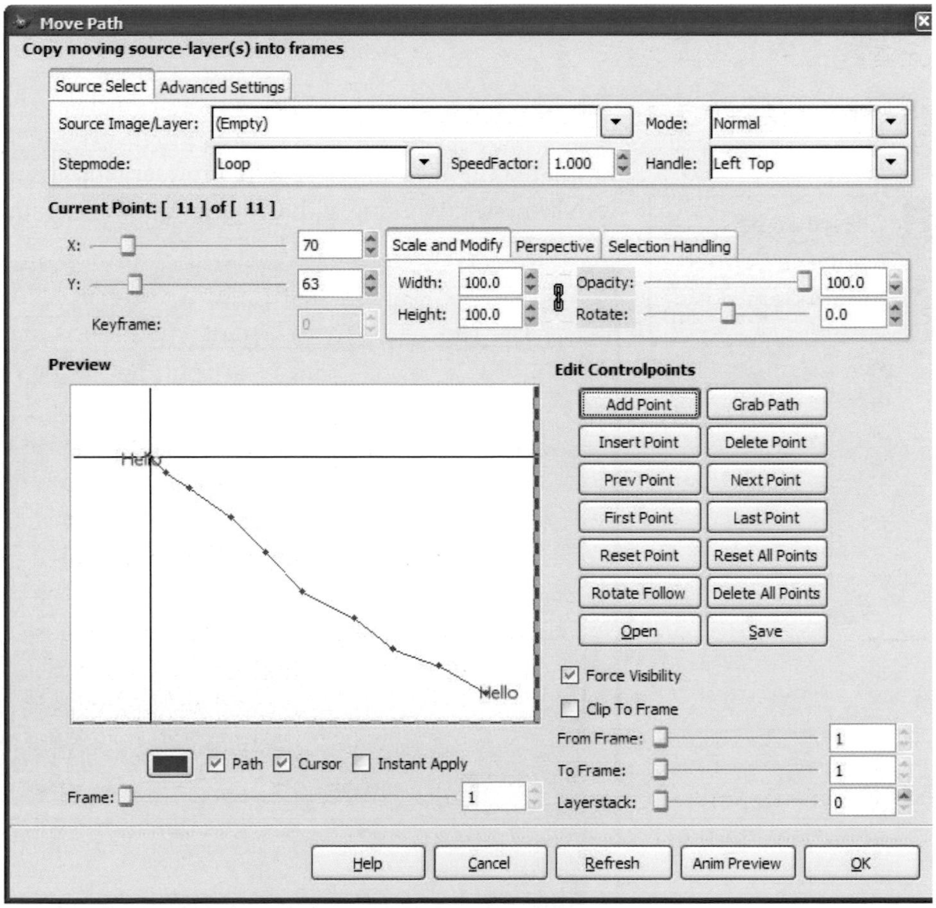

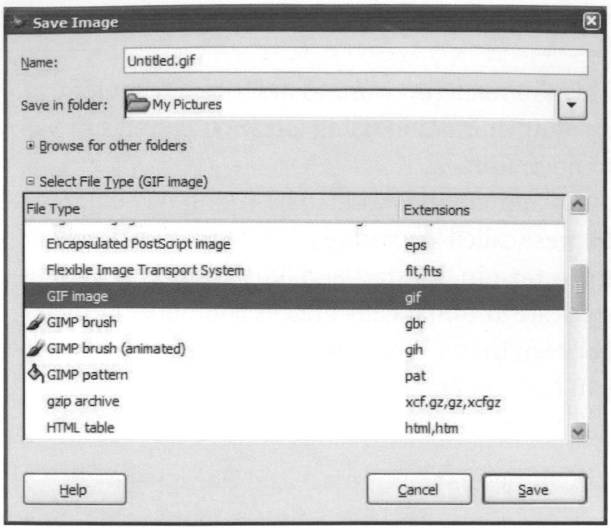

Figure 10.64

On the CD, the final GIF can be seen on the page helloanim.htm in the folder animation2.

4 Return to the image and choose save – select the GIF option.

This will bring up the GIF animation option. Choose **Save as Animation** and Export. This will create an animated gif.

Figure 10.65

Animated GIF files

ACTIVITY

Create a GIF using the Script-fu function.

Animated GIF files do not require browser plug-ins, so they are accessible to all web browsers. Working with GIF animation files requires no extra programming

Figure 10.66

expertise – they are inserted just like a static image. Animated GIF files can be made to loop, to play only once, or to play a fixed number of times.

You can create animated GIFs in GIMP by creating each element in a different layer. When you have all the layers in place, you then save as a GIF animation in the same way as before.

Alternatively GIMP can create some animation effects from a still image. To do this, load up any image and choose **Script-fu Animators**. This will allow you to create a range of interesting effects automatically.

User interface

Aims

■ To reinforce the previous discussion on user interface

Previous units on design have already looked at aspects of the user interface. The purpose of this unit is to serve as a checklist before you finalise your product.

Using a consistent layout

As previously mentioned in Unit 10.5, good products have a consistent layout. This includes:

► a colour scheme that is coordinated
► menus in the same place on each screen
► a logo, if used is placed on each page
► navigation buttons, if used, are in the same area of each screen
► a limited range of fonts.

Using graphics to illustrate a message

Graphics can be used instead of words for a variety of reasons:

► To save space.
► To make the product attractive to young children.
► For consistency.
► To avoid clutter.
► To improve visual appearance.

Adding prompts or messages to help users find their way around

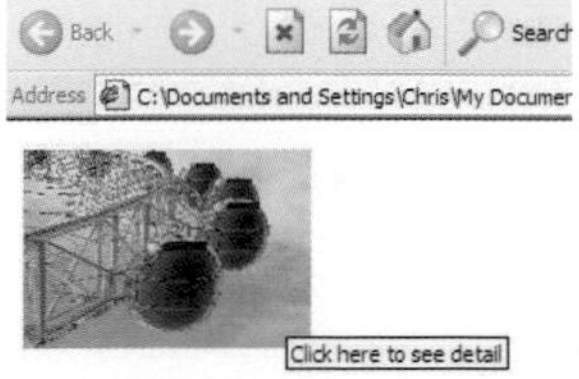

During development, popup messages such as the one shown in Figure 10.67 can be used to help the user to navigate around the package. When the mouse pointer is hovered over the image of the wheel a message pops up to indicate what the user can do. Little touches like this can make your product much easier to use.

■ Figure 10.67

Using interactivity features to allow users to initiate certain procedures

If you want people to be attracted to your product, you need interactivity. This can be as simple or as complicated as you want. An interactive element is a way for the user of your product to make things happen on screen.

There are several ways you can achieve this:

▶ hyperlinks in text
▶ buttons
▶ rollover images
▶ images that are hot spots
▶ image maps.

Testing

Aims

- To emphasise the importance of testing
- To look at strategies for testing

portfolio_tip

Testing is often the poorest section of work done by students for assessment. Plan your testing carefully and follow a plan to ensure that your multimedia product is completely tested.

Testing is one of the most important stages in the development of a product. All software should be tested before the user is given the final product. All possible outcomes must be tested so you should plan carefully how you will test the product. When testing make sure that you test all aspects of your product, not just the links and menus. You should test that multimedia components appear as designed and function correctly.

Does the product meet all the requirements listed in the functional specification?

ACTIVITY

Devise a questionnaire for the users of the multimedia product to collect their opinions of the solution.

At the start of the development process, a functional specification was drawn up. This needs to be looked at again during the testing process to ensure that all the aims and objectives have been met. You should try to involve the user in this part of the testing to answer the question, 'Does the product do what you expected?' It is often difficult to test the product under real conditions, but every effort should be made to do this if possible: perhaps testing it on a different specification of machine.

The final product should be reviewed carefully alongside the original specification. Feedback from the user might mean changing a few things at this stage, but it is better to make changes before the product is released. Consider which aims have been met and the extent to which they have been met. Are there any aims that have not or could not be met?

Do all the interactive features work correctly?

Testing the navigation system in an extensive multimedia product can be very repetitive but each option needs to be tested. Can the user navigate the structure efficiently or are there dead links? Every menu should have a way to reach the menu above, if there is one, and the main menu.

portfolio_tip

At some point during final testing, copy the product to a CD and try to run it from the CD. If it fails it could be that you have linked to something on your PC and forgotten about it. The product must be self-contained.

During the design of the product, a map of the menu structure should have been drawn up. This should be used to check the route through all the menus to make sure nothing has been missed out.

Does every link go where it should, with no dead-ends?

portfolio_tip

When you have a complete product copy it to CD and test it on another system, that way you will know that the product is self-contained and is not relying on items in your network area or development system.

Every link should work and every page should have a route back. Check that this is so. The user should not be left down a dead end with no way back. Use the menu plan from the initial design to check the actual structure. If your product works in a web browser then you should not simply rely on the forward and back buttons for navigation. The navigation should be built in to your product.

Is the product robust or can it be made to fail?

It is easy to say a product works well if you test what you already know works. During testing, you should set out to try and make the product fail, by trying to do unexpected things. For example try shutting down a video in the middle – do you go back to a point where you can still see the menu?

Can other people use the product without help?

portfolio_tip

Produce prototypes as you go along and get feedback along the way. Do not leave it all until the end or there will be too much to do.

The best way to see how easy a system is to use is to test it out on others. Someone who has not seen your multimedia product before should try it out to see how easy it is to use. Feedback on ease of use can then be looked at to review the product. It is often the case that someone else will see issues that you as the designer did not see because you are so familiar with the whole thing. It is a bit like spotting your own spelling mistakes.

Try to find some people who will match the profile of the end user and ask them to review your product.

For the assessment, you are required to involve others in the testing and evaluation process and to use that feedback to modify your product.

Distribution

Aims

- To examine issues surrounding the distribution of your product
- To consider different ways of distributing your product

The specification requires that you create a multimedia product that is self-contained and that your eportfolio must be capable of being viewed in a web browser.

You will also need to make sure that all the necessary files are contained on the media you use to distribute the product.

As you have seen in the preceding units, multimedia files can take up lots of space. This is particularly true for video content and this can place constraints on the format you use for distribution.

Software

You have created your multimedia product using specialised software. It is quite possible that your target users will not have this software available to run the product. Products like GIMP and Audacity use their own file formats to save files, unless you switch to a recognised format. Make sure that you choose formats that are universal when saving files from these products. Guidance on this was given in the relevant units.

Run time version

This is the final version of your product, which is completely self-contained. All pages, images and videos should be organised so that nothing is linked out to a folder left on your PC.

The safest way to produce files that are universally readable is in a format that can be read into browser software such as Internet Explorer or Netscape Navigator. All computers that have the capability to run multimedia will then be able to access your product.

It is likely that the product is going to need a lot of storage space so think about the medium you are going to use. For assessment, it will need to go onto a CD, so you should have tested it on one during your development and testing.

Instructions for users

To access the higher marks, as part of the distribution pack for your product, you need to have comprehensive instructions that demonstrate how to get started with your product. The instructions should enable a novice user to install and use the product.

Evaluation

Aims

- To examine the success of the software product
- To examine personal performance in the production of the product

portfolio_tip

Make sure you refer to your own skills and development in the evaluation.

In the course of this unit, you should have produced a multimedia software product that someone else can use. You should have gone through all the usual planning stages that software developers use when they are producing solutions professionally. You should have designed and developed a multimedia product and documented it for the user. At the same time as producing this solution, you will have been learning new skills and processes. For the purpose of this unit, you should have been paying attention to your own performance, to see if you have been making the best use of your time.

The product

This will have been produced to fulfil the requirements of a user. It will have involved a lot of liaison with the user or other person who requires the multimedia product. This stage will have ended with the production of a functional specification – a document that sets out what the product must do.

When the product is complete, it is necessary to go back to the functional specification and ask whether the requirements have been met. You, the developer, should ask yourself that before handing over the software to the client or user.

If, for example, the solution is supposed to contain a slide show with a musical background, you need to verify that it does indeed have this.

You should also ask whether the solution is a good one, does it make the best use of the multimedia facilities available to you and is it of the best quality? You should ask yourself whether the same or better results could have been achieved by using a different approach. Have you made the product too complicated?

Your performance

You should consider how well you tackled this unit. Ask yourself what you can now do compared with when you started. How did you find out the things you needed to know? Did you consult:

- teachers
- websites
- the software help system
- books?

Did your research show you pointers about how you can best find things out in the future? Did you encounter many dead ends that you will be able to avoid?

The assessment

The evaluation stage of a project like this one is a good time to look at what you have produced in terms of what needs to be produced for assessment.
  The specification says:

> For this unit you will produce:
>
> ● A runtime version of a fully working multimedia product with instructions for users.

Check that this is in fact what you did. You must have used multimedia objects in your system. There must be some evidence of things like videos, sounds and images in your product.

> Your eportfolio for this unit should include:
>
> **a** A functional specification which describes the context, purpose and audience for your product. You will need to describe in detail the product and set out clear measurable success criteria.

Right at the beginning of the project, the functional specification should be clearly set out, quite possibly as a set of bullet points. These will form the basis for your final evaluation of the product.

> **b** A design for the product that meets the functional requirements and makes good use of multimedia design. It needs to include different multimedia components both ready made and some you made yourself. You will also need evidence of prototype solutions, which have been evaluated and improved on.
>
> There should be evidence of your use of prototyping to improve and refine the design.

Check that there is evidence that your designs closely match what the client wants. Does the solution make proper use of multimedia?

> **c** A runtime version of a fully working multimedia product with instructions for users.

There should be plenty of screen shots showing the product in use. Your solution must be documented for the user. Your actual product ready to run should also be in your portfolio.

> **d** Evidence of formative and summative testing.

> **e** An evaluation assessing:
>   ● the multimedia
>   ● your own performance and current skill level and identifying areas for improvement.

UNIT 11
Using spreadsheet software

Spreadsheet applications

Aims

- ■ To introduce Unit 11
- ■ To examine uses for spreadsheets

Introduction

This is an optional unit which is user focused. It is intended for students who would like to develop higher level skills in spreadsheet design and production by designing and testing a complex spreadsheet. In Unit 3 you used a complex spreadsheet to help reach a decision based on information you had been given and data in a spreadsheet model. In this unit, you will develop your skills further and use similar complex techniques to create a spreadsheet that will help someone else. You will be assessed on your ability to design, produce and evaluate a complex spreadsheet. You might like to use this unit as a focus for Unit 8 – Managing ICT projects. If you do, remember that you are completing two portfolios and will need to plan your time accordingly.

You will be testing and making sure that the spreadsheets you create are reliable and will produce accurate information in all circumstances. When a user enters data into any system the potential for data entry errors exists. Humans often make mistakes. The phrase 'garbage in, garbage out' applies to spreadsheets as well as to any other computer system. If a user enters incorrect data, then the result of the processing will be incorrect. A good spreadsheet design will allow for future proofing. For example, if VAT is calculated by your spreadsheet, there should be an easy way for the user to alter the rate should the government change it. You should seek and make use of feedback from others to help you in your work.

Assessment evidence

For this unit, you will design, produce, test and evaluate a complex spreadsheet to meet a set of functional requirements that fulfil the user requirements for a scenario you will be given.

Your work will be assessed on the following evidence:

a A functional specification which describes the context, the problem and explains what the spreadsheet is required to do.
b An initial design that fulfils the functional requirements. You will need to describe the data to be entered and the processing that is required. There should be adequate measures to ensure that the data is structured and

validated so as to prevent common data entry errors. Functions and formulae must both be included to analyse some complex data. Your design should consider screen layout and presentation to make the spreadsheet easier to use. Your design must include a user interface and presentation of results. There must also be evidence showing that you used prototyping to improve and refine the design.

c A fully working spreadsheet solution that meets all the functional requirements, together with user and technical documentation.

d Evidence of testing the spreadsheet, both formative and summative.

e An evaluation which measures the success of the spreadsheet and your own performance and skills.

Uses of spreadsheets

Spreadsheets can be used in many different ways and this unit sets out some examples that may help you.

Modelling

Using spreadsheets for computer modelling allows the user to enter data and a set of rules, and then look at how changing the data or the rules affects the situation. A computer model of the Livewires budget, for example, might show that if extra staff are hired, the firm will run out of money before the end of the year.

CASE STUDY

Livewires wants to know, if it reduces the price of its stock and sales increase by 10% as a result, will it make more money?

Using a spreadsheet, it can vary the data in the Price column and the data in the Income column will automatically be recalculated. Then when the data in the Number sold column is adjusted, the Income data will again be recalculated.

Of course they could always just go ahead and change the prices and see what happens, but then if it was wrong it might be out of business. Using a model is a good idea because there are no risks involved and you can change things as often as you like.

Advantages of spreadsheets for modelling include:

▶ You can make alterations and quickly see the outcomes.
▶ You can repeat tests as often as you like.
▶ You can look at 'what if?' scenarios.
▶ You can model dangerous situations safely.

In addition to financial modelling, spreadsheet software can be used for many other kinds of model:

▶ Modelling the stresses which will be borne by a new building
▶ Modelling traffic flow in a new road system
▶ Modelling coastal erosion.

Statistical analysis

The analysis of numbers often involves the production of statistics. Many organisations perceive the need to analyse statistics – not that statistics are always right but they can help find trends in data.

Spreadsheets have many functions built in to help with generating statistics including:

▶ average
▶ maximum
▶ minimum
▶ standard deviation.

In addition to functions, pivot tables, graphs and charts can also be used for statistical analysis.

An examination body is analysing the way that two questions performed in an examination. They want to find out if candidates who scored high marks in Question 2 also scored high marks in Question 3.

	A	B
1	Score Question 2	Score Question 3
2	3	8
3	15	5
4	7	8
5	9	3
6	15	22
7	12	4
8	3	3
9	13	17
10	7	14
11	15	22

 Figure 11.1

The marks for 200 candidates are entered into a simple spreadsheet. Looking at the marks in the columns does not provide any meaningful information. So a chart called a scatter graph is produced.

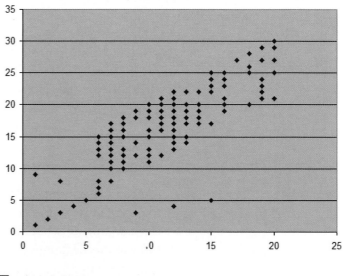

 Figure 11.2

The graph plots the marks for Question 2 against the marks for Question 3. Looking at the graph shows that apart from a few candidates there is a relationship between the two questions.

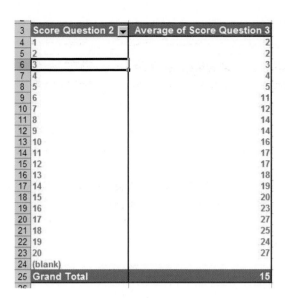

	Score Question 2 ▼	Average of Score Question 3
3		
4	1	2
5	2	2
6	3	3
7	4	4
8	5	5
9	6	11
10	7	12
11	8	14
12	9	14
13	10	16
14	11	17
15	12	17
16	13	18
17	14	19
18	15	20
19	16	23
20	17	27
21	18	25
22	19	24
23	20	27
24	(blank)	
25	Grand Total	15

■ **Figure 11.3**

A pivot table can be produced that shows each possible mark for Question 2 and the average score on Question 3 for candidates with that mark. The candidates who scored 8 on Question 2 on average scored 14 on Question 3. This confirms that there is a relationship between the two questions.

Cost-benefit analysis

Cost-benefit analysis is used to see how good or bad a planned action might turn out to be. Although a cost-benefit analysis can be used for almost anything, it is normally used on financial questions. Generally speaking in the world of business, if you spend money on something then benefits must result otherwise it is not worth spending the money.

> **CASE STUDY**
>
> Livewires is thinking about longer opening hours for its new retail store. The big question is – should Livewires hire additional sales staff or have existing staff work overtime? The salary figures can be put into a spreadsheet and the likely costs worked out. The benefits in terms of increased sales and profit can also be calculated. Additional running costs such as electricity and heating can also be included. This sounds simple, but there are many other factors that the computer simulation cannot take into account, such as: are the staff willing to work overtime, what effect will it have on their work–life balance, and will the extra pressure of working longer hours result in more sick leave?

Simulation

On the CD is a spreadsheet called Dice simulation.

Simulation refers to a method of analysis that attempts to imitate a real-life system. Without simulation, a spreadsheet model will only reveal one outcome based on the figures in the spreadsheet. The Monte Carlo method is one type of spreadsheet simulation; numbers are randomly generated to represent uncertain variables over and over again to simulate a real-life situation.

ACTIVITY

Load the spreadsheet called Dice simulation. Look at the formulae used for the simulation.

One classic example is to simulate the rolling of a die to look at the probability of a particular number being obtained. One way would be to roll a die say 100 times, write down the number each time then count them up and produce a chart of the results. This is obviously time-consuming and tedious. Using the Monte Carlo method, 100 random numbers can be generated between 1 and 6 and the spreadsheet can count the values and produce the chart in seconds. This leaves you free to analyse the results.

Figure 11.4 shows how a spreadsheet can be used in the above situation.

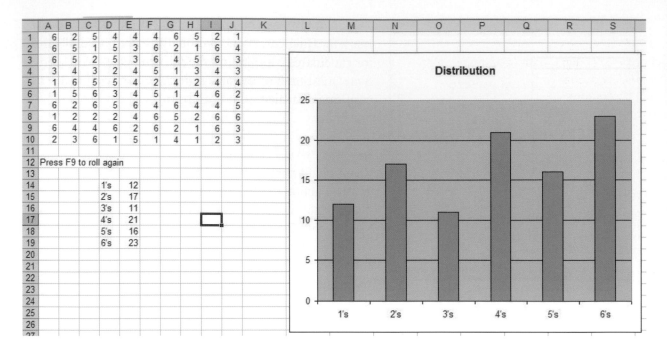

	A	B	C	D	E	F	G	H	I	J
1	6	2	5	4	4	4	6	5	2	1
2	6	5	1	5	3	6	2	1	6	4
3	6	5	2	5	3	6	4	5	6	3
4	3	4	3	2	4	5	1	3	4	3
5	1	6	5	5	4	2	4	2	4	4
6	1	5	6	3	4	5	1	4	6	2
7	6	2	6	5	6	4	6	4	4	5
8	1	2	2	2	4	6	5	2	6	6
9	6	4	4	6	2	6	2	1	6	3
10	2	3	6	1	5	1	4	1	2	3
11										
12	Press F9 to roll again									
13										
14				1's	12					
15				2's	17					
16				3's	11					
17				4's	21					
18				5's	16					
19				6's	23					

Figure 11.4

Forecasting

Forecasting is a process of using existing and historical data to try to forecast future events and trends. It is often used in the business world to predict cash flow. By analysing the cash flow, a business can plan for loans to be available, or money to be set aside for seasonal variations in sales. Forecasts help build a picture of the way in which cash moves within an organisation.

Budgeting

Budgeting is the process of predicting and controlling the spending of money within an organisation. Depending on the level of detail, budgeting can be taken over different periods of time ranging from day-to-day monitoring to annual budgeting.

Spreadsheets can be used to calculate the cost of a major purchase over a number of years, and calculate the impact of overheads on the running of a business.

Planning

All businesses need to have a business plan which describes the business, its aims, and its financial forecasts. It is used as a way of measuring the success of a business and for obtaining external funding.

As part of a plan, the business will need to have a set of financial forecasts which gives an indication of how the finances are expected to look over the next

17	
18	Premises (rent, rates)
19	Power (light, heat, electricity, gas)
20	Telephone
21	Insurance
22	Postage and carriage
23	Interest and bank charges payable
24	Stationery
25	Drawings, wages, or salary
26	Equipment hire
27	Motor expenses
28	Accountancy fees
29	Legal/professional fees
30	Depreciation

■ **Figure 11.5**

three to five years. The level of detail depends on the size and experience within the business. Ideally the first year's planning should have the most detail. The following years might have less detail as less is known about the future.

Spreadsheet design

The inputs into the system and the methods used to validate it

When studying a spreadsheet you need to look carefully at the inputs to the system. Data can be entered into a spreadsheet in several ways, and not just by entering a number directly into a cell. Data can be entered using forms, dialogue boxes, from other programs via links, using scroll bars and spinners. You will examine some of these ways in later units.

All data entered into a complex spreadsheet should be validated in some way. You will look at validation methods in Unit 11.3.

The processing that takes place

The purpose of entering data into a spreadsheet is to process that data and produce useful information. Processing takes a variety of forms. You will be expected to use different techniques in your spreadsheet such as formulae, functions, lookup tables and charts. These techniques are described in later units.

How information is presented

The final presentation of information in a spreadsheet should match the requirements of the user. You will see in later units a variety of ways that presentation can be enhanced using colour and formatting.

Functional specification

Aims

■ To examine the importance of a functional specification

■ To examine what needs to be included in a functional specification

Introduction

Often, when we need a solution to a problem that involves using a spreadsheet, we simply go to the computer, fire up Excel and get to work. We try things out this way and that and often we end up with something that will do the job. This is all well and good if the solution is just for yourself or the job is an easy one. The plan of this book was made by entering the units and sub-headings onto a spreadsheet, plus notes about who was going to write what and what resources could be useful on the CD. The spreadsheet design needed no planning – it was basically making a list and a spreadsheet is great for that because you can re-order things and sort them and add extra ideas.

Often though, a spreadsheet is used to tackle a more complex job. It is set up in such a way that it is effectively a new application. It may also be set up for other people to use, so if there are flaws in it, this could be very annoying for them. When this is the case, it is much safer to plan what the spreadsheet is going to do and how it is going to do it. An initial overview can help to clarify some general plans that will make the finished product more organised, easier to produce, more pleasant to use and easier to maintain.

This starting point is called the functional specification. This sets out what the finished product must do. Without this, it will be impossible later on to decide to what extent you have succeeded. You need to keep this in mind all the time while you are developing your spreadsheet so that you do not go off at a tangent and produce something that isn't needed.

Another reason why a functional specification is valuable is that you can use it to communicate your plans to others. It can form the basis of discussions with potential users so that they are clear about what it is you are producing and they can comment on whether the product will be useful to them.

If you are using this unit alongside Unit 8 – Managing ICT projects, then you will need to present your functional specification to the project board for approval. As a result of this communication, the form of the functional specification may change over time. This is normal and means that the document can provide a useful means of making sure that the client and the developer always understand each other.

We shall now consider the functional specification needed to produce a useful system for the Livewires company that we met in earlier units.

The context

The first thing that is necessary to understand is the context in which the solution will work. It is no use making an impressive spreadsheet solution to a problem if you do not take an overview of the company and the situation in question.

IT solutions do not exist in a vacuum. They are produced in order to solve a real-world problem. If they are produced in a business context, they will need to be directed towards the aims of the business. The best software developers never lose track of what their creations are for. To this end, the best software developers are able and willing to communicate effectively with their clients so that they always address their needs.

> **CASE STUDY**
>
> Livewires is a company that installs computer networks. The core of their activities has been on a business to business basis for many years. They conduct surveys of clients' premises and analyse the computer networking problems or potential they have. They design network solutions and install them, using their specialist teams of network engineers.
>
> Recently, it also opened some retail stores in order to capitalise on the growing demand for home networking among the general public. We saw in Unit 8 how it used a variety of project management methods in order to arrive at some solutions to the new problems posed by its expansion into the retail trade.
>
> It also receives many orders from customers who know what they want and simply need to put together an order for network components when they visit the store, phone up or ask for a quote online.

The nature of the problem

It is essential that having understood the context in which a system is to be produced, the developer also arrives at a clear idea of exactly what problem needs to be addressed. This might be to speed up the answering of enquiries, the production of an efficient traffic control system that minimises motorists' waiting time at traffic lights or to produce invoices. It is important that the problem's boundaries are clearly identified so that effort is not wasted solving problems that do not need to be addressed.

> **CASE STUDY**
>
> Livewires needs a quick way to produce quotes and invoices to deal with customers who are buying a range of components.
>
> It needs a system to prepare an invoice for a customer who has bought some of its goods. This can be achieved in many ways:
>
> - a specially written programmed solution
> - a generic sales system, as used by similar businesses but adapted to suit the company
> - a customised database solution using a DBMS such as Access
> - a spreadsheet solution.

For this situation, there is no need to produce a solution to look after stock control or staff wages. These are dealt with by other systems.

The preferred option would, in reality, be chosen on the basis of compatibility with other systems as well as cost-benefit comparisons. However, a spreadsheet will do the job perfectly well and has the virtue of being quick to develop and test. All it needs is a copy of Excel and someone in the company or working for the developers who has a bit of know-how.

The tasks you want the spreadsheet to perform

Once the overall purpose has been understood, the next thing to do is to break the problem down into sub-tasks. These can then be tackled separately which makes the whole project a lot easier to tackle. It also reduces the chances of making mistakes.

The Livewires spreadsheet solution must allow:

- the entry and storage of customer details such as names and addresses
- the entry and storage of stock details such as the name of the item and its cost
- the selection of a number of items that the customer wants
- the automatic looking up of prices
- the calculation of invoice totals
- the production of an itemised invoice
- the clearing of invoice details ready for the production of the next one.

It could be pointed out that as a component of a complete sales and stock control system, this leaves a lot out, but if the limits are agreed, it is possible to set to work to make the spreadsheet.

While work on the spreadsheet is in progress, it is likely that the developer will liaise with the users in order to check that what is being produced is satisfactory. Also, it is very likely that new ideas will crop up and the final product may be more ambitious than originally planned. If this happens, the functional specification will have to be updated so that a realistic final evaluation can take place.

How to judge the effectiveness of the solution

There are two main considerations in deciding whether your solution has been effective:

▶ Does it fulfil the original requirements specification?
▶ Does it satisfy the user or client?

In the first case, this will be assessed as the result of thorough testing. The test plan will have been written to cover all the requirements and the spreadsheet will be tested with a full range of normal, boundary and unusual data.

The second aspect is less objective but it is also important if you are to have a satisfied customer. It is useful to enquire from the client or the user to what extent the system fulfils requirements from their points of view. It may be that at this stage, there are ways to make the product easier to use or to add some extra functionality.

Spreadsheet design

Aims

■ To understand the issues involved in planning a spreadsheet

■ To look at various aspects of the design of a spreadsheet

Introduction

Even with fairly complex projects, it can be very tempting to go straight to the computer and start to try out ideas. This is usually a bad idea because you will start putting formulae and data straight down in the first convenient place, feeling confident that if you need to move things around, the formulae will automatically adjust to whatever you decide to do. For example, you can create a block of data with references to other cells and if you cut and paste it somewhere else, the spreadsheet knows about this and will adjust so that the formulae still point to the right places.

Often, this is completely reliable and you do indeed get the freedom you want to adjust layouts. Where this approach can let you down is when you want to move references to different sheets or maybe duplicate them, and when, before long, you will have links that may or may not be the correct ones and more importantly, *you* will lose track of what is going on. It is therefore crucial to organise the spreadsheet well for the sake of understanding it as well as ensuring that it will do what is expected.

There are some general principles that you should always bear in mind:

ABSOLUTE CELL REFERENCES
When you copy or move a formula or any other cell that refers to another cell, the references are adjusted to take account of the new position. If you do not want this to happen, for example when you always want a formula to get a value from a constant, you use dollar signs to stop the reference adjusting. So, instead of using a formula such as =A12*A20, you could use =A12*A20 to stop the A20 being adjusted.

▶ Time spent in planning is rarely wasted. It can be boring but makes things much easier later on.

▶ You should separate things as much as possible. This includes using separate worksheets whenever it seems reasonable.

▶ Never accept default names – this is particularly true of the workbook name and also the worksheet names.

▶ Add worksheets whenever you need them. Conversely, delete sheets that you do not need.

▶ Name data ranges or cells that you often reference. It saves having to keep looking up cell references or worrying about using ABSOLUTE CELL REFERENCES.

▶ Be generous in your use of labels – they help a lot for the user to understand what to do.

▶ Make good use of formatting such as colours. On a large sheet this helps make things stand out. Give some thought to the printing of your spreadsheet. Some colours may not show up so well on paper. Also, a large sheet that you can easily navigate on screen will not fit onto a sheet of A4 paper – use print preview to see how to divide up the blocks of data.

Processing

Processing is what the computer does to data. Data is input, the computer does something to it and produces information as output. A spreadsheet does its processing by using a range of basic tools.

Formulae

These are the expressions that you build into cells that instruct the spreadsheet to do fairly simple things. Typically, they involve simple mathematical relationships such as

```
=(A12+A20)*2
```

This simply means add together the contents of cells A12 and A20, then after that, multiply by 2. We often use brackets in order to force a calculation to proceed in a particular order.

The computer carries out calculations using something called algebraic logic. It carries out a calculation using a set of rules, rather than using the order in which the calculation is set out.

> **ACTIVITY**
>
> Try the following on as many different calculators as possible.
>
> ```
> 4 + 2 × 4 =
> ```

Some calculators will give 24 as the answer, some will give 12. This is because some calculators, normally the cheaper ones, will not follow the correct mathematical rules.

	A	B	C	D
1	4	2	4	=(A1+B1)*C1
2	4	2	4	=A2+B2*C2
3				
4				

	A	B	C	D
1	4	2	4	24
2	4	2	4	12
3				

■ **Figure 11.6**

> The correct order for calculations is Brackets, Indices, Division, Multiplication, Addition, Subtraction or BIDMAS for short. This means that calculations do not happen simply from left to right. The correct answer to 4+2*4 is 12. You multiply 2 by 4 then add 4.

Figure 11.6 shows the effect of using brackets in a calculation.

We can make formulae as complex as we want by embedding bracketed expressions inside each other, but there comes a point where these get difficult to read and then it is best to split the stages of a calculation into different cells.

Formulae do not have to be mathematical. Text strings can be joined together by setting up an expression such as

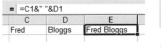

	C	D	E
	Fred	Bloggs	Fred Bloggs

■ **Figure 11.7**

```
=C1 & " " & D1
```

This joins together the contents of cell C1 and D1 with a space in between. This is called concatenation. '&' is a concatenation operator.

Functions

These are ready-made packages of calculations or other operations that the spreadsheet provides for you. They save you having to make complex expressions and they also help to make a spreadsheet a lot more understandable. They all have names and they are all followed by brackets. The brackets contain the arguments or parameters that the function needs to work on. The function name says what to do, the parameters say what to do it to. For example:

```
=SUM(A12:C30)
```

means use the function SUM to add up all the values that occur in the range starting at cell A12 and finishing in the cell C30. SUM needs to be supplied with a cell range as a parameter.

Another common function is IF. For example:

```
=IF(A12>49,"PASS","FAIL")
```

This means look in the cell A12 and check whether it is greater than 49. If it is, insert the word PASS, otherwise insert the word FAIL. The IF function therefore needs three parameters. If you don't supply them, you will get an error message.

ACTIVITY

On your spreadsheet, click the f_x button and look at the wide range of functions that are available. Notice that the use of each one is explained and also the number and type of parameters that it requires.

Macros

Often, you have to carry out the same sequence of actions in order to accomplish a task. You may need to format different ranges of cells in different ways, some to show currency, some to show zero decimal places. Or, maybe you often have to plot the same graph from a range of values. In these cases, it is worth producing a macro, which is a stored sequence of actions – a computer program in effect.

You can record a macro, so that all you have to do is to perform the relevant actions and they will be stored.

The macro can be played back from the Tools → Macro menu options or it can be attached to a button or a menu item.

Macros are also useful to incorporate into a spreadsheet solution for others to use. Not only do they automate tasks and save effort, they also ensure that the actions are carried out the same way every time and this can reduce errors.

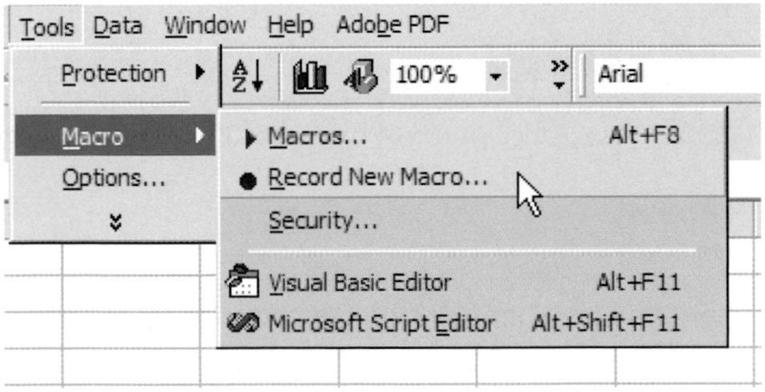

Figure 11.8

Programmed modules

When a macro is recorded, it generates some program code, in a programming language called Visual Basic for Applications (VBA). The useful thing about this is that the code is easily understandable and also it can be added to or adjusted to refine the macro yet further.

For example, you may want a certain action to occur again and again, such as moving the cursor to a particular cell. You can record this happening once and you can take a look at the program code produced.

```
Sub Macro1()
'
' Macro1 Macro
' Macro recorded 06/02/2006 by Sean O'Byrne
'

'
    Range("A2").Select
End Sub
```

■ **Figure 11.9**

With a little bit of programming knowledge, you can write your own macro to make things happen repeatedly. In the next example, a simple loop is written to write out the three times table into the cells of a spreadsheet.

```
Sub Macro1()
'
' 3 times table

Dim Counter As Integer

For Counter = 1 To 20
    Cells(Counter, 1).Select
    ActiveCell.Value = Counter * 3
    Next Counter
End Sub
```

■ **Figure 11.10**

	A
1	3
2	6
3	9
4	12
5	15
6	18
7	21
8	24
9	27
10	30
11	33
12	36
13	39
14	42
15	45
16	48
17	51
18	54
19	57
20	60
21	

■ **Figure 11.11**

The result of running this macro is shown in Figure 11.11.

This unit is not intended to cover much in the way of programming, although you will find some more examples in Unit 11.6. It should be realised though, that adjusting macros by writing a few lines of program code can often achieve results that are hard to do any other way.

The structure of the spreadsheet

Layout is important. Not just from an aesthetic point of view, but also in order to:

▶ make the spreadsheet easy to use
▶ make the spreadsheet easier to design.

One of the first decisions you should make when designing a spreadsheet is how many pages (worksheets) you need. Many users of spreadsheets never bother to make use of multiple pages and this misses a great opportunity to divide up the different functions and thereby make them clearer and easier to understand.

If we take the Livewires scenario, we will recall that we need to take information about customers and information about the stock for sale and then work out some prices and present the results as an invoice. The invoice should look like an invoice, so its format will probably be rather different from a basic grid-like spreadsheet page. All this suggests three separate worksheets, one to store customer details, one to store stock details and one to create the invoice. This is so much easier than trying to place all the details in different blocks of data all on one worksheet.

Once we have decided this, we should name the three worksheets so that there is no effort later in trying to remember what we did on each worksheet.

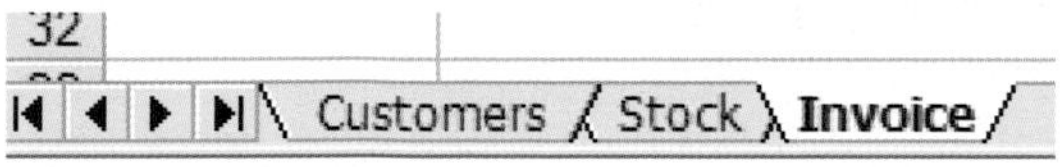

Figure 11.12

Data entry and validation

It is usually not good enough to expect users of a spreadsheet solution to have to enter data straight into cells. If you do require this, the cells should be very well labelled so that there is no doubt what must be done. Because spreadsheets potentially have thousands of places where data can be entered, this is a significant design point. Entry of data into the wrong cells needs to be prevented unless you have a very informal and trusting relationship with your users. To do this, you will need to lock some cells and hide others.

Validation is the checking of data by the software as it is input to ensure that it is reasonable. It can check that the data conforms to certain rules such as the type of data entered. It can, for example, make sure that stock numbers are selected from a list rather than typed in. This reduces the risk of making mistakes that could lead to unreliable outputs. There are various ways to perform validation in a spreadsheet:

▶ Use the Validation option from the Data menu. This provides a wide variety of validation rules that can be applied to a selected range of cells.
▶ Use drop-down boxes from the Control toolbox. For example, a combo box can be set to display data from any part of the workbook and the user chooses which item to enter.
▶ Use macros, which can be set to insert pre-planned data and this reduces the chances of making errors.
▶ Use formulae and functions to highlight expected errors.
▶ Write program code – with specially written code, it is possible to guard against errors in a highly customised way.

We shall examine these in more detail in Unit 11.6 and further examples are also shown in Unit 11.12.

Layout and presentation

portfolio_tip

Your assessment will take into account the attention that you pay to the spreadsheet layout, so make sure that it is easy to use by trying out your designs on others.

For personal use, you can set up a spreadsheet without bothering to emphasise the different blocks of data and data entry points. With other users, you should take a lot of care to make the use of the spreadsheet as foolproof as possible. This means using colours, borders and blanking out gridlines in order to concentrate the mind of the user on the important points. As usual, it is best to take some care with this right from the outset, although you will want to change your ideas as you develop the spreadsheet.

The issues of layout are considered in more detail in Unit 11.5.

Output

It is possible for a spreadsheet to output data all over the place. After all, it is made from thousands of cells and these can accept data, process data or output data. Often this is exactly what it is required to do and the user will want to read the results of calculations from many cells. However, a complex spreadsheet will benefit from having the output directed to a designated part of the workbook. This helps to concentrate the mind of the developer as well as making it easier to use.

Sometimes the positioning of the output is obvious from the purpose of the spreadsheet. For example, in the Livewires invoice system, all the important output will go onto the invoice.

The workbook can be set up to perform the calculations and lookup functions wherever is logical, but at the end, the important data is copied to the invoice sheet, which is also formatted to look like an invoice.

The issue of presenting the results will be returned to in Unit 11.8.

Livewires
Invoice

To:
Customer Number: 101
          Mr   James   Raybould
Flat 1
34 Jersey Close
Oldham
OL9 8YU

Details

ITEM CODE	ITEM	PRICE	QUANTITY	TOTAL
AE424657	Netsolutions OfficeConnect wireless 54 Mbps travel router	189	1	189
AE424707	Supernet 10/100 PCI adapter	189	5	945
AE424711	Supernet 10/100/1000 PCI adapter	189	1	189
AF524775	Supanet 56k External Modem	189	1	189

■ **Figure 11.13**

Future-proofing

If you make a complex spreadsheet and put a lot of effort into its design and creation, you will not want the product to be used just for a short period and then abandoned. You need to design into the spreadsheet some adaptability so that as much of it as possible will be re-usable if the needs of the users change or grow.

This means, as we saw before, the subdivision of the workbook into sensible sections so that it is easy to change parts of the whole without having to redesign everything.

It is a common practice in making many products, but especially in computer systems, to work using the concepts of 'layers'. What this means is that a system is built so that one layer acts through another and another, eventually to carry out its purpose. For example, the computer user works with an application (the word processor) to write and print a document. The word processor does not control the hardware of the computer but works through another layer, the operating system. The operating system acts on the hardware and works through yet another layer – the printer driver – to operate the printer. The advantage of all this layering is that updates can be made to a particular layer, such as the operating system, without having to rebuild all the other components that work with it.

In the spreadsheet that is set up for the invoice system, it is best if the invoice sheet contains little else apart from the invoice format. It will do little apart from look up data and generate the customer's invoice. All other functionality, such as looking after the data stores, can be kept separate and updated without having to make too many adjustments to the invoice itself.

Future-proofing will be examined in more detail in Unit 11.7.

Testing

The spreadsheet must be tested as thoroughly as possible. Much of this will happen along the way, while it is being developed. It makes sense that if you add a combo box to a worksheet and set it to pick up data from a data range, that you immediately test it to see whether it does in fact pick up the right data and allow the user to make a choice.

When the workbook is finished, it should be tested in its entirety. This is because although we can be reasonably sure that each individual part works, we need to be certain that the parts interact together as intended and the output is in fact correct.

This can be a lengthy process and it really needs a properly thought out test plan to make sure that all possible outcomes are tested.

Testing will be dealt with in detail in Unit 11.9 and the issues are also covered in Units 12.9 and 12.10. Even though Unit 12 as a whole covers the programming module, the important points about testing remain the same.

Prototyping and iteration

Spreadsheets are infinitely flexible – this is probably one of the reasons why they were among the very first items of software available on PCs when they were invented in the early 1980s.

Because of this, there are countless ways of solving problems when using them. You can gradually work towards a solution by creating lots of columns to hold intermediate data or you can create more complex formulae to carry out several operations in one cell. Despite your careful designs, you will find that spreadsheets take on a life of their own once you start to develop them.

This is no bad thing. You can use the intermediate stages as *prototypes*. A prototype is a partially working model of the finished article. That means you can get a good idea about the final outcome before it is finished. Better still, you can show your end users what the product will look and feel like and they can get a much better idea about what you are making. A partly completed product can convey much more than a requirements specification written in words.

A prototype allows your users to give you valuable feedback on the product so that you can make improvements. Do not forget who has to use the product in the end, so user feedback is vital if you want the final spreadsheet to be used.

Refine your initial design and try out alternatives

Repeatedly trying out refinements with constant user feedback is known as iterative development. Iteration means repetition – you design and consult and design again. The same happens during the creation of the spreadsheet.

The waterfall model

One way that system analysts and designers look at the development of a system is through a representation known as the *waterfall model*. This shows how each stage of the analysis and design process leads onwards to the next until you arrive at a finished product. The waterfall model can be adapted to include iterative techniques that show how at any stage, it is possible, and in fact can be desirable, to re-visit earlier stages to keep on refining the product until it meets all needs. The waterfall diagram in Figure 11.14 shows some of the iterations that are possible.

Figure 11.14

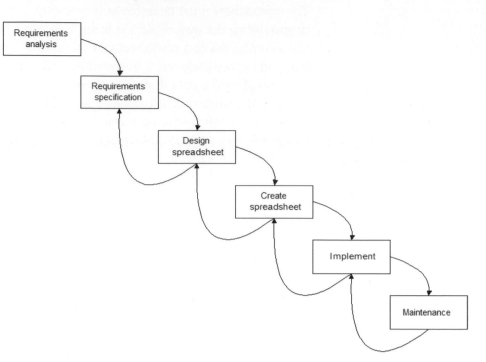

Test that the formulae are working properly and that the underpinning logic is correct

Iterative development means that you can keep checking that all is well. You immediately test each formula and function as you build the spreadsheet and then periodically re-check with your users that the spreadsheet is performing as it should.

Check for ease of use

As the spreadsheet develops, the iterative approach can be useful in making sure that the users actually like what you are doing. You cannot test for ease of use by yourself. You need to get feedback from someone who is not close to the development process and is only interested in using the finished product.

Further aspects of testing will be dealt with in more detail in Unit 11.9.

Test for robustness

What happens if users do unexpected things with the spreadsheet? Will they get impenetrable error messages?

You need to make sure that the product is robust. This means that it will not generate system error messages. As far as possible, ensure all actions are anticipated with either custom error messages produced – ones that you have written – or that wrong actions are prevented – by locking cells or hiding them.

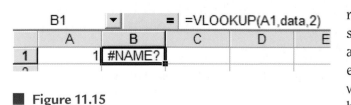

Figure 11.15

Processing

Aims

■ To examine a range of processing activities that can be achieved with a spreadsheet

The whole point of any computer system, including a spreadsheet, is to process data and give back the results of the processing to the user, or to output to a device. Most people know that spreadsheets are particularly useful at performing calculations, but not everyone is aware that spreadsheets have a wide range of processing abilities that go a long way beyond performing calculations.

Many of the activities that can be performed by writing program code can also be performed by using spreadsheet functions. Of course, it is possible to write program code as well, which allows a spreadsheet to do almost anything of which the computer is capable.

Calculating

Numerical processing is what most users expect from a spreadsheet and indeed, this is what they are particularly useful for. Calculations can be performed very easily on a spreadsheet because:

▶ the stages of a calculation can easily be separated
▶ the results of one calculation can be fed into another
▶ changing the data produces immediate recalculation.

We have already seen that the most common ways of performing calculations involve the use of formulae and functions. The difference between them is explained in Unit 11.3. Both formulae and functions start with the equals (=) sign in most spreadsheets including Microsoft Excel. The equals sign says 'do this' rather than 'display this'.

Formulae

These are built up by the user by constructing expressions. These expressions can include constants, variables and operators. Expressions can embed other expressions. For example, the expression

```
=A1+B1
```

takes two variables (the contents of cells A1 and B1) and adds them together, displaying the result in the cell that contains the expression.

ACTIVITY

Work out the result of the expression both with and without the brackets.

The expression

```
=(A1+B1)*5
```

adds together the contents of the two cells as before, but then multiplies the result by the constant 5. The brackets make sure that the addition takes place first and then the multiplication.

Operators

Operators are the components of an expression that carry out actions. A range of operators is available. Arithmetic operators perform calculations. The arithmetic operators are:

Arithmetic operator	Meaning	Example
+ (plus sign)	Addition	3+3
– (minus sign)	Subtraction Negation	3–1 –1
* (asterisk)	Multiplication	3*3
/ (forward slash)	Division	3/3
% (percent sign)	Percent	20%
^ (caret)	Exponentiation	3^2 (the same as 3*3)

Reference operators are used to combine cells into ranges for calculations.

Reference operator	Meaning	Example
: (colon)	Range operator, which produces one reference to all the cells between two references, including the two references	B5:B15
, (comma)	Union operator, which combines multiple references into one reference	SUM(B5:B15,D5:D15)

Functions

Functions are groups of instructions that simplify the work of setting up a spreadsheet. Instead of creating lots of linked cells, each of which carries out a separate stage in a calculation, a function combines all the work into one named package. Functions have names and the data that they are intended to work on is presented to them inside brackets as a set of arguments or parameters.

There are many pre-designed functions available in spreadsheets. They are categorised according to their general area of importance.

Most users of Excel have experience of some of the functions such as SUM, AVERAGE and IF. Some examples of their use were given in Unit 11.3.

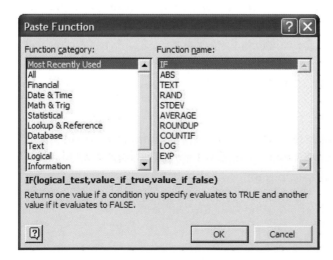

■ Figure 11.16

Click on the f_x (function) button on Excel and explore the functions available.

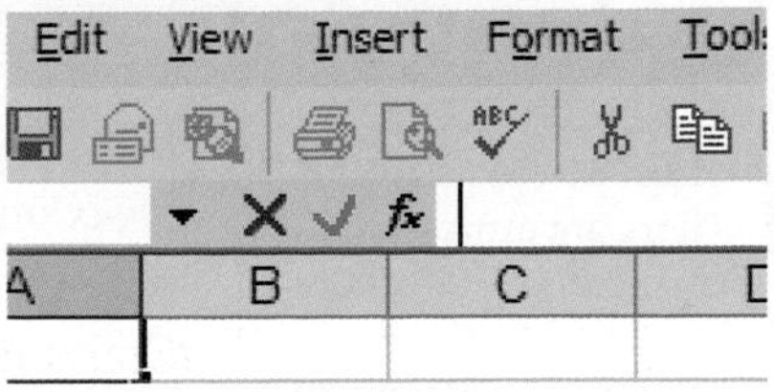

Edit   View   Insert   Format   Tool

■ Figure 11.17

Merging data from different sources

Spreadsheets are often required to combine data from various sources. These sources may be internal to the particular workbook or they may come from outside.

Excel has several ways in which it can access external data. These methods are available from the menu sequence Data → Get External Data. From here, it is possible to import tables from databases, text files or web pages.

■ Figure 11.18

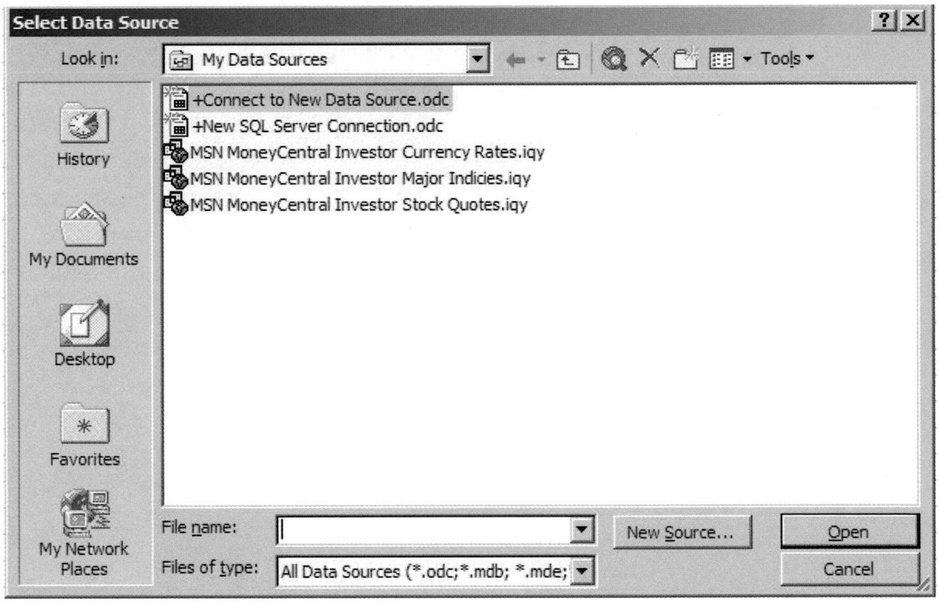

Figure 11.18 shows some of the external data sources that can be merged with Excel data.

Once the data is imported, it can be processed together with any data already in the workbook.

We have seen in Unit 11.3 that there is an operator that can join text strings together. It is called the text concatenation operator. With it, we use the ampersand (&) to join, or concatenate, one or more text strings to produce a single piece of text:

```
"North" & "wind"
```

produces

```
"Northwind"
```

Making comparisons

BOOLEAN EXPRESSIONS
These are expressions that evaluate to either true or false. For example, the statement A1=B1 is ether true or false – it cannot be anything else.

It is often necessary to compare items of data and to make decisions on the basis of such comparisons. For example, the result of a series of examinations may be compared with a preset value to see if a pass has been attained. Comparisons invole the use of BOOLEAN EXPRESSIONS.

You can compare two values with *comparison operators*. These are also known as *Boolean operators*. When two values are compared by using these operators, the result is a logical value, either TRUE or FALSE.

Comparison operator	Meaning	Example
= (equal sign)	Equal to	A1=B1
> (greater than sign)	Greater than	A1>B1
< (less than sign)	Less than	A1<B1
>= (greater than or equal to sign)	Greater than or equal to	A1>=B1
<= (less than or equal to sign)	Less than or equal to	A1<=B1
<> (not equal to sign)	Not equal to	A1<>B1

B2	▼	=	=IF(A2>500,A2*0.15,A2*0.1)

	A	B	C	D
1	Takings	Earnings		
2	£499.00	£ 49.90		
3	£501.00	£ 75.15		
4				

■ **Figure 11.19**

Boolean expressions are often used in conjunction with the IF function. They are also crucial to the design of most programs. The IF function takes three parameters, the first of which is a Boolean expression, the second is what to put in the cell if the expression is true, the third is what to put in if it is false. In the following example, the IF function checks to see what a salesman has taken. If it is greater than £500, he is paid commission of 15% of the earnings, otherwise, he is paid only 10%.

```
=IF(A2>500,A2*0.15,A2*0.1)
```

Nested IFs

You can make IF statements achieve more by embedding further IFs inside. For example, suppose that some students take two examinations, paper 1 and paper 2. They must pass paper 1 with a minimum score of 50. They must also get a total for the two papers of at least 100.

■ **Figure 11.20**

	A	B	C	D	E	F
1	Surname	Forename	Paper 1	Paper 2	Total	Pass/Fail
2	Jenkins	Mike	22	101	123	PAPER 1 FAIL
3	Atkinson	Joe	51	56	107	PASS
4	Smith	Emma	65	76	141	PASS
5	Dodd	Louise	45	46	91	FAIL
6	Epson	Nathan	34	34	68	FAIL
7	Hewlett	Thelma	21	50	71	FAIL
8	Packard	Rose	20	100	120	PAPER 1 FAIL
9						

The spreadsheet can be set up to do this with the following statement in column F:

```
=IF(E2>=100,IF(C2<50,"PAPER 1 FAIL","PASS"),"FAIL")
```

This first checks the value in cell E2 to see if the total score is greater than or equal to 100. If it is, it then checks to see if the value for the first paper, in cell C2, is less than 50. So, if the candidate scores more than 100 in total, but less than 50 in paper 1, the cell displays 'PAPER 1 FAIL'. If he gets more than 50 in the first paper and at least 100 in total, he gets 'PASS'. If, however, he gets less than 100 in total, the word 'FAIL' is displayed.

This combined function is then copied down for all the candidates.

■ Figure 11.21

	A	B	C	D	E	F
1	Surname	Forename	Paper 1	Paper 2	Total	Pass/Fail
2	Jenkins	Mike	22	101	=C2+D2	=IF(E2>=100,IF(C2<50,"PAPER 1 FAIL","PASS"),"FAIL")
3	Atkinson	Joe	51	56	=C3+D3	=IF(E3>=100,IF(C3<50,"PAPER 1 FAIL","PASS"),"FAIL")
4	Smith	Emma	65	76	=C4+D4	=IF(E4>=100,IF(C4<50,"PAPER 1 FAIL","PASS"),"FAIL")
5	Dodd	Louise	45	46	=C5+D5	=IF(E5>=100,IF(C5<50,"PAPER 1 FAIL","PASS"),"FAIL")
6	Epson	Nathan	34	34	=C6+D6	=IF(E6>=100,IF(C6<50,"PAPER 1 FAIL","PASS"),"FAIL")
7	Hewlett	Thelma	21	50	=C7+D7	=IF(E7>=100,IF(C7<50,"PAPER 1 FAIL","PASS"),"FAIL")
8	Packard	Rose	20	100	=C8+D8	=IF(E8>=100,IF(C8<50,"PAPER 1 FAIL","PASS"),"FAIL")
9						

portfolio_tip

At A2 level, you should make use of some complex functions. However, you should also add notes to the cells to explain what is going on if they are not immediately clear.

When an IF function contains another IF function, this is called *nesting* the function. It can be done any number of times within the outermost IF.

You can mix and match any spreadsheet functions so that the parameters are other functions. This allows a spreadsheet solution to be very sophisticated and powerful. On the other hand, the more you make use of complex functions, the more unreadable the spreadsheet becomes. Sometimes it is easier to split the results of a complex action into separate cells so that you can see exactly what is going on.

ACTIVITY

Using the values in the Figure 11.19, show using manual calculations that the IF function has worked correctly. What would the result be if cell A2 contained the value £500.00?

Conditional formatting

Spreadsheets allow comparisons to be made in many other circumstances apart from in an IF function. One example is in the use of conditional formatting. A cell or range can be set up to compare the contents of the cells with some pre-set value and alter the display in some way according to the result. Maybe the colour will be highlighted or the font size increased.

■ Figure 11.22

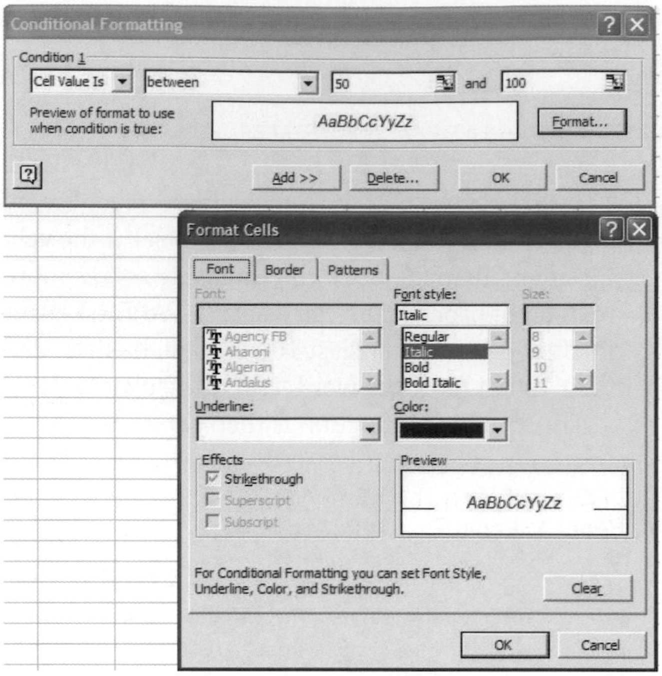

You can experiment with this feature on the spreadsheet file Pass_Fail which is on the CD.

In Figure 11.23, the result of an exam is shown in red if it is a fail.

■ Figure 11.23

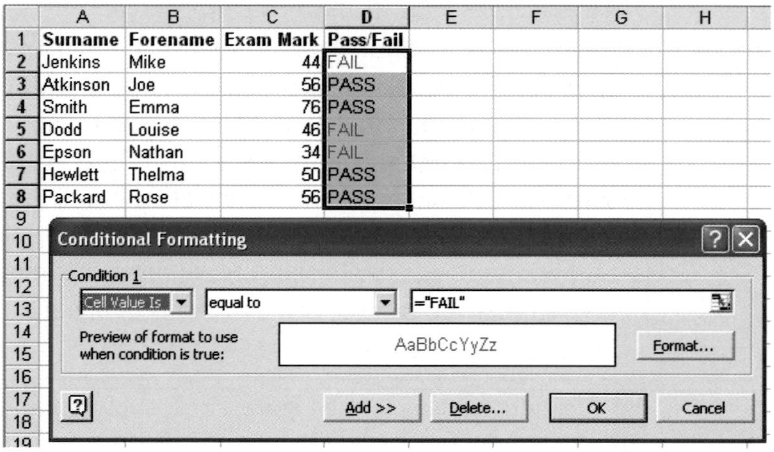

Sorting, grouping, filtering and pivoting data

Sorting

Spreadsheets are good at manipulating data in a host of useful ways. Data can be sorted very rapidly in any way required. All you need to do is to highlight the data you need to be sorted and then choose the Data → Sort menu sequence. You can sort by up to three criteria.

	A	B	C	D	E	F	G
1	Job No.	Customer	Project mana	Date starte	Date finished	On time	Charge
2	234	Johnson Motors Ltd	Alex	20-Mar-00	29-Mar-00	Y	£ 10,245.06
3	235	Siegfried Metal Works	Steve	9-Apr-00	19-Apr-00	Y	£ 5,417.11
4	236	Sunni Bank Inc	Sean	30-Apr-00	6-May-00	Y	£ 5,644.41
5	237	Price's Health Foods	Steve	20-May-00	28-May-00	Y	£ 18,025.39
6	238	Figaro Hairdresser Salons	Chris	9-Jun-00	20-Jun-00	Y	£ 11,596.61
7	239	Dulcamara Wine Importers	Sean	30-Jun-00	6-Jul-00	Y	£ 14,522.00
8	240	Turandot Games and Puzzles	Chris	21-Jul-00	26-Jul-00	Y	£ 4,830.09
9	241	Johnson Motors Ltd	Steve	10-Aug-00	19-Aug-00	Y	£ 516.57
10	242	Megacorp plc	Sean	31-Aug-00	12-Sep-00	N	£ 17,482.50
11	243	Johnson Motors Ltd	Alex	21-Sep-00	1-Oct-00	Y	£ 19,826.60
12	244	Figaro Hairdresser Salons	Sean	11-Oct-00	22-Oct-00	Y	£ 1,299.70
13	245	Fred & Joe Hairdressers	Steve	1-Nov-00	12-Nov-00	Y	£ 8,560.17
14	246	Turandot Games and Puzzles	Sean	21-Nov-00	26-Nov-00	Y	£ 13,612.92
15	247	Sunni Bank Inc	Chris	11-Dec-00	20-Dec-00	Y	£ 16,739.87
16	248	Siegfried Metal Works	Chris	1-Jan-01	9-Jan-01	N	£ 6,445.77
17	249	Winnit Betting Shops	Alex	22-Jan-01	30-Jan-01	Y	£ 8,115.41
18	250	Binge Wine Bars	Alex	11-Feb-01	20-Feb-01	Y	£ 5,711.38
19	251	Bobson Publisher	Chris	3-Mar-01	14-Mar-01	Y	£ 15,711.27

Sort

Sort by
Job No. — ◉ Ascending ◯ Descending

Then by
Customer — ◉ Ascending ◯ Descending

Then by
— ◉ Ascending ◯ Descending

My list has
◉ Header row ◯ No header row

Options... | OK | Cancel

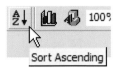

■ Figure 11.24

Sort Ascending

■ Figure 11.25

You have to be careful to make sure that all the data that needs to be sorted is included in the highlighted area or the items will no longer be in the correct rows. You also have to make it clear whether the data range contains a header row or not, otherwise the headers are sorted with the data.

There is also a shortcut button to do a sort on the standard toolbar.

Grouping

You often need to group data so that related items are collected together. There are various ways to do this.

Use separate worksheets to hold data that forms a logical whole. It makes sense to keep data about stock on a separate sheet from that about customers.

Another useful way to group data is to name a range. If you highlight a range of data such as the prices of a set of articles, you can then give the set a name by using the sequence Insert → Name → Define. This block of data can then be referenced very easily by lookup functions or other objects such as combo boxes.

Filtering

With large collections of data, you often need to show only a small subset of the whole. You can do this on the spot or you can send a subset to another part of the workbook. The autofilter is a convenient way to highlight a subset.

Microsoft Excel - jobs

File Edit View Insert Format Tools Data Window Help Adobe PDF

Sort...
Filter ▸ ✓ AutoFilter
Form... Show All
Validation... Advanced Filter...
Consolidate...
Group and Outline ▸
PivotTable and PivotChart Report...
Get External Data ▸

G17 = 8115.414

	A	B			Date finish	On time	Charge
1	Job N ▾	Customer			Date finish ▾	On time ▾	Charge ▾
2	234	Johnson Motors Ltd			29-Mar-00	Y	£ 10,245.06
3	235	Siegfried Metal Works			19-Apr-00	Y	£ 5,417.11
4	236	Sunni Bank Inc			6-May-00	Y	£ 5,644.41
5	237	Price's Health Foods			28-May-00	Y	£ 18,025.39
6	238	Figaro Hairdresser Salon:			20-Jun-00	Y	£ 11,596.61
7	239	Dulcamara Wine Importe			6-Jul-00	Y	£ 14,522.00
8	240	Turandot Games and Puzzles	Chris	21-Jul-00	26-Jul-00	Y	£ 4,830.09

■ Figure 11.26

It puts a drop-down box at the head of each data range so that you can select the items you need to display.

Figure 11.27

	A	B	C	D
1	Job N ▼	Customer ▼	Project ma ▼	Date sta ▼	Dat
6	238	Figaro Hairdresser Salons	(All)	9-Jun-00
8	240	Turandot Games and Puzzles	(Top 10...)	21-Jul-00
15	247	Sunni Bank Inc	(Custom...)	11-Dec-00
16	248	Siegfried Metal Works	Alex	1-Jan-01
19	251	Bobson Publisher	Chris	3-Mar-01
25	257	Price's Health Foods	Richard	4-Jul-01
30	262	Dulcamara Wine Importers	Sean	16-Oct-01
32	264	Fred & Joe Hairdressers	Steve	26-Nov-01
33	265	Bobson Publisher	Chris	16-Dec-01
34	266	Price's Health Foods	Chris	5-Jan-02
35	267	Figaro Hairdresser Salons	Chris	25-Jan-02
39	271	The Academic Standards Agency	Chris	17-Apr-02
52	284	Price's Health Foods	Chris	8-Jan-03
53	285	Yummy Biscuit Company	Chris	29-Jan-03
57	289	The Academic Standards Agency	Chris	21-Apr-03
66	298	Megacorp plc	Chris	23-Oct-03
75	307	Sunni Bank Inc	Chris	24-Apr-04
83	315	Winnit Betting Shops	Chris	5-Oct-04
87	319	Price's Health Foods	Chris	26-Dec-04
89	321	Fred & Joe Hairdressers	Chris	5-Feb-05
90	322	Greenfinger Garden Centres	Chris	25-Feb-05
93	325	The Academic Standards Agency	Chris	28-Apr-05

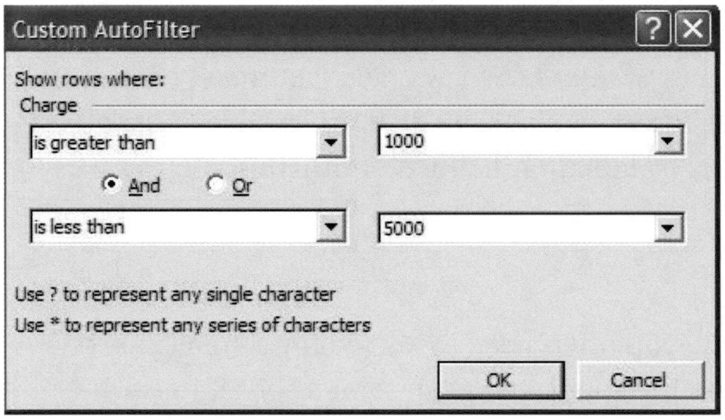

Figure 11.28

The autofilter is quite powerful as it allows selection in a wide variety of ways. You can use comparisons here too.

Pivoting

This is grouping of data in order to produce summaries. These summaries can be calculated in many different ways. Pivoting data involves either counting cells of a certain value or adding up a range of figures.

232

CASE STUDY

Livewires has a worksheet that contains a list of details about all the installation jobs it has carried out.

	A	B	C	D	E	F	G
1	Job No.	Customer	Project manager	Date started	Date finished	On time	Charge
2	234	Johnson Motors Ltd	Alex	20-Mar-00	29-Mar-00	Y	£ 10,245.06
3	235	Siegfried Metal Works	Steve	9-Apr-00	19-Apr-00	Y	£ 5,417.11
4	236	Sunni Bank Inc	Sean	30-Apr-00	6-May-00	Y	£ 5,644.41
5	237	Price's Health Foods	Steve	20-May-00	28-May-00	Y	£ 18,025.39
6	238	Figaro Hairdresser Salons	Chris	9-Jun-00	20-Jun-00	Y	£ 11,596.61

Figure 11.29

The directors want to know which project managers have been working with which companies.

A pivot table can show this very easily.

The pivot table wizard asks you to drag and drop the fields you are interested in to the pivot table. In this case we want to summarise the projects for each customer and see which project managers were responsible for each one.

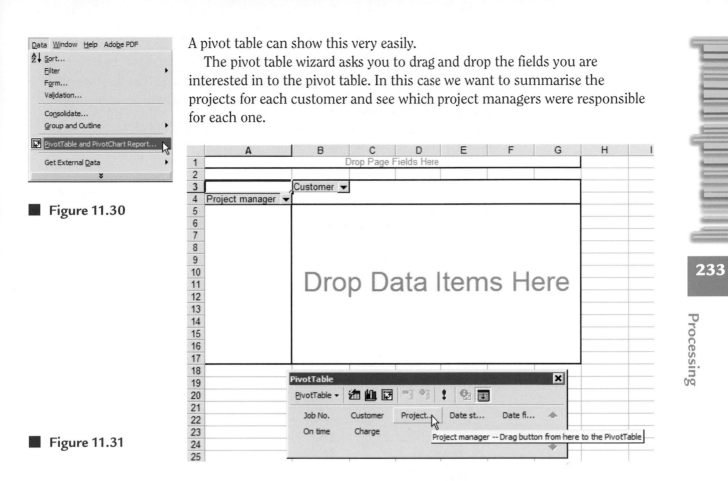

233

Figure 11.30

Figure 11.31

You also drag in the data that you want to be summarised. In this case, we want to see the number of projects that have been led by each project manager for each customer, so we drag in the projects as the data to be summarised.

Count of Project manager	Customer			
Project manager	Binge Wine Bars	Bobson Publisher	Dulcamara Wine Importers	F
Alex	4	2		
Chris		2	1	
Richard		1		
Sean		2	1	
Steve				
Grand Total	4	7	2	

Figure 11.32

Pivot tables are endlessly fascinating and can be used in many powerful ways to see patterns and trends that would otherwise take a lot of studying. Pivot tables are often at their most useful when you do a lot of trial and error, summarising tables in many different ways. Surprising facts can often be seen with very little effort.

Importing and exporting data

Spreadsheets are so useful in manipulating tables of data that they are often used on data that has originated from other sources. There are numerous examples of this:

▶ Data from scientific experiments that has been collected by data-logging instruments can be imported and analysed in a variety of ways. Graphs can be plotted as well.

▶ Data can be obtained from mainframe databases and sorted or filtered in order to see trends, or used in mail merge operations.

▶ Downloaded bank statements can be loaded into a spreadsheet to track your individual spending patterns.

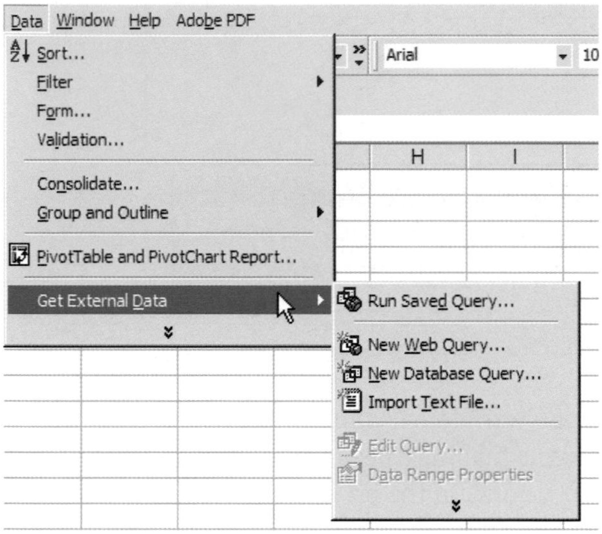

Spreadsheets have a variety of ways in which they can import data.

A wizard guides you through the steps when you import data so that the spreadsheet treats headings in the right way and separates the rows and columns correctly.

If you are able to choose a file export format from another application where a table is generated, you will always be able to use the data in a spreadsheet if you save it as a CSV (comma separated values) file. Most software can do this.

The process can also be done in reverse. You can export data from a spreadsheet to be used by different software or on a totally different platform. Again, CSV is always a safe way to do this as most software can read it. The easiest way to do this is to use the many file format options available in File → Save As.

■ Figure 11.33

■ Figure 11.34

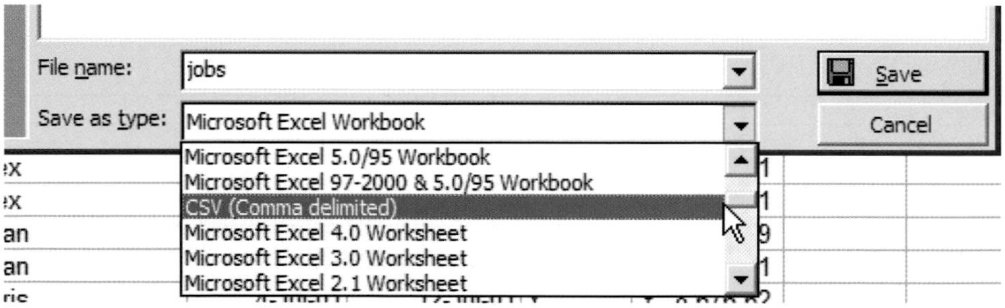

Layout and presentation

Aims

- To look at ways to set out a spreadsheet to make it easy to understand

A simple spreadsheet can be set out very clearly, with data in neat rows and columns and useful headings and labels. However, it does not take long for a spreadsheet to grow – more data is accumulated and more functionality is built in. Before long, it can become complex, cluttered and difficult to use.

Fortunately, spreadsheets come with plenty of features that can help you to make them easier to use and to cut out the complexity for the typical user, leaving much of the workings out of the way so that they do not cause the user confusion. These features should be used together with a careful construction plan so that the overall result is easy to use.

Fonts

When you are setting up a spreadsheet, you tend to concentrate on its functionality. Few of us take much trouble to change much in the way of its appearance. This can be a good thing – if you start changing different parts of a spreadsheet to fancy fonts, the result can be a total mess. The example in Figure 11.35 gives totally the wrong impression for a spreadsheet and would put most users off.

■ Figure 11.35

	A	B	C	D	E	F
1	CUSTOMER_NUMBER	TITLE	SURNAME	FORENAME	INITIALS	ADDRESS1
2	101	MR	RAYBOULD	JAMES	J	FLAT 1
3	132	MR	ALLEN	TOM	T	8 GLEBE DRIVE
4	176	MR	TOMLINSON	JACK	J	9 IRONBRIDGE ROAD
5	254	MR	BARNABY	IAN	I	75 CATHEDRAL CLOSE

coursework_tip

Use font changes sparingly – just to highlight headings.

The default font for most spreadsheets is Arial, which is not an accident. It is a sans serif font which has been found to convey information clearly and with the minimum effort from the reader. Serif fonts such as Times New Roman are better suited to long text passages.

However, you can make creative use of fonts to a small extent in order to highlight certain parts of a sheet. The very least you can do is to use bold or possibly a larger font size to make headings stand out.

■ Figure 11.36

	A	B	C	D	E	F
1	Customer_Number	Title	Surname	Forename	Initials	Address1
2	101	Mr	Raybould	James	J	Flat 1
3	132	Mr	Allen	Tom	T	8 Glebe Drive
4	176	Mr	Tomlinson	Jack	J	9 Ironbridge Road
5	254	Mr	Barnaby	Ian	I	75 Cathedral Close
6	266	Dr	Washbourne	George	G	75 Caravan Road

	A
1	name
2	fred
3	bill
4	sue
5	chris
6	peter

	A
1	bill
2	chris
3	fred
4	name
5	peter
6	sue

	A
1	**name**
2	bill
3	chris
4	fred
5	peter
6	sue

Making headings bold also has a bonus when sorting. Look at Figure 11.37.

Notice how the column heading 'name' has been sorted with the data in the second image, but in the third, because it was in bold face, the heading was not sorted.

■ **Figure 11.37**

Styles

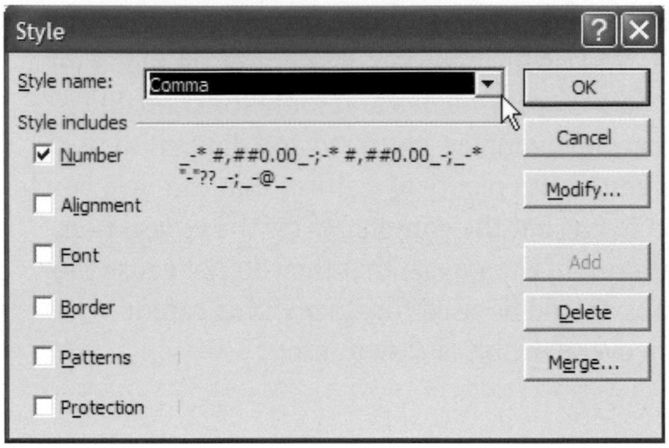

■ **Figure 11.38**

There are choices available for displaying data. These are available though the format menu and some of the more common choices are also available on the formatting toolbar. These choices are of significance with numeric data and also dates. Numeric data can be set to display commas or not in order to separate digits in numbers of 1000 or more. This is largely a matter of personal taste.

Styles can also be applied to the display of dates so that they can be in US (mm/dd/yy) or UK (dd/mm/yy) format and with the months displayed as numbers or names. Amounts of money can usefully be displayed using the currency format. That ensures that the right number of decimal places is always displayed and the values look right too. It is also easy to change the international settings so that the currency symbol displayed is the one you want.

Colours, borders and shading

The use of colour can be very helpful in making different regions of a spreadsheet look distinct. When there is a mass of figures and a total, the total can easily get lost. A colour highlight can be useful in making it stand out.

99	331	Price's Health Foods	Steve	29-Aug-05	9-Sep-05	Y	£	13,153.61
100	332	Sunni Bank Inc	Sean	18-Sep-05	28-Sep-05	Y	£	5,851.34
101	333	Price's Health Foods	Richard	9-Oct-05	15-Oct-05	Y	£	2,675.61
102		**Total to date**						£ 1,041,011.36
103								

■ **Figure 11.39**

Putting a border around a block of data can be useful in demarcating it. This can be useful to highlight an address block on a document such as an invoice.

■ Figure 11.40

Livewires
Invoice

To:

Customer Number: 101

Mr	James	Raybould
Flat 1		
34 Jersey Close		
Oldham		
OL9 8YU		

Shading can be very helpful in making different areas clear. There is even a feature which can automate this. It is particularly useful if you do not have a good 'eye' for graphic design. Many of us tend to make a mess of choosing colour schemes so it is useful that there are some well-thought-out schemes all ready to choose from.

■ Figure 11.41

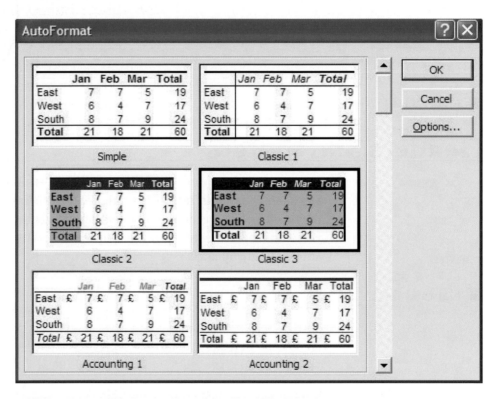

Applying an autoformat can make a big difference in appearance.

	A	B	C	D	E	F	G
1	Job No.		Customer	Project manager	Date started	Date finished	On time	Charge
2	234	Johnson Motors Ltd	Alex	20-Mar-00	29-Mar-00	Y	£ 10,245.06
3	235	Siegfried Metal Works	Steve	9-Apr-00	19-Apr-00	Y	£ 5,417.11
4	236	Sunni Bank Inc	Sean	30-Apr-00	6-May-00	Y	£ 5,644.41
5	237	Price's Health Foods	Steve	20-May-00	28-May-00	Y	£ 18,025.39
6	238	Figaro Hairdresser Salons	Chris	9-Jun-00	20-Jun-00	Y	£ 11,596.61
7	239	Dulcamara Wine Importers	Sean	30-Jun-00	6-Jul-00	Y	£ 14,522.00

■ Figure 11.42

Conditional formatting

It is possible to make the appearance of a cell vary according to the value that is in it. We saw how to do this in Unit 11.4. There are many potential uses for conditional formatting. One is to make cells containing negative sums of money stand out in a different colour. On the AS level CD, there are checklists that students can use to track how far they have progressed in doing their eportfolio. Conditional formatting is used to highlight the tasks remaining.

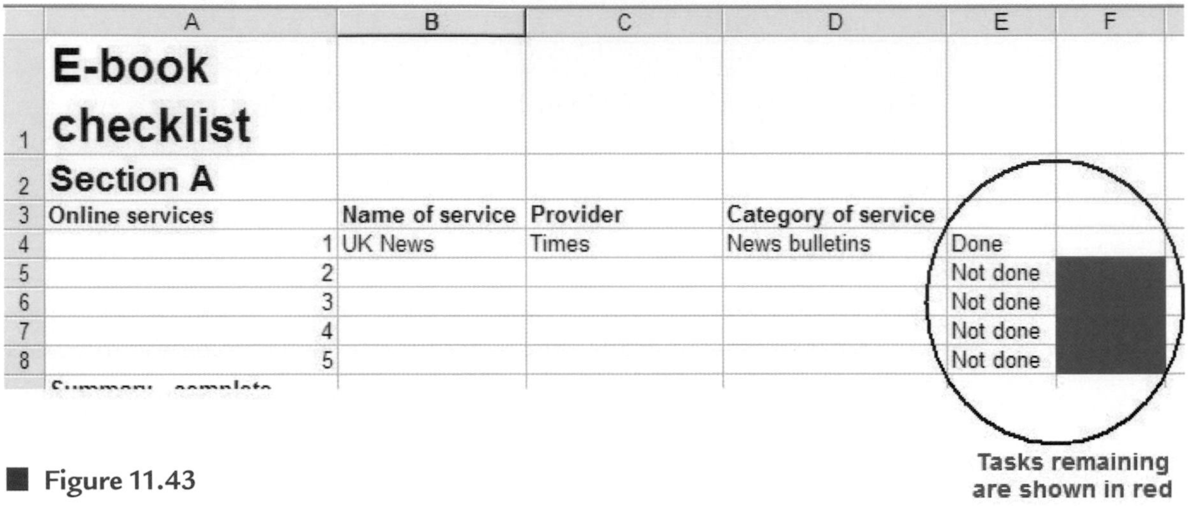

	A	B	C	D	E	F
1	**E-book checklist**					
2	**Section A**					
3	**Online services**	**Name of service**	**Provider**	**Category of service**		
4	1	UK News	Times	News bulletins	Done	
5	2				Not done	
6	3				Not done	
7	4				Not done	
8	5				Not done	
	Summary: complete					

Tasks remaining are shown in red

■ **Figure 11.43**

Headers and footers

Just as with a word-processed document, headers and footers can make a spreadsheet easier to read. They can give an impression of where the sheet fits into a series. The headers and footers can be customised to show whatever you want and some items such as page numbers and dates can be automatically updated.

■ **Figure 11.44**

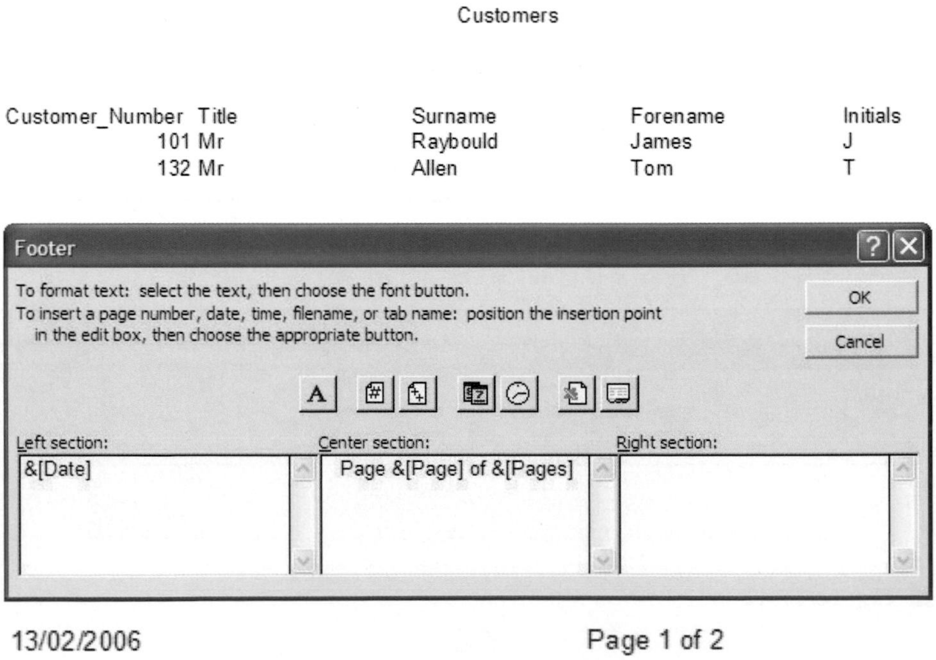

Customers

Customer_Number	Title	Surname	Forename	Initials
101	Mr	Raybould	James	J
132	Mr	Allen	Tom	T

Footer [?][X]

To format text: select the text, then choose the font button.
To insert a page number, date, time, filename, or tab name: position the insertion point in the edit box, then choose the appropriate button.

OK

Cancel

Left section:	Center section:	Right section:
&[Date]	Page &[Page] of &[Pages]	

13/02/2006   Page 1 of 2

Graphics

Just like all modern GUI-based software, spreadsheets allow the addition of graphics to their text content. This can mean simply adding a picture to a spreadsheet.

Also, it means that you can use drawing tools to highlight parts of your spreadsheet or a chart that goes with it. Figures 11.46 and 11.47 have used data summaries from a pivot table to show how graphics can be added.

	A	B	C	D	E
1					
2					
3	Sum of Charge				
4	Customer ▼	Total			
5	Binge Wine Bars	£ 38,569.72			
6	Bobson Publisher	£ 78,823.78			
7	Dulcamara Wine Importers	£ 19,032.67			
8	Figaro Hairdresser Salons	£ 77,191.66			
9	Fred & Joe Hairdressers	£ 55,758.63			
10	Greenfinger Garden Centres	£ 77,437.00			
11	Johnson Motors Ltd	£ 83,119.09			
12	Megacorp plc	£ 43,232.06			
13	National News Corporation	£ 33,568.43		Good	
14	Passmore Examinations Syndicate	£ 66,581.72		customer!	
15	Price's Health Foods	£ 138,174.11			
16	Siegfried Metal Works	£ 18,834.92			
17	Sparky's Electrical Stores	£ 20,680.70			
18	Sunni Bank Inc	£ 55,352.71			
19	The Academic Standards Agency	£ 39,811.84			
20	Tone and Def Music Stores	£ 35,186.87			
21	Traditional Furniture Stores	£ 30,143.88			
22	Turandot Games and Puzzles	£ 39,415.72			
23	Winnit Betting Shops	£ 59,914.63			
24	Yummy Biscuit Company	£ 30,181.22			
25	Grand Total	£ 1,041,011.36			
26					

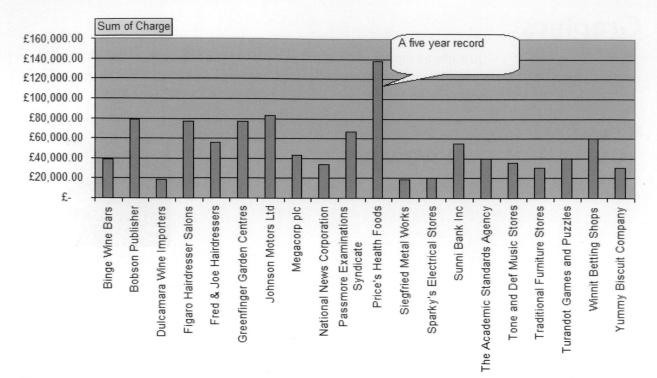

■ Figure 11.47

Data entry and validation

Aims

- To explore ways to make a spreadsheet easy to use
- To reduce the likelihood of making errors when putting data into a spreadsheet

As with any other IT system, it is essential that the data entered into a spreadsheet is accurate, otherwise the output cannot be relied upon. Spreadsheets provide a number of ways in which you can validate data entry and prevent unreasonable or impossible data being input. You can also protect the parts of a spreadsheet that the user should not alter so that data is only input into the correct cells.

Restricting input to acceptable data values

Spreadsheets have a useful validation feature that is flexible in what it allows to be entered. It also makes data entry easier for the users as they do not have to type it in.

In Figure 11.48, the cells in column C are being validated against the list of allowable items as indicated on the sheet in cells I1 to I5.

■ **Figure 11.48**

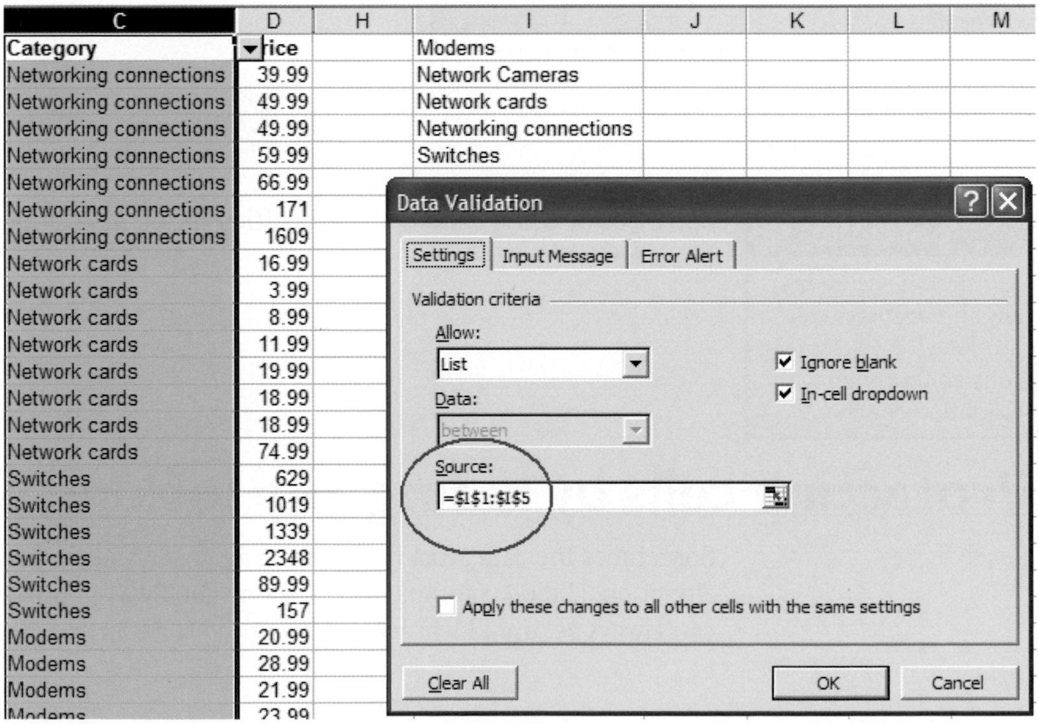

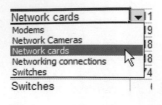

■ Figure 11.49

When the user wants to make an entry in the cell, a drop-down box appears.

If a user attempts to type in an item that is not allowed, a customised error message can be set to appear.

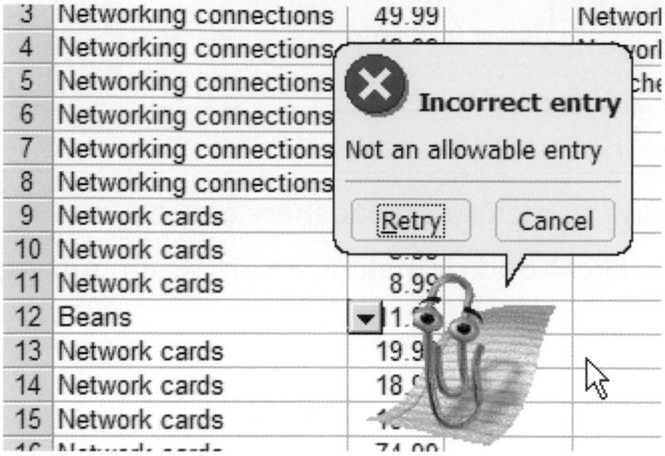

3	Networking connections	49.99	Networl
4	Networking connections		
5	Networking connections		
6	Networking connections		
7	Networking connections		
8	Networking connections		
9	Network cards		
10	Network cards		
11	Network cards	8.99	
12	Beans	1.	
13	Network cards	19.9	
14	Network cards	18.	
15	Network cards		

Incorrect entry
Not an allowable entry
[Retry] [Cancel]

■ Figure 11.50

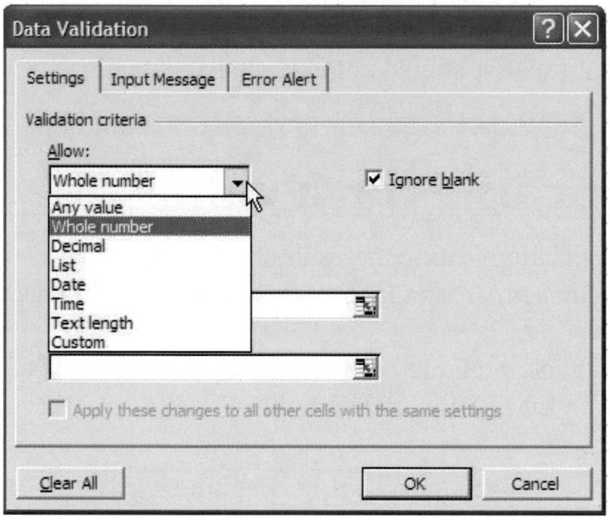

■ Figure 11.51

The validation feature can be set to enforce the entry of values within a range or of a certain data type.

Validation is so important that the designer of a spreadsheet should do everything possible to ensure that the data entered is acceptable. As we saw in Unit 11.3, there are many ways to do this as well as using the validation option from the menu. For example, suppose that cell A1 must contain a value – it must not be left blank. You can put an IF function in the cell next to it, B1, which checks for this and displays a message if the cell is blank. If there is something in it, then nothing is displayed.

```
=IF(A1="","This cell must be filled in","")
```

This can be further enhanced by using conditional formatting in cell A1 to show a different colour if it is left empty.

portfolio_tip

You should ensure that any spreadsheets you produce for assessment contain thorough validation checks.

Protecting cells by hiding and locking them

Sometimes the data must be protected against accidental deletion or alteration. Hiding columns or cells is one good way to prevent accidents. They can always be 'unhidden' again if they need to be amended.

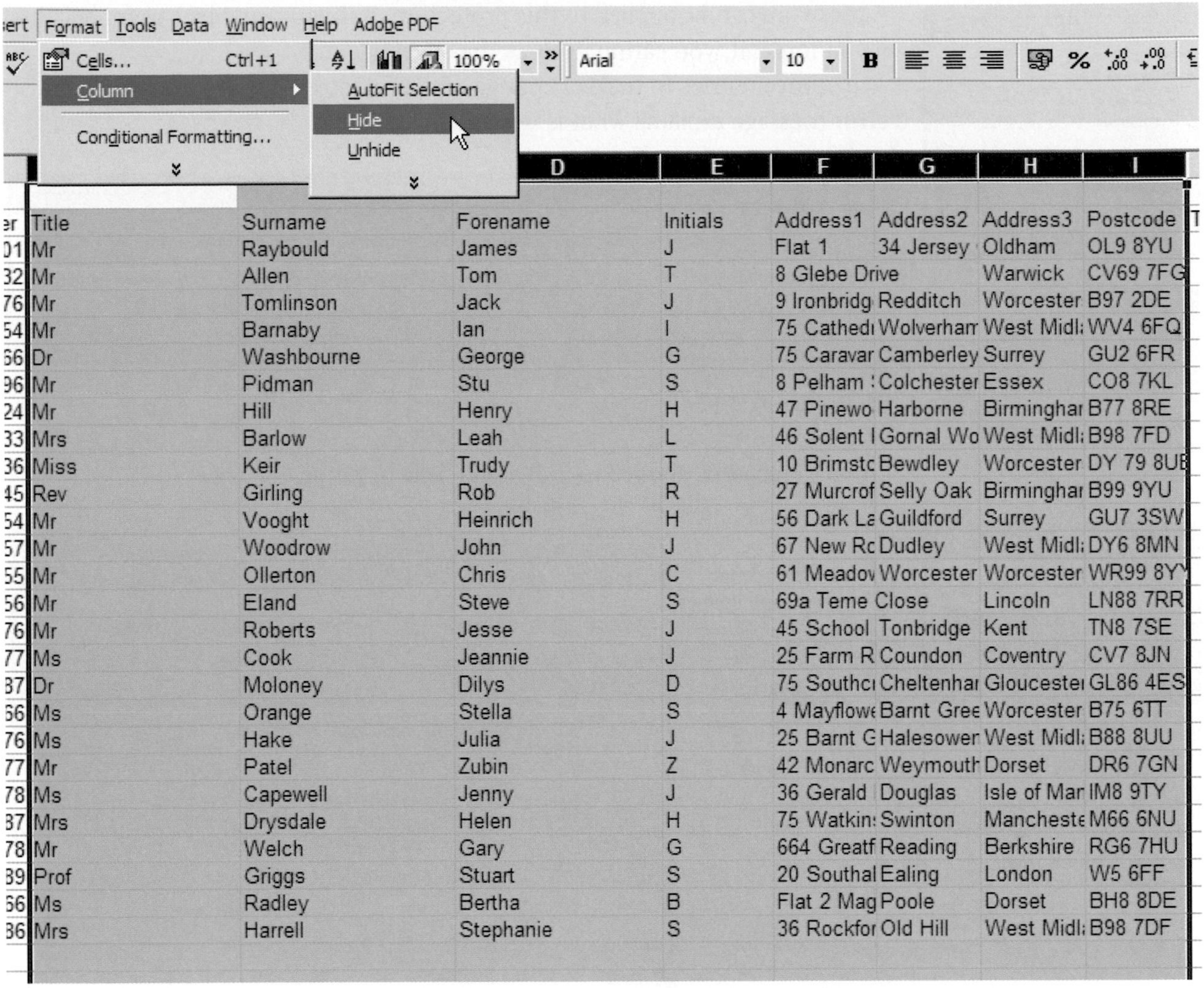

	Title	Surname	Forename	Initials	Address1	Address2	Address3	Postcode	T
01	Mr	Raybould	James	J	Flat 1	34 Jersey	Oldham	OL9 8YU	
32	Mr	Allen	Tom	T	8 Glebe Drive		Warwick	CV69 7FG	
76	Mr	Tomlinson	Jack	J	9 Ironbridg	Redditch	Worcester	B97 2DE	
54	Mr	Barnaby	Ian	I	75 Cathedi	Wolverham	West Midli	WV4 6FQ	
56	Dr	Washbourne	George	G	75 Caravar	Camberley	Surrey	GU2 6FR	
96	Mr	Pidman	Stu	S	8 Pelham :	Colchester	Essex	CO8 7KL	
24	Mr	Hill	Henry	H	47 Pinewo	Harborne	Birminghar	B77 8RE	
33	Mrs	Barlow	Leah	L	46 Solent I	Gornal Wo	West Midli	B98 7FD	
36	Miss	Keir	Trudy	T	10 Brimstc	Bewdley	Worcester	DY 79 8UE	
45	Rev	Girling	Rob	R	27 Murcrof	Selly Oak	Birminghar	B99 9YU	
54	Mr	Vooght	Heinrich	H	56 Dark La	Guildford	Surrey	GU7 3SW	
57	Mr	Woodrow	John	J	67 New Rc	Dudley	West Midli	DY6 8MN	
55	Mr	Ollerton	Chris	C	61 Meadov	Worcester	Worcester	WR99 8YY	
56	Mr	Eland	Steve	S	69a Teme	Close	Lincoln	LN88 7RR	
76	Mr	Roberts	Jesse	J	45 School	Tonbridge	Kent	TN8 7SE	
77	Ms	Cook	Jeannie	J	25 Farm R	Coundon	Coventry	CV7 8JN	
37	Dr	Moloney	Dilys	D	75 Southci	Cheltenhar	Glouceste	GL86 4ES	
56	Ms	Orange	Stella	S	4 Mayflow	Barnt Gree	Worcester	B75 6TT	
76	Ms	Hake	Julia	J	25 Barnt G	Halesower	West Midli	B88 8UU	
77	Mr	Patel	Zubin	Z	42 Monarc	Weymouth	Dorset	DR6 7GN	
78	Ms	Capewell	Jenny	J	36 Gerald	Douglas	Isle of Mar	IM8 9TY	
37	Mrs	Drysdale	Helen	H	75 Watkin:	Swinton	Mancheste	M66 6NU	
78	Mr	Welch	Gary	G	664 Greatf	Reading	Berkshire	RG6 7HU	
39	Prof	Griggs	Stuart	S	20 Southal	Ealing	London	W5 6FF	
56	Ms	Radley	Bertha	B	Flat 2 Mag	Poole	Dorset	BH8 8DE	
36	Mrs	Harrell	Stephanie	S	36 Rockfor	Old Hill	West Midli	B98 7DF	

■ Figure 11.52

Sheets or whole workbooks can be locked or protected, so that the user cannot change the data. This is particularly useful when applied to a worksheet that contains all the lookup data or the calculations for a project.

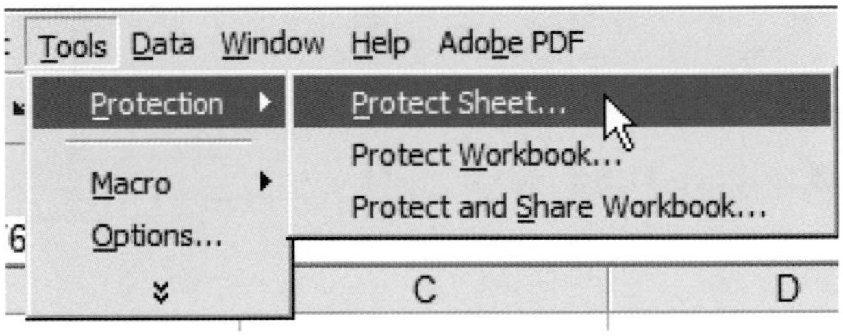

■ Figure 11.53

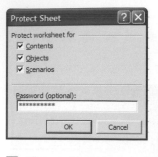

■ **Figure 11.54**

A password can be applied to this protection, but you must be careful because if you forget it, you cannot unlock the sheet again.

If someone tries to make a change on a protected sheet or workbook, an error message explains what is wrong.

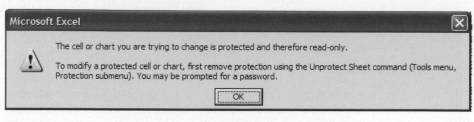

■ **Figure 11.55**

Protection can be applied to individual cells or ranges.

portfolio_tip

If you are going to password protect any of your portfolio work make sure you note down the password. It is a good idea to give it to your tutor, so that if you do forget your password, development will not be delayed.

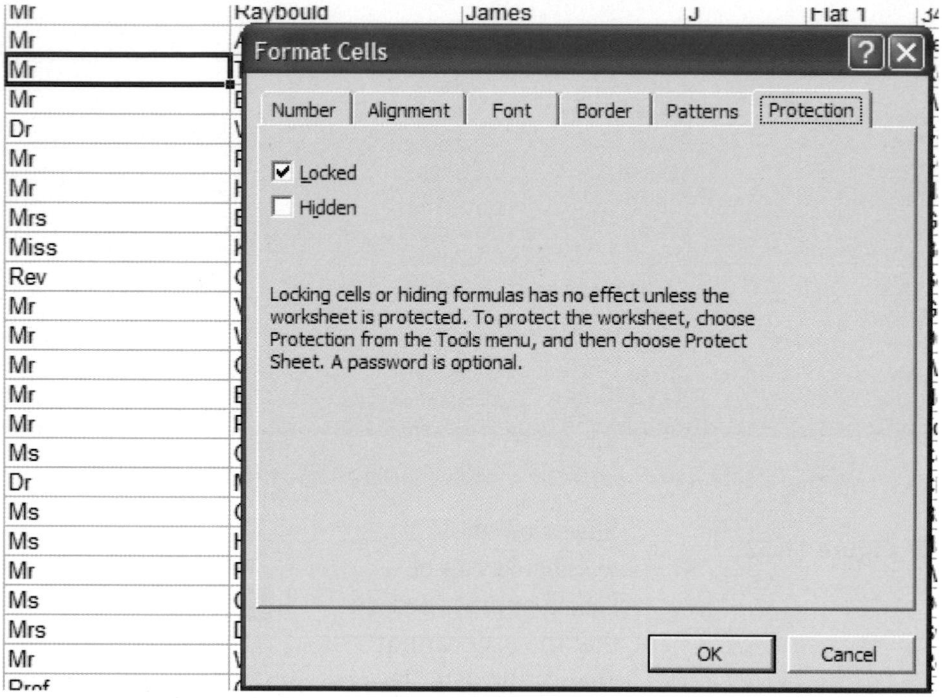

■ **Figure 11.56**

Automated data transfer from another sheet or application

Copying data from another sheet is easy. All you have to do is to go to that sheet, highlight what you want, select Edit → Copy or Ctrl-C, go back to the sheet where you want to place the data and select Edit → Paste or Ctrl-V.

If you often perform this operation, you can make it into a macro. All you have to do is to switch on the macro recorder, give the macro a name, then carry out the actions. You stop the recorder and you can replay this whenever you want.

If you go to Tools → Macro → Macros and select Edit, you can see the Visual Basic code that has been automatically generated. If you want to run this from a button next time, you can paste the code into the event procedure of a button on the worksheet.

```
Sub copy()
'
' copy Macro
' Macro recorded 13/02/2006 by Sean O'Byrne
'

'
    Sheets("Customers").Select
    Cells.Select
    Selection.copy
    Sheets("Sheet2").Select
    ActiveSheet.Paste
End Sub
```

■ **Figure 11.57**

When you have done this and the data is in the spreadsheet, you can stop the recorder and apply the program code to a command button on the sheet or a new button on the toolbar.

If you right-click on a toolbar and select Customize, then Macros, you can then drag a new button onto the toolbar.

You can then click on the new button and choose the macro that you want it to run.

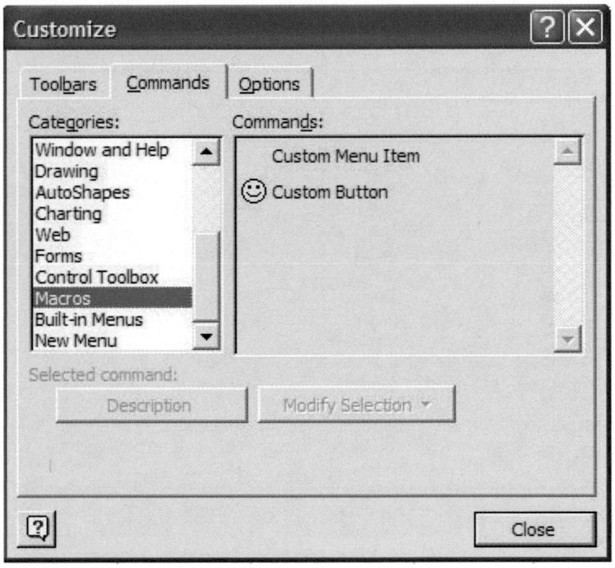

■ **Figure 11.59**

Figure 11.57 shows the code recorded for copying the data from a whole sheet and pasting it onto another called Sheet2.

If you want to get data that has been originated in another application, the process is much the same. Suppose you want automatically to bring in a CSV file that has been saved from a database application. You record a new macro and carry out the actions Data → Get External Data → Import Text file, then navigate to the source and answer the questions that the wizard asks about how to format the data and where to put it.

Customize

| Toolbars | Commands | Options |

Categories:

Window and Help
Drawing
AutoShapes
Charting
Web
Forms
Control Toolbox
Macros
Built-in Menus
New Menu

Commands:

Custom Menu Item

☺ Custom Button

Selected command:

Description   Modify Selection ▾

Close

■ **Figure 11.58**

Assign Macro

Macro name:

different_app

copy
different_app

Macros in: All Open Workbooks

Description
Macro recorded 13/02/2006 by Sean O'Byrne

OK

Cancel

Edit

Record...

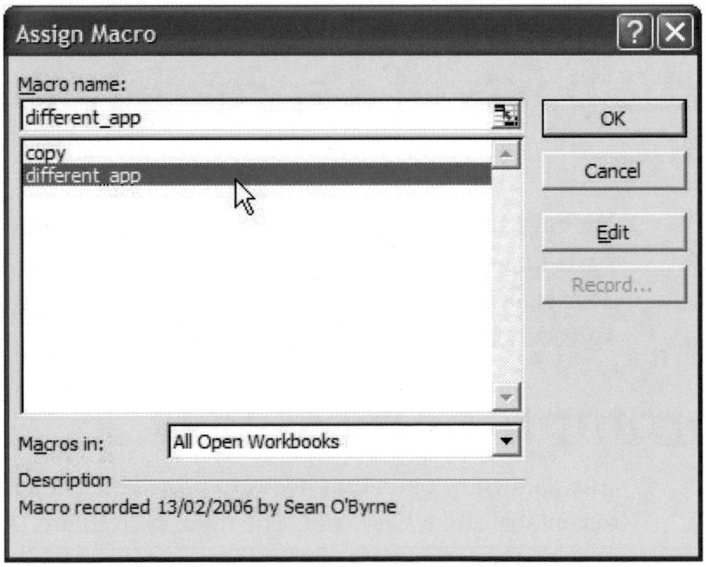

■ **Figure 11.60**

Using forms

Sometimes, it can be confusing for a user to understand exactly where data is supposed to go. You can make things easier by using forms. You can create forms from the Visual Basic environment as described in Unit 12, but there is a quick and easy way as well.

Often a spreadsheet is used as a simple (flat file) database. Some or all of the data on a worksheet can be arranged as a data table, with field names as headings and each row representing a record. In this case, you must have no space between the header row and the data itself. You can highlight the data range and then select Data → Form, and a form appears which makes it clearer what the user is typing in or editing. Although the data must be selected first, this action can be assigned to a macro if necessary.

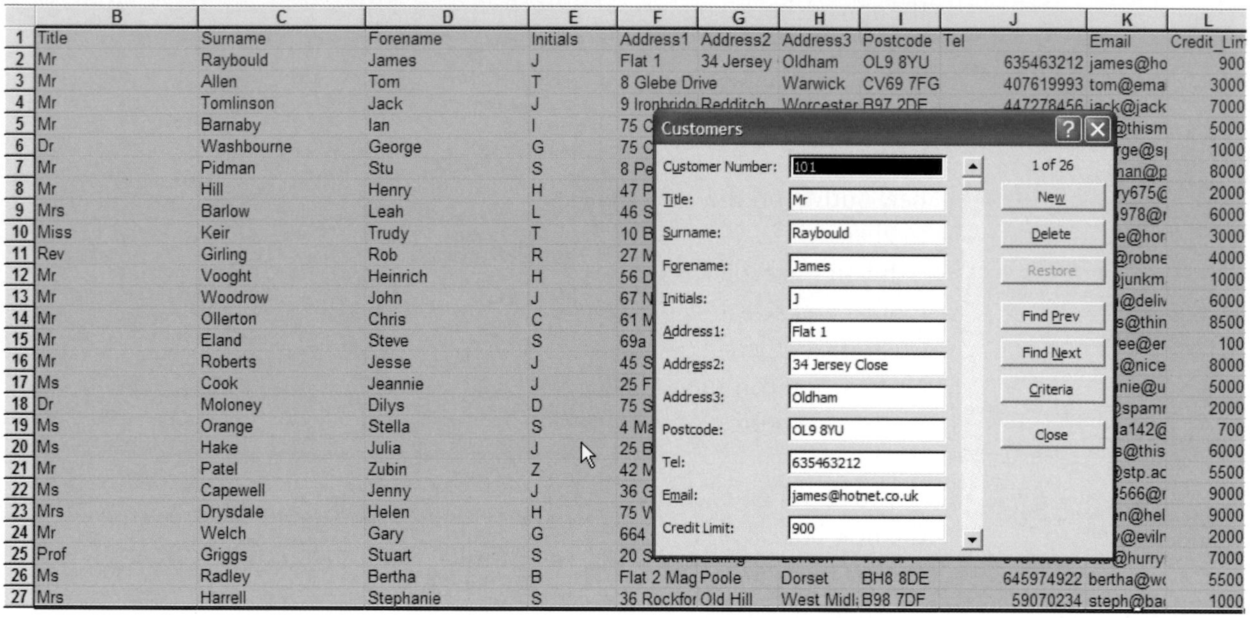

■ **Figure 11.61**

Limiting the parts of a spreadsheet the user can change

We have seen on page 242 that it is possible to hide and/or lock to protect parts of a spreadsheet so that the user cannot alter the data or the formulae. This is always a wise move when unknown users may have to make use of a spreadsheet containing valuable data.

Adding prompts or messages

Any data entry operation needs to provide users with hints as to what is acceptable and what is not. The more help that is given, the less likely it is that mistakes will be made.

On a spreadsheet, this can be provided in all sorts of ways.

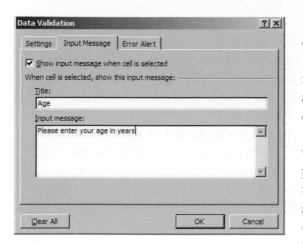

■ Figure 11.62

Text boxes can be placed at strategic places containing the instructions.

Prompts can be added by setting an input message for data validation. When a cell is selected a message appears to help the user decide what to put in the contents of the cell.

Comment boxes can be helpful in various ways. In the next unit we examine how they can be useful to provide reminders about what a certain cell is designed to achieve. They can also be helpful to the user of a spreadsheet. The comments appear when the mouse cursor passes over a cell and this can serve as a useful reminder if any special action or precaution needs to be taken.

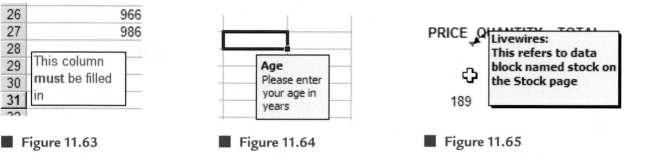

■ Figure 11.63   ■ Figure 11.64   ■ Figure 11.65

Using forms controls

If you select View → Toolbars → Control Toolbox, you get a small set of useful objects that you can place on a worksheet, some of which can be useful to validate data entry and make it easier for the user.

List boxes and combo boxes are good for providing a choice from a set of limited options. If you right click on the box to set the properties, you can set the source of the data in the ListFillRange field and the place where the data is

■ Figure 11.66

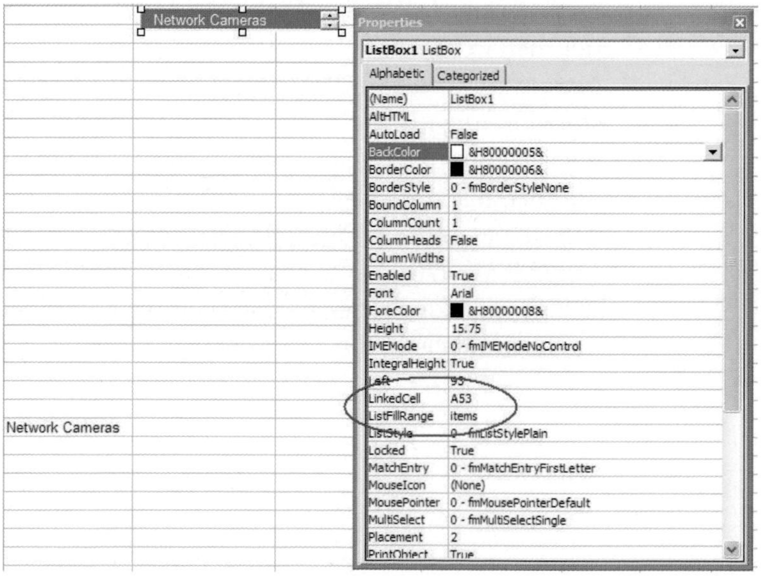

■ Figure 11.67

to go in the LinkedCell field. Exactly the same can be applied to a combo box, but the user is free to type in their own choice as well as what is in the list.

The control toolbox gives a wide variety of ways in which users can be helped to make the best use of a spreadsheet solution. You can easily customise a worksheet to be very user friendly by providing such aids as drop-down boxes, check boxes and radio buttons.

For example, the customer numbers on the Livewires spreadsheet can be selected by the user and VLOOKUP functions used to find the details of that particular customer.

	A	B	C	D	E	F
1				Livewires		
2				Invoice		
3			To:	176	▼	
4		Customer Number:	176			
5		Mr	Jack	176		
6		9 Ironbridge Road		254		
7		Redditch		266		
8		Worcestershire		296		
9		B97 2DE		324		
10				333		
11				336		
12			Details	345		
13	ITEM CODE	ITEM	PRICE	QUANTITY	TOTAL	
14	AE424657	Netsolutions OfficeConnect wireless 54 Mbps travel router	189	1	189	
15	AE424707	Supernet 10/100 PCI adapter	189	5	945	
16	AE424711	Supernet 10/100/1000 PCI adapter	189	1	189	
17	AF524775	Supanet 56k External Modem	189	1	189	
18						

If you use a combo box to select a number, it converts it into text. If you send the user's choice to fill in a particular cell, using the linked cell property, this text will not then work if you

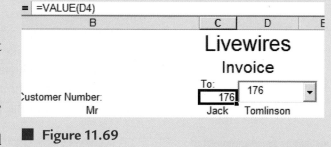

■ Figure 11.69

need to perform a VLOOKUP to a block of data where the numbers are stored in true number form. One way round this is to set the combo-box-linked cell to one cell, then use the function VALUE to convert this to a true number in another cell.

In the example in Figure 11.69, the combo box has looked up 176 but has stored it as "176", i.e. as character data in cell D4. In cell C4, we use the VALUE function to change it back into a proper number so that it can look up the numbers in the customer data block.

Remember that if you have a sheet that has controls on it and you want the data selected to appear without the controls, you can simply use the = (equals) sign on a different sheet to copy the cells you want to a new location.

By changing the appearance of a worksheet – by removing grid lines and adding controls – you can produce a wide variety of useful documents such as:

▶ invoices
▶ order forms
▶ tax summaries
▶ bank statements.

A worksheet does not have to end up looking like a worksheet!

Using buttons to initiate procedures

We have seen that it is possible to set up buttons on a worksheet to activate a macro. Similarly, a button can be placed on the toolbar to do the same. Buttons are intuitive and most users find them easy to cope with. Buttons can also be placed on user forms set up in the Visual Basic environment. Unit 12 shows many examples of how they can be used to carry out any process required. Designing a user interface to make use of buttons is an essential step in the process of setting up a spreadsheet application.

Future-proofing

Aims

■ To design a spreadsheet in order to make it easy to update

Introduction

MAINTENANCE The altering of a system after it has been implemented.

In Unit 11.3, we took a brief look at how a spreadsheet can be set up in such a way to make it useful for as long as possible. We do not want the effort that goes into constructing a complex spreadsheet to go to waste, so we have to bear in mind the MAINTENANCE issues.

We examined how the concept of 'layering' can help greatly in the designing of a complex system. Networks are built from several layers which focus attention separately upon functions such as the cabling used, the way in which the data is packaged up to be sent, the ways in which errors are corrected, the way that data is routed through the network and the way in which applications place data on the network and retrieve it.

One well-known model upon which networks are designed is known as the OSI seven layer model. This divides functionality into seven separate areas including those mentioned above. The good thing about this is that any layer can be updated without having to worry about doing anything to other layers.

The same approach can be designed into your spreadsheet. A complex spreadsheet involves stores of data, input and output and processing. As far as is possible, these functions should be kept physically apart – on different worksheets if you can.

This is not always possible to do – some sheets are interactive, where there will be input and output on the same page. There will be times when an output page has processing embedded in it. All this is inevitable, but as a general rule, activities should be kept separate.

The advantage is the same for the spreadsheet as it is for a network. You can change parts without having to worry about the effects on other parts. A network engineer can install a new network operating system without having to renew the cabling. A spreadsheet used for creating invoices can have new types of charges added in without having to alter the list of customers.

Storing values which change frequently

Suppose a spreadsheet is used to calculate the cost of items on sale. The items are subject to Value Added Tax (VAT). Suppose at the moment the VAT rate is 17.5%. You can set up a sheet with this figure incorporated into the formulae you use.

Price	VAT
39.99	=D2*0.175
49.99	=D3*0.175
49.99	=D4*0.175
59.99	=D5*0.175
66.99	=D6*0.175
171	=D7*0.175
1609	=D8*0.175
16.99	=D9*0.175
3.99	=D10*0.175
8.99	=D11*0.175
11.99	=D12*0.175

■ **Figure 11.70**

Price	VAT
39.99	=D2*VAT
49.99	=D3*VAT
49.99	=D4*VAT
59.99	=D5*VAT
66.99	=D6*VAT
171	=D7*VAT
1609	=D8*VAT
16.99	=D9*VAT
3.99	=D10*VAT
8.99	=D11*VAT
11.99	=D12*VAT

■ **Figure 11.72**

One day, the VAT rate may change. Think of all the effort in finding all references to 0.175 and changing them to the new rate. You will probably have forgotten many of them and your spreadsheet will start giving wrong answers. It is much better to set up a cell which stores this rate and name it VAT. While you are at it, you should label this cell by entering what it is in an adjacent cell.

It is a good idea to keep items like this stored on a separate sheet. You could call it 'Lookup' and any adjustments will be easy to find.

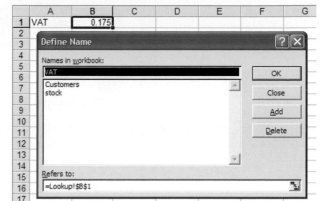

■ **Figure 11.71**

This way, when you need to work out the VAT for an item, you enter a formula that refers to the named cell. If the VAT rate changes, you just change it once on the lookup worksheet.

This approach is suitable for a wide range of purposes such as discount rates, commissions and currency conversion rates.

Creating templates for standard layouts

A spreadsheet can take a lot of effort to set up. Sometimes, the hardest work is involved with making it look right. If you have designed something that will be reused again and again, such as an invoice, you may want to save it as a template.

■ **Figure 11.73**

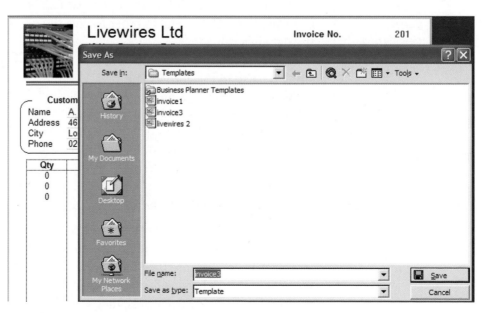

Then, when you next select File → New, you will be able to start a new spreadsheet based on the contents and layout of the template.

Figure 11.74

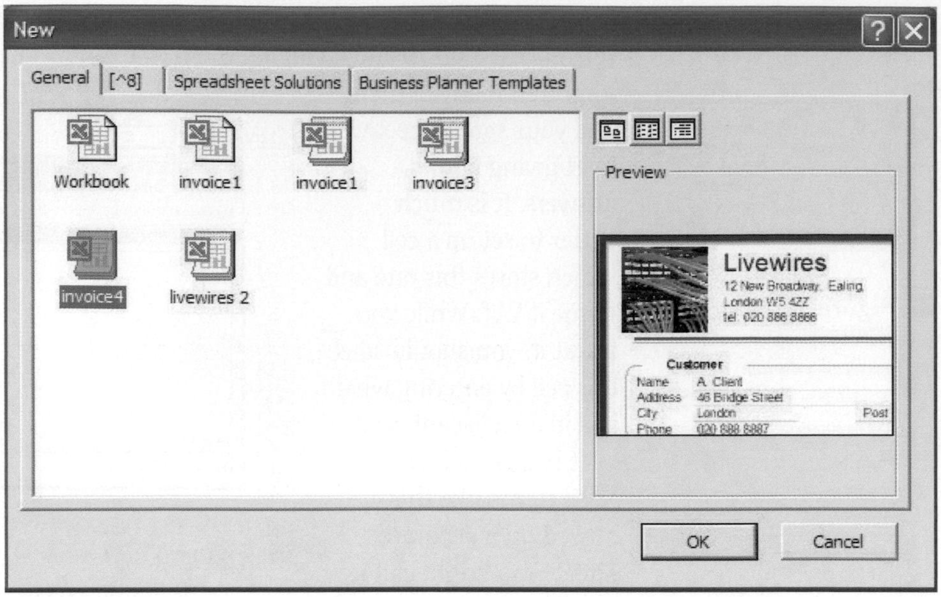

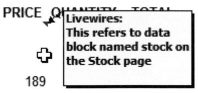

There are lots of free spreadsheets and templates available on the web. You can also make your own so that future projects are made easier.

http://www.exinfm.com/free_spreadsheets.html

Documenting spreadsheets by adding comments

When programmers write program code, there is always the certainty that as the program grows, they will forget a lot of the logic that went into the creation of the program. For this reason, programmers always embed comments along with their code so that there is a constant reminder why things were done in the way that they were.

Producing a complex spreadsheet is just the same. It is easy to put comments into cells so that their purpose can be easily understood. Comments are also useful in order to give the users extra information about the data in a cell.

Cells containing comments have a small red flag in the corner. The comments can be seen by moving the mouse cursor over the cell or by selecting View → Comments from the menu.

Figure 11.75

Figure 11.76

Locking and protecting cells

We have already looked at how to protect cells, worksheets and workbooks in Unit 11.6. You should always remember to do this when setting up a spreadsheet for others to use, because they could accidentally or deliberately make changes to the logic or the underlying data that would result in wrong results being produced. As with any passwords, they should be chosen to be remembered by you and any support staff, but not easy to guess by the users. Another useful technique is to hide cells so that the user is not aware that they are there.

Presentation of results

Aims

- To consider the importance of good presentation design
- To look at examples of design

In this unit, you will learn about some of the ways good graphic design can help present your results. Good design will make your spreadsheet much more user friendly. It is not difficult to achieve using quite simple techniques combined with a careful approach to layout.

Page layout

The way you lay out your page is very important. If your layout is confusing, mistakes will be made and incorrect results will follow. Also the users will be put off using the spreadsheet.

Some ideas for good design:

- ▶ Do not have too much on any one screen.
- ▶ Arrange items symmetrically.
- ▶ Use word wrap to avoid very wide headings in cells.
- ▶ Group similar data items together.
- ▶ Use borders and shading to group data.

Most spreadsheets have a very wide range of fonts and styles available. Some very fancy some very plain. If you look at a few professional spreadsheets you will notice that they use simple fonts most of the time.

 http://www.exinfm.com/free_spreadsheets.html

Font styles

The word *style* can refer to the use of bold, italic and underlining when using text. It is often better to use a change in style rather than changing the font to make something stand out.

Charts and graphs

Spreadsheets can produce many different chart types, which can lead to some confusion when deciding which chart type you need for a given set of data. The most common types of chart and their uses are explained in the table on page 254. One of the advantages of a chart is that trends can be displayed. Also when you create charts using a spreadsheet they can change as values change in the spreadsheet.

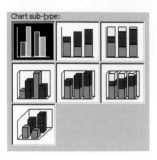

■ **Figure 11.77**

Pie chart

Pie charts are often misused. They should only be used if you want to show proportions. An example of this would be to display data on what form of transport people use to travel to school or college. Take care not to have too many categories or the chart becomes meaningless. If you have lots of categories, you should consider combining them to reduce the overall number.

Bar chart

The bar chart is perhaps the most frequently used of all chart types. It is simple and easy to understand so it is useful for a range of data types. There is a variety of ways that bar charts can be displayed. If you have long names for the data items consider turning the labels sideways.

A bar chart is best used if you need to compare values. For example the number of a particular item sold each month.

Scatter chart

Scatter charts are used to display two sets of data on a chart, to see if there is a relationship. You saw an example of one on page 210.

Line chart

Line charts are most often used where there is a period of time involved. It is also useful for showing all sorts of relationships, e.g. expansion against temperature. These charts are perfect for displaying trends. For example, plotting a graph of how long it takes for a room to warm up on a cold day.

Purpose of the Chart	Appropriate Chart Type
Compare data that is in categories	Column chart, bar chart, radar chart
Compare data over time	Area chart, line chart, column chart (stacked), high-low chart
Percentage of total comparisons	Pie chart, doughnut chart, stacked bar or column
Relationship between two variables	Scatter plot

Graphics

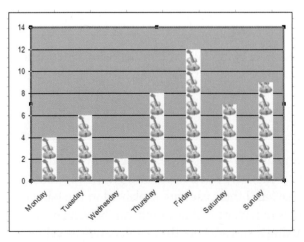

■ **Figure 11.78**

Graphics can be used in a number of ways on a spreadsheet. They can be used to enhance the appearance or give the sheet a corporate look. If a company has a logo then it is likely that this will appear on all the pages somewhere so plan for this in your design.

Graphics can also be used as buttons to run macros, for example a picture of a printer could have a macro assigned to it that prints out the current page. If you are designing a spreadsheet for young people then this is a good technique to use.

Graphics can also be used to produce a pictogram which is a type of chart using pictures or graphics to represent numeric values rather than just bars.

Animation

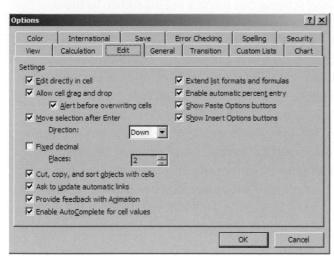

■ Figure 11.79

You can add animation to your workbooks by changing the options in the Tools menu. So that, instead of seeing a new column just appear when you add it, the animation makes the column slide into position, by moving existing columns to the right.

It is also possible to simulate animation in graphs and charts using scroll bars. It is possible to investigate change to variables and see the changes animate on the graph.

The following web link shows how this can be used to teach population dynamics. There are several sliders used in this example which enable you to model population dynamics by varying factors using scroll bars.

 http://sunsite.univie.ac.at/Projects/ demography/DemoMovie.xls

ACTIVITY

Load the spreadsheet from the web link and experiment with it to see how animations can be used.

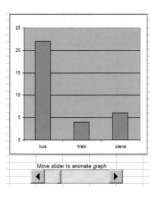

■ Figure 11.80

Colours, borders and shading

Background and borders

Borders can be used to make things stand out or to separate out groups of data. A user can easily be guided to look at a particular part of the sheet by using borders.

Emphasis

There are several ways you can emphasise something so that someone's attention is drawn in a particular direction. You can use:

▶ **bold**
▶ colour
▶ highlighting
▶ negatives

Colours and shading

Choosing the correct colour scheme can make a big difference to the appearance and readability of a spreadsheet. People's attention is drawn to bright, basic colours but after a short time the eye becomes tired. If you want to get attention very quickly, then use bright colours. However if you are trying to present specific information that needs to be well understood or the page needs to be read carefully, bright colours will not help.

Eye fatigue is more likely to occur at the yellow and red end of the spectrum, and will spoil concentration as well as increase the risk of errors. Only use bright colours for important information that must stand out.

Conditional cell formatting ,when combined with the use of colours, can be used to draw attention to an event. For example, on the Livewires spreadsheet if a customer exceeds the credit limit then a red box appears with the words 'OVER LIMIT' in it. Red is used as it is a colour associated with warnings that something is wrong.

■ **Figure 11.81**

		Credit limit
Total	945	OVER LIMIT

Testing

Aims

■ To emphasise the importance of testing

■ To look at strategies for testing

Testing is one of the most important stages in the development of a spreadsheet. All software should be tested before the user is given the final system. All possible outcomes must be tested so you should plan carefully how you will test the spreadsheet.

Spreadsheets can be complicated systems. When it comes to testing, they will have many instances of formulae and data. The formulae are connected to data in various parts of the workbook. One small error in a formula can produce a useless jumble of numbers.

Does the solution meet all the requirements listed in the functional specification?

ACTIVITY

Devise a questionnaire for the user of the spreadsheet to collect opinions on the solution.

At the start of the development process, a functional specification was drawn up. This needs to be looked at again during the testing process to ensure that all the aims and objectives have been met. You should try to involve the user in this part of the testing to answer the question, 'Does the spreadsheet do what you need it to do?' It is often difficult to test the spreadsheet under real conditions, but every effort should be made to do this.

The final spreadsheet should be reviewed carefully alongside the original specification. Feedback from the user might mean changing a few things at this stage, but it is better to make these changes before it is handed over. Consider which aims have been met and the extent to which they have been met. Are there any aims that have not or could not be met?

When anlaysing the final spreadsheet you should refer back to the prototyping and final testing you carried out.

Is the underlying logic of the spreadsheet correct?

This refers to the way in which the spreadsheet operates and carries out the calculations. Logic errors can result when you have used an incorrect formula or if you have written a function and the ALGORITHM for that function is wrong. You might have the correct algorithm but have implemented it incorrectly.

One of the most common causes of errors in formulae is a result of not understanding the order in which a spreadsheet will carry out calculations. See page 218 for coverage of algebraic logic. The best way to check out the logic is to use some simple data so that you are able to calculate the answer by using a calculator. You can then compare your results with that of the spreadsheet.

Do all the functions and formulae work correctly?

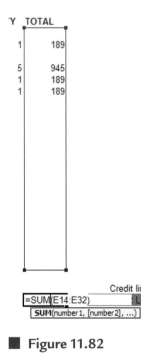

Figure 11.82

It only needs one wrong formula to make the whole spreadsheet useless. Careful testing of all parts of the workbook is required to be sure of the end result in all circumstances.

Formulae can be checked in a number of ways. The sheet can be viewed with all the formulae displayed, or individual cells can be examined by double-clicking them. The sheet then displays the formula and highlights all the cells connected with it. Figure 11.82 shows a section of the Livewires invoice with the formula displayed in this way.

Functions must follow the correct syntax for them to work. The order in which the function's variables are entered must be correct. For example when using the IF function, check that the logic is correct and the actions are in the correct sequence:

IF (condition, TRUE action, FALSE action).

ACTIVITY

Look carefully at the following statements:

```
IF(A2>A3,"Greater","Less")
IF(A2<A3,"Greater","Less")
IF(A2<A3,"Less","Greater")
IF(A2>A3,"Less","Greater")
```

The aim is for the cell containing the formula to display 'Greater' IF the value in A3 is higher than the value in the cell A2 and 'Less' IF the value in A3 is lower than the value in the cell A2.

Devise some suitable test values for A2 and A3 and decide which of the statements will achieve the aim.

If you have followed the advice in Unit 11.3 and built your workbook in a modular way, then each section should be tested as you build the workbook.

Does the built-in validation prevent unacceptable data values from being entered?

The Livewires workbook on the CD has some cells that use methods of validation.

When testing the spreadsheet, the validation methods must be tested for correct functioning. The level of stock for any item will never exceed 200 and cannot be less than 0.

To test this, attempts should be made to enter values that will be rejected and values that will be accepted. For example:

- ▶ 0 (zero) should be accepted
- ▶ −2 should be rejected
- ▶ 250 should be rejected.

ACTIVITY

Load the spreadsheet and try the above values in the No_in_stock column of the stock sheet.

Take some screen shots of your results.

Planning is vital. All validation rules should be tested. It is easy to make a mistake and have a field that is not able to accept good data due to a simple mistake such as using the wrong symbol e.g. >100 instead of <100. Such mistakes are easy to make but can be hard to correct once the spreadsheet has been handed over to the user.

ACTIVITY

Load the sheet and look at the **ITEM CODE** column on the invoice sheet. Notice how the sheet provides a list of stock codes.

Look at the validation rule for this column and try to test it with invalid codes.

Can the spreadsheet cope with normal, extreme and abnormal data?

The testing needs to cover all possible data that could be entered into the workbook.

The stock level is always between 0 and 200. The column is set up to validate the number entered.

- ▶ **Normal data** such as 23 or 115 will be accepted and should not produce an error message. Numbers at the limits should also be checked. 0 and 200 are examples of normal data at the limits.
- ▶ **Extreme data** falls outside the normal limits. −5 and 210 are examples that could be used here. Data that is just outside the boundaries should also be entered −1 and 201 are the numbers to use in this case.
- ▶ **Abnormal data** is types of data that are not expected. For example, a user might enter the letter 'O' instead of a zero or hit the space bar in the middle of a number such as 25.

Only by testing with the three types of data can you be confident that your workbook will stand up to a user when it is in use. Here is an example of a test plan for the No_in_stock column:

Reason for test	Data type	Data entered
Not an integer	Abnormal	Letter O
Out of range	Extreme	–3
Out of range	Extreme	200
Good data	Normal	32
Boundary	Normal	200
Boundary	Normal	0
Boundary	Extreme	–1
Boundary	Extreme	201

Is the spreadsheet robust or can it be made to fail?

It is easy to say a system works well if you test what you already know works. During testing, you should set out to try and make the workbook fail, by trying to do unexpected things. Try pasting a formula from one cell into the wrong place. The formula should be locked so that this cannot happen.

Can other people use the spreadsheet without help?

portfolio_tip

Produce prototypes as you go along and get feedback along the way. Do not leave it all until the end or there will be too much to do.

The best way to see how easy a system is to use is to test it out on others. Someone who has not seen your workbook before should try it out to see how easy it is to use. Feedback on ease of use can then be looked at to review the system. It is often the case that someone else will see issues that you as the designer did not see because you are so familiar with the whole thing.

For the assessment, you are required to involve others in the testing and evaluation process and to use that feedback to modify your spreadsheet.

Documentation

Aims

- To understand the importance of documentation
- To examine what needs to be included in documentation

All computer systems need documentation. There are two major categories of documentation, which fulfil different needs:

- ▶ user documentation
- ▶ technical documentation.

A software solution is a combination of software and documentation. An excellent spreadsheet might be difficult to use, if the documentation is poor.

To produce good documentation, you should think of it as an extension of the spreadsheet system itself and try to work on it as part of the development process. You are using feedback from the user in the development of the spreadsheet and the same should apply to documentation. When the spreadsheet is tested by the user, be sure to test the documentation as well.

How to use the application

Documentation should be matched to the users and their likely level of experience. If the users are computer specialists, the documentation will be written differently from that for users without computer experience.

Your user documentation should be well laid out with a contents page. This should lead to section headings that will probably include some of the ones suggested here.

- ▶ **System requirements** Your spreadsheet will be written using a particular spreadsheet application. Your user will need that application installed to use your spreadsheet. This will need to form part of your specification.
- ▶ **Prior knowledge** Your user may not have used spreadsheets before. You need to make clear what skills you expect your user to have in order to use your spreadsheet.
- ▶ **Installation instructions** Most spreadsheets will open without any special installation procedures. However, if you have used macros in your spreadsheet, the user might need to know how to enable them. They are often disabled for security reasons, particularly on a network.
- ▶ **Getting started** This should show the user what needs to be done to open the spreadsheet. This might include copying the spreadsheet from the disk it is supplied on to the hard drive of the computer.

See also Unit 12.10

▶ **Entering data** How does your user enter data into your spreadsheet? Describe any methods such as entering into cells directly or how to use any forms you might have set up.

▶ **Amending or deleting data** If the user needs to change any data, it should be clear how this is best done. For example, there may be important data items that can be amended, such as the rate of VAT.

▶ **Backups** How the user backs up the spreadsheet should be made clear. There may be external data items that need to be backed up as well.

Good documentation will include screen shots and numbered instructions to help the user.

Menus and data-entry forms

Good documentation should include screen shots of the interface that the user will see. These make it much clearer what has to be done than simply relying on words alone. You can make screen shots just by pressing the Prt Scrn key and then using 'paste' to place the screen capture into your document. It is much better if you have specialist graphic software to prepare screen shots so that you can focus in on a small part of the screen and save just that part. Saving the shot in an uncompressed format such as TIFF or BMP will produce a better quality image. The screen shots in this book were taken with such software.

The GIMP software provided on the CD for Unit 10 will do this task for you. Figure 11.83 shows how to activate this feature in GIMP.

Software for capturing screen shots also provides ways of annotating the shot. For example, you can highlight a part of the screen to draw attention to it or add arrows to the image to point to a particular feature.

Images combined with good numbered instructions and examples of data to try are an effective way to provide documentation.

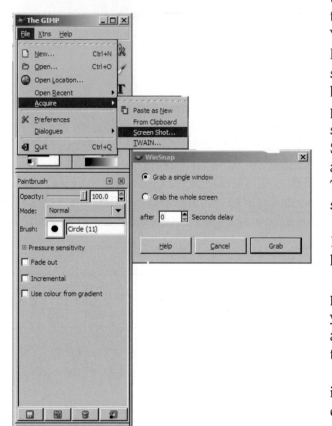

■ **Figure 11.83**

Error messages

To reach the higher mark ranges for your spreadsheet, the data entered by the software should be validated. If a user enters invalid data by mistake then you should provide meaningful error messages on screen. A good clear message will not need further explanation. However your documentation should give some guidance on how the user can avoid errors and there should also be explanations of any system error messages that your spreadsheet might display.

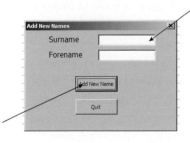

■ **Figure 11.84**

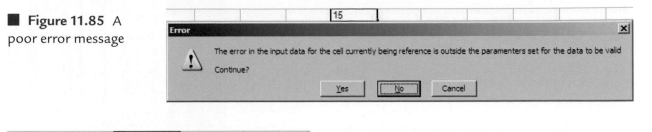

■ **Figure 11.85** A
poor error message

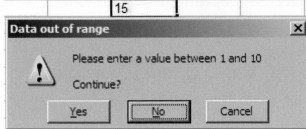

■ **Figure 11.86** A better error message

In Figure 11.85 not only is the message confusing but it also contains spelling errors which will reduce the confidence of the user in the quality of the system.

What the message really means is better explained by the message in Figure 11.86.

The user might need guidance on what the choices 'Yes' 'No' and 'Cancel' will do with the data.

Troubleshooting strategies

Even the best software will sometimes give unexpected errors and maybe malfunction. Possibly this could be the result of problems with the computer. Your documentation should give some ideas to try out when things do not work as they should. For example if the spreadsheet freezes when it is open, what can the user try to rescue any data or restart the program?

Technical documentation

At some point your spreadsheet might need to be updated, and you might not be available to do the job. The users will probably not have enough experience to do the job themselves and so will employ a specialist to do the job for them.

They might be able to work things out for themselves but it will be much quicker and less expensive if you have left sufficient information to allow someone else to adapt and maintain your system.

Technical documentation for a spreadsheet should include:

► the final design specification
► the hardware and software required
► how to open the spreadsheet
► a copy of calculations and formulae
► functions used
► names and code for any macros used
► details of cells with validation
► details of any forms used for input
► copies of test results
► details of any hidden and protected cells
► names and ranges of any tables defined.

Evaluation

Aims

- To examine the success of the spreadsheet
- To examine personal performance in the production of the spreadsheet

In the course of this unit, you should have produced a complex spreadsheet ready for someone else to use. You should have gone through all the usual planning stages that software developers use when they are producing solutions professionally. You should have designed and developed a spreadsheet and documented it for the user. You will also have produced technical documentation to enable someone else to maintain your spreadsheet.

At the same time as producing the spreadsheet, you will have been learning new skills and processes. For the purpose of this unit, you should have been paying attention to your own performance, and the new skills you have developed.

> **portfolio_tip**
>
> Make sure you refer to your own skills and how they have developed in this evaluation.

The spreadsheet

This will have been produced to fulfil the requirements of a user. The process will have involved a lot of liaison with the user or other person who requires the spreadsheet system. This stage will have ended with the production of a functional specification – a document that sets out what the system must do.

When the spreadsheet is complete, it is necessary to go back to the functional specification and ask whether the requirements have been met. You, the developer, should ask yourself that before handing over the software to the client or user.

If, for example, the solution is supposed to produce a set of graphs you need to verify that it does this accurately and in the manner specified.

You should also ask whether the solution is a good one and does it make the best use of the spreadsheet facilities available to you?

You should ask yourself whether the same or better results could have been achieved by using a different approach. Have you made the spreadsheet too complicated?

Your performance

You should consider how well you tackled this unit. Ask yourself what you can now do compared with when you started. How did you find out the things you needed to know? Did you consult:

- ► teachers
- ► websites
- ► the software help system
- ► books?

What skills in developing a spreadsheet have you acquired as you have gone along? What new knowledge have you developed about spreadsheets?

The assessment

The evaluation stage of a project like this one is a good time to look at what you have produced in terms of what needs to be produced for assessment.
   The specification says:

> **For this unit you will:**
> Design, produce, test and evaluate a solution to a complex problem involving the use of spreadsheet software.

Check that this is in fact what you did. You must have a spreadsheet that will enable someone to solve a complex problem. Evidence will be in the form of the completed spreadsheet, documentation, screen shots showing development and screen shots showing that testing has been completed.

> **Your eportfolio for this unit should include:**
> **a** A functional specification that describes the problem and explains what the spreadsheet is required to do.

Right at the beginning of the project, the functional specification should be clearly set out. Quite possibly this will be as a set of bullet points. These will form the basis for your final evaluation of the product. Check that your specification includes a clear description of the problem you set out to solve.

> **b** An initial design that satisfies the functional requirements and describes the data to be entered and the processing that is required. It must include some measures to structure and validate data and use functions and formulae to analyse complex data. You must have considered screen layout and presentation, the user interface and presentation of results.
>   You also need evidence that you produced some prototypes then improved and refined the design using feedback on these prototypes.

Check that there is evidence that your designs closely match what the client wants. Does the solution make proper use of complex facilities available in your spreadsheet software?

c A fully working spreadsheet solution that meets all the functional requirements, with supporting user and technical documentation.

There should be plenty of screen shots showing the spreadsheet in use. Your solution must be documented for the user. You also need to have produced documentation for a technical user that is sufficient for someone with a technical background to able to maintain your spreadsheet at some point in the future.

d Evidence of formative and summative testing.

e An evaluation assessing:
- the spreadsheet
- your own performance and current skill level, identifying areas for improvement
- use of feedback from others.

ICT skills

Aims

- To illustrate the skills needed to set up a complex spreadsheet
- To reinforce some of the skills already covered in this unit

This section is essentially a 'how to do it' section. It looks at the skills you will require to build a complex spreadsheet for this unit. There are examples of the use of these facilities in other parts of the chapter.

To gain high marks, the spreadsheet will be a complex one, with some complicated formulae. It will need to use several linked sheets and include some macros to aid the user. You will need to test the sheet, document it and then make it available to a user.

Combining complex information and linking to other applications

Exporting and importing data

Exporting data is preparing the data for use in other pieces of software. Importing data is loading data into your spreadsheet from another package.

There are a number of formats that you can use to export data from Excel. To access them, use the Save As option and use the pull-down list to choose your format.

Figure 11.87

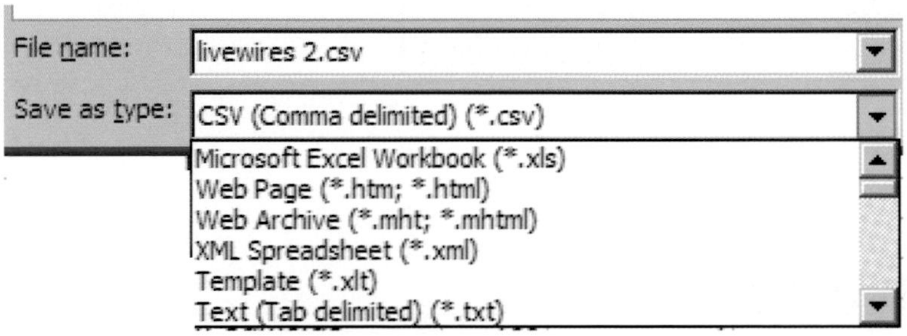

One method of exporting data is to make a comma separated values (CSV) file from your spreadsheet. This will produce a file containing the data from your spreadsheet with a comma between each item. See Figure 11.88. This method of saving data is widely used and files in this format can be imported into most software.

If you turn formula view on first, then the CSV contains your formulae instead of your data.

A	B	C	D	E	F	G
Part_Numl	Description	Category	Price	No_in_stock	Re_order_level	Re_order_quantity
AE424657	Netsolutions OfficeConnect wireless 54 Mbps travel router	Networking connections	39.99	26	22	30
AE424658	Netsolutions OfficeConnect wireless 54 Mbps print server	Networking connections	49.99	90	87	100
AE424665	Netsolutions OfficeConnect wireless 54 Mbps gateway	Networking connections	49.99	15	14	20

```
Part_Number,Description,Category, Price ,No_in_stock,Re_order_level,Re_order_quantity
AE424657,Netsolutions OfficeConnect wireless 54 Mbps travel router,Networking connections,39.99,26,22,30
AE424658,Netsolutions OfficeConnect wireless 54 Mbps print server,Networking connections,49.99,90,87,100
AE424665,Netsolutions OfficeConnect wireless 54 Mbps gateway,Networking connections,49.99,15,14,20
```

■ **Figure 11.88**

> **portfolio_tip**
>
> Exporting to a web page is a suitable format to use for portfolio.

Link objects

Many different types of objects can be linked to a spreadsheet. This section covers some of the ones you might find useful in your project.

You can create links between cells in different workbooks:

1 Open both the workbooks.
2 If you are creating a formula, press = (equals sign).
3 In the Window menu, click the name of the other workbook.
4 Select the cells you want to link to.
5 When you finish entering the formula, press ENTER.

You can link or embed objects from other programs using Object Linking and Embedding (OLE). This is supported by many different programs. For example, you can insert an Adobe Acrobat (PDF) document into Microsoft Excel.

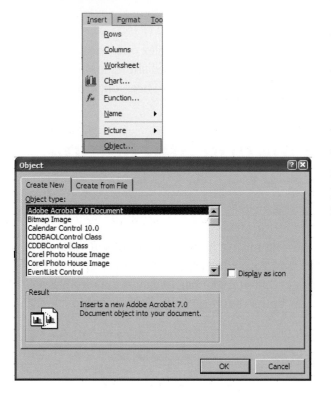

■ **Figure 11.89**

Organising data

■ **Figure 11.90**

In Microsoft Excel, when you open the spreadsheet you are starting a **workbook**. Just like an ordinary book, this contains separate pages. A workbook can contain several **worksheets**. These are single pages within a workbook.

When you first run a spreadsheet program such as Excel, you start off with three worksheets.

Figure 11.90 shows the three tabs for the three worksheets at start up.

You should always give your worksheets names that have sensible meanings. This is another standard and sensible way of working. If you look at the example workbook in the Livewires model, the names look like this:

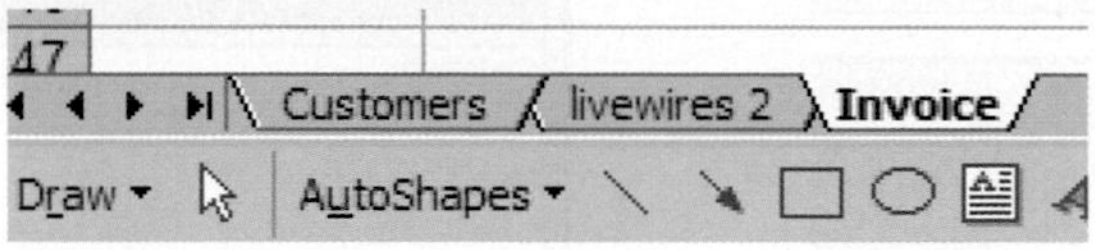

■ Figure 11.91

Using meaningful names means that most people who look at the workbook will be able to understand the thinking behind the system that you have used.

Linked sheets

Cells on different pages can be linked in a workbook.
   You can create links between cells in different sheets:

1 Open the workbook.
2 If you are creating a formula press = (equals sign).
3 At the bottom of the screen, click on the name of the other sheet.
4 Select the cells you want to refer to.
5 When you finish entering the formula, press ENTER.

You can link cells on any number of sheets in a workbook so that changing data on one sheet changes the linked cells on others.

Lookup tables

Lookup tables are used in the Livewires example on the CD. The invoice uses a lookup table to find data for the customer's name and address as well as prices and item descriptions.
   The formula used for the customer's title is:

```
=VLOOKUP($A$4,Customers,2)
```

This looks up the value in A4 (the customer's number) in the lookup table called Customers, it then returns the value from the second column, which holds the customer's title. The image shows part of the lookup table.

	A	B	C	D	E
1					
2	Customer_Number	Title	Surname	Forename	Initials
3	101	Mr	Raybould	James	J
4	132	Mr	Allen	Tom	T
5	176	Mr	Tomlinson	Jack	J

■ Figure 11.92

To define a lookup table:

1 Highlight the area to be used.
2 Click on Insert.
3 Choose Name.
4 Choose Define.
5 In the pop-up window, give the table a meaningful name.

ICT skills

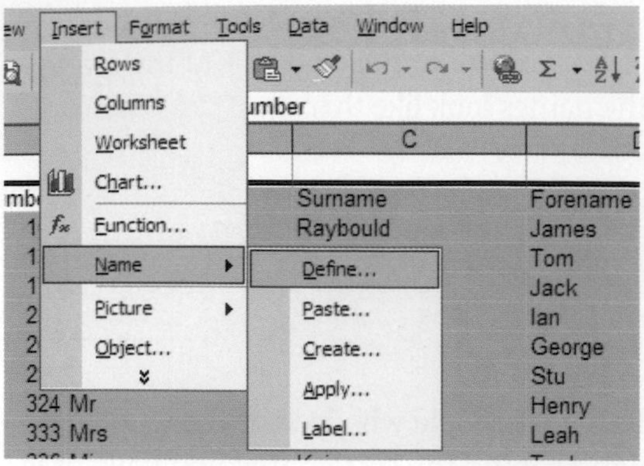

Figure 11.93

Figure 11.94

Entering and editing data

Absolute and relative cell referencing

An absolute cell reference refers to a fixed cell location. References to it will not alter if they are copied or moved. To do this a dollar sign is added in front of the row and column references:

```
=C2*$F$3
```

This is called absolute cell addressing.

When you use relative cell referencing and you copy a formula down, it adjusts to reflect its new position. The spreadsheet works like this because that is usually what the user wants. In Figure 11.96 the formula to calculate the total cost of a number of items on the invoice is entered as =D14*C14 and then copied down the column.

```
=VLOOKUP($C$4,Customers,2,2)
=VLOOKUP($C$4,Customers,6,1)
=VLOOKUP($C$4,Customers,7,1)
=VLOOKUP($C$4,Customers,8,1)
=VLOOKUP($C$4,Customers,9,1)
```

Figure 11.95

TOTAL
=D14*C14
=D15*C15
=D16*C16
=D17*C17
=D18*C18
=D19*C19
=D20*C20
=D21*C21
=D22*C22
=D23*C23
=D24*C24
=D25*C25
=D26*C26

Figure 11.96

Inserting data into multiple cells simultaneously

To enter the same data into several cells at once quickly:

1 Select the cells where you want to enter data. The cells do not have to be adjacent. (If they are not adjacent, you will need to use Ctrl+Click to select each cell.)
2 Type the data and press Ctrl+Enter.

Using multiple worksheets

To organise your workbook and make it easier to use, you should set up worksheets for different aspects of the tasks. For example, in the Livewires workbook there are three sheets:

► customers
► stock
► invoice.

Each sheet holds part of the system. This makes it easier to maintain and use.

Formatting

Cell formats

Setting the cell data type is an important step in the refinement of a spreadsheet. If you leave it up to the spreadsheet then odd things might happen.

If you enter a telephone number such as:

    0123457654222

the spreadsheet will change it to:

    1.23458E+11

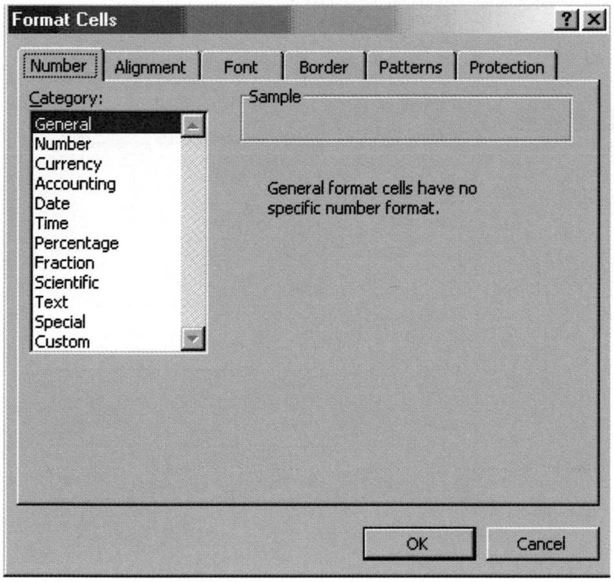

Figure 11.97

Because the spreadsheet assumes the data is a number, it removes the zero from the beginning. Then, because the number is a long one it changes it into something called **standard form** (otherwise known as scientific notation). Clearly this is no use for displaying a telephone number. If you need to store a telephone number, then you should format the cell to hold **text**.

There are many choices in Excel for the formatting of data. To format a single cell, right-click the cell and choose **format cells** from the pop-up menu. To format a range of cells, first highlight the range required then choose **format cells** from the menu.

- ▶ **General** has no specific format. This is the default and the program tries to pick what it decides is the best format.
- ▶ **Number** defines the data as a number. This allows you to choose how many digits come after the decimal point.
- ▶ **Currency** defines the cell as holding a money value. The default in the UK is to use a £ sign and two decimal places. This means that £2.50 is displayed correctly and not as 2.5.
- ▶ **Accounting** lets you choose the currency symbol. You might not want £s and the standard number of digits after the decimal point.
- ▶ **Date** allows you to store dates in a variety of formats. People from different countries have different ways of writing dates so there are several formats to choose from. You can also do calculations with dates, such as how many days are there between two dates.
- ▶ **Time** allows hours, minutes and seconds to be entered and then to be used for calculations.
- ▶ **Percentage** lets you use the number as a percentage without dividing by 100 every time.

Colours

Another useful way to make a spreadsheet easier to read is to use colours to make the rows and columns stand out on screen. The Livewires sheet is an example of this.

It is also possible to use borders to make the cells stand out as needed.

Conditional formatting

Conditional formatting can be used to make a cell change when a condition is true. This can be used to make things such as errors stand out. In the Livewires spreadsheet, if the customer's invoice total exceeds the credit limit on the account, the cell next to the total changes colour and displays a message.

This is achieved using conditional formatting, which is found on the Format menu of Excel. Choose this option and then complete the two pop-up windows to set up the cell. To apply this to a range of cells, highlight the cells before choosing conditional formatting.

■ Figure 11.98

Total	945

■ Figure 11.99

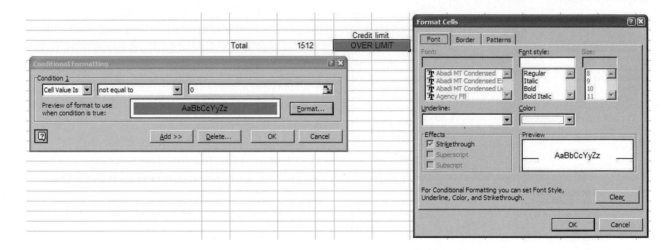

■ Figure 11.100

Using functions and formulae to solve complex problems

Functions are used to do things such as calculate totals. For example:

```
=SUM(A3:A23)
```

will calculate the total of all the cells in the range A3 to A23. It is less effort than using =a3+a4+a5+a6+...+a23 and better practice.

Functions always have names and they expect **arguments**. These are the values that they need to work on. **SUM** is a function; (A3:A23) are the arguments.

If you are stuck and do not know how to use a function then you can use the function help facility.

An array formula can perform multiple calculations and then return single or multiple results. Array formulae act on two or more sets of values known as array arguments. These arguments must have the same number

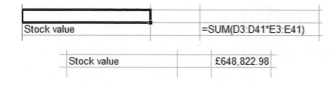

Stock value | =SUM(D3:D41*E3:E41)
Stock value | £648,822.98

Figure 11.101

of rows and columns. You create array formulae in the same way that you create other formulae, except you press Ctrl+Shift+Enter to enter the formula.

On the Livewires spreadsheet, the total value of all the stock can be calculated using an array combined with the SUM function.

Figure 11.101 shows the formula and the result of the calculation on the spreadsheet.

To select cells containing a particular value or data, highlight the range that includes the type of cells you want to select. Then:

1 On the **Edit** menu, click **Go To**.
2 Click **Special**.
3 Do one of the following:
   - To select blank cells, click **Blanks**.
   - To select cells that contain comments, click **Comments**.
   - To select cells that contain constants, click **Constants**.
   - To select only cells that are visible in a range that crosses hidden rows or columns, click **Visible cells only**.
   - To select the current region, such as an entire list, click **Current region**.

Validating and checking data

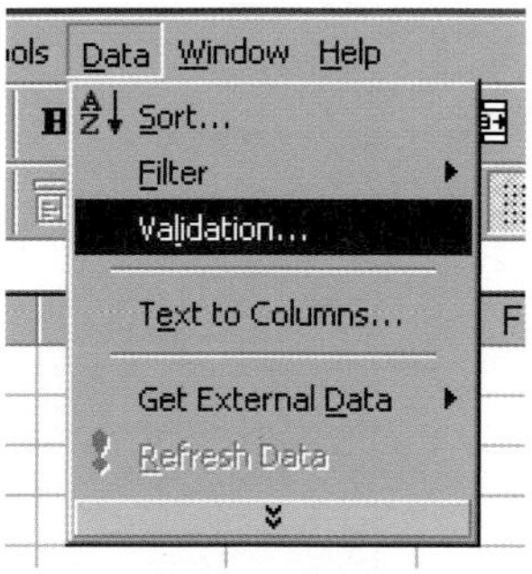

It is also necessary in any model to check that the data is reasonable. It is possible to get the spreadsheet to do this for you by setting up validation rules.

Validation rules check to see if the data that you input matches certain conditions that you have set for a particular cell or range.

For example, to set cell A1 to accept whole numbers between 1 and 10 only, from the menu choose **Data** then **Validation**.

The next step is to fill in the form that follows with the validation rule, as in Figure 11.103.

The other tabs on the form allow you to set a message to appear when the cell is chosen and the **error alert** is the message that appears when the value is wrong.

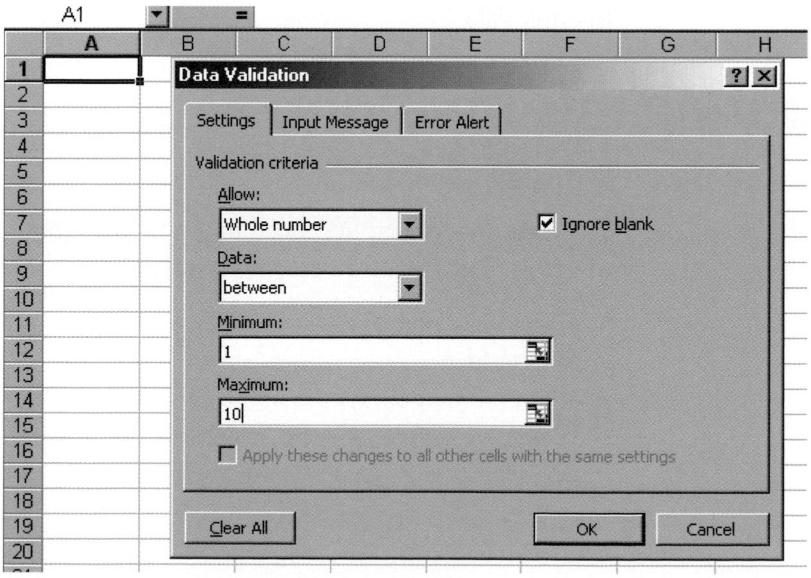

Figure 11.102

Figure 11.103

Analysing and interpreting data

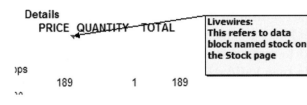

	Score Question 2	Average of Score Question 3
3		
4	1	2
5	2	2
6	3	3
7	4	4
8	5	5
9	6	11
10	7	12
11	8	14
12	9	14
13	10	16
14	11	17
15	12	17
16	13	18
17	14	19
18	15	20
19	16	23
20	17	27
21	18	25
22	19	24
23	20	27
24	(blank)	
25	Grand Total	15

■ **Figure 11.104**

Pivot tables

Pivot tables can be used to provide a summary of the data in a spreadsheet. They are used to analyse related totals, where you have a long list of figures to total and you want to compare facts about each of the items. PivotTable reports are interactive, so if you change the data, the pivot table updates. You can also produce different summaries, such as counts or averages.

Figure 11.104 shows the scores for candidates in an examination. The score for Question 2 is in the first column. The second column shows the average scores for Question 3. The people who scored six marks for Question 2 averaged 11 marks on Question 3.

There are other examples of pivot tables on pages 232–3.

Adding messages to data

Messages can be added in the form of comments to help the user with a particular cell or piece of data.

Details
PRICE QUANTITY TOTAL

Livewires:
This refers to data block named stock on the Stock page

)ps
189   1   189
)

■ **Figure 11.105**

To add a comment, right-click the cell and choose Insert Comment. The comment box appears for you to type in your comments.

Comments can also be used to help a user to input data into the spreadsheet by giving details of the type of data to be entered or an example of how to enter data.

Cut
Copy
Paste
Paste Special...
Insert...
Delete...
Clear Contents
Insert Comment
Format Cells...
Pick From List...
Add Watch
Hyperlink...

■ **Figure 11.106**

Presenting information

Views

To create a view, you first need to get the workbook set up the way you want to see it. Then create a custom view name:

1 In the View menu, select Custom Views.
2 Click Add.
3 In the Name box, type a name for the view.
4 When you display a view, Microsoft Excel switches to the sheet that was active when you created that view.

Graphs and charts

Graphs and charts are a good visual way to present numeric information. Often a chart in a report or presentation gives a much clearer picture of any pattern or trend. Often the wrong type of chart or graph is chosen. For example, pie charts are not much use if there are a lot of different items to show.

■ **Figure 11.107**

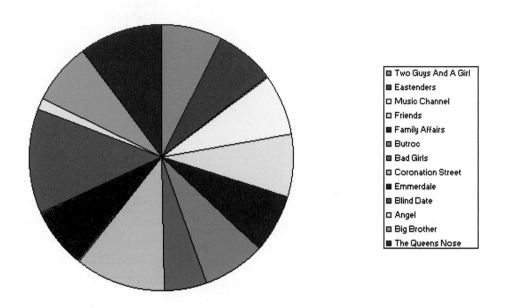

This set of data would be much easier to follow as a bar chart (see Figure 11.108.

■ **Figure 11.108**

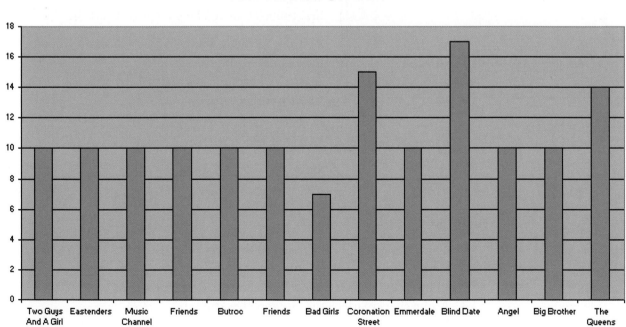

portfolio_tip

Charts and graphs are a very useful way to simplify information and show trends. If appropriate to your system try to include them in your work.

To add a chart or a graph in Excel, select the data by highlighting and then use the chart wizard to format the chart according to your needs.

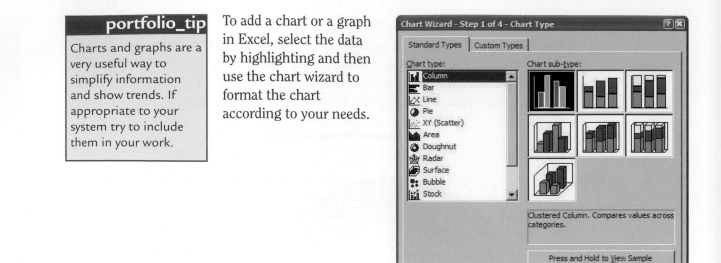

■ **Figure 11.109**

Limiting access

■ **Figure 11.110**

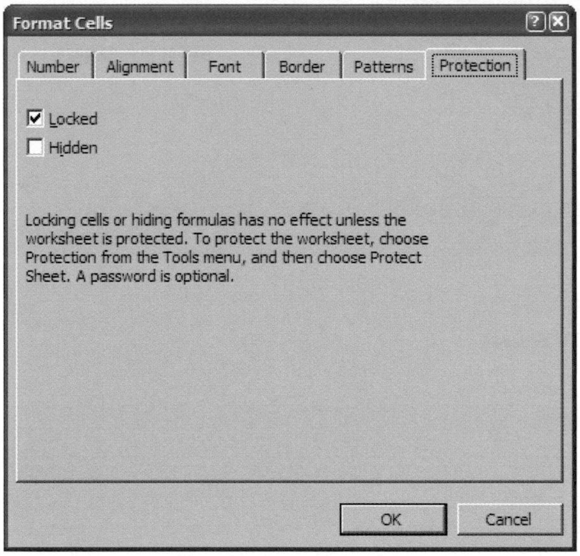

Select the worksheet you need to protect, choose Tools → Protection → Protect Sheet. You can provide a password if you want to. This is a good idea if the spreadsheet is going out to a user, but for your project work only do this with a copy of your original.

Each cell has two attributes: locked and hidden.

The default is that all cells are locked but not hidden. These attributes only work when the worksheet is protected. To allow a particular cell to be changed when the worksheet is protected, you must first unlock that cell by changing its attributes.

1 Choose the cell or cells that you want to unlock.
2 Choose Format Cells.
3 In the Format Cells dialog box, click the Protection tab.
4 Remove the checkmark from the Locked checkbox.

Locking or unlocking cells has no effect unless the worksheet is protected.

To hide a cell:

1 Choose the cell or cells that you want to hide.
2 Choose Format Cells.
3 In the Format Cells dialog box, click the Protection tab.
4 Add a checkmark to the Hidden checkbox.

Changing the Hidden attribute of a cell has no effect unless the worksheet is protected.

Customising and automating

Templates

A template is a predefined spreadsheet layout complete with formulae, ready for the user to enter data. They are used in situations where the user will need to start new versions of the spreadsheet on a regular basis. When a template is opened, a new and untitled spreadsheet is created with the properties of the original template, but it will take on the title of 'untitled spreadsheet' rather then the name of the template. This means that when the user saves the spreadsheet, it does not replace the original.

To save as a template, first set up the spreadsheet and then select template in the drop-down menu.

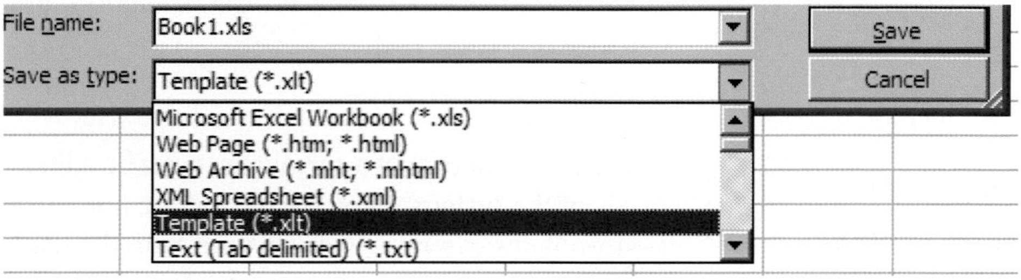

■ Figure 11.111

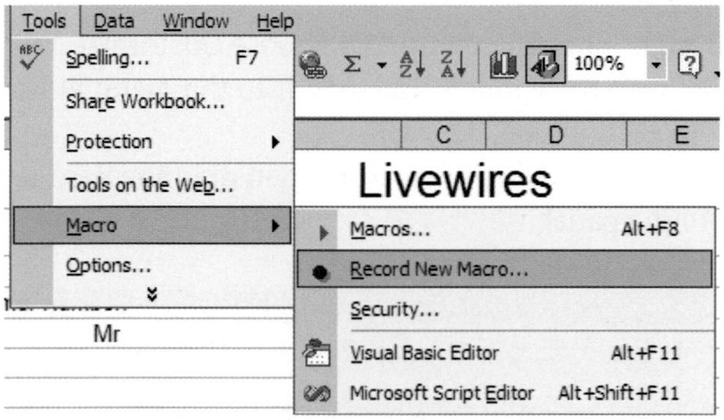

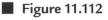

Macros

Macros are used where a series of commands needs to be repeated, or to provide access to complex command sequences for a user. For example, the Livewires spreadsheet will require the invoice to be printed and then cleared ready for the next user. A macro could be recorded which prints the invoice, clears the page, and sets the cursor ready for the next customer number to be entered.

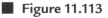

■ Figure 11.112

Always remember to stop recording the macro before you add the button to the page.

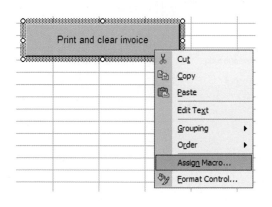

■ Figure 11.113

portfolio_tip

In your technical documentation, you should include the code for each macro, and details of how it is used.

Forms

Further details can be found in Unit 12.7.

Data entry forms can be used to assist the inexperienced user in entering data into a spreadsheet system. Instead of the user entering the data directly into the cells, a form can be used which accepts the data and adds it to the cells as needed.

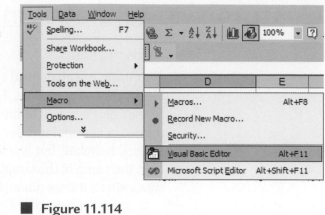

■ **Figure 11.114**

Forms can be produced via the Form option in the Data menu. Forms are constructed using VBA.

Menus

The menu structure of a spreadsheet can be edited and customised to suit the needs of the system. Menu items that are not needed can be removed and custom items can be added. This can help the user by removing anything that might cause confusion or cause problems with your spreadsheet if they are used inappropriately.

To add an item to a menu, right-click the menu and choose Customize.

Then select the item to add from the window and drag it to the menu at the top of the screen.

To remove any menu item, open the Customize form then drag the item to be removed from the menu to the panel.

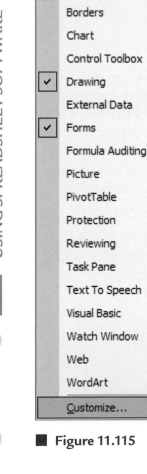

■ **Figure 11.115**

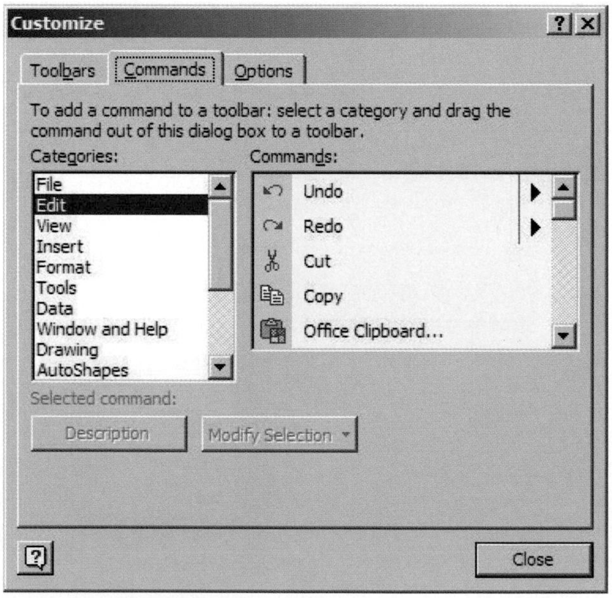

■ **Figure 11.116**

UNIT 12
Customising applications

Introduction to the unit

Aims

■ To recognise when a problem needs extra coding to be undertaken

Introduction

Most users of computers become skilled to a greater or lesser degree in common office applications such as spreadsheets, word processors and database applications.

For most people, this is enough to fulfil their everyday IT needs. Indeed, these applications can be customised quite easily to suit individual requirements. A spreadsheet is no use at all until it has been customised by entering data and formulae. Sometimes, however, all the 'up front' facilities are still not enough to make for an easy life.

Fortunately, there are always ways to take the functionality further. Microsoft Office provides its own built-in programming language called Visual Basic for Applications (VBA) and with this pretty well anything is possible.

You can produce a customised solution for a client and use this unit to provide a software development project for the deliverables required in Unit 8 – Managing ICT projects.

Do not be put off doing this unit if you have never programmed before. Programming is not difficult and it can be very satisfying to produce something that works *exactly* as required. Also, programming skills may give you an edge later on in applying for employment.

Modern office software such as is provided by Microsoft Office or Star Office can do an amazing range of jobs. So many that most users probably only ever use at the most about 20% of the functionality.

If you are about to write a document, you start up a word processor and get typing. It works 'straight out of the box'. After a while, you get to realise that all sorts of time-saving features are available, such as search and replace, tables and drawing tools.

With spreadsheets, it isn't quite so immediate. A spreadsheet isn't a lot of use until you understand about formulae and functions. The empty grid that you start with is not quite 'ready to use'.

Database software is even less immediately available. Software such as Access can't do anything at all until you have planned the tables and entered data. Even then, it isn't much use until you have made some queries and probably forms and reports as well. Users cannot make the best of software like this unless they have at least some understanding of how relational databases work.

Even so, with some training and experience, users can set up some quite sophisticated systems. Very soon it becomes apparent that to get really powerful functionality, you need to go beyond the basic tools. In other words, eventually you need to do some programming. Even if you simply place a command button on a form, you will become aware of the programming that goes on beneath.

It does not take long for someone using a product such as Excel or Access to have a brand new product created by using these tools. That is why they are sometimes called 'Application Generators' rather than just 'Applications'.

Clicking on the event properties of even a simple Find Next button created by the button wizard will reveal some VBA code that has been generated automatically.

```
Private Sub cmdFindNext_Click()
On Error GoTo Err_cmdFindNext_Click


    Screen.PreviousControl.SetFocus
    DoCmd.FindNext


Exit_cmdFindNext_Click:
    Exit Sub


Err_cmdFindNext_Click:
    MsgBox Err.Description
    Resume Exit_cmdFindNext_Click


End Sub
```

Code which has been generated automatically is usually excessively long as it is designed to work in all sorts of situations. In the example above, the intention of the user is to find the next record in a table or query. This is achieved with the line

```
DoCmd.FindNext
```

which is the program's way of saying 'Do command find next'.

The rest of the program code is there 'just in case' of errors.

We have, even if we have not written the code ourselves, added a nice bit of extra ease of use to an application: a button progresses us to the next record in a set.

In some cases then, a little bit of coding can add much needed simplicity in the operation of software. Coding can of course go much farther than this. It can lead to the production of highly customised and easy-to-use applications. But this may be at the cost of expending a lot of effort in development time. In a typical office, most staff do not have the time, let alone the expertise, to write a lot of program code.

The context

> MAINTENANCE The alteration of a system after it has been implemented.

Often, enthusiasts will code up a solution to a problem without giving it a lot of thought. This can be a problem if it leads to the production of something big. A big system that was developed in that way will probably be inefficient and very difficult to MAINTAIN. Suppose an enthusiastic amateur programmer, who is really employed as a bookkeeper, creates a system that other people eventually depend upon. If he leaves, there will be nobody around to update the system or fix errors.

It is really important that systems used by others are produced in a formal and reliable way. They must be easy to understand so that they can be maintained.

So, even when planning an internal system, it is best to go through the formal stages of system development. They have been developed because they help to make sure that everything important is covered and that different practitioners can communicate with each other. You will have examined these in some depth in Unit 8 – Managing ICT projects.

Before deciding to develop an application, it is advisable to look carefully at the situation from an analyst's point of view, even if you are not a proper analyst.

The situation needs to be looked at carefully and some questions answered, preferably in consultation with those who will use it.

▶ What, exactly, does the software need to do that it cannot do already?
▶ Is the software difficult to use for beginners? Would it make it easier if it were customised?
▶ Would the customised solution promote uniform practices across a department, thereby making for more efficient work?
▶ Would a customised solution irritate expert users who can already do what they need to do?

CASE STUDY

The Headteacher of a school wanted all the student reports to be printed out neatly and in the same way so that they gave a better impression to parents. He decided that it might look good if all the teachers typed them up instead of handwriting them. Some of them already used computers but they all had their own favourite ways of doing this and the printed output was not consistent. So, one of the IT technicians produced a system where the students' details and the comments were all fields in a flat file database, using Excel.

When the reports were produced, they were mail-merged onto a standard report form.

The trouble was, some staff had not used Excel very much. Many of them did not feel the need to use it. The technician customised a spreadsheet with a data entry form so that all the teachers had to do was to type comments into boxes. He thought that this would be much quicker for them. The underlying data sheet was locked and inaccessible. The data entry form transferred the comments from a text box into the appropriate spreadsheet cell when the teacher clicked a button labelled 'Update'.

Those who knew Excel then found that they were limited to 200 words per comment. They sometimes had to cut down their comments to fit the limit. Also, they often wanted to say the same thing to lots of parents. Previously they would simply have used 'fill down' and a bit of minor editing. They felt that the new system created extra work.

So, nobody was satisfied, stress levels went up and this led to frustration with the system. It could all have been avoided if a proper study of the requirements had been made before implementing the system. It is possible that *no* system was needed.

When all the stakeholders have been consulted, it is worth looking at whether the customisation of the software is even desirable. Often it is not worth the effort.

If the effort *is* worth it, then a proper functional specification should be drawn up. This should make it totally clear what needs to be done and why.

The context of the problem in the case study was that, at that time, reports were going out to parents in all sorts of different formats. This did not look good. Also it was a nightmare for tutors to collate these reports because they did not all have the same information on them. The names of the students had to be typed or written in by each teacher. Sometime names were spelt differently by some teachers on reports belonging to the same student, for example Anne instead of Ann. This wasted time, as these details could easily be merged from the school student database. Reports involve repetitive work so computers are an obvious solution. But, some of the teachers were not familiar with the techniques they needed.

The nature of the problem

There is no need to make an application if there is no problem to solve. The problem might be an existing frustration or inefficiency such as the case of the school reports. The problem might be that some new procedure is needed or insisted upon by management. Maybe the business is entering into new territory and information is required from the company database in a way that it is not set up to deliver.

Here are some examples of real-life situations which have necessitated the customising of ordinary software:

▶ An examinations board is moving to online assessment. It needs to create a flat file database of past questions, organised by category and subject matter.
▶ A list of products in stock needs to be produced so that no item appears more than once.
▶ A company merger takes place. The customers from one company need to have new customer numbers generated so that they can be processed by a new joint system.

In many cases, the problem is a one-off as in these examples. Programming can help to produce a quick fix.

Other examples are more complex.

▶ A university needs a quick lookup facility for phone numbers and email addresses that can be accessed through a browser both on its website and its intranet.
▶ A business needs a system that allows each department to contribute information to its monthly newsletter in exactly the same format and upload it onto the company website without any further intervention by IT staff.

<table>
<tr><td>ACTIVITY</td><td>Think of three different situations where the normal facilities of a spreadsheet or a database application would not be adequate and further development work would be necessary. Show your examples to someone else who will attempt to identify a non-programmed solution.</td></tr>
</table>

What the custom solution is required to do

The nature of the problem often suggests the solution. But, if the problem is complex, it may be necessary to go through the usual system development processes of breaking the problem down into solvable steps.

Take the case of the university telephone number lookup system. To solve this problem adequately, the following subproblems must be solved:

► The data – the phone numbers and email addresses – must be collected.
► The data must be stored in a data file in a consistent way.
► Software must be created to allow this data to be edited and new data input – this must be validated to prevent inconsistent entries.
► The software must be able to sort or index the numbers so that users can look up phone numbers and email addresses by name or department.
► The software must be able to upload the edited data onto the website.

> **ACTIVITY**
>
> Choose a different scenario, such as one that you suggested in the last activity. Break it down into subproblems.

How the success of the custom solution can be measured

Any new system should be evaluated to see whether the effort was worth it and whether things are better than they were before.

> **CASE STUDY**
>
> In the case of the school reports on page 282, the technician who created the reporting system was very pleased with his efforts. The system worked well, the teachers were unable to write excessive amounts, each report contained the requisite data fields and the mail-merge process produced beautiful neat reports with the school logo looking good in the corner. A success!
>
> The teachers hated it! They had to go and collect a floppy disk with the names of their students already on it. They had to rework their reports whenever they wrote too much. Sometimes, the disks became corrupted and they had to get another one and start again. Sometimes they got so fed up that they copied and pasted the same remark into each report or pasted one of two or three standard reports according to the students' test results.
>
> The parents were not too impressed. For example, Lydia Jones's IT report said *He has worked to Level 5 this year. He selects the information they need for different purposes, check its accuracy and organise it in a form suitable for processing.*
>
> Lydia's parents showed this to their friends, whose son Ben was in the same class. His report was exactly the same. Nobody understood a word of it.

So, was the customised solution a success? It depends who you asked!

A proper evaluation would be measured against the original specification. All the stakeholders would be asked. Maybe the IT technician who made the report system should have sent out evaluation forms to all staff and a selection of parents.

The need to code

Aims

- To look at the alternatives to writing program code
- To identify functionality that will require coding

Remember, standard office software is not just a collection of applications – it is also a collection of application generators. That is, you can use the facilities to create totally new software products.

To program or not to program?

A small amount of program code can be added to an application very easily. Programming is not difficult and can be fun. The satisfaction of producing something that *exactly* fits your requirements is very rewarding. Programming is *not* a last resort. However, before undertaking anything fairly major, it is advisable to look at what the software has to offer without resorting to writing program code. This is because as soon as you start writing significant amounts of code, the work does tend to expand and take up a lot of time. Also, it is inevitable that you will make mistakes when programming; everyone does. This adds to the inconvenience and time taken because of the need to fix bugs.

Making use of the software's inherent capabilities means that although you may not get quite the result you want, you will have routines that are already tested.

We shall now examine some of the features that may help to reduce the need to write new code.

Macros

Microsoft Office provides a way of storing keyboard and mouse operations. These can be stored under a macro name and activated when required. The means of activating macros are quite varied: you can attach a macro to a button on a toolbar, make a new menu item, assign it to a key combination such as Alt-Z, or select it from the Tools → Macro menu.

Macros are invaluable ways of personalising your copy of the software. The number of uses is limitless. Here are some examples.

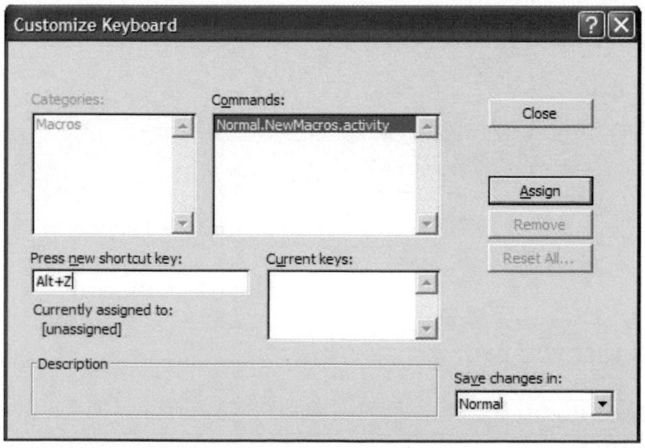

■ Figure 12.1

Word-processing macros

Adding a name and address at the top of a letter

This can be combined with adding a standard sign off such as *Yours faithfully*. The font can be set and the usual printer selected. This method is often preferable to using a template, because it is just so quick and easy.

Setting out the layout of a standard document

A standard document such as a meeting agenda can be activated as a macro, so that, every time it is run, the layout and the headings are in place.

Saving typing effort on repetitive items

When this book was being written, every time the authors wanted to include an activity, they indicated this to the typesetters by enclosing the activity in angle brackets like this:

<activity>
|
<end activity>

■ Figure 12.2

<activity>
Think of other reasons you might want to have a macro set up in a word processor.
<end activity>

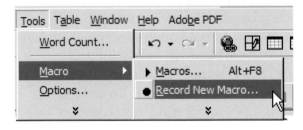

■ Figure 12.3

It is a moment's work to set up a macro that puts in the angle brackets and the headings then moves the cursor into place ready for the text to be typed.

This was created in a moment by using the macro recording facility. You just go through the actions and the macro is created.

Apart from being really easy, another advantage of recording a macro is that it creates VBA code which you can look at. Select Tools → Macro → Macros and then select the macro Edit name and click the button to see the code. In this case, it looks like this:

```
Sub activity()
'
' activity Macro
' Macro recorded 08/01/2006 by Sean O'Byrne
'
    Selection.TypeText Text:="<activity>"
    Selection.TypeParagraph
    Selection.TypeText Text:="<end activity>"
    Selection.MoveUp Unit:=wdLine, Count:=1
    Selection.TypeParagraph
End Sub
```

The great thing about this is that you can:

► make changes to the macro if you want
► learn how to write some VBA.

ACTIVITY

Go through this example of program code and write down what you think each line does.

Later, when you want to write more extensive program code, it is often the best plan to record some macros then paste the resulting code into your own routines.

Spreadsheet macros

There are lots of reasons you might want macros in spreadsheets. A common use is to highlight a set of figures and then record a macro as you go through all the chart-plotting steps. Then, when you want to draw a similar chart, all the routine steps of formatting, adding axes, labelling axes, choosing legends and titles etc. are done automatically.

Another use is to set out headings, for example for sales figures by category, on a new worksheet. You can do this in other ways, but a macro is more flexible.

Database macros

Macros are rather different in a database application because you cannot record them.

Wizards

These are utilities that can set up standard features in an application or other project by asking the user questions. After the questions are all answered, the wizard creates the facility required. We have already made much use of wizards in Unit 7, where they were a great help in setting up parts of a database application.

Wizards are normally activated automatically

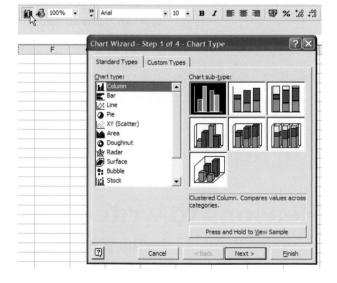

■ Figure 12.4

when certain actions are selected from a menu. One well-known example appears when you select the chart button from the Excel toolbar.

Functions

Functions are particularly useful in spreadsheets and database applications. They are pre-made collections of expressions and commands that can be called up by name. Also, if there is not a suitable function for something you want to automate, you can always write your own.

The most well-known function is the SUM function in Excel, which adds up a set of values. The syntax of this is

```
=SUM()
```

The equals sign tells Excel to do something other than just display it. The word SUM is the name of the function and the brackets are there to contain the *arguments* to the function. The arguments are the data that the function is required to work on. So, if we enter

```
=SUM(A1:A12)
```

this adds up all the values starting at cell A1 and finishing at cell A12. This function saves us the bother of entering all the intermediate cell references.

■ Figure 12.5

There are many functions available in Excel and Access. You can see them all by clicking on the function button in Excel. You have probably already used many of them.

The syntax and use of these functions can be looked up when you click this button.

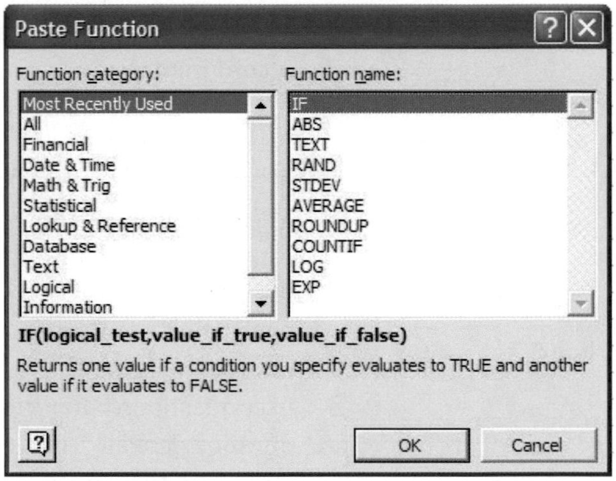

■ Figure 12.6

Reasons to write program code

Despite all the powerful features at your disposal, there will still be reasons why you sometimes need to write your own program code. There are some things that just can't be done 'out of the box'. There may be a way if you look hard enough but writing your own code might be a more elegant solution.

The following sections consider some of these reasons.

Iteration

Programmers regularly write code that repeats itself. Getting a spreadsheet to do this is not possible in most cases. You may want to move the cursor down a column of cells that contain values until you get to the next free space in order to add a new entry. If you need this to happen automatically, you will

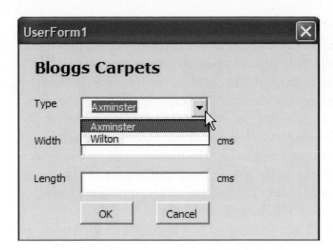

Figure 12.7

need to write some code that starts at a given position and makes its way down until it encounters a blank cell.

Forms

If a spreadsheet is being set up for a non-expert user, it is sometimes more user friendly to provide an on-screen form to be filled in which transfers the data to specific cells in the spreadsheet when it has been entered. One example could be to let a carpet salesperson enter details of a customer's requirements and transfer these to an underlying spreadsheet for the production of an estimate or an invoice.

This is not possible unless some program code is written.

Validation

Excel allows a wide variety of validation techniques, obtainable by highlighting the cells concerned and selecting Data → Validation. Sometimes however, you will want to validate data in a very specific way that is not allowed for in the basic rules provided.

Transpose data

You may want to copy data to another location on a spreadsheet depending upon some complex set of circumstances. You can always do this with nested IF statements but sometimes coding it is more flexible.

Improve the performance and efficiency of an application

Often repeated commands can be tedious and writing program code can save the user the trouble of working out complex expressions. Suppose that it is necessary to go down a long list of customers and check to see if they have paid their bills. If they have, you can delete them from the list, then close up the empty row. They could be identified by IF statements and then you could go through the list and delete the rows. A specially written routine could do this automatically.

> **ACTIVITY**
>
> Think of a complex set of procedures that might be carried out on a spreadsheet that could usefully be automated with a specially written routine.

Provide enhanced security

There is nothing to stop you writing routines to protect your data in ways that would be unexpected to someone who viewed the data. It is easy to write an encryption algorithm that is entirely your own invention and unlikely to be cracked by any but the most determined hackers.

Automate complex tasks

If a set of actions has to be performed at intervals, it is often worth the trouble to write some program code to do this. That way, there is no need to remember all the actions necessary and this reduces the time wasted in re-learning them and also reduces the chances of error.

Someone might keep a record of all the income and expenditure for his business. The expenditure would include miles driven by car, office supplies bought, training courses attended and so on. The income might come from several different sources. At the end of the tax year, he is required to group together all the different categories of expenditure and income and present them to his accountant so that a tax return can be done.

It is possible to write code to do all this and that obviates the need to remember all the steps. As this only happens once a year, it would be easy to forget what to do.

Add finesse to a solution

Sometimes it is worth writing code simply to produce a better result. Although it may be perfectly all right to produce a graph of sales figures by using the wizard, consistency can be applied by using program code. This can then incorporate other features that may be required such as a corporate logo or other data files.

Facilitate data sharing between applications

You may need to import data from an application that creates file formats other than those supported by the standard software. Perhaps a mainframe database application produces lists in its own format which is not compatible with Excel. You may need to write code that reads some proprietary file format and converts it to something that Excel can read such as CSV.

Objects, control properties and events

Aims

- To understand the meaning of event-driven languages
- To understand the meaning of objects

Introduction

Most modern software is event-driven. This means that when it is running, it sits there waiting for something to happen. When something does happen – *an event* – it responds in the way that it has been programmed.

Events are mostly actions carried out by a user. They are things like clicking a mouse on a button, passing the mouse cursor over something, selecting an item from a list or menu, speaking into a microphone or any of hundreds of actions. Some events are not as obvious. A car being photographed by one of the London congestion charge cameras is an event; the deviation of an aircraft from its intended course is also an event; as is the loading of a screen in an application.

This approach to computer use is relatively new. Computers used to be loaded with the relevant software and data, and then be left to process the data – so called *batch processing*. This still happens, but most users are more familiar with event-driven software. Event-driven software is enormously common and popular because it behaves more like real-life human interactions. This makes it easy to understand and learn.

Objects

Part and parcel of the event-driven environment is the use of objects. In ordinary life, an object can be pretty well anything – a table, a cat, an invoice. Objects are identifiable entities, separate from other entities. We recognise objects because of what they are like – their *properties* – and what they can do – their *methods*. For example, a cat has properties such as colour and name. The cat has methods such as run and purr. Objects are themselves made up from other objects, each with its own properties and methods. So, the cat object is made up from other objects such as legs and fur.

This familiar idea of objects has been applied to the development of computer software. Everything you see when you run a modern piece of software is an object. The application Microsoft Word is an object. It has

ACTIVITY

List some more objects that can be seen in a typical Word session.

properties such as position on screen and methods such as check spelling or resize. Word is made up from many other objects such as menu bars, toolbars, an editing window and scroll bars, plus many more. All of these have their own properties and methods.

ACTIVITY

Look up some more methods that Word has. You can find them by following links from:

http://msdn.microsoft.com/library/

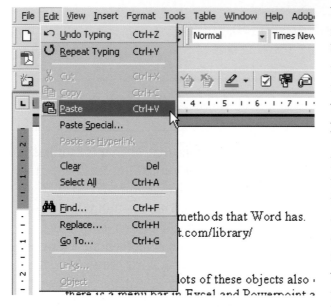

■ Figure 12.8

You will notice that lots of these objects also occur in other applications. For example, there is a menu bar in Excel and PowerPoint as well as in Word. In many ways, these menu bars are similar – they may have slightly different choices, but they all work in the same way. You click on an item and you get a drop-down menu of further choices.

It is no coincidence that they are so alike. They have been designed this way because people find them intuitive to use. Also, they really belong to the Windows (or other) operating system. The operating system has many blueprints for objects called *classes* and the application just creates an instance of them – an object based on them – when it is running. This is not just helpful for the user, who does not have so much to learn, it is also helpful to the programmers who created the application. They can just 'borrow' things that already exist and are already tested. This saves time both for the user and for the programmers.

When you write your own code, using an event-driven programming language such as VBA, you have access to all these Windows objects and can use them for your own purposes. This means that you can very easily create something that looks good and familiar to users. All the Microsoft Office applications (application generators) provide a toolbox that contains some of the more regularly used objects that users see on the screen. They may be called *screen objects* because of this or they are sometimes called *controls*.

If you are working on a network you may not be able to access these tools. Your network administrator may have disabled them for security reasons.

These toolboxes are accessible from many places throughout Microsoft Office. One quick way to see them is to select View → Toolbars → Control Toolbox in Excel or Word.

coursework_tip

If you are working on this unit then you will need to have this option enabled, so see your network administrator.

■ Figure 12.9

■ Figure 12.10

This brings up a small set of common screen objects.

The name of each object in the toolbox can be seen as a tool tip if you hover the mouse cursor over it.

Object-oriented languages

Most programs are now written using objects, and programming languages have developed to make it easy to create new classes and objects from them. The latest development tools from Microsoft – Visual Studio.Net – are all designed around this concept. This technique is called object-oriented programming. C++ and Java are common object-oriented languages.

A fully featured object-oriented programming language makes it easy to produce your own classes. It will also come with a lot of pre-made classes that you can make use of. Remember, you create objects from classes. Objects are realities within a program; classes are a blueprint for making objects.

VBA is designed to provide you with a rich set of pre-made objects from which you can make an application.

Form objects

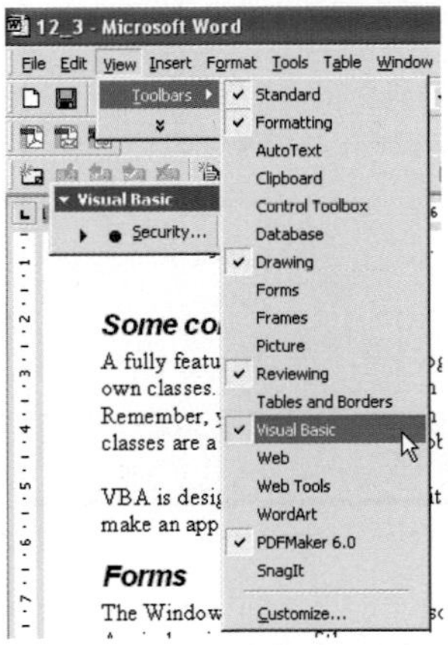

The Windows operating system is so called because it produces windows on the screen. A window is an area of the screen in which an application or part of an application is running. You make windows when programming by creating a *form*. In VBA, the way you make a form is to first make sure that the Visual Basic toolbar is visible. Do this by selecting View → Toolbars → Visual Basic.

You will then be able to see the buttons that give you access to VBA. You will then need to click on the Visual Basic Editor button.

When you have the Visual Basic Editor open, you can select Insert User Form.

The form will appear together with a toolbox of common screen objects.

■ Figure 12.12

■ Figure 12.13

■ Figure 12.11

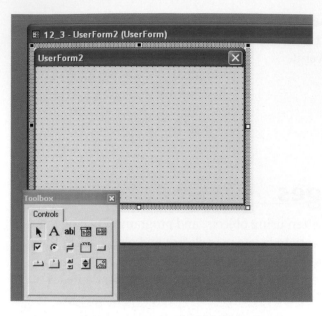

A form is known as a *container object*. This means that it can contain other objects. The objects available in the toolbox are examples of objects that can be placed on a form.

To place an object on a form, you click on it then drag it out to the desired size on the form.

■ Figure 12.14

Label objects

■ Figure 12.15

Labels are objects that provide information on a form for the user to read. Figures 12.15 and 12.16 show how to put a label on the screen.

Once the label is on the form, you should immediately change some of its properties. The system will name it something like Label1 by default. This will make it hard to remember later, so you change the name property.

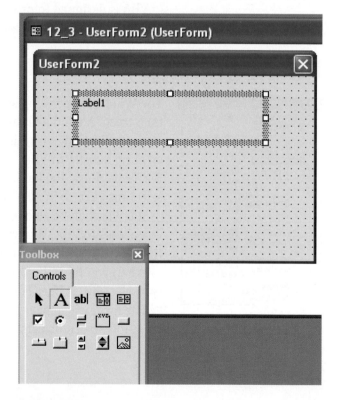

■ Figure 12.16

Changing an object's properties

To change the properties of an object, you right-click on the object and select the properties field from the properties box.

You should always change the name of the object to something meaningful.

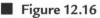

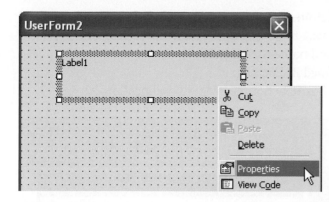

■ Figure 12.17

■ Figure 12.18

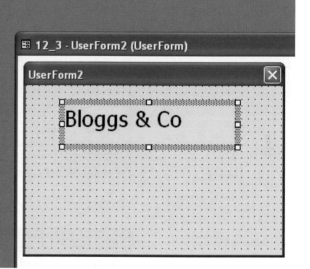

Create a form and change the properties as described above.

It is also good practice to use a convention that identifies the type of object that you are using. So this label has been renamed lblHeading. 'lbl' means label. We have also changed the caption, which is what the label displays on the form and then the font to make it stand out more. You can make other changes if you want.

Combo box objects

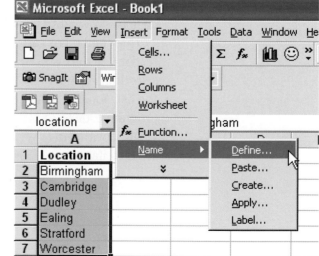

■ Figure 12.19

A very common screen object, called the combo box, allows users to make selections from a list. This is particularly useful when creating a database or, for example, choosing products on a spreadsheet to be entered into an invoice.

You select a combo box from the toolbox in the usual way.

Figure 12.20 shows a list of places that can be selected from a combo box. You first need to

■ Figure 12.20

rename it – say as cmbLocation. Then you need to tell it where to get its information from. An easy way to do this on an Excel spreadsheet is to make a list of the data on a sheet and name the range.

In this case, we have named it 'Location'.

You then set the combo box Row Source property to Location.

■ Figure 12.21

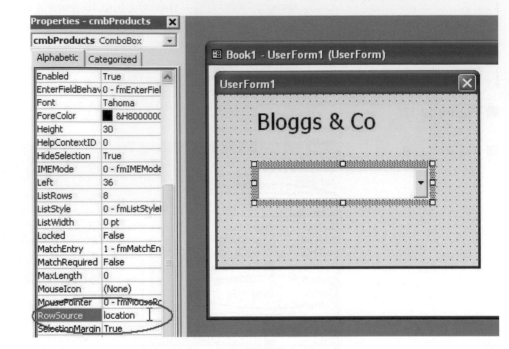

You can test this by clicking on the Run Macro button.

■ Figure 12.22

The combo box will now show the data although we have not yet written any code to say what to do with it! That will come later.

This combo box can respond to the event of selecting a value from the list. You can write program code to say what do with the selected item.

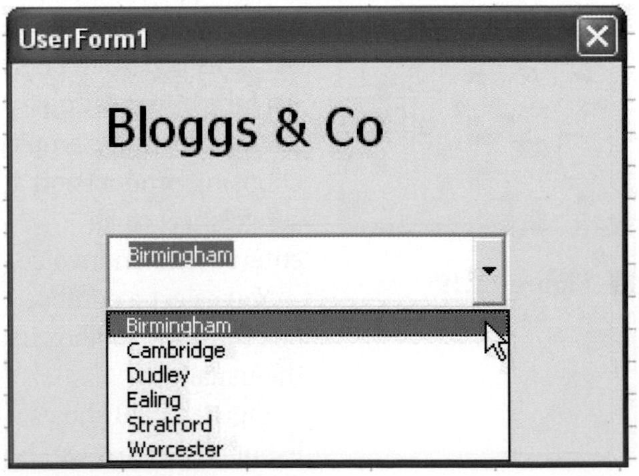

■ Figure 12.23

Button objects

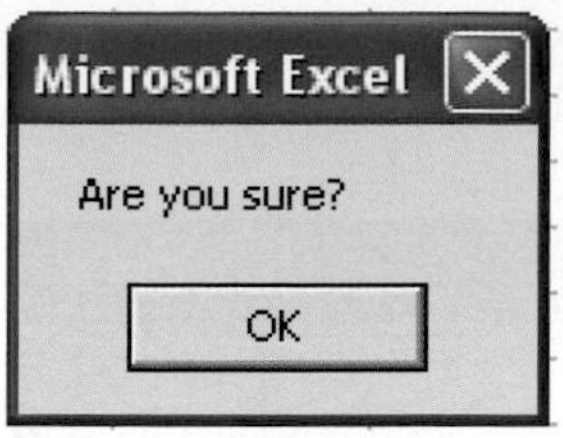

Microsoft Excel
Are you sure?
OK

■ **Figure 12.24**

Command buttons are among the most familiar objects on modern PC screens.

Any application has rows of buttons for common actions, known as toolbars. In most applications you can add or remove buttons so that the toolbar is customised to your needs. Dialogue boxes, where the user can make several related choices, always have at least OK and Cancel buttons.

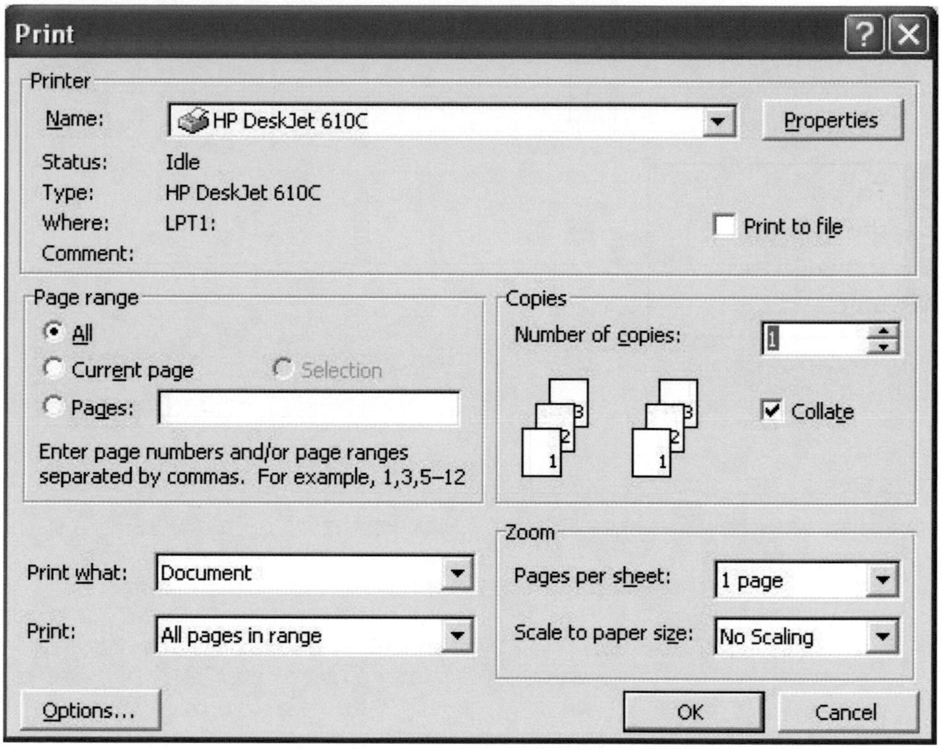

Print
Printer
Name:
HP DeskJet 610C
Properties
Status:
Idle
Type:
HP DeskJet 610C
Where:
LPT1:
Print to file
Comment:
Page range
All
Current page
Selection
Pages:
Enter page numbers and/or page ranges separated by commas. For example, 1,3,5–12
Copies
Number of copies:
1
Collate
Print what:
Document
Print:
All pages in range
Zoom
Pages per sheet:
1 page
Scale to paper size:
No Scaling
Options...
OK
Cancel

■ **Figure 12.25**

You place buttons on a form in the same way as any other object. You should immediately rename them in their property box. The one in Figure 12.26 is

Book1 - UserForm
UserForm1
Bloggs
Next
Cut
Copy
Paste
Delete
Properties
View Code
Align
Make Same Size
Group
Bring Forward
Send Backward
cmdNext

■ **Figure 12.26**

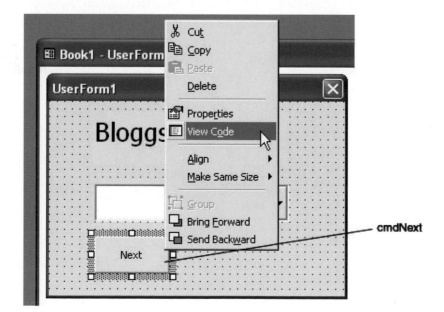

named cmdNext. You can write the program code to be run when the button experiences a 'click' event, i.e. when someone clicks the button, by going to the View Code window that you can see if you right-click the button.

You can try this out by writing a simple line of code like this:

■ **Figure 12.27**

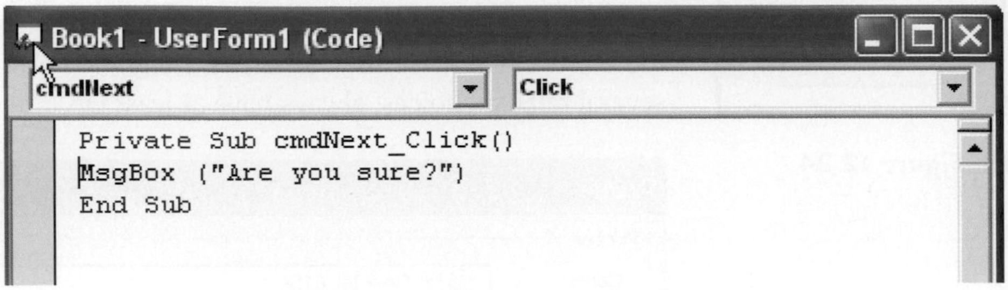

```
Book1 - UserForm1 (Code)

cmdNext                    ▼    Click                    ▼

    Private Sub cmdNext_Click()
    MsgBox ("Are you sure?")
    End Sub
```

ACTIVITY

Try out some of the examples shown in this unit.

CUSTOMISING APPLICATIONS

298

Designing routines

Aims

■ To understand some program-planning methods

When people who are not normally programmers want to make a customised and programmed add-on to their office software, they often make the mistake of just writing a bit of code and developing it as they see fit. This is only all right if the project is a very small one. For even a moderately ambitious project, it pays to do some careful planning before opening up the code windows. There are plenty of ways to make errors which can magnify to such an extent that it might even mean starting again! Time spent on careful design is never wasted.

In Unit 8, you examined the need to produce a design specification before embarking on a project. Units 7.2 and 8.6 cover some of the issues involved in this.

Data modelling

If a proposed solution involves the production of a database, then considerable preparation is needed in order to get the structure efficient. You will need to go through data-modelling processes such as producing entity–relationship diagrams and carrying out normalisation to the third normal form (Unit 7.4) to ensure that there is minimal data redundancy. It is only when the data requirements have been identified and planned that it is worth looking at the processing required.

Processing

Much of the processing required when you make an application using office software is carried out by the inbuilt capabilities of the packages themselves. For example, many database projects only require the construction of queries and perhaps a few simple macros to do the jobs required. Spreadsheet systems can carry out many tasks using formulae and functions.

If a project is going beyond the in-built functionality, it is necessary to make a plan of what jobs need to be done. It might be that only some of these need programming.

The tasks that need programming must also be broken down into easily understood parts. If you write big chunks of code, it can become extremely difficult to fix errors later.

If you place an object on a form, you can go to the View Code option and write some program code to tell the object what to do if a certain event happens. Each object will have its own 'package' of code. However, you will want to write more code than just that associated with screen objects and you should subdivide this extra code so that it is easy to understand and maintain. You will at least want to write some extra procedures. You may need to create extra modules, themselves containing procedures.

Each procedure should only do one job. This has implications for your program design that we shall look into later.

You can plan your modules and procedures and inspect them at any time by using the project explorer. In Figure 12.28, you can see a view of an Excel project that has recently been started. You can see in the left window that there are three worksheets in a workbook which still have their default names and one module has been started. Some of the procedures in this module are visible in the right-hand window.

It is vital to keep a close eye on the parts making up a project as it develops so that you can see how the component parts relate to each other.

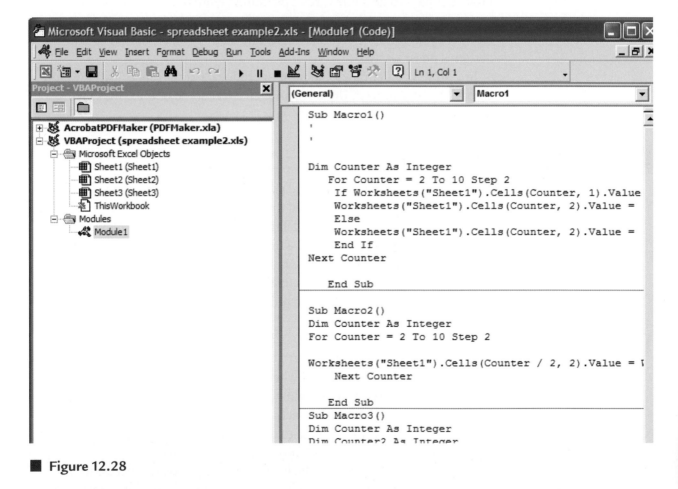

■ Figure 12.28

Planning your procedures

The number of procedures or other subroutines that you require will probably be more than you expect. It is important to try to keep each process separate so that errors are easy to find.

There are many ways of making diagrammatic representations of your plans. One way is to use a structure diagram.

In Figure 12.29, you can see how the process of printing a pay slip has been broken down into stages. Firstly, three main jobs are identified and they are placed on the diagram in the order that they will take place, arranged left to right.

One of these jobs, the production of the body of the pay slip, is decomposed into three further steps, progressing from left to right.

■ **Figure 12.29**
Example of a screengrab

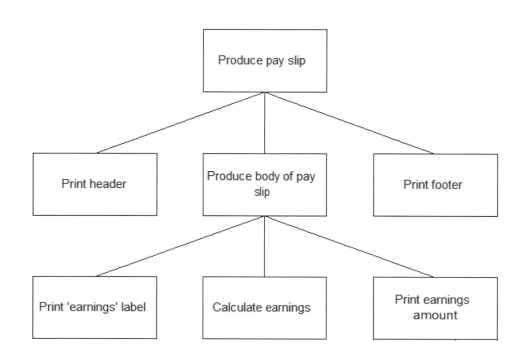

You can break down the jobs that need to be done until you have such simple jobs that they can be coded in a short procedure.

> Producing structure and other diagrams is something that students often don't like doing, but they really do help you to produce a better solution. Plus, they *can* be fun! It is *much* easier to set them up and adapt them if you use proper drafting software such as Microsoft Visio.

In the past, programmers used to make great use of a drafting tool called a structured flow chart. It is not so much in favour nowadays, but it can help to produce a sensible algorithm to solve a small part of a problem. Rectangles are used to denote processes, diamonds denote decisions and curved boxes denote terminators. The flow chart in Figure 12.30 shows the steps involved in validating a login.

■ **Figure 12.30**

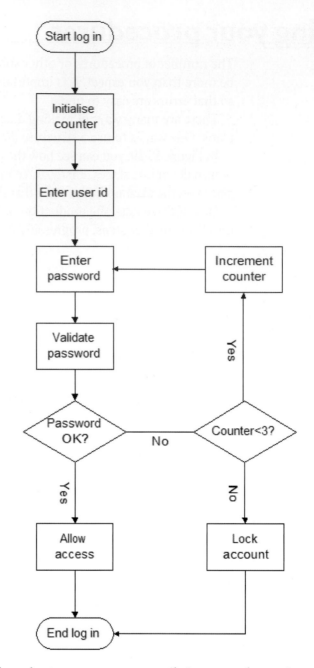

Structured flow charts can grow very easily in a complex project and there soon comes a point at which they stop being helpful and become messy.

Prototypes

Another approach to planning and developing a system is to make use of prototypes. These are partly working mock-ups of the intended system. Prototypes are easy to make with modern development software. Even with office application development tools such as Access, it is very easy to produce some forms, perhaps with the help of the wizard, which give an impression of how the finished software might look.

There are many advantages in using prototypes as well as a few disadvantages, which we shall now consider.

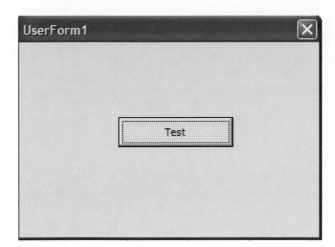

UserForm1 ☒

Test

Improve and refine your initial design

A form can be set up in most office packages and it is a simple matter to place a dummy command button on a form just for the purpose of trying out the code segments that you have written.

The code behind this calls up a procedure that you want to test. In this case, it is a one-line procedure:

```
Private Sub Display_Form()
frmDataEntry.Show
End Sub
```

Set up forms as in this example. Try out this line of code, then create a new form and adapt the code to show the new form.

This procedure is designed to call up a form where customer details can be input. So, when the button is clicked, this can give a good impression of how the finished application might behave and look.

Customer details ☒

Bloggs & Co

Customer details

Surname ☐☐☐☐☐☐☐☐☐☐

Forename ☐☐☐☐☐☐☐☐☐☐

Address ☐☐☐☐☐☐☐☐☐☐

☐☐☐☐☐☐☐☐☐☐

☐☐☐☐☐☐☐☐☐☐

Telephone ☐☐☐☐☐☐☐☐☐☐

| Accept | | Cancel |

■ Figure 12.32

Functionality can be added to the two buttons on this form to show their behaviour, although at this stage you would not write the full code for processing the data.

It is easy to go back to the forms and improve their designs without having to worry about any knock-on effects yet. For example, extra fields will probably need to be added.

Test that your routines work properly

A prototype can be set up to demonstrate that subroutines that you have written are working correctly. The form we set up in Figure 12.31 can be redirected to run a different piece of code.

The following example is testing values in a spreadsheet to see if they are even or odd and to report the fact on the sheet. By connecting this code to a button, we can run it very easily and make corrections if necessary.

```
Sub Macro1()

Dim Counter As Integer
  For Counter = 2 To 10 Step 2
    If Worksheets("Sheet1").Cells(Counter, 1).Value Mod 2 = 0 Then
      Worksheets("Sheet1").Cells(Counter, 2).Value = ("The value is even")

Else

      Worksheets("Sheet1").Cells(Counter, 2).Value = ("The value is Odd")
    End If
  Next Counter

End Sub
```

	A	B	C	D	E	F	G	H
1	1							
2	2							
3	3							
4	4							
5	5							
6	6							
7	7							
8	8							
9	9							
10	10							
11								
12								
13								
14								
15								

UserForm1

Test

Click the button and we can see if the logic is correct.

	A	B	C	D	E	F	G	H	I
1	1								
2	2	The value is even							
3	3								
4	4	The value is even							
5	5								
6	6	The value is even							
7	7								
8	8	The value is even							
9	9								
10	10	The value is even							
11									
12									
13									
14									

UserForm1

Test

The odd values have not been identified, so the code needs to be checked and fixed.

ACTIVITY

Look at the code from this example and follow its logic.
Find out what MOD means.
Can you fix the error?

Check for ease of use

The design of the user interface is one of the hardest things to get right when developing an application. Ideas that may have occurred to you may turn out to make a very hard-to-use application. The use of prototypes will allow you to move objects around and add or remove them in order to make a better working experience for the users.

The developer might decide that the form in Figure 12.35 needs a little alteration!

Figure 12.35

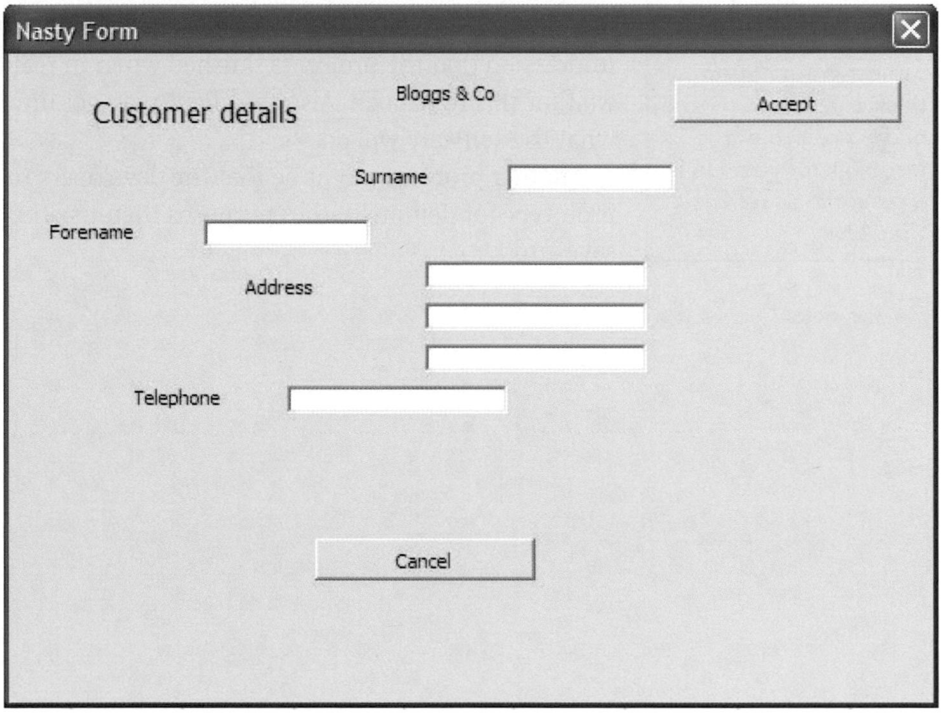

ACTIVITY

Imagine you are a user reviewing this form at the prototyping stage.
Write a letter to the developer with your thoughts about this form.

Test for robustness

Robustness is the ability of an application to withstand all the mistakes and silly things that a user might do to it. If a user enters some impossible data or clicks the wrong button, it is no good if the application crashes and some system message flashes up (see Figure 12.36). The user won't know what to do and certainly won't be impressed.

Microsoft Visual Basic

Run-time error '28':

Out of stack space

| Continue | End | Debug | Help |

Get feedback from others

Prototypes are particularly good for communicating with the users or clients. They can far better understand what you are planning if they see a semi-working model in front of them instead of a long description. They can also make much more of a contribution to the development of the project which will give them more 'ownership' and, consequently, more satisfaction.

The drawbacks of using prototypes in this way are that they may give the impression that the project is finished when in reality there may be quite a wait for this to happen. Also the client may get unrealistic expectations about what the software will do.

Another problem might be that the developers make a quick and inferior prototype for demonstration purposes then use this in the real application to save effort.

---

portfolio_tip

If you are using this unit alongside Unit 8 remember to organise a meeting with your end user and also the project group. Show them the prototype and make a record of the feedback for your Unit 8 portfolio as well as Unit 12.

Programming structures

Aims

■ To learn some standard programming structures

Introduction

Whatever programming project you work with, there are some standard techniques that are commonly used. They all help you to produce programs that are effective with the least effort.

Programs consist of a series of statements which are instructions to the computer. As a basic rule, these statements are executed (carried out) one after another. This orderly sequence of events is often changed by the programmer in order to make programs more flexible. Nowadays, programs are built up from objects as explained in Unit 12.3, but within the objects, the same rules still apply in nearly all programs.

In order to try out the examples and exercises which follow, you will need to set up a project in Excel or Word. Excel is much to be preferred although most of the commands will work in either application. The examples assume you are working with Excel.

> You should try all the exercises which follow. You will get more out of this if you alter the exercises and experiment.

Setting up a project

ACTIVITY

As before, the first thing to do is to start a new workbook.

Make sure that the Visual Basic toolbar is showing.

■ **Figure 12.37**

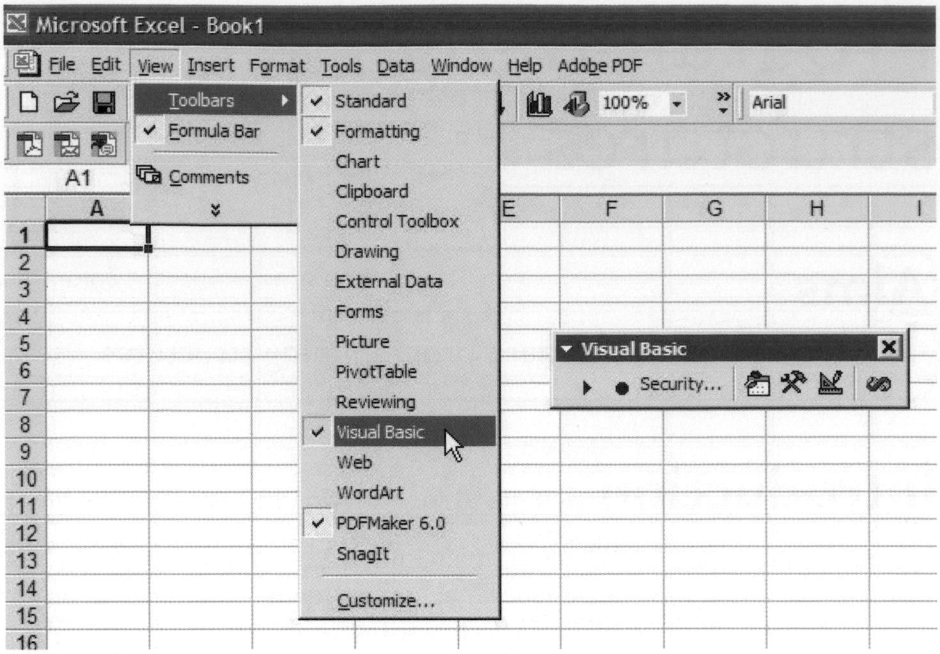

■ **Figure 12.38**

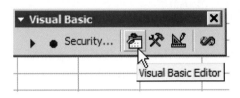

■ **Figure 12.39**

You then need to click on the Visual Basic editor.

An easy way to try out a few ideas is to Insert a new User Form. Use the properties window to change the name of the form to frmTest. You may as well change the caption to Test as well.

Make sure that the toolbox is visible – click View Toolbox if it is not.

Then place a text box onto the form. Use the properties window to change its name to txtOutput. It is very important to take care with this – if you spell it wrongly, you will probably get errors later.

Set its Multiline property to True. This is so that any output can be made to run vertically down the box.

Now put a command button on the form. Change the name to cmdTest and the caption to Click Me.

Double-click on the button to get the editor window where you write the program code. There will be a space where you can write the code that will be activated when the button is clicked. The beginning and end lines will already be there for you. This is called an *event procedure*. Just enter one line. It will then look like this:

```
Private Sub cmdTest_Click()
Call Times_Table
End Sub
```

The line Call Times_Table will run another procedure that we have not yet written so we cannot test it yet.

Iteration

INTEGER A whole number – it has no fractional part. 10 is an integer, 10.6 is not.

VARIABLE A named area of storage in memory that holds a value which can change during the running of a program.

ACTIVITY
Use the spreadsheet that is already set up.
We shall add to the program to output the 3 times table.

Often it is necessary for part of a program to repeat itself. There are many reasons why this might be necessary, possibly something is being counted or maybe each word in a word-processed document is examined in turn for spelling errors.

Iteration is a term that means repetition. Iterative program development means regularly returning to earlier stages of development in order to make improvements or consult with the client. In programming, iteration refers to repeating a section of code. A part of a program that repeats is called a loop.

There are basically four ways of programming a loop. Some of them make use of an INTEGER VARIABLE to count the number of iterations that have occurred.

While and until loops

A loop that starts with `While` tests for a condition before it executes. So, if it has `While counter <= 10` at the start, the loop will not occur at all unless the value of the counter is less than or equal to 10. In VBA, the end of the loop is indicated by the word `Wend` or `Loop`.

An *until* loop tests for a condition at the end of the loop, so it will have to be executed at least once. In VBA, it starts with `Do`.

Below the button's event procedure, type in the following code. When you have finished, a line will divide it off from any other code.

```
Private Sub Times_Table()
Dim Counter As Integer
Counter = 1


While Counter <= 10
txtOutput.Text = txtOutput.Text & Counter * 3 & vbCrLf
Counter = Counter + 1
Wend


End Sub
```

DATA TYPE The computer just stores 0s and 1s. We have to assign data types so that the computer handles the data in the way that we want.

In this code, we have *declared* a variable called *Counter*. This sets up memory for the variable and gives it the DATA TYPE *integer*. We *initialise* it by giving it the value of 1.

The main work in this procedure occurs with the line

```
txtOutput.Text = txtOutput.Text & Counter * 3 & vbCrLf
```

This works on the text box that we put on the form. This text box has a property called *text*. Just like all properties, we can either change them using the property window or from within a program. We are saying here, 'put into the text box called txtOutput whatever was there before concatenated with the value obtained by multiplying counter by 3' (Counter * 3). We also add something else – vbCrLf. That is a useful CONSTANT which stands for 'carriage return, line feed'. This is exactly what happens when you press the 'Enter' key. We use it here to make the output go to a new line, each time the loop iterates.

CONSTANT A named value held in memory that does not change during the running of a program.

We then increment the counter with the line

```
Counter = Counter + 1
```

so that next time the while condition is executed, the value is one more. The loop will continue until the value of `Counter` becomes 10.

The syntax for writing an *until* loop in VBA is

```
Do Until ....
.
.
.
Loop
```

We shall make a procedure to count down from 10.

Attach another button to the form. Call it cmdCountdown and change the caption to Count Down.

Write its event procedure as follows:

```
Private Sub cmdCountdown_Click()
Dim Counter As Integer
Counter = 10

Do Until Counter = 1
txtOutput.Text = txtOutput.Text & Counter & vbCrLf
Counter = Counter – 1
Loop

End Sub
```

Why is the output not quite what we expected? Try to fix it.

For...next loops

If we know in advance how many times we need a loop to iterate, we use a for...next loop. We can write the 3 times table in a different way.

Create a new button called cmdForNext. Write its event procedure as follows:

```
Private Sub cmdForNext_Click()
Dim Counter As Integer

For Counter = 1 To 10
txtOutput.Text = txtOutput.Text & Counter * 3 & vbCrLf
Next Counter

End Sub
```

You will see that this is an easier way to write a loop as long as you know you will always need 10 iterations.

Try adding the words `Step 2` after `For Counter = 1 to 10`.

Improve the usability of the form by adding a button called cmdExit. Make its event procedure just one word – End. You can now exit cleanly from the form.

You can clear the text box with the line

```
txtOutput.text=""
```

You may like to have this on a button or make it part of other procedures.

You can write loops within loops. These are called nested loops. The following code is attached to a button called cmdMore and it uses a nested loop to display the 2, 3 and 4 times tables.

```
Private Sub cmdMore_Click()
Dim counter1 As Integer
Dim counter2 As Integer

For counter1 = 2 To 4
For counter2 = 1 To 10
txtOutput.Text = txtOutput.Text & counter1 * counter2 & vbCrLf
Next counter2
Next counter1

End Sub
```

Selection

Often, a programmer needs to make a program behave differently according to different circumstances. There are various constructs available to allow this to be carried out in a variety of ways. The process of choosing a course of action according to the results of a test is called selection.

if...then...else

The idea behind this construct is 'if something is true, then do this, or else do something else'. There are many occasions where you will have to use this method.

We shall demonstrate this on a new form.

ACTIVITY

Set up a new form and call it frmSelect.

Add a text box called txtOutput and a button called cmdGo. Also add a button called cmdExit. Change the captions to match Figure 12.40.

The event procedure for cmdExit is simply the word End. ☛

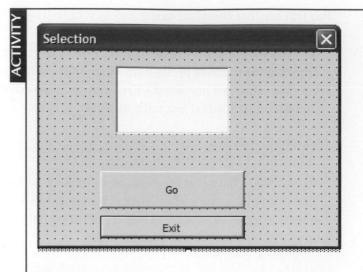

■ Figure 12.40

The event procedure for cmdGo is:

```
Private Sub cmdGo_Click()
Dim BookChoice As String
BookChoice = InputBox("Which A level books are the best?")

If BookChoice = "Hodder" Then
txtOutput.Text = "Absolutely right!"
Else
txtOutput.Text = "Wrong. Try again."
End If


End Sub
```

Run and test the buttons. Try altering the code.

STRING This is a data type that stores any characters such as letters, numbers and symbols.

It is possible to nest 'if' statements so that a series of circumstances can be catered for, but if there are too many choices, the 'case' construct is better.

Case

This is useful when there are several options, not just one or two.

Use the 'Select' form that you used in the previous activity. Set the txtOutput text box Multiline property to True.

Add a new command button called cmdDinner. Change its caption to something suitable. Enter the following event procedure: ☞

```
Private Sub cmdDinner_Click()
Dim Money As Single
Dim Message As String

Money = InputBox("How much money do you have?")
Select Case Money
Case Is > 4
Message = "You can have fish and chips"
Case 2 To 3
Message = "You can have fish but no chips"
Case Else
Message = "You will have no dinner"
End Select

txtOutput.Text = Message
End Sub
```

SINGLE This is a number data type that accepts decimal places.

Sub-programs

Programs are always built up from smaller units. You can call these units sub-programs. We have already seen how this makes writing and debugging them easier. There are several different types of sub-program. They are written and used in different ways.

Sub-routines

The sub-routines that we write in VBA are usually better known as *procedures*. We have already made use of many in the earlier examples. Each button we create comes ready with a sub-routine otherwise known as an event procedure. The whole project consists of all of these routines plus any others that we have written.

We have also seen how we can call procedures from other procedures. Earlier, we wrote a procedure called Times_Table and called it from a button event procedure.

```
Private Sub cmdTest_Click()
Call Times_Table
End Sub
```

There is a great advantage to doing this. A procedure that is called from another procedure can be re-used throughout the program, thereby saving a lot of work.

Functions

These are sub-programs that produce a single value. A function has a value after it has been run. We have already used some ready-made functions such as MsgBox and InputBox.

In VBA it is generally called *in-line*, which means that it is used as part of a statement.

```
Money = InputBox("How much money do you have?")
```

In this case, InputBox is the function. It takes the value that is given to it in the brackets and displays it as a message. The user's response is passed to the variable Money.

We can easily write our own functions.

ACTIVITY

We shall write a simple function to cube a number and then we shall display it.

Set up a new form and name it frmCube. Set up one text box called, as before, txtOutput, one button called cmdCube and another called cmdExit. Put appropriate captions on the objects.

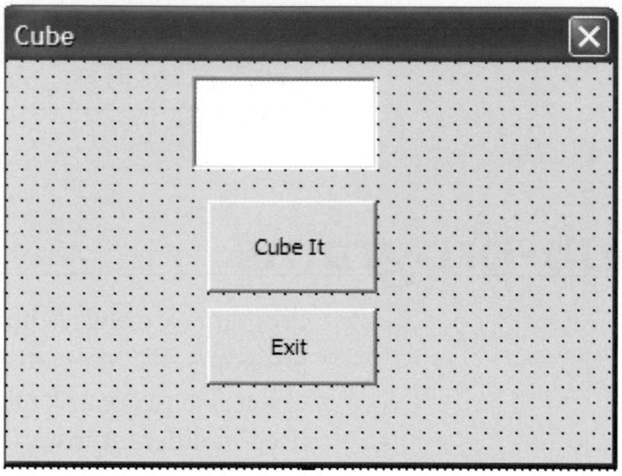

First, we write the function that will cube a number. Go to the code editor and type in as a separate sub-program:

■ **Figure 12.41**

```
Function Cube(Number)
Cube = Number * Number * Number
End Function
```

This function – called Cube – takes the value of a number and multiplies it by itself twice to give the cube. The function now receives the value of this calculation.

Then, enter the following event procedures.

First, for the cmdCube button:

```
Private Sub cmdCube_Click()
Dim Number As Integer

Number = InputBox("Enter an integer number")
txtOutput.Text = Cube(Number)
End Sub
```

We use the ready-made function InputBox to get a number from the user and we store it in the variable Number. We then use our own function Cube to cube the number that has been entered.

Finally for a clean exit, we write this for the exit button:

```
Private Sub cmdExit_Click()
End
End Sub
```

Test this function with different numbers.

Passing parameters

A parameter is a value that we give to a procedure or a function. Procedures and functions in VBA always have a pair of brackets after their names. You may have noticed that VBA will put these in even if you don't. The parameters are placed in the brackets both for sending and receiving.

We have already done some parameter passing in the last example. The function Cube was written as Function Cube(Number). That means it expects a value to be passed to it when it is called and it will be called Number.

We called the function by giving it a number in brackets in the line

```
txtOutput.Text = Cube(Number)
```

When a value is passed to a procedure or function, unless you tell it otherwise, it is only a copy that gets passed. The original value remains unchanged even if the procedure makes changes to the copy. This is called passing a parameter by value. You can pass a parameter by reference. In this case, the original is worked on by the procedure or function and can be changed.

Nested structures

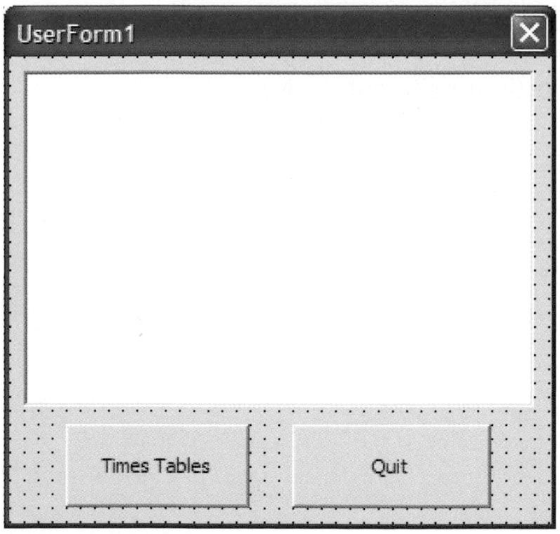

■ **Figure 12.42**

We have in this unit examined how to use loops and selection techniques. It is often useful to embed these structures inside one another. It is possible to embed loops within loops, if structures within if structures, if structures within loops and loops within if structures. There is not space here to consider all these possibilities but an example can show a typical case.

Suppose we wanted to print out all the multiplication tables from 2 to 12. We can first write a loop to multiply all the numbers up to 12. Another loop placed outside this loop steps through all the multipliers from 2 to 12.

For demonstration purposes, we can set this up on a form with one text box, called txtOutput and two command buttons, one called cmdTimesTable and one called cmdQuit. Make sure that the text box is big enough and that the Multiline property is set to true.

The following code shows how it is done:

■ Figure 12.43

```
Private Sub cmdExit_Click()
End
End Sub
```

```
Private Sub cmdTimesTable_Click()
Dim counter1, counter2 As Integer
Dim result As Integer

result = 0

'start outer loop
For counter1 = 2 To 12

'start inner loop
For counter2 = 1 To 12

result = counter1 * counter2
txtOutput.Text = txtOutput.Text & Str(result) & " "

'end inner loop
Next counter2

'new line for next multiplier
txtOutput.Text = txtOutput.Text & vbCrLf

'end outer loop
Next counter1
End Sub
```

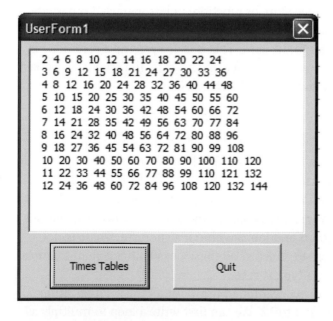

■ Figure 12.44

The output to the text box will now be as in Figure 12.44.

We could, if we wanted, add if statements within these loops in order to select particular results such as odd numbers or to add comments. The point is that the basic programming structures are infinitely flexible and, by using them creatively, it is possible to achieve a lot with only a small amount of code. This makes for easier program maintenance as well as saving memory and enabling programs to run faster.

Human–computer interface

Aims

■ To learn some techniques for designing a user-friendly interface

Introduction

An interface is the boundary between two systems. A modem is the interface between a PC and the telephone system. An analogue to digital converter is the interface between an analogue sensor, such as a thermistor, and a computer.

The boundary between a human and a computer is called the human–computer interface (HCI). It is made up of all the items that allow the human to control the computer and the computer to send information back to the human.

The design of the HCI is one of the most critical aspects of systems design. Although the data processing must be right, it is often easier to see a way to do this than to get the interface right. Developers often design interfaces based on what they know rather than on what the user knows.

Here are a few tips for a good HCI:

▶ Do not have too many functions at the top level – this will confuse. A good rule is that the range of options or choices should never be more than five or six.
▶ Be consistent. For example, if you have several screens put the 'back' button in the same position on all of them.
▶ Try to make the HCI symmetrical.

If you could look at a TV or video from around 15 years ago, you would see lots of buttons and controls on the front. Look at a modern TV – there are very few buttons, perhaps only on/off, volume and channel. Have you noticed how Windows XP hides buttons and menu choices that you do not use very often? It helps simplify the interface even if it is annoying at times.

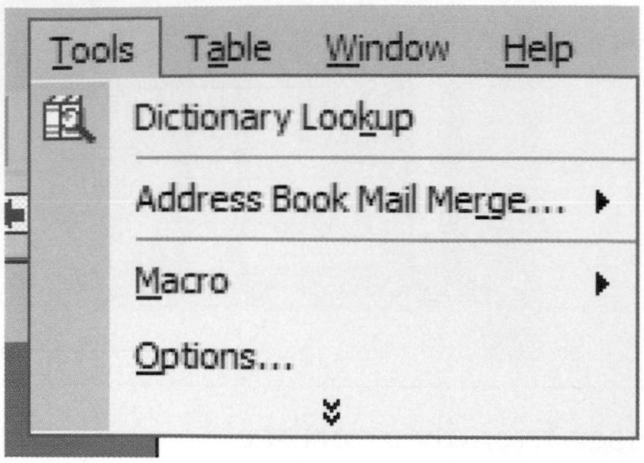

Tools   Ta**b**le   **W**indow   **H**elp

Dictionary Loo**k**up

Address Book Mail Me**r**ge...   ▶

Macro   ▶

Options...

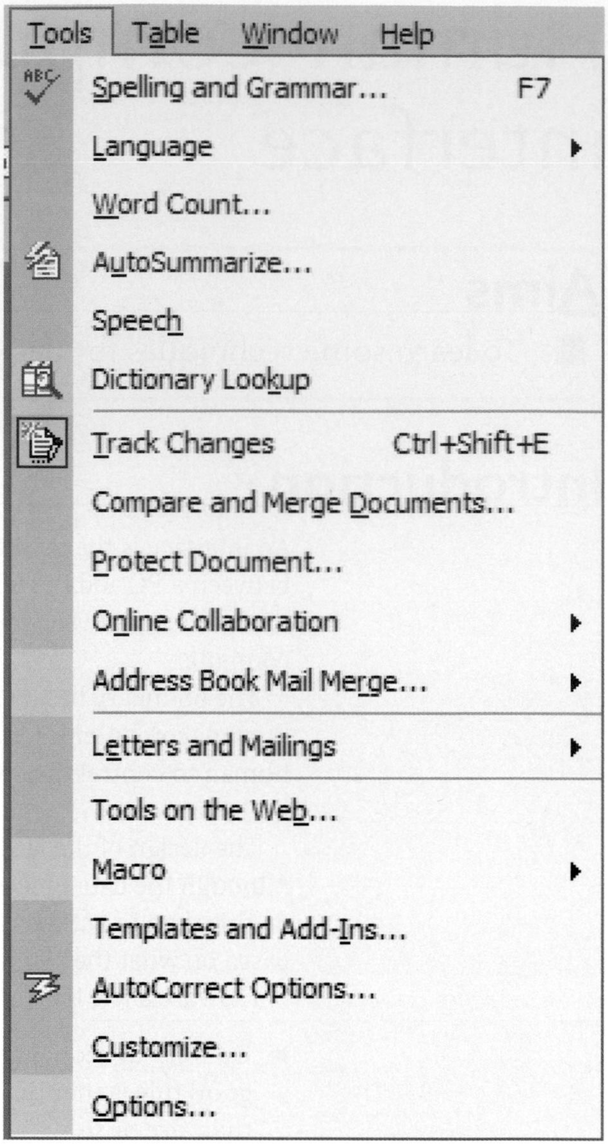

⌄⌄

Tools   Ta**b**le   **W**indow   **H**elp

Spelling and Grammar...   F7

Language   ▶

Word Count...

A**u**toSummarize...

Speech

Dictionary Loo**k**up

Track Changes   Ctrl+Shift+E

Compare and Merge **D**ocuments...

Protect Document...

O**n**line Collaboration   ▶

Address Book Mail Me**r**ge...   ▶

L**e**tters and Mailings   ▶

Tools on the We**b**...

Macro   ▶

Tem**p**lates and Add-**I**ns...

AutoCorrect Options...

Customize...

Options...

■ **Figure 12.45**

GUIs

The best interfaces are intuitive. That means that it is fairly obvious how to use them – they do not require a lot of prior learning. By far the dominant HCI in use at the moment is the graphical user interface (GUI). This is an interface where most actions and objects are represented by pictures. We have encountered many of these throughout this course. There are many GUIs in existence, but the most widely known is Windows, from Microsoft. This has developed over the years to reflect the way that most people want to work and its success has been largely based on the fact that it makes use of a metaphor. The Windows *metaphor* is a desktop. It behaves in the way you would like a real desktop to behave. You can drag things around to reposition them and drop them in the bin if you want to get rid of them.

The desktop is better than a real desktop because it has windows where different activities can be going on. Material can be *copied* and *pasted* (more metaphors) between the activities (applications) in the windows.

So successful has this metaphor become that versions of it exist in Apple computers (in fact they had it first!) and there are plenty of GUIs available for Unix and Linux systems as well.

The Windows metaphor has many very powerful features:

▶ **Consistency** – each application has a familiar look and way of working.

▶ **A natural sequence** – you select something then do something to it.

▶ **Error prevention** – only valid options are available to the user.

▶ **Drop-down menus** – headings lead to related options that do not appear until the heading is selected.

▶ **WYSIWYG (What You See Is What You Get)** – the graphical nature of the interface allows an exact display of the output – the printout is the same as the screen representation. This may sound pretty obvious these days but it was not always so. Computers used to display only a standard size and type of character. Formatting did not always show up on screen. You had to remember that something was bold, underlined or centred.

Application Generators and Windows programming environments make it as easy as possible to create your own GUIs for applications. But, just because it is physically easy, does not mean that your interfaces will be a success. Some sense of design and a bit of know-how are required to make the best interfaces.

The Gestalt principle

The Gestalt principle is that people use a top-down approach to organising data. This principle should influence how you organise graphical information on the screen. The Gestalt Principle identifies the criteria people use to group items together when displayed. Correct grouping makes it easier for a user to locate an item. For example, all the buttons to do with navigating the menus such as back, forward, and main menu should be grouped together. This allows the user to learn the interface more quickly. There are a number of ways that items can be grouped to make access easier. Colour, drawing frames and highlighting are frequently used.

Other considerations

Making screens less crowded improves clarity and readability. A good design will display only what the user needs to perform during the current operation. This reduces errors and improves performance.

Properties of forms

As we have already seen in this unit, modern applications are built up from objects. These objects have properties and methods. When working in Microsoft Office, we can set the properties of objects at design time, using the properties window, or at run time from within the program. This allows us great flexibility in producing a good dynamic interface that can vary according to circumstances.

It is worth having a good look at the properties that are available for pre-designed items such as those you can get from the toolbox.

Form	
Format	Data	Event	Other	All
Caption	
Default View	Single Form
Views Allowed	Both
Scroll Bars	Both
Record Selectors	Yes
Navigation Buttons	Yes
Dividing Lines	Yes
Auto Resize	Yes
Auto Center	No
Border Style	Sizable
Control Box	Yes
Min Max Buttons	Both Enabled
Close Button	Yes
Whats This Button	No
Width	9.998cm
Picture	(none)
Picture Type	Embedded
Picture Size Mode	Clip
Picture Alignment	Center
Picture Tiling	No
Grid X	10
Grid Y	10
Layout for Print	No
Subdatasheet Height	0cm
Subdatasheet Expanded . . .	No
Palette Source	(Default)

■ **Figure 12.46**

Form	
Format	Data	Event	Other	All
On Current	
Before Insert	
After Insert	
Before Update	
After Update	
On Dirty	
On Delete	
Before Del Confirm	
After Del Confirm	
On Open	
On Load	
On Resize	
On Unload	
On Close	
On Activate	
On Deactivate	
On Got Focus	
On Lost Focus	
On Click	
On Dbl Click	
On Mouse Down	
On Mouse Move	
On Mouse Up	
On Key Down	
On Key Up	
On Key Press	
Key Preview	No
On Error	
On Filter	
On Apply Filter	
On Timer	
Timer Interval	0

■ **Figure 12.48**

The form itself has a rich set of properties. In Access, if you create a new form and look at the properties window, you will see an amazing array of things you can change. They all have a default setting and most of the time we don't change the defaults.

Figure 12.46 shows one of four pages of properties for an Access form. It is concerned with the format of the form – the aspects of it that will be apparent to the user when looking at it. The Data properties relate to where the data on the form will come from and what the user is allowed to do with it.

There are ways to set the size, whether scroll bars are visible, or if the caption is at the top, and many more aspects of the form. The close and resize buttons can be turned off by selecting 'No' for the control box property. We often want to change the colour of a form. We go to the 'Detail' properties for this.

Section: Detail	
Format	Data	Event	Other	All
Force New Page	None
New Row Or Col	None
Keep Together	No
Visible	Yes
Display When	Always
Can Grow	No
Can Shrink	No
Height	5.402cm
Back Color	-2147483633
Special Effect	Flat

■ **Figure 12.47**

The Event (Figure 12.48) shows a huge variety of actions that the form can respond to.

ACTIVITY

Start up Access. Use any convenient file that you already have or create a new one. Create a new form without using the wizard and try changing some of the form properties. Remember – what you can change in the properties window, you can also change in a program.

Positioning of objects

We saw in Unit 12.4 how it is very easy to make a total mess of a form by just dropping objects wherever you feel like doing so. There are many ways that the form design software can help you position objects accurately, but you also need to know a few things.

A user will not want to use a form if it is badly laid out or badly thought out. It is worth the effort to make a form as attractive as possible right from the outset.

■ Figure 12.49

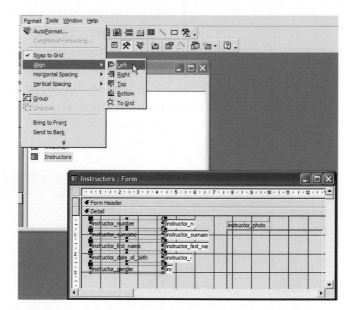

If you have a lot of text boxes or any other object and you want them to line up, you can highlight them all and align them.

You can also use the Snap to Grid feature to help you drag objects to the right position.

Another consideration is the route that a user will take while working through a form. If there are lots of text boxes to fill in, it is more natural to work down the screen and if there are other columns, it is easiest to follow a path as if you were reading a newspaper. (See Figure 12.50.)

■ Figure 12.50

Apart from designing the form this way, you will also have to make sure that when the user presses Enter or Tab, the focus moves to the correct next field. After all, most users will not want to use the mouse to move to the next field. It may be that you did not place them in order in the first place. If the user is entering data from something like an application form, then laying out the screen in a similar way will help.

In Access, you can set this right either manually or automatically by selecting Tab Order from the View menu.

Another consideration is where you put your command buttons. The eye naturally moves down the page when working on it. If you have buttons to confirm or abort or move to the next record, you will want these at the bottom of the screen. It is not natural for people to go back up to the top of the page to perform an action on data already entered.

Notice how this is the case in the dialogue box in Figure 12.51. Also, people read from left to right (in most languages!). Usually at the end of a form they

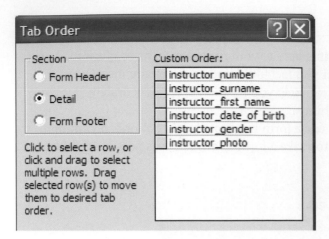

will want to confirm their actions. So, you should make the OK button the one on the left. Cancel goes to the right as you will probably have to think more about it.

When there is a set of buttons, one of them can be set up to respond to the Enter key. Notice in Figure 12.51 that the OK button has a thicker border to indicate that it has the focus. You should take the trouble to set the focus to the most likely button to click. You can do this most easily from code.

The screen in Figure 12.52 has the focus set to the Customers button. This button has been named cmdCustomers.

This was achieved by setting an event procedure to run when the form was opened. We use the On Load event.

The code is just one line.

■ Figure 12.52

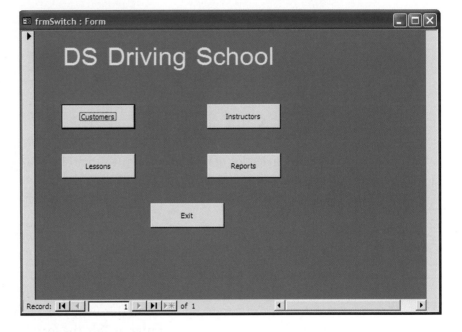

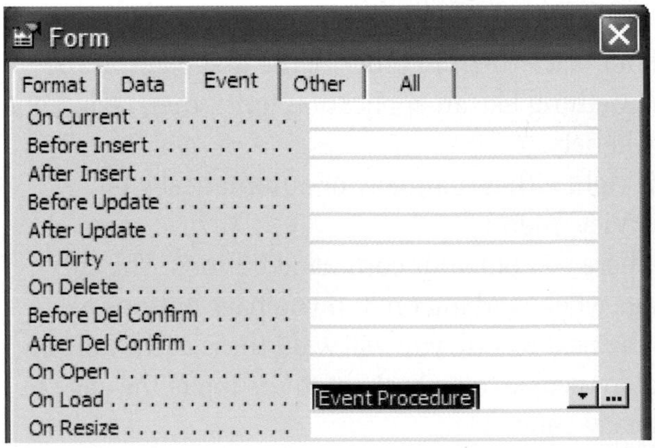

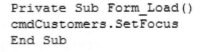

```
Private Sub Form_Load()
cmdCustomers.SetFocus
End Sub
```

■ Figure 12.54

Notice how when we want to set the property or invoke a method of any object in VBA (and many other object-oriented languages), we use what is called the 'dot notation'. To invoke the command button method SetFocus, we state the object – in this case the command button cmdCustomers – and then type a dot followed by the method we want.

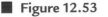

■ Figure 12.53

Fields and labels

In databases and many other applications, we frequently make forms with lots of text boxes on them. These text boxes are used to accept and edit data, which is subsequently saved to a data table or otherwise processed.

A text box on its own is not particularly helpful to a user. It needs a label placed by it or above it to indicate exactly what it is for. It may be enough simply to say something like 'Surname' or it may be better to supply help if its meaning is not obvious. In the dialogue box in Figure 12.51, (a dialogue box is a form too), we have some explanation of how to use the form in the message that starts with 'Click to select a row...'.

You should take care where you place labels. When you place a text box on an Access form, you automatically get a label created with it. The position of the label may or may not be satisfactory. The caption of the label almost certainly will not be. It will probably say something like Text4 in a very small font. You need to keep a close eye on this and make changes as necessary.

Labelling fields so that the user can immediately see what has to be done is one of the most significant parts of form design.

Validation

You have already seen how to perform validation in many ways. In databases, you can set this up at the table design stage. On spreadsheets there is a very useful validation facility under the Tools → Options → Error Checking menu option.

With forms, you can customise the validation much more accurately. One way is to use the validation property for a text box. Suppose that there are two types of report that can be requested, 1 and 2.

You can rule out any illegal response by setting the validation property of the relevant text box as in Figure 12.56.

Enter the type of report you require

2

■ Figure 12.55

■ Figure 12.56

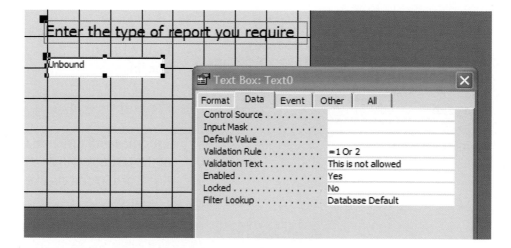

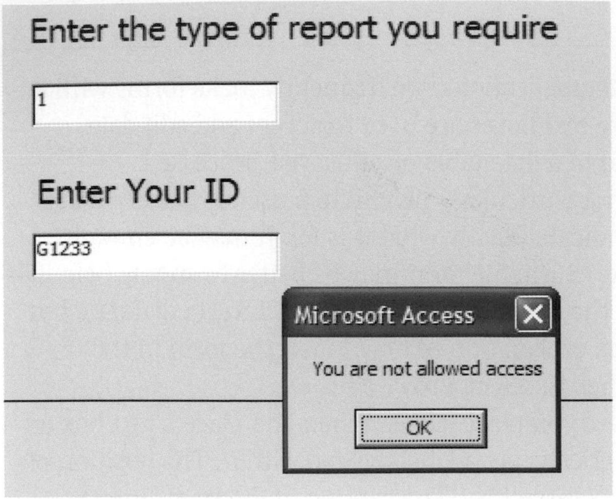

Enter the type of report you require

`1`

Enter Your ID

`G1233`

Microsoft Access

You are not allowed access

OK

■ Figure 12.57

The validation text is also set so if an invalid entry is made, the user gets a customised response.

We can do even better than this if we write some code. Suppose that requesting a report is only allowed to users who have access codes beginning with the letter 'A'. (We can make up any rule we want.)

We can use the Update event to check what has been entered. We can check it in any way we like.

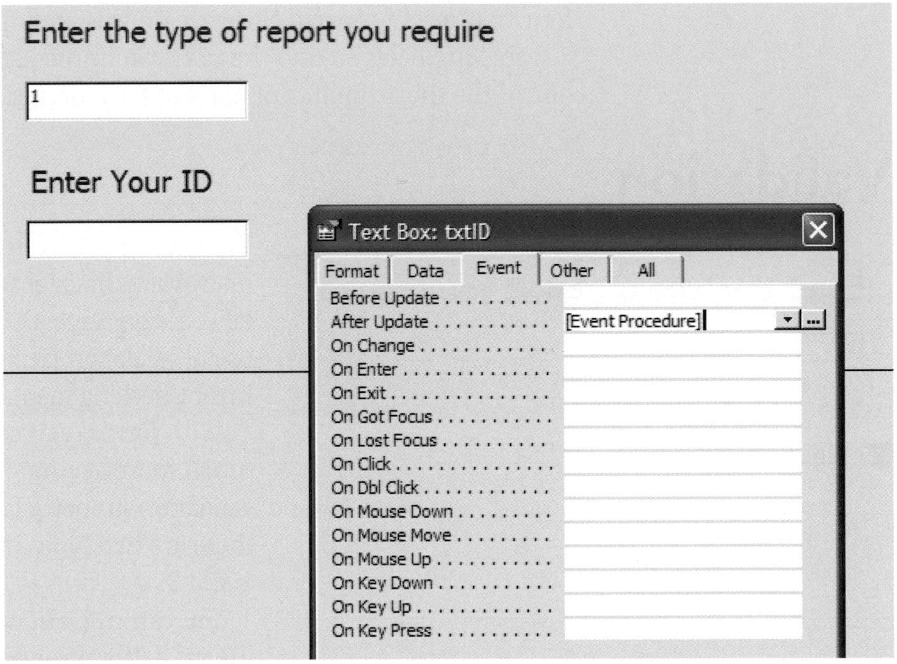

Enter the type of report you require

`1`

Enter Your ID

Text Box: txtID

| Format | Data | Event | Other | All |

Before Update . . . .
After Update . . . .   [Event Procedure]
On Change . . . .
On Enter . . . .
On Exit . . . .
On Got Focus . . . .
On Lost Focus . . . .
On Click . . . .
On Dbl Click . . . .
On Mouse Down . . . .
On Mouse Move . . . .
On Mouse Up . . . .
On Key Down . . . .
On Key Up . . . .
On Key Press . . . .

■ Figure 12.58

```
Private Sub txtID_AfterUpdate()
If Left$(txtID.Text, 1) <> "A" Then
MsgBox ("You are not allowed access")
End If
End Sub
```

■ Figure 12.59

Three lines of code are enough (as shown in Figure 12.59).
The line

```
If Left$(txtID.Text, 1) <> "A" Then
```

uses the Left$ function to check the text property of the text box called txtID. It looks at the left of the text typed in and checks the first character to see if it is an 'A'.

```
txtID.Text, 1
```

You can make absolutely anything happen if you write code!

Programming in a database

Aims

■ To use programming techniques to perform actions on databases

Introduction

Office software provides programming capabilities in each of its applications. Microsoft Office provides a version of VBA in Word, Excel, Access, PowerPoint and other applications too. There are certain differences between these types of VBA, because the applications have different jobs to do. Also, each application has its own object hierarchy which relates to its own capabilities and purposes. To get the most out of programming any of the applications, it is necessary to have a reasonable knowledge of the objects that are available and where to look up information about them. The Access version of VBA has many features which set it apart from the other versions. For example, the Access version of VBA has features to create, search and manipulate data sets. Access VBA programs also often make use of another programming language – Structured Query Language (SQL) – a version of which is used in many other database management environments.

Learning Access VBA can be rather more difficult than other versions of VBA because you need to have many objects set up before you can write any programs to manipulate them.

In this unit, we shall try out a few Access VBA techniques on the DS Driving School database that we met in Unit 7. If you want to save time, all the objects and programming code are available on the CD. You can either enter the code yourself or make use of the examples. If you use the examples, you should make lots of alterations in order to gain first-hand knowledge of how the language works.

This unit has only a limited amount of space, so the examples given are only a starting point. The capabilities of Access VBA are more or less limitless. Also, many professional programmers would write their code using the VB programming language and make a link into the Access objects and manipulate them. That way, they can compile their applications without the users having access to their source code or even needing to have a copy of Access themselves.

The example database

The DS Driving School database is not complete. Only some of the functionality has been written. When you have worked through the example code, you should be able to add more to it if you want to.

The starting point for anyone using this database is the switchboard.

■ Figure 12.60

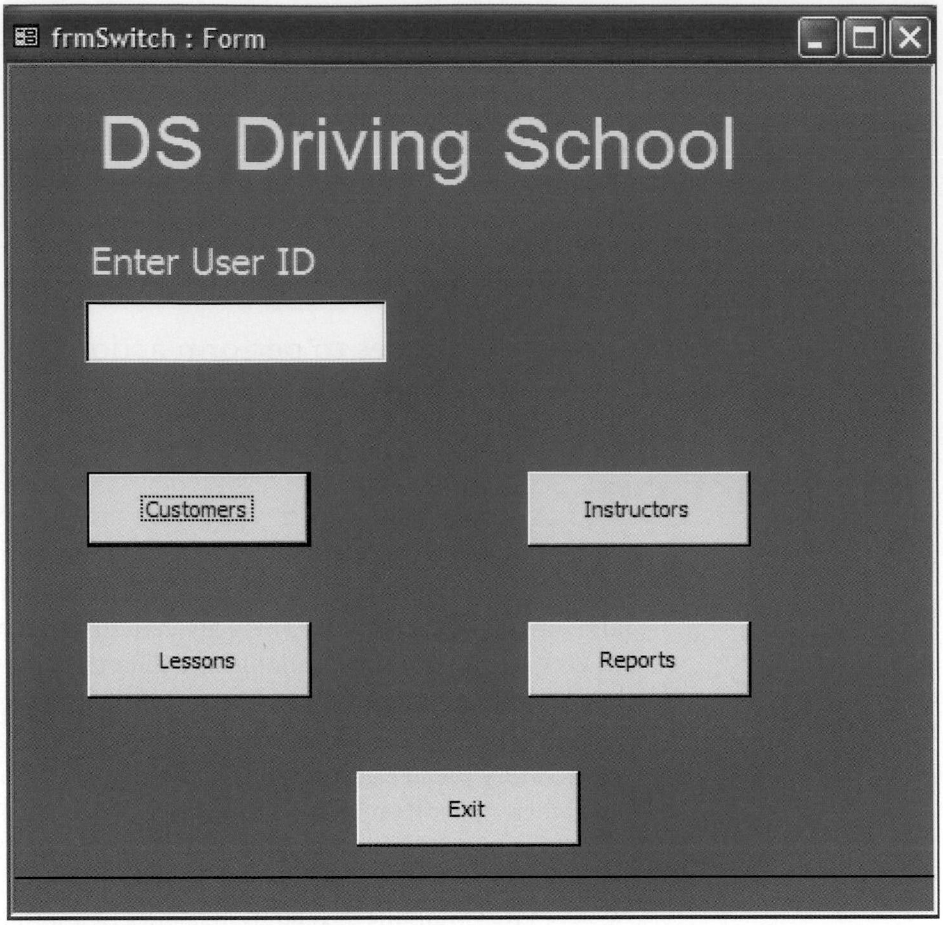

This switchboard is, of course, a form which contains five command buttons, two labels and a text box. Notice that some of the form's properties have been changed from the default; there are no scroll bars, record selectors or navigation buttons – these have all been set to False. Also, the background colour has been changed and the form has been named frmSwitch. This has been left as a caption to the form, so you can see it at the top of the form. You could change that if you wanted.

There are data tables behind this application and for the purposes of this chapter, we shall be working with one called tblCustomer. This contains personal information about the driving school customers.

Handling database objects and controls

Remember, anything you can do to a form or any other object with the property box, you can also do through a program. We shall start by looking at what happens if you click the button with the caption 'Customers'. Basically it is set up to open another form, frmCustomers. If you enter a user ID such as B123 then click 'Customers', you get a typical view of the customer form.

Note that this form does show scroll bars, the record selector and the navigation buttons.

The code lying behind the Customers button is as follows:

```
Private Sub cmdCustomers_Click()
On Error GoTo Err_cmdCustomers_Click

    Dim stDocName As String
    Dim stLinkCriteria As String

    txtID.SetFocus
    If txtID.Text <> "" Then
    stDocName = "frmCustomers"
    DoCmd.OpenForm stDocName, , , stLinkCriteria
    Else
    MsgBox ("You must enter your User ID")
    End If

Exit_cmdCustomers_Click:
    Exit Sub


Err_cmdCustomers_Click:
    MsgBox Err.Description
    Resume Exit_cmdCustomers_Click


End Sub
```

The main work is in the highlighted section. This sets the focus to the text box and validates that there is in fact something in it. A suitable message is shown if not. Otherwise, the variable stDocName is set to frmCustomers and the form is opened. frmCustomers is already linked to the data table tblCustomer, so when it appears, all the data from that table is available. Notice that the navigation buttons (Figure 12.61) refer to 27 records.

There is a second event procedure running here as well. We have had one event from the user so far – clicking the Customers button. When the form frmCustomers opens it initiates that form's Open event.

We have written an event procedure for that as well. This event procedure is part of the form's collection of procedures.

```
Private Sub Form_Open(Cancel As Integer)
Dim ID As String
ID = [Forms]![frmswitch]![txtID]
If Left$(ID, 1) = "A" Then
txtsurname.Locked = True
txttelephone.Visible = False
Else
txtsurname.Locked = False
txttelephone.Visible = True
End If


End Sub
```

The idea of this procedure is to show how you can manipulate controls on a form from within a program. This procedure sets up a variable called ID. It gives it a value taken from the switchboard form:

```
Dim ID As String
ID = [Forms]![frmswitch]![txtID]
```

It then examines the first letter to see if it is A.

```
If Left$(ID, 1) = "A" Then
txtsurname.Locked = True
txttelephone.Visible = False
Else
txtsurname.Locked = False
txttelephone.Visible = True
End If
```

If it is, it locks the surname field and hides the telephone field. This could be because of the rights of different users with different IDs but it is included just to show what can be done.

■ Figure 12.62

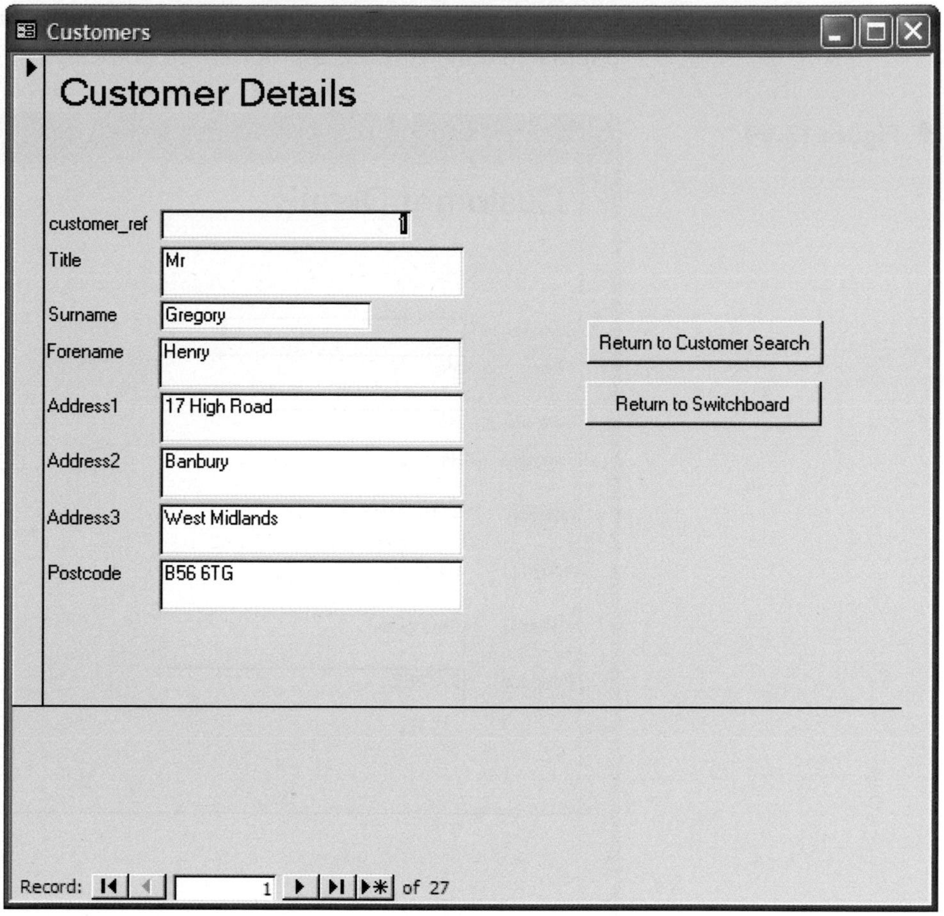

ACTIVITY

Try changing the colour of the form according to some aspect of the user ID.

Accessing tables

One of the great advantages of writing programs for a database application is the fine degree of control you get over the data itself. You can do anything to it and it is often much easier to write code than to struggle over using the various features of queries.

RECORDSET A subset of the data in a table.

The easiest way to access data in tables is to first create a RECORDSET. It can be all the data in all the tables or data selected from one or more tables – it is in fact what you get when you use a query, but here we shall write a little code to manipulate it.

You create a recordset by using an SQL statement.

We shall use SQL to make a subset of customer data according to where they live. The form VBA_Test has been set up to show you how.

coursework_tip

Go to any query you have made before and view the SQL version to see the code you need. In fact, if you don't know the SQL syntax to create a recordset that you need, you can always make a query and paste the SQL code into your own program.

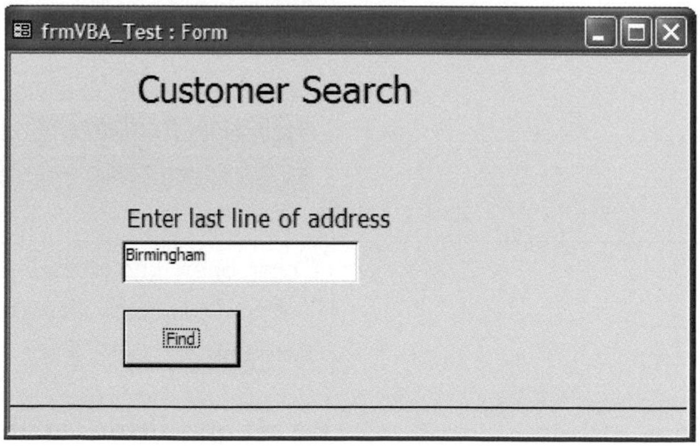

■ Figure 12.63

If you click the button 'Find', you get the same customer form as before but populated only with the appropriate customers.

■ Figure 12.64

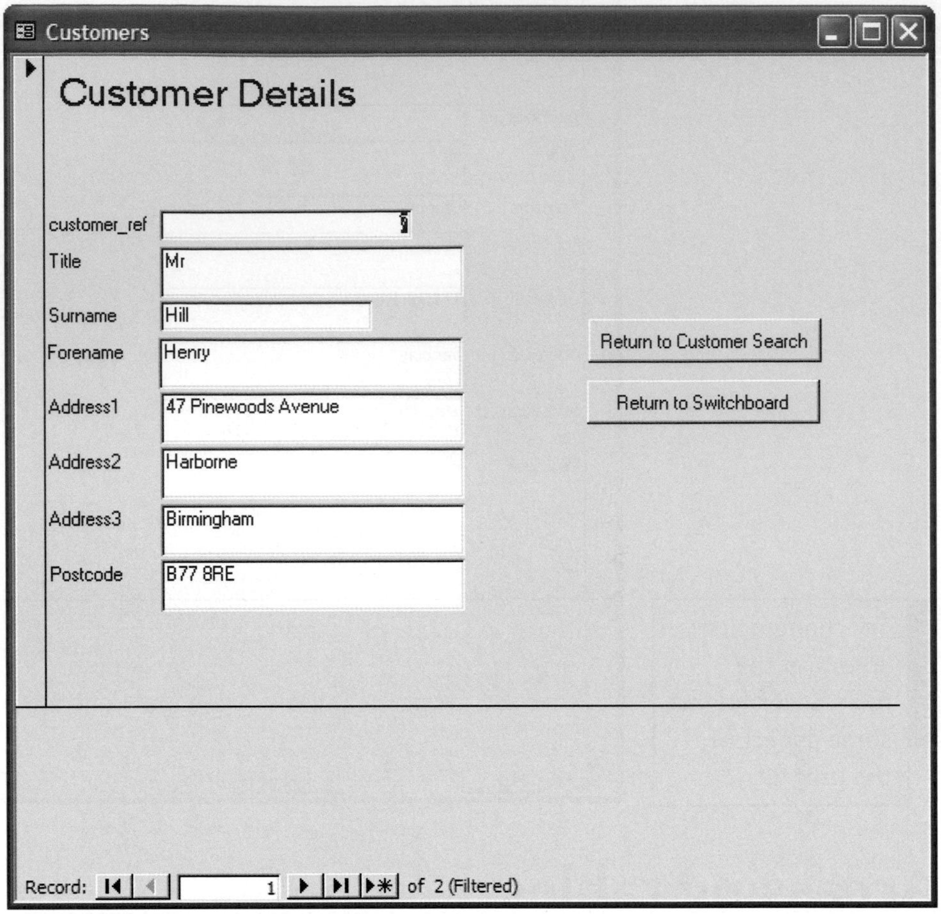

Notice how we only have two records selected. Scrolling through with the navigation buttons will show only two results.

The code that we used for this was put in the button's event procedure.

```
Private Sub cmdTest_Click()
Dim Strsql As String

'first clear the SQL variable
Strsql = ""

'then give it the SQL statement
Strsql = "SELECT * from tblCustomer WHERE_
tblCustomer.address3=[forms]![frmVBA_Test]![txtCity];"

'now open the form, applying the SQL conditions
DoCmd.OpenForm "frmCustomers", acNormal, Strsql
End Sub
```

We set up a string variable called Strsql – this is to hold the SQL statement that we shall write.

Write code to produce a list of customers whose surnames begin with a certain letter.

The highlighted SQL statement selects all fields (*) from the customer table where the address3 field contains the specified data. Notice the use of exclamation marks and square brackets to reference a particular field on a particular form. The form is part of the 'forms' collection and this is why we also need to reference [forms].

Modifying forms

We have already seen that we can control the appearance and functionality of forms from within a program. We made the telephone field invisible. Remember that you can make any changes you want from within a program. This is often useful if you want to re-use a form but only certain operations are permissible at a particular time.

Some useful changes could be to:

▶ lock fields that must not be changed under certain circumstances
▶ hide details from certain users
▶ show different sets of buttons to different users.

Modifying reports

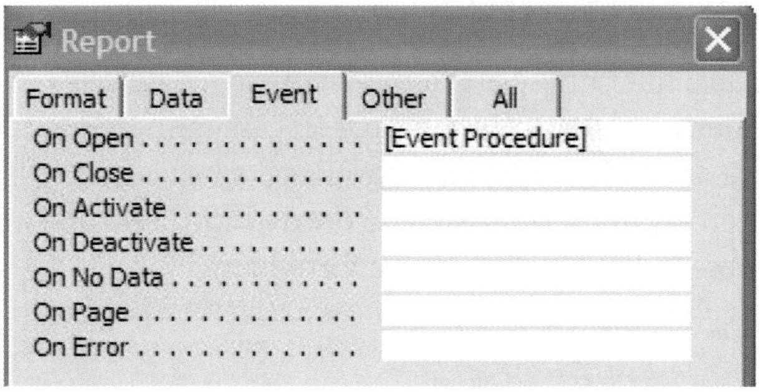

Reports can be modified 'on the fly' by program code exactly as can forms. You can write event procedures to respond to various circumstances. The most useful one is On Open, but it is also useful to take some action if there is no data in a report. You can stop the print process and flag up a warning.

The following code checks the user ID just as we did when opening the customer form earlier. This time, it removes the surnames from the report if the ID starts with an 'A'. This could relate to the department that someone works in.

Figure 12.65

```
Private Sub Report_Open(Cancel As Integer)
Dim ID As String
ID = [Forms]![frmswitch]![txtID]
If Left$(ID, 1) = "A" Then
instructor_surname_Label.Visible = False
instructor_surname.Visible = False
Else
instructor_surname_Label.Visible = True
instructor_surname.Visible = True

End If

End Sub
```

It is possible to change the appearance or headings or how the data is grouped according to circumstances.

Validating and verifying data

We have used code in several of our examples in this unit to validate data entered. We can most easily do this by using the if...then construct. We then write code to block data entry and display a suitable message.

In the following block of code, which we used in the Customer button's event procedure:

```
If txtID.Text <> "" Then
stDocName = "frmCustomers"
DoCmd.OpenForm stDocName, , , stLinkCriteria
Else
MsgBox ("You must enter your User ID")
End If
```

the customer form (frmCustomers) is only opened if there is something in the txtID text box. The code effectively says 'if the text in txtID doesn't equal nothing ("") then open the form, otherwise just put up an error message'.

It is far more flexible to write your own validation routines than to rely on the built-in validation properties of tables and forms. You can also make more customised responses to the entry of bad data.

Searching tables and external files

Sometimes it is useful to be able to examine and amend data in a database that has been created by a different system. Nowadays, you can connect say an Access system to an Oracle database, a text file or an Excel spreadsheet. Once the connectors have been set up, it is possible to create recordsets and manipulate the data as if it were in the DBMS's native format.

In the case of Access, the technology involved is called ActiveX Data Object Data Base (ADODB).

You first need to declare a variable to hold the connector and tell it the sort of external object to which you want to connect.

CONNECTION STRING The type, name and location of the file to be read.

You also have to provide a CONNECTION STRING (in this case `C:\customers.xls`).

We have also told the connector that the top row of the sheet is occupied by the field names (`FirstRowHasNames=1`)[1 means true, 0 means false].

```
Dim cn As ADODB.Connection

Set cn = New ADODB.Connection

With cn
    .Provider = "MSDASQL"
    .ConnectionString = "Driver={Microsoft Excel Driver (*.xls)};" & _
    "DBQ=C:\customers.xls; FirstRowHasNames=1;
    ReadOnly=False;"
    .Open

End With
```

Once we have established a connection with the external data, we can write a normal SQL string in order to extract the data that we want. In this case, we shall extract all (*) from the worksheet called Customers.

```
StrQuery = "SELECT * FROM [Customers]"
```

The complete code is as follows:

```
Private Sub cmdGetData_Click()

Dim cn As ADODB.Connection
Dim rstData As Recordset
Dim rs As ADODB.Recordset
Dim StrQuery As String
Dim strtemp As String

Set cn = New ADODB.Connection

With cn
    .Provider = "MSDASQL"
    .ConnectionString = "Driver={Microsoft Excel Driver (*.xls)};" & _
    "DBQ=C:\customers.xls; FirstRowHasNames=1;
    ReadOnly=False;"
    .Open

End With

StrQuery = "SELECT * FROM [Customers]"

Set rs = New ADODB.Recordset

rs.Open StrQuery, CurrentProject.Connection, adOpenKeyset,
adLockOptimistic


rs.MoveLast

If rs.RecordCount = 0 Then
MsgBox ("no records")
End If

MsgBox (rs.RecordCount)
MsgBox (rs.Fields.Count)

If rs.EOF Then Exit Sub

rs.MoveFirst

Do Until rs.EOF
```

```
strtemp = rs![surname]

MsgBox (strtemp)


rs.MoveNext
Loop

rs.Close
Set rs = Nothing


End Sub
```

The code above shows how you can sequentially step through an external data source. If you needed to make changes to the data, you would output the details onto a form and use the recordset update method in order to write the changes back to the data file.

Programming in a spreadsheet

Aims

■ To use programming techniques to manipulate a spreadsheet

Introduction

Programming is easier in a spreadsheet than in a database. The development of a spreadsheet has much in common with programming, which makes the cross-over from using formulae and functions to writing code less of a jump.

Another reason why programming a spreadsheet is easy is because so much of its potential can be achieved by recording macros. These macros can be pasted into your own code and, as well as saving effort, they can be a very good way of learning the syntax of the language and the nature of the objects available.

One of the main reasons to use programming in a spreadsheet is when iteration is required because it is not possible to achieve this other than programmatically.

You may have noticed by now that when you use the editor to write code, if you type the name of an object and then a dot, the possible properties and methods appear in a drop-down box. This feature is called intellisense. It can help a lot in learning what can be done to and by an object.

VBA does, unfortunately, allow you to use variables before you have declared them. This is not good practice and also, if you do declare them, intellisense can pick up on this when you write code and suggest possible properties and methods for your own variables.

Handling spreadsheet objects

Spreadsheets have a rich set of objects in their object hierarchy. It is possible to use them to control every aspect of a spreadsheet's behaviour. You can see what is available, how the objects can be changed and what they can do by looking in the object browser.

Start a new Excel workbook, make sure that the Visual Basic toolbar is switched on, add a new user form and click the object browser button.

Spend a short while looking at the properties and methods of a few objects, just to get a feel for what is there.

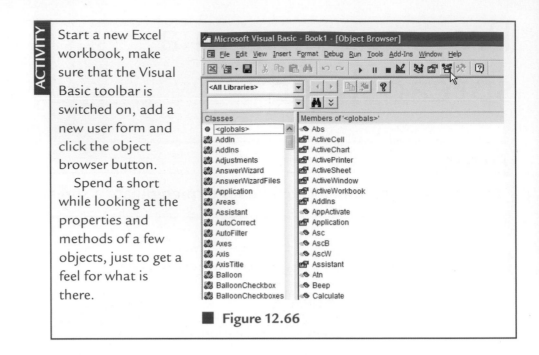

■ Figure 12.66

Manipulating a worksheet or a cell

There are some examples of interaction between program code and a spreadsheet in Unit 12.4. We saw how a column of numbers was checked for being odd or even. It is possible to interact with the cells of a worksheet in any way you wish.

To try out some of these examples, the easiest thing to do is to create a new workbook, switch on the Visual Basic Toolbar and immediately make a new form. You can then place a command button on the form and double-click on it to get the code-editing window.

Manipulating a worksheet

It is possible to alter worksheet properties from within a program. One such property is the sheet's name. If you start a new workbook, it automatically creates three worksheets by default. It calls them Sheet 1, Sheet 2 and Sheet 3. Even assuming that you want three sheets, the sheet names may not be as you require. You can write code to make some quick changes.

Put the following code into an event procedure and try it out. The easiest way is to put it in the event procedure of a button.

Remember, the lines following the ' are comment lines. These are put in so that humans can understand what is going on. The compiler ignores them.

```
'first declare variables to hold the number of sheets and a counter
'to hold the position of the current sheet in the loop
Dim iSheetNumber As Integer
Dim iSheetCounter As Integer
```

```
' Count is a property of Worksheets (which is in turn a property of
' ActiveWorkBook)
' It tells us how many sheets there are.
' We assign this to the variable iSheetNumber
iSheetNumber = Worksheets.Count

' We loop through the sheets to the maximum number that we stored in
' iSheetNumber
' We use iSheetCounter to count our way through the sheets
For iSheetCounter = 1 To iSheetNumber

' We activate that sheet
Worksheets(iSheetCounter).Activate

' We change the sheet's Name property to "My Sheet"
' and add in the current value of iSheetCounter
Worksheets(iSheetCounter).Name = "My Sheet " & iSheetCounter
Next iSheetCounter
```

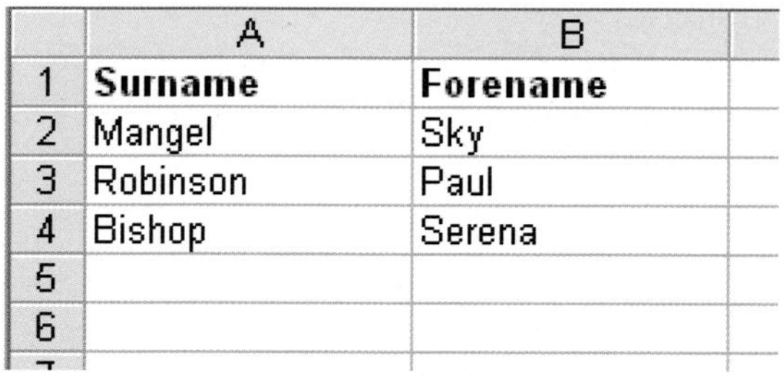

	A	B
1	**Surname**	**Forename**
2	Mangel	Sky
3	Robinson	Paul
4	Bishop	Serena
5		
6		
7		

■ **Figure 12.67**

Manipulating a cell

A worksheet cell, just like anything else, can be handled via program code. You can change the values in it, lock and unlock cells or simply detect what the contents are. The following example shows how you can use a form to add data to a sheet.

Suppose you have a list of data, such as people's names in a sheet.

You can set up a form so that a user has a more intuitive way of entering data.

This example is trivial, but the principles used have wide implications if you are building an application for others to use.

■ **Figure 12.68**

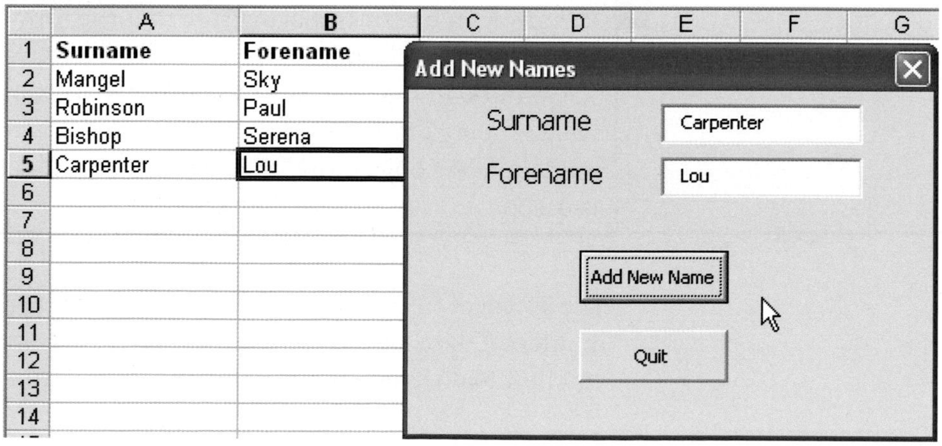

	A	B	C	D	E	F	G
1	**Surname**	**Forename**					
2	Mangel	Sky					
3	Robinson	Paul					
4	Bishop	Serena					
5	Carpenter	Lou					
6							
7							
8							
9							
10							
11							
12							
13							
14							

Add New Names

Surname   Carpenter

Forename   Lou

Add New Name

Quit

We can plan the code with a set of steps. This is an alternative to doing a proper structured flow chart and is perfectly acceptable for a simple macro or piece of program code.

1 The active cell has to start at the top left of the sheet.
2 It examines the contents to see if they are blank.
3 If they are, it copies the names from the text boxes on the sheet to the relevant cells.
4 Otherwise it moves on and looks at the next cell down.

The only way to do this apart from programming is to do it manually.
Some code that will do this is as follows:

```
Private Sub cmdAddNew_Click()
Dim iCurrRow As Integer

    iCurrRow = 1
    Cells(iCurrRow, 1).Select

    Do While Not IsEmpty(ActiveCell.Offset(1, 0))
    Cells(iCurrRow, 1).Select
    iCurrRow = iCurrRow + 1

    Loop

    ActiveCell.Offset(1, 0).Select
    ActiveCell.Value = txtSurname
    ActiveCell.Offset(0, 1).Select
    ActiveCell.Value = txtForename

End Sub
```

ACTIVITY

Create the form behind this code. Name all the objects appropriately and try out the code.

Note that if you make any mistakes in writing the code, it won't work. It is always a bit tricky making sure that the form objects are spelt exactly the same as in the code.

Go through the code line by line and make sure that you understand what is going on.

Identify the objects and the methods and also the single function that is used in it.

The potential to build powerful and easy to use applications is more or less limitless. Take a look at the many websites that people have set up to show you how to do simple and more complex things in Excel VBA.

CUSTOMISING APPLICATIONS

338

Modifying charts and graphs

Making charts is a common use for a spreadsheet. Most users can use the chart wizard to make successful charts. It may be useful to create some programmed procedures for chart making if you want your users always to produce consistent results. The following example is just one possibility. As before, there are limitless opportunities to customise your own spreadsheets with code.

The example takes a spreadsheet of sales figures.

■ **Figure 12.69**

	A	B	C	D	E	F	G
1	Sales by region (thousands)						
2							
3	Region	January	February	March	April	May	June
4	North	3.4	6.5	3.4	7.5	3.8	7.6
5	South	6.4	5	3.6	6.9	5.4	5.4
6	East	8.3	4.3	4.3	9.6	3.7	3.4
7	West	2.1	9.5	3.2	5.5	2.4	3.1
8							
9							
10							
11							
12							
13	Column						
14	Line						
15							

The entries in cells A13 and A14 will serve as data for a combo box that we shall use. In reality you would probably put them on a different sheet or even hide them.

The idea is to make a graph of the sales figures, where the user can choose either a column or a line graph. The user can also type in a title that will appear on the chart.

A user interface is made by setting up a form as in Figures 12.70 and 12.71. The user enters a title in the text box.

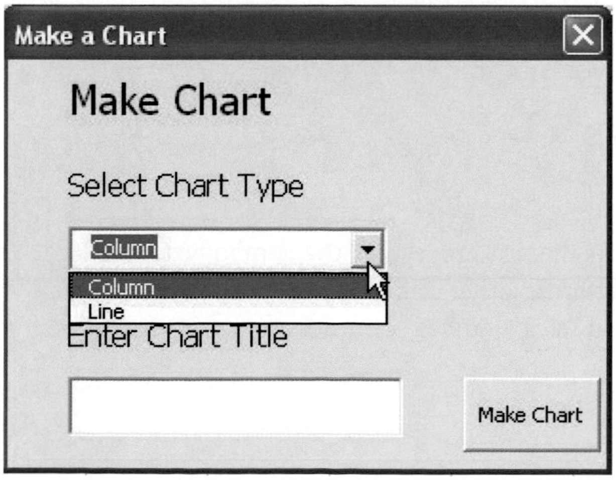

■ **Figure 12.70**

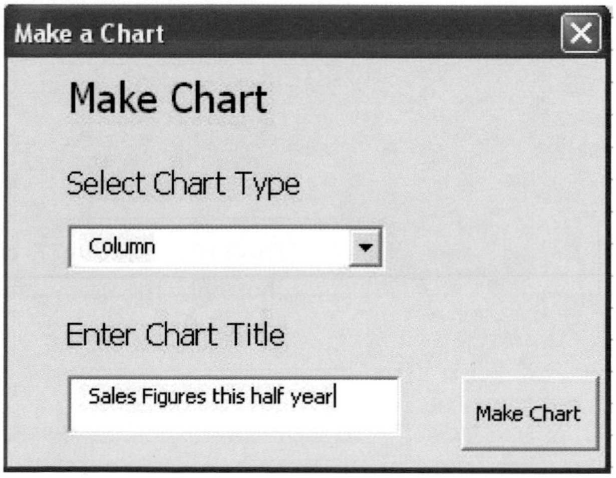

■ **Figure 12.71**

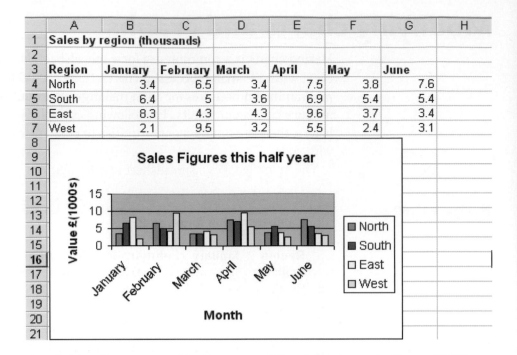

	A	B	C	D	E	F	G	H
1	Sales by region (thousands)							
2								
3	Region	January	February	March	April	May	June	
4	North	3.4	6.5	3.4	7.5	3.8	7.6	
5	South	6.4	5	3.6	6.9	5.4	5.4	
6	East	8.3	4.3	4.3	9.6	3.7	3.4	
7	West	2.1	9.5	3.2	5.5	2.4	3.1	

On clicking the command button, we get the chart shown in Figure 12.72.

We could have asked for any data and incorporated it into the chart. The way this works is as follows.

First, we record two macros, one for a column chart and one for a line chart.

We then set up a user form with labels, a combo box, a text box and a command button as in Figure 12.71. We naturally take the trouble to set up the names and captions as appropriate. The command box has its RowSource property set to point at the chart type choices that are already on the sheet. It is easier to do this if you name the values (highlight the cells then Insert → Name → Define); then you can enter that name as the property.

We then write an event procedure to go in the command button's On Click procedure.

```
Private Sub cmdDoIt_Click()
If cmbType.Text = "Column" Then
Call sales_graph2(txtTitle)
Else
Call sales_graph(txtTitle)
End If
End Sub
```

This procedure simply checks the text property of the combo box – the item chosen by the user – and performs either one or the other sub-routine. We named them sales_graph and sales_graph2.

Just to make it a bit neater, we also took the user's choice of title from the text box txtTitle and passed it as a parameter to the relevant sub-procedure.

One of the sub-procedures has the following code. The other one is much the same.

Notice how the parameter is received by the procedure in the brackets after its name.

```
Sub sales_graph(strChartTitle)
    Range("A3:G7").Select
    Charts.Add
    ActiveChart.ChartType = xlLineMarkers
    ActiveChart.SetSourceData Source:=Sheets("Sheet 2").
        Range("A3:G7"), PlotBy _:=xlRows
ActiveChart.Location Where:=xlLocationAsObject, Name:="Sheet 2"
With ActiveChart
    .HasTitle = True
    .ChartTitle.Characters.Text = strChartTitle
    .Axes(xlCategory, xlPrimary).HasTitle = True
    .Axes(xlCategory, xlPrimary).AxisTitle.Characters.Text = "Month"
    .Axes(xlValue, xlPrimary).HasTitle = True
    .Axes(xlValue, xlPrimary).AxisTitle.Characters.Text = _
    "Value £(1000s)"
End With
ActiveChart.Legend.Select
Selection.Delete

End Sub
```

The title is added by the highlighted line. You could have made any other change you wished.

```
Option Explicit
Dim strChartTitle As String
```

In the module's General tab, we added these lines:
Option Explicit ensures that we will be warned if we don't declare a variable. Then we declare the variable to take the chart title. By declaring it here rather than in a procedure, all the sub-procedures can use it. This is called declaring it as a *global* variable.

Searching worksheets and external files

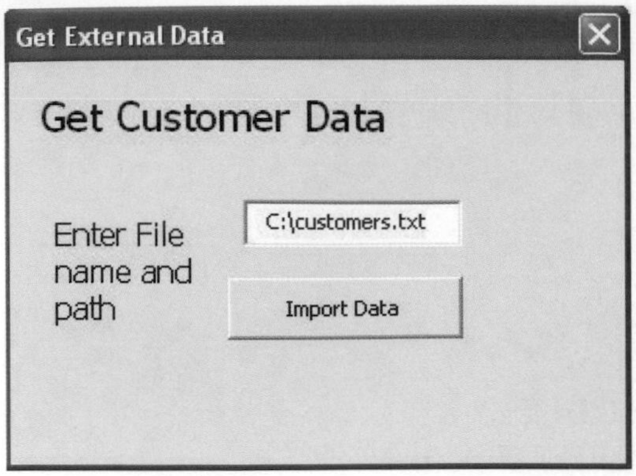

We can get a spreadsheet to import a particular text or other data file. Naturally, this can be automated.

In this simple example, we have typed in the pathname and file name of the text file to import. In a properly developed application we would add a common dialogue box in order to let the user navigate to the file required.

The code to import this data is as follows:

■ Figure 12.73

```
Private Sub cmdGetData_Click()
With ActiveSheet.QueryTables.Add(Connection:= _
    "TEXT;" & txtFileName, Destination:=Range("A1" ))
    .Name = "Customers"
    .FieldNames = True
    .RowNumbers = False
    .FillAdjacentFormulas = False
    .PreserveFormatting = True
    .RefreshOnFileOpen = False
    .RefreshStyle = xlInsertDeleteCells
    .SavePassword = False
    .SaveData = True
    .AdjustColumnWidth = True
    .RefreshPeriod = 0
    .TextFilePromptOnRefresh = False
    .TextFilePlatform = xlWindows
    .TextFileStartRow = 1
    .TextFileParseType = xlFixedWidth
    .TextFileTextQualifier = xlTextQualifierDoubleQuote
    .TextFileConsecutiveDelimiter = False
    .TextFileTabDelimiter = True
    .TextFileSemicolonDelimiter = False
    .TextFileCommaDelimiter = False
    .TextFileSpaceDelimiter = False
    .TextFileColumnDataTypes = Array(1, 1, 1, 1, 1, 1, 1, 1, 1)
    .TextFileFixedColumnWidths = Array(13, 264, 25, 255, 255,
    255, 255, 255)
    .Refresh BackgroundQuery:=False
  End With
End Sub
```

There is more code than is really needed because it was generated by recording a macro – by far the easiest way to find out how to program something!

The highlighted section shows how the file name is obtained from the user form.

Browsing data

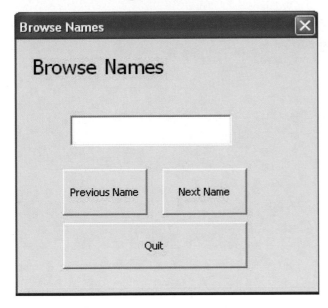

■ Figure 12.74

You may want to display data sequentially on a form. This can be set up quite easily as in the following example. It is set up to work on the list of names shown in Figure 12.68.

The surnames will be displayed in the text box. The text box is named txtSurname and the command buttons are cmdPrev, cmdNext and cmdQuit.

First, we want the active cell to be the first name on the sheet – that is cell A2 in our example.

We can make this happen automatically without the user having to do anything. All we need to do is to write an event procedure which will run as soon as the form is opened. If we call the procedure UserForm_Initialize, it will run automatically. The following code selects the cell in row 2, column 1 and copies the name into the form's text box.

```
Private Sub UserForm_Initialize()
Cells(2, 1).Select
txtSurname = ActiveCell.Value
iRow = 2
End Sub
```

The following code is attached to the cmdPrev button:

```
Private Sub cmdPrev_Click()
If ActiveCell.Offset(-1, 0).Row <> 1 Then
    iRow = iRow — 1
    Cells(iRow, 1).Select
    txtSurname = ActiveCell.Value
End If

End Sub
```

ACTIVITY

Add code to allow edits to be used to update the spreadsheet.

It checks to see if the previous row is the first row using the row property. If it is, it won't do anything. Otherwise, it decrements the row counter and selects that cell. Then it displays its contents in the text box. If we wanted to, we could add code that copies any changes made to the text box back to the spreadsheet cell.

To move forwards, we do the reverse, but this time, we check that the next cell contains something before we move on using the value property.

ACTIVITY

Try out some of these examples of code. They are all to be found in the file **Ch 12_3 SS examples** on the CD, if you don't want to type them in.

```
Private Sub cmdNext_Click()

If ActiveCell.Offset(1, 0).Value <> "" Then
    iRow = iRow + 1
    Cells(iRow, 1).Select
    txtSurname = ActiveCell.Value
    Else
    MsgBox ("Can't go there")
End If


End Sub
```

Testing

Aims

■ To understand how to carry out formal testing

Introduction

When you develop a solution to a problem using application generators, you should, ideally, have a well-thought-out specification to work from. You then develop the screen objects and program code. As you write each procedure, you naturally try it out to see if it works according to plan. This is a fairly easy way to proceed and it should lead to the production of mostly quite serviceable code. However, just because you 'tried it out' does not mean that what you have produced is good enough. There may well be all sorts of hidden problems that you didn't notice:

> ▶ There may be some circumstances where a procedure fails.
> ▶ There may be problems when the procedures are linked together.
> ▶ The user interface may be difficult for others to understand.

If you are producing a serious product for others to use, you need to be thorough in your testing. It is one thing for a 'buggy' product to be used only by its creator, where problems might be fixed while it is in use, but it is quite something else if a company starts to rely on the product and gives it to other staff to use.

portfolio_tip

If you are completing this unit alongside Unit 8 you should call a project group meeting to review the product when testing is complete.

The reasons for testing

It is worth thinking for a moment about why you do testing. There are obvious intuitive answers – 'to see that the software works' or 'to check that the software performs the tasks expected of it'. This is all well and good, but it is best to take a step back for a moment and look at it in a slightly different way. It is better to be brutally honest and look at testing in a more destructive and negative way.

portfolio_tip

You must include feedback from others in developing your product.

The purpose of testing is to discover errors.

This is a different point of view. If you deliberately set out to 'break' the software, you are more likely to be rigorous in checking all possible circumstances. Often, it is best to get others to test the software because they may be more motivated than you are to find faults.

It does not take long for a project to grow. The more it grows, the more links there will be between different modules. This produces an exponential growth of potential problems as the project progresses. This requires ever more testing to check all the different pathways through a system. It is not at all surprising that software of any degree of complexity has faults in it even after it has been released. With proper testing, we try to keep this to a minimum.

It is not possible to test everything – even in relatively trivial software. Although we try to cover it all, there will always be circumstances that we have not thought of or allowed for. It is usual for commercial and other software to come with a disclaimer about its performance, simply because it is so difficult to test everything.

PATCH Extra code that is added to software post-release, in order to fix a problem or improve performance.

Many software companies regularly issue updates or PATCHES to cover eventualities that were not apparent when the software was first released.

If you use a machine with Windows XP, you will be aware of the number of times the automatic update process loads a patch.

Types of testing

Testing can take place at various stages of development and in quite different ways. It may be carried out by the developers or their appointed testers before the client ever gets to see it. This is called alpha testing.

Once the software is complete and tested extensively by the developers, it might be handed over to a user who puts it to work in its intended environment on the understanding that it may still have errors. The user may get special incentives to take this responsibility and report the findings back to the developers. This is called beta testing.

The developers may adopt one of two types of approach themselves. They may test that a particular set of inputs produces the correct outputs, without looking inside the procedures. When you concentrate on inputs and outputs, this is called black-box testing – because you are not interested in what goes on inside the 'box' or the procedure or object.

Another approach is to inspect the goings on inside each procedure, by checking the intermediate values of variables as the program is being stepped through. This 'internal' testing is called white-box or clear-box testing. This can only be done by the developers. Beta testing is always black box.

Where a single procedure or module is being tested, this has to be white-box testing because it is only a part of the finished product. This is called *unit testing*. *Package testing* is where a group of modules is tested together.

Integration testing takes place when all the modules have been put together to uncover errors that may exist in connecting them. This can show up occasions where there are errors in parameter passing.

System testing is checking for errors in the whole package against the original specification. This is a form of black-box testing.

Acceptance testing is also checking against the requirements but it is carried out by the client and not the developers.

Usability testing is investigating how well users can relate to the software and its ease of use.

portfolio_tip

Testing is often done very badly by students when they do their projects. It may help you to devise a better test plan if you divide up your testing according to some of the categories outlined in this section.

The test plan

To be methodical, it is necessary to devise a test plan. The idea of a test plan is to make sure that all aspects of the system are tested properly and nothing important is left out. Test plans will not normally be necessary to pick up faults such as syntax errors, because the interpreter or compiler will warn of these. The test plan is more aimed at logical errors where the program runs but gives the wrong results.

A test plan should include the following headings:

▶ the parts of the system to be tested
▶ the data that will be entered
▶ the expected result.

Aspects that need to be tested

White-box testing should cover:

▶ correct values produced by the module
▶ correct behaviour of application such as cursor movement, worksheet selection
▶ behaviour if no data entered.

Black-box testing should cover:

▶ screen layout
▶ form design
▶ validation checks
▶ files created or amended correctly
▶ all error situations
▶ all outputs
▶ ease of use.

Your own test plan may include different aspects depending on the nature of your software. You need to decide:

▶ how far you are going to go with the testing
▶ what methods you will use
▶ the order in which you will carry out your tests.

The plan can include quite a large number of headings such as:

▶ an identification number for each test
▶ the features of the software that will be tested, such as the passing of a parameter from one procedure to another
▶ dependencies – does the procedure involve interaction with other procedures?
▶ an approach, such as supplying a particular type of test data
▶ pass/fail criteria
▶ results
▶ hardware required
▶ what needs to be documented about the test.

portfolio_tip

When you carry out testing for work in your portfolio, you should also make sure that there are references in your test plan to where the evidence of the results is to be found. Perhaps an extra column or heading can be inserted that holds the page number where there is a printout or a screen dump to confirm the success of a test.

Tests should be well documented. This is to ensure that others can understand what has and, more crucially, has not been carried out. If there are any disputes with the client later on, the documentation can be referred to as evidence that testing has been properly carried out.

It is easy to miss out on important aspects of the working of software when devising tests. In the last unit, there is a very simple set of procedures that simply moves down through a list of surnames in a spreadsheet and displays them on a form. Each time the 'Next' button is clicked, the focus moves to the next cell and copies the name onto the form. Similarly, the 'Previous' button moves the focus back up.

■ **Figure 12.75**

	A	B	C	D	E	F	G
1	Surname	Forename					
2	Mangel	Sky					
3	Robinson	Paul					
4	Bishop	Serena					
5	Carpenter	Lou					

Browse Names [×]

Browse Names

Robinson

[Previous Name] [Next Name]

[Quit]

Initially, this was tested very superficially as follows:

Test	Expected Result	Actual Result
Form open	Active Cell is A2	OK
Click Previous button	No movement – because header row is detected	OK
Click Next button	Robinson displayed	OK
Click Next button again	Bishop displayed	OK
Click Quit	Application ended	OK

Everything looks OK, but is it really? Later it was found that when the form was loaded, although the active cell was indeed A2, no name was displayed. The test didn't take that into account.

Also, there was no test to see if the 'Previous' button worked after having worked through the data forwards. In fact it didn't work. The active cell returned to cell A2 instead of going back one by one. This fault only emerged later by accident – it hadn't been planned for or tested. This is such a simple scenario but there are quite a lot of possible progressions through it.

It is no easy matter to think of all the possible things that might happen. This is why it is a good idea if you get other people to try their best to break it!

Test data

Most tests of data-processing systems will involve the need for test data. This is data that has been invented specifically to uncover possible errors.

Often, the data that is expected in an application must fall within a certain range. We often write validation routines to ensure that this is the case. If this is the case, we should test the routine for data that would normally be expected to be used in ordinary operation. We also need to show that the highest and lowest acceptable values are indeed accepted. It is so easy to write a condition such as <10 where we really need to include the value stated and should write $<=10$.

We also need to check that data just outside the range is rejected as is data that is the wrong type.

Suppose that a module is written that checks the value of an order placed on an ebusiness website. If the value of the order is £20 or more, the carriage is free. Suitable test data could be:

Test data	Reason	Intended Result
1	boundary acceptable data	accepted but no free carriage
10	well in range for no free carriage	accepted but no free carriage
19	boundary acceptable data	accepted but no free carriage
20	acceptable for free carriage	free carriage
100	well into range for free carriage	free carriage
0	not an order	should be flagged as error
-1	unacceptable data	should be flagged as error
zz	unacceptable data	should be flagged as error

> **portfolio_tip**
>
> It is the unacceptable data that many students leave out. To gain high marks, you must include – and show that you have used – data that will be rejected by the system.

A test should – if appropriate – include data that is acceptable, data that is on the boundaries, date that is beyond the boundaries and data that is unacceptable.

Involving others

> **portfolio_tip**
>
> Make sure that you include evidence of feedback from others in your eportfolio.

We have seen that it is a good idea if testing is carried out by those who did not develop the software. This is to avoid 'being soft' on the software because you are involved with its creation. Also, it is essential that black-box testing is carried out by a user or someone who is playing the part of a user. We need the opinions of those who do not know about the software internals and only see the end result.

> **portfolio_tip**
>
> Your portfolio must contain evidence of what the specification calls 'formative' and 'summative' testing. All this means is that there should be some evidence that you have tested as you have developed your solution (formative) and also you have tested the completed product in its entirety (summative).

Ideally, the external testers should provide written feedback that can also be incorporated into the testing documentation. The more thoroughly the testing is carried out – and documented – the fewer problems there are likely to be if there are any disputes later about the quality of the product.

Program documentation

Aims

■ To understand the importance of documentation

■ To examine what needs to be included in documentation

All computer systems need documentation. There are two major categories of documentation, which fulfil completely different needs:

▶ user documentation
▶ technical documentation.

User documentation is produced to provide instruction in how to use the system. This has a different purpose from technical documentation and it is aimed at a different category of person. User documentation may or may not assume technical expertise – it depends on the system in question.

Technical documentation is aimed at IT professionals – programmers, project managers, network managers, installers – and its language and approach can assume a certain level of technical expertise of its readers.

Instructions on how to use the application

Most people still expect software to come with a printed manual. They may not look at it much, but they rely on it for looking things up that are not obvious. If they are very diligent, they may use the manual properly and read it in advance before they start work with the software product.

When you buy a well-known software product such as a virus killer or an office package, the amount of printed documentation will probably be small. This might be because the software does not need a lot of user interaction. Once a firewall is set up, you may not need to do much to it. It may be because the product is familiar and so often updated that it is impractical and expensive to print a fat manual that will quickly be out of date. In this case, it makes more sense to provide documentation on a CD or better still on the website of the manufacturer.

Web-based documentation is easy to update and it is also easily searchable. Microsoft Office is a huge suite of programs; a single manual to cover everything would be totally impractical and it would put the cost of the product up. The Microsoft knowledge base is a far more useful way to present the instructions that are required.

For widely known software, there are plenty of books available too, in order to help people get started.

Specialised software such as the applications that might be produced in-house using applications generators are a different matter. They need some basic documentation because they will cover business practices that are not necessarily familiar to the user. They also are more focused on a particular activity and are not big general-purpose tools.

On the CD is a package called GIMP. The developers use web-based documentation. Here is a link:

http://docs.gimp.org/en/

Your user documentation should be well laid out with a contents page. This should lead to section headings that will probably include some of the ones suggested here:

▶ **System requirements** The user may install the software themself. If so, then it is necessary to check that the hardware and operating platform is correct for the application. It will probably be necessary to remind users that Excel or Access is needed to run your particular application. In reality, in most organisations installation will be done by technical staff.

▶ **Prior knowledge** In some cases it may be helpful to itemise the sort of experience that is desirable before attempting to start work with the software. It may be difficult for someone with no Windows experience to work with a Window-based application.

▶ **Installation instructions** This may require instructions on where to locate the software. If the application is a compiled one, you will probably supply it with an installation wizard which will prompt the user through all the important decisions.

▶ **Getting started** Some introductory details will help the user become familiar with what the product is all about and how to access it. The location of any associated files may be included here plus comments on the approach taken or the component parts of the system.

▶ **Entering data** The user needs to be instructed in how to make use of the interface in order to enter data into the system. In most cases, this will be via on-screen forms.

▶ **Amending/deleting data** Most applications require data to be changed in some way by the user. There should be instructions in the documentation to cover the business activities that need to be performed using the product.

▶ **Backups** It will often be the responsibility of the user to make backups of the work in case of accidental deletion or corruption. There should be a section in the documentation that suggests good ways of doing this.

portfolio_tip

You must produce user documentation for your software product. It should be very clear and easy to follow with plenty of screen shots.

Menus and data-entry forms

Good documentation should include screen shots of the interface that the user will see. These make it much clearer what has to be done. You can make screen shots just by pressing the Prt Scr key and then using 'paste' to place the screen capture into your document. It is much better if you have specialist graphic software to prepare screen shots so that you can focus in on a small part of the screen and save just that part. Saving the shot in an uncompressed format such as TIFF or BMP will produce a better quality image. The screen shots in this book were taken with such software. One good example is SnagIt which is very easy to use.

■ Figure 12.76

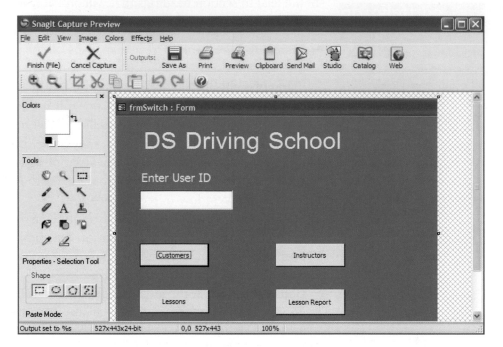

Software for capturing screen shots also provides ways of annotating the shot. For example, you can highlight a part of the screen to draw attention to it.

■ Figure 12.77

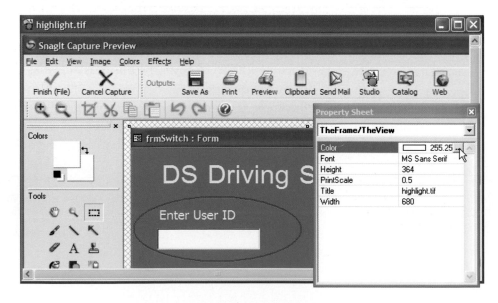

Error messages

Any application that you produce ought to be as 'bullet-proof' as possible. You don't want errors to occur that cause the operating system to kick in and display a cryptic message that will confuse your user. If the user does make a mistake, it is best if you can anticipate this as far as possible so that you can provide your own customised and meaningful error messages. There is only a small space on a screen, so if an error needs further explanation, then it can be documented in a separate section where all error messages are categorised and fully explained.

Further details can be provided with suggestions on what to do about preventing errors.

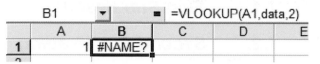

■ **Figure 12.78**

Troubleshooting strategies

Your documentation can include suggestions about how to fix any anticipated problems. For a small application, there should not be too many serious problems, but possibly there may be cases where backup data needs to be restored or a file might have been saved in the wrong location and a few suggested ideas for solving the problem may help.

Another good approach would be to include the URL of a website where problem-solving strategies can be found. That way, any new problems that occur after the documentation was written can be added.

Layout

Users will not want to read through every section of a manual. They will dip into it to find out what they want at a particular time. You should therefore pay particular attention to the way that the manual is laid out. You should break down the material into lots of headings and related sub-headings. For example, a suitable heading might be 'Producing reports'. This could contain sub-headings such as 'Instructor Lists' and Lesson Lists'.

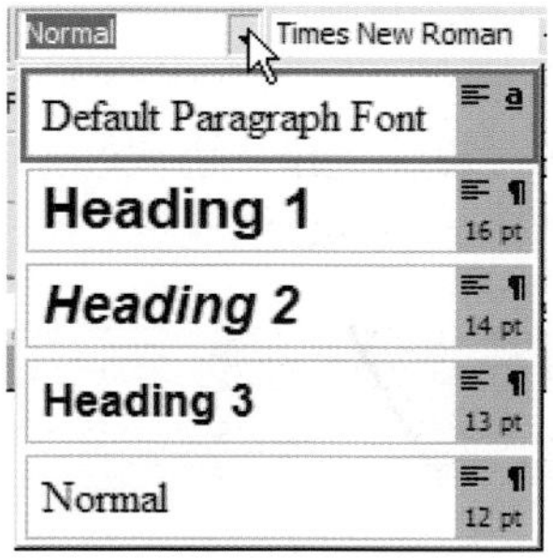

A useful way to set out the headings and sub-headings is to use the styles that are available in your word processor. The normal template will have a small range of styles that will probably be enough.

You can alter or add to these if you need more. One advantage of using styles is that you always have a clear idea what level of material you are working on (Heading 1, 2 or 3, etc.) and you can use these styles to form the basis of an automatic contents page later. If you don't like a style, you can change them globally whenever you want.

You can also set the headings and sub-headings to be numbered automatically. This can make it a lot easier for the reader but it also makes it easier for the writer of the manual. By indenting headings using the tab key, automatic numbering of sub-sections can also be done. Updates are automatically corrected as you go as well.

Figure 12.80 shows the dialogue box you can use to choose a type of numbering system.

■ **Figure 12.79**

portfolio_tip

The advice for good layout in a user manual is also good advice for setting out your report.

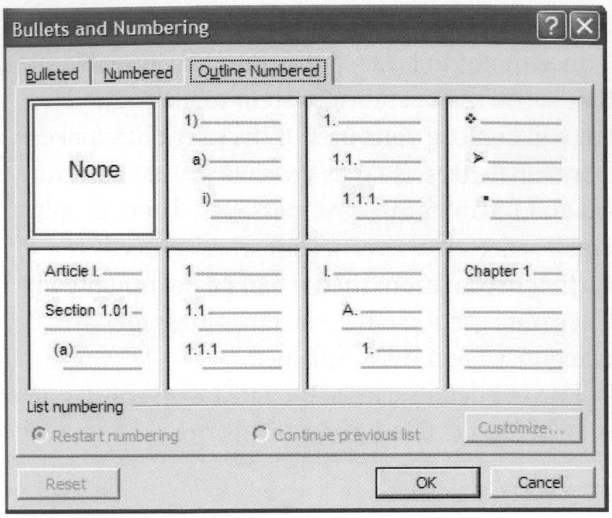

Figure 12.81 shows the result of choosing one of the numbering styles.

Bullets and Numbering dialog box

Figure 12.80

1. First Main Heading

1.1.   *First Sub Heading*

1.2.   *Second Sub Heading*

1.3.   *Third Sub Heading*

2. Second Main Heading

Figure 12.81

Technical documentation

All activities involved with the development and installation of a computer system need to be documented. This means that records have to be kept about exactly what has happened and also the reasoning behind the actions. This documentation – which is sometimes generally referred to under the heading 'technical documentation' – exists for various reasons:

▶ to ensure that proper procedures are followed
▶ to provide evidence that procedures have been followed
▶ to provide information for anyone who has to maintain the system.

Software development companies take a great deal of trouble over producing the right documentation and this extends to the production of documents about documents as well! Figure 12.82 shows a template for one company's documents for testing procedures.

Figure 12.82

DOCUMENT HISTORY

Version	Date	Updated by	Details
1.0	09 December 2005	A.N. Other	Draft
1.1	12 January 2006	A.N. Other	Updated following Review with Joe Mangel
1.2	19 January 2006	A.N. Other	Updated Timescales/Dates

Companies keep large manuals detailing the exact nature of the documentation that must be produced for every stage of a project. This attention to detail is of the greatest importance to ensure that the products produced are as reliable as possible. If staff change, it doesn't matter so much as long as everything is properly documented.

Technical documentation will include a host of detail. All the departments that are responsible for a project will have their own areas of responsibility in the production of documentation.

The programmers – or possibly their team leaders – will produce a record of the program code that has been written and how it is divided up into modules. Records will be needed of how the modules link together and dependencies upon other resources such as external pre-compiled code.

Detailed records such as this are essential if at a later stage the system is to be updated as it almost certainly will be. If records are not kept, the program code will probably be extremely difficult to understand. If the same programmers are involved in an update, they will have forgotten about it all; if new programmers are involved, someone else's code will prove to be a nightmare to read unless there is good documentation.

Some of the documentation is embedded within the code itself. When writing code, you should always include comments so that the purpose of different lines or sections is obvious.

Testing is also thoroughly documented. Figure 12.83 shows the contents page of a testing documentation manual from one company's software development unit. You will see that nothing is left to chance.

There are examples of commented code listings on pages 336–7

■ Figure 12.83

CONTENTS

Evaluation

Aims

■ To examine the success of the software product

■ To examine personal performance in the production of the product

portfolio_tip

Make sure you refer to your own skills and development in the evaluation.

In the course of this unit, you should have produced a software product that someone else can use. You should have gone through all the usual planning stages that software developers use when they are producing solutions professionally. You should have designed, developed and fully tested a useful solution to a problem and documented it for the user and for a technical reader.

At the same time as producing this solution, you will have been learning new skills and processes. For the purpose of this unit, you should have been paying attention to your own performance, to see if you have been making the best use of your time.

The product

This will have taken root from an investigation into a situation that can be helped by the provision of an IT solution. The investigation would have involved a lot of liaison with the user or other person who requires the computer system. This stage will have ended with the production of a functional specification – a document that sets out what the system must do.

When the software is complete, it is necessary to go back to the functional specification and ask whether the requirements have been met. You, the developer, should ask yourself that before handing over the software to the client or user.

If, for example, the solution is supposed to produce a list of driving lessons for each instructor in a driving school, in time order, you need to verify that it does indeed do this. Also, that it is easy for the user to generate these lists without a lot of trouble.

You should also ask whether the solution is a good one – for programmers it is often not enough just to make something that works, they want it to be elegant as well. A well-crafted solution is not just pleasing for its creator, it will probably be more efficient in its use of the computer's resources and also be easier to maintain.

You will have made use of at least some programming in the production of this solution. You should take a last look and ask yourself whether the same or better results could have been achieved simply by using the existing features of the software, without writing any code. You may have to ask others in case there are features that you didn't know about. Possibly, you could have achieved a similar result but the use of some program code allowed the solution to be easier for the user or provided extra validation or processing capability.

Ultimately, you must get feedback from the client. You may well be satisfied that the software does what is required, but in case of misunderstandings, the person who is to use the product is the one who matters most.

Your performance

You should consider how well you tackled this unit. Ask yourself what you can now do compared with when you started. How did you find out the things you needed to know? Did you consult:

- ▶ teachers
- ▶ websites
- ▶ the software help system
- ▶ books?

Did your research show you pointers about how you can best find things out in the future? Did you encounter many dead ends that you will be able to avoid?

The assessment

The evaluation stage of a project like this one is a good time to look at what you have produced in terms of what needs to be produced for assessment.

The specification says:

For this unit you will:
Design, produce, test and evaluate a working solution to a problem involving the use of applications software enhanced by programmed events.

Check that this is in fact what you did. You must have done some event-driven programming. There must be some evidence of event procedures in your documentation.

Your eportfolio for this unit should include:
a A functional specification that describes the problem to be solved and explains what the custom solution is required to do.

Right at the beginning of the project the functional specification should be clearly set out, quite possibly as a set of bullet points. These will form the basis for your final evaluation of the product.

b An initial design that:

- ● satisfies the functional requirements
- ● uses appropriate data structures
- ● responds appropriately to events ☞

- identifies the functions to be programmed, using diagrams to show the structure of each
- considers form design.

Plus evidence of your use of prototyping to improve and refine the design.

Check that there is evidence that your designs closely match what the client wants. Does the solution make proper use of data storage? This means in particular, that if you are producing a database system, the tables should have been properly designed and normalised to the third normal form, with correct links established between primary and foreign keys.

If your solution is based on some other form of data storage, you may need to check that the relevant files are sensibly named and stored within a usable directory tree.

You should provide evidence that the events you intended to detect are in fact correctly responded to and that other events are not inadvertently causing unexpected side effects. For example, does the selection of an item from a combo box trigger an event or does the user have to click a button first? You should have made a list of all the required events and what procedures they were supposed to run. There should be test plans designed to cover these eventualities.

The functionality of the solution should be mapped to the procedures and functions that were written. For example, the generation of a list might be the result of an event procedure attached to the On Click method of a button, but that event procedure may then in turn call another procedure or function in order to sort the data into order or produce a suitable record set. There is much to be gained from writing the code in small chunks that are linked together. Your documentation must show how these links are made. A set of diagrams mapping this out can be a great help.

■ **Figure 12.84**

Your solution will almost certainly make use of forms – user forms as they are called in VBA. There should be evidence that you actually planned and designed these forms rather than just put them together as the project progressed! Hand-drawn designs are often a good way to show that the correct processes have been adhered to.

You will probably have produced some prototypes or non-working or partly working early drafts of your solution. These should have been shown to your client or user and there should be evidence of suitable feedback.

c A fully working custom solution that meets all the functional requirements, with supporting user and technical documentation.

There should be plenty of screen shots showing the product in use. Your solution must be documented both for the user and for those who may need to perform maintenance later. As well as a professionally produced user manual, there must be a complete listing of the program code, fully documented with comments for each event procedure and other procedures and functions.

If you followed the suggestions made in Units 12.9 on testing and 12.10 on documentation, you should have plenty of evidence that your product was tested thoroughly.

As stated at the beginning of this unit, you need to consider the success of the software you produced, with feedback from the user or client. You should also assess your own skills and identify any skills relevant to this task that you feel are still lacking.

Aims

■ To recap on the programming skills demonstrated in this unit

During the course of producing your software solution in this unit, you will have made use of a variety of programming techniques. You will also know the correct terminology to describe these techniques and some of the component parts of a computer program. If you have worked through the examples in this book for this unit, you will already have encountered all of the following points. In this chapter, we shall re-visit and summarise them.

Constants, variables and arrays

A constant is a named portion of memory, set up to hold a value that does not change throughout the running of a program. We use constants to save having to remember things that are repeated in many places throughout a program.

We can declare a constant like this:

```
Const Vat = 0.175
```

This sets a value to the constant Vat which we can use elsewhere in the program.

A variable is also a named portion of memory, but we can change its contents during the running of a program. We should always declare variables before using them although VBA allows you not to do this. When you declare variables, you set up what data type they will be and you enable the compiler to detect errors such as using the wrong data type later or using the same variable name twice.

If you add the line `Option Explicit` to the top level of your modules, you will force yourself to declare variables.

You can declare a variable in various ways in VBA such as by using the Dim statement:

```
Dim iCounter as integer
```

This statement sets up a variable called iCounter and requires it to hold an integer value.

An array is a data structure which is declared similarly to a simple variable, but it consists of more than one *element*. This allows you to refer to a set of related data by using the same name.

For example, you can set up an array of surnames with the following statement:

```
Dim strSurname(10) As String
```

This sets up an array called strSurname which can hold ten surnames as string variables.

Each 'cell' in an array is called an *element* and each position – designated by a number – is called an *index* or *subscript*.

You can put data into the array elements with statements like these:

```
strSurname(1) = "Smith"
strSurname(2) = "Jones"
```

You can then visualise the array as in Figure 12.85:

strSurname

array element	Smith	Jones								
array index	1	2	3	4	5	6	7	8	9	10

■ **Figure 12.85**

Arrays can be any data type. They can also be multi-dimensional. A statement such as:

```
Dim iMark(10,10) As Integer
```

sets up a table with ten rows and ten columns to hold integer values.

Loops

We have seen in Unit 12.5 how to create programming loops. You should remember that a loop is a portion of program code that repeats. Each time a loop is gone through is called an *iteration*.

Remember there are four main ways in which loops can be set up.

Precondition (Do While)

You can test for a condition before the loop is executed. In VBA this is written as:

```
Do While [condition is true]
    .
    .
    .
Loop
```

The next example shows how a Do While loop can be used to output the contents of an array of surnames. (NB There is a deliberate error in this program.)

```
Dim iCounter As Integer

Dim strSurname(10) As String

iCounter = 1

strSurname(1) = "Smith"
strSurname(2) = "Jones"
strSurname(3) = "Black"
strSurname(4) = "Blue"
strSurname(5) = "Pink"
strSurname(6) = "Green"
strSurname(7) = "White"
strSurname(8) = "Grey"
strSurname(9) = "Yellow"
strSurname(10) = "Purple"

Do While iCounter < 10

MsgBox (strSurname(iCounter))

iCounter = iCounter + 1

Loop
```

A loop written in this way may not have to execute at all if the condition on the first line is not met.

We can also use the structure While...Wend as we did in Unit 12.5.

ACTIVITY

What do you think will happen when this code is run? Do you think that the programmer intended this? If not, what is the error?

Post-condition Do Until

Sometimes it is best to test a condition at the end of a loop. In VBA we do this with the Do Until statement.

We could re-write the first line of the last example with

```
Do Until iCounter=10
.

.
Loop
```

A loop written in this way must iterate at least once as the test is at the end.

Fixed iteration (For...Next)

You can make a loop always iterate a fixed number of times. In VBA you use the For...Next structure.

If we wanted to output **all** the surnames in the last example, we could have written:

```
For iCounter = 1 To 10

MsgBox (strSurname(iCounter))

Next iCounter
```

That is less work but there is no flexibility if the number of names varies.

Recursion

It is also possible to use recursion to iterate a section of code. This is where a procedure calls itself.

Selection

We have seen in Unit 12.5 that there are two common methods for determining the direction of flow in a program. We can use the If...Then...Else method, where a condition is checked and a consequence is provided for depending on what the result of a test is.

The Select...Case structure allows for many possible outcomes.

Routines and functions

We have seen that programs are written in small sections. The terminology for these component parts varies. We can call a sub-part of a program a *routine* or a *sub-routine*. In VBA, when you write a procedure, you will normally head it with the word Sub as in

```
Private Sub cmdGo_Click()
```

This is the start of a sub-routine that forms an event procedure. The word procedure is often used instead of sub-routine.

Functions return just one value and they are often called in-line – that is, they form part of another statement as in

```
iNumber = Cube(iValue)
```

This calls the function Cube and assigns its value to the variable iNumber.

Nowadays, it is common to write programs as a series of *objects*, where packages of program code are bundled together with relevant data and the resulting package can be linked to other objects and re-used without having to keep examining what is going on inside. This allows for great productivity from programmers.

Passing parameters

In Unit 12.5 we passed values to functions. The example with the Cube function shows how the value of the variable called iValue is being handed to the function Cube, where it will be multiplied by itself twice.

Remember that parameters may be passed by value or by reference. If you pass them by value, a copy of the value is handed to the procedure or function. The original will not be changed by any processing that occurs in the function. If you pass by reference, you hand the address of the variable to the procedure or function. It works with the actual variable itself so if it changes its value, it stays changed.

Input/output methods

No program is worth writing if there is no input or output. That is what computer systems are for – to take input, process it and output the results.

This is so important that it is no surprise that there are many, many ways to do this. We have made use of several methods in the examples earlier in the unit.

Examples of input methods include:

▶ InputBox
▶ take the text property from a text box
▶ select an item from a combo box
▶ respond to a button click event
▶ read from a file.

Output methods are equally diverse:

▶ use the immediate window
▶ output to a label's caption property
▶ change the caption of a button
▶ output to a printer
▶ output directly onto a form
▶ use the MsgBox feature.

You will have experienced a wide range of techniques in doing this unit. Some of them may have taken some learning in order to get them just right, but you should have had a lot of fun in learning!

Index

INDEX